Global Climate Change and Natural Resources

2010

Also by Emil Morhardt

Ecological Consequences of Global Climate Change: Summaries of the 2009 Scientific Literature

Global Climate Change and Natural Resources: Summaries of the 2008-2009 Scientific Literature

Global Climate Change and Natural Resources: Summaries of the 2007-2008 Scientific Literature

Biology of Global Change

Global Climate Change: Summaries of the 2006-2007 Scientific Literature

Research in Natural Resources Management

Clean Green and Read All Over

Research in Ecosystem Services

California Desert Flowers

Cannon and Slinkard Fire Recovery Study: A Photographic Flora

Global Climate Change and Natural Resources

2010

A Roberts Environmental Center Annual Snapshot

J. Emil Morhardt, Editor

The Roberts Environmental Center Press

Roberts Environmental Center Press
Claremont McKenna College
925 N. Mills Avenue
Claremont, California 91711
(909) 621-8190

Morhardt, J. Emil
    Global Climate Change and Natural Re-
    sources 2010: A Roberts Environmental
    Center Annual Snapshot/ J. Emil Mor-
    hardt, Editor.

    ISBN 978-0-9843823-1-6 (paper)

Table of Contents

Introduction

J. Emil Morhardt

Over the past few years, studying global warming has become one of the biggest scientific endeavors ever undertaken; the scientific literature on it has gone from a trickle to a flood, and the results—which can be thought of as clues is a an astoundingly complex mystery story—are being serialized weekly in *Science*, *Nature*, the *Proceedings of the National Academy of Science*, and other top scientific journals.

But for most readers these papers are out of reach; most journals are only freely accessible through accounts at college and university libraries, and worse, the articles are often extremely difficult to read. It is not uncommon, for example, for it to take me three to five hours to fully understand a three-page paper on some aspect of the topic in *Science* or *Nature*, and I read hundreds of such papers a year. In addition, the nature of cutting edge science is that it is messy; the papers contradict one another, fail to address the contradictions since they are contemporaneous, and often assume full familiarity with details of, say, earth orbital climate forcing, or the significance of different relative concentrations of the stable atomic isotope, oxygen-18 ($\delta^{18}O$ is what the journals cryptically print) in buried marine mollusk shells. This leads to trips to other scientific papers and Wikipedia to sort out the details.

Most of us are reduced to reading newspaper or magazine accounts—or denunciations—of the research, listening to short presentations on radio and television, discussions on talk radio, or scanning blogs. I'm betting that few of the people making these presentations read the original papers carefully; even if they did and have the original scientists in tow, the commentaries are mostly limited to sound bites. And only a tiny number of studies ever gets any publicity at all.

On top of that, the whole issue has become highly political. It is hard for scientists to understand how scientific findings could become political—they produce, after all, just data; and if they have important implications, other scientists will immediately try to verify or discredit them. The main thing that science does, by hook or by crook, is get to the truth, and the more important the issue, the more scientists will jump on board and the faster the science will move. They are jumping on board this issue with both feet, so the science is moving rapidly indeed.

Nevertheless, even commentators as nominally responsible as editorial writers for the Wall Street Journal are willing to look at *The Guardian*'s account of two scientific papers—rather than actually trying to read them—with conflicting views on the rate of Arctic ice melt, and conclude, for no apparent reason, that the one fitting the no-global-warming school of thought must be correct. That commentator pronounced that "...global warming is dead, nailed into its coffin one devastating disclosure, defection and re-evaluation at a time" (Stephens 2010). That was this morning. Next week there will be more papers, though, and global warming will turn out not to be dead, or even moribund. More likely it will be alive and well from what the papers in this book show.

The State of the IPCC

I thought I'd use this forward to comment on the Intergovernmental Panel on Climate Change (IPCC) which is having a few health problems of its own, though it is by no means moribund either. Given the recent political assaults, you might be thinking "Isn't the IPCC just a political organization controlled by liberal European governments?"

It is decidedly not. Rather, the IPCC is a very large professional peer review group, maybe the largest that has ever existed. Its working groups include hundreds of scientists, engineers, economists, and other specialists who compile all the available technical literature relating to climate change, examine it minutely, and once in a while produce a massive literature review. The last one was published in 2007 and consists of three volumes, each weighing about five pounds and running to about 1,000 pages of very small print citing thousands of technical journal articles and other publications. But, instead of you having to purchase a printed version, the IPPC makes it freely available for download online, so you can easily examine it yourself if you are skeptical about its technical content. To give you a sense of the detail involved let's just take a look at Chapter 10 of Volume I, Climate Change 2007: the Physical Science Basis (Solomon *et al.* 2007).

Chapter 10 covers global climate projections. It has two coordinating authors, 12 lead authors from 13 countries, and 78 contributing authors from research laboratories around the world. *All* of the authors are scientists specializing in global climate projections who have published peer-reviewed technical journal articles on the subject. The chapter is 100 pages long, is filled with technical graphs and climate maps, and cites about 600 technical journal articles, many by the authors of this chapter, and more than most scientists are likely to read carefully in several years—many more than most scientific review articles would attempt to cover. It is clearly written, carefully reasoned, cautious about making conclusions, and entirely open about what is and is not known.

Is there a conspiracy here? It's hard to imagine. That so many scientists—almost a hundred for Chapter 10 alone—who are actively conducting and publishing this research can agree on this material, makes me believe that the ideas are entirely in the scientific mainstream and not influenced by political considerations. Scientists, in general, are not very political anyway, and don't like putting themselves in positions in which their work can be challenged on other than scientific grounds; they tend to be very careful in pushing conclusions beyond the science, especially when they already know it is likely to be challenged by non-scientists. Apparently though, a few overzealous statements crept in (about the rate of glacial melt in the Himalayas, and maybe a few other things) making an opening which was vigorously exploited by global warming skeptics.

Climate Change Skeptics

Should we take the climate change skeptics seriously? Some, we should; especially the ones with scientific credentials. There is nothing wrong with skepticism about climate change or any other technical issue. All scientists are professional skeptics, and a good bit of scientific training and practice consists of carefully reading research papers trying to find anything that might be wrong with them. Typical problems include lack of appropriate experimental controls, lack of (or incorrect) statistical analysis, unreasonable assumptions, and conclusions that are not supported by the results. All of these problems should be caught during peer review, but they can be subtle, and sometimes find their way into published papers, even those in the most prestigious scientific journals. So it is entirely appropriate that published scientific results be examined fully and if the results are inconclusive, they should be recognized as such, even if the scientists publishing them are convinced that they are correct. And obviously, if scientists draw conclusions beyond what their data can support, they should be called to account, which is what much of the current brouhaha about the IPCC stems from. What matters in science is getting to the truth, and if the data and analysis supporting a particular position are flawed, then the work needs to be redone, perhaps using entirely different techniques, until it is reproducible and unassailable, or alternatively, shown to be irreproducible and therefore meaningless. This is, in fact, the way all important science is done, and the more attention fellow scientists pay to potential flaws, the more quickly those flaws are corrected and the doubts assuaged. It is very much the way global warming and climate change is being pursued, so sooner or later, everyone *is* going to agree on the basic facts. But we can expect it to be in flux for a while longer. This book is as much about that flux as anything else.

J. Emil Morhardt

The Approach Used in this Book

Think of this book as a Readers Digest of the current scientific literature on global warming and its effect on natural resources. Each chapter is about one of the important issues, and consists of short journalistic summaries of eight technical journal articles, most published in the past year. The summaries are bite-sized, independent of one another, and can be browsed and read profitably in any order. As the editor, I have tried to get the authors to make the summaries accessible and interesting, and to capture the essence of the underlying research without being overly complicated or opinionated. For the most part they have succeeded. I think this book is an excellent way to begin to understand the complexities of global warming and climate change. It might even lead you to tackling some of the original science which is, indeed, fascinating.

References Cited

Solomon, S., Qin, D., Manning, M., Chen, Z., Marquis, M., Averyt, K., Tignor, M., Miller, H., 2008. Climate change 2007: the physical science basis. Cambridge University Press Cambridge and New York.

Stephens, B., 2010. What's next on global warming? Editorial Page, Wall Street Journal. 6 April 2010.

Section I—Physical Effects and Drivers of Climate Change

1. Diminishing Ice Sheets and Glaciers

Grace Beck

Glaciologists are striving to understand both the causes and the consequences of increased rates of glacier retreat in the present decade. Since glacier flux is dependent on a combination of geological processes, researchers are investigating the roles of climate, solar radiation, and precipitation. Some researchers have conducted field studies on specific glaciers and used their findings to make general conclusions about worldwide glacier retreat, while others have compared glacier mass balance values around the world to determine retreat trends. Several studies, such as one performed by Koch *et al.* (2009), suggest that glacier retreat is occurring at an alarming rate, and suggest that if we don't make immediate changes in our environmental policies, global glacier area will be significantly reduced in the next several decades. The results of other studies, however, are not nearly as concerning. Although glaciers are retreating, retreat rates may be occurring at a much slower rate than previously thought. Since the approaches, methodologies, and findings of current studies greatly differ, apparently it will be a while before we gain a full understanding of the causes and effects of glacier retreat.

Although glaciologists disagree about the severity of glacier retreat in the present decade, most researchers do agree on the cycle of glacier flux since the Little Ice Age. During the Little Ice Age, a cool period from about 1550 to 1850, glaciers grew. From 1850 to 1940, glaciers gradually retreated as the climate warmed. Glacier recession declined and reversed in many cases from 1950 to1980 as slight global cooling occurred. Since 1980, however, glacier retreat has become much more rapid and ubiquitous than in past years. Glaciers around the world are losing mass and many natural habitats are at risk. Glacier retreat is also affecting the availability of fresh water for irrigation and domestic use as well as the level of the oceans. The World Glacier Monitoring Service has documented 17 consecutive years of negative mass balances that indicate volume loss.

A glacier consists of an accumulation zone, where the accumulation of ice persists during the summer, and an ablation zone, where snow cover is seasonal. To be sustainable, a glacier must have a consistent accumulation zone. When a glacier increases in volume due to climate cooling or increased snowfall, the positive mass balance results in glacial advance. This advance also increases the glacier's area at low-level elevations where ablation is highest, returning the glacier to equilibrium. Climate warming or a decrease in snowfall leads to negative mass balance and glacier retreat. To reestablish equilibrium, a retreating glacier must lose enough of its highest melting (ablating) sections, usually at the lowest elevations, so that accumulation in the accumulation zone once again balances ablation, reestablishing equilibrium. If a glacier cannot retreat to a point where equilibrium is established, it is in disequilibrium with the climate system. A glacier in disequilibrium with present climate will thin and eventually melt away if there is no decrease in temperature. Since glaciers take a few years to respond to climate change, they will continue to retreat in the foreseeable future regardless of climate.

On the Rise: The Effect of Climate Fluctuation on China's Monsoonal Temperate Glacier Region

China's monsoonal temperate glaciers are losing mass due to climate fluctuations in the past several decades. Increased incidence of mudflows, rock falls, and floods in the region indicate that rising temperatures are increasing the rate of glacial retreat. Zongxing *et al.* (2009) studied eight glaciers and two basins in the Chinese monsoonal temperate glacial region, which they considered representative of the whole of China's monsoonal temperate glacier region because the glaciers varied in size, altitude, location, and sun exposure. After analyzing the melting patterns of the glaciers in response to fluctuating climate changes, they concluded that glaciers in the region were stationary or advancing from 1900 to 1930 and from 1960 to 1980, but were retreating between 1930 and 1960 and the present. These periods of glacial retreat are likely due to climate warming and a decline in precipitation in China's monsoonal temperate region.

Zongxing *et al.* undertook their study in three steps. First, climatic changes in the past 100 years were explored using previous studies, including the ice core record, tree ring indices, and observation data from 16 climate stations. Second, the changes in eight monsoonal temperate glaciers in the last several decades were studied based on previous reports and field investigations. Third, runoff variation in the Hailiuogou and Yanggong basins since the 1980s was also analyzed using observational data. Based on their findings, Zongxing *et al.* concluded that retreat rates vary from glacier to glacier depending on latitude, thickness, and degree of climate fluctuation. During the current warming period, however, changes in glacial surface features and meltwater runoff appear to be more pronounced than in past warming periods. Glacier mass and surface thickness have been rapidly decreasing while glacial runoff depth has been correspondingly increasing. Such changes in China's water cycle are on the rise due to the increase in temperature and decline in precipitation during the past several decades. Further glacial melting and increased runoff could lead to serious water and soil erosion in high altitude zones, and may threaten soil systems and the ecological environment in China and around the world.

20th Century Climate Warming and Glacier Retreat in British Columbia

Fluctuations of glaciers during the 20th century in Garibaldi Provincial Park, in the southern Coast Mountains of British Columbia, were reconstructed from historical documents, aerial photographs, and fieldwork. While over 505 km², or 26%, of the park was covered by glacier ice at the beginning of the 18th century, ice cover decreased to 297 km² by 1987 and to 245 km² by 2005 (Koch *et al.* 2009). Glacier recession was found to be greatest between the 1920s and 1950s, with typical frontal retreat rate of 30 meters per year. Many glaciers advanced between the 1960s and 1970s, but all glaciers have been in retreat ever since. The record of 20th century glacier fluctuations in Garibaldi Park is similar to that in Southern Europe, South America, and New Zealand, suggesting a common, global climatic cause. Koch *et al.* conclude that global temperature change in the 20th century explains the behavior of glaciers in Garibaldi Park and elsewhere.

During the first two decades of the 20th century, all of the glaciers were found to be retreating slowly, interrupted by small periods of advance or standstill. Between the 1920s and 1960s, glaciers rapidly retreated, but again advanced between the 1960s and early 1980s. Since the 1980s, however, glaciers have been in retreat. The data show that periods of glacier recession coincide with warm and relatively dry periods, whereas advances occurred during relatively warm periods with variable precipitation. The findings not only indicate a strong correlation between climate change and glacier retreat, but also a 5–10 year lag time in the response of glaciers to a change in climate.

Observed historical ice loss in Garibaldi Park and in mountain regions around the world is broadly synchronous and attributed to global 20th century climate warming. If warming continues at the present rate, glaciers in Garibaldi Park will become smaller and may even vanish. Not only will recreation and tourism be affected, but also our water supply, fishers, and aquatic ecosystems.

Glacier Recession Since the Little Ice Age

Glaciers in the Andes are particularly sensitive to both large and small-scale changes in climate. Espizua and Pitte (2009) investigated glacier fluctuations since the maximum "Little Ice Age" advance in the upper part of the Rio Grande basin in the El Azufre, El Peñón, Las Vacas, and Gussfeldt valleys. Based on marine morphology (size and height of glaciers), stratigraphic relationships, minimum radiocarbon ages obtained from peat on the glacial deposits, and proximity to active glaciers, the researchers found that the maximum Little Age Ice advance in the area occurred during AD 1550–1720, with a subsequent advance around AD 1830. In general, the studied glaciers have been in of retreat ever since despite a brief period of advance between 1980 and 1990.

The studied valleys lie between the arid and semiarid Central Andes of Argentina to the north, and the more humid conditions in Patagonia to the south. The researchers chose to examine glaciers in this area because few studies have recorded glacier fluctuations in this part of the Andes. The identification of the glacial deposits related to the Little Ice Age was based mainly on relative age criteria, such as topographic position of the end moraines, the relationship of tills to outwash deposits, geographic differences, and radiocarbon ages. In addition to examining aerial photographs and performing field investigations, the minimum age of glacier advance was determined by collecting samples of peat from basal peat logs on each of the moraines.

Espizua and Pitte also determined area and length variations of glaciers in each valley since the 19th century. The total glacier area loss in the El Peñón glacier was found to be 0.87 km^2 between 1894 and 2007, while the length reduction was determined to be 1.12 km. In the same period, the El Azufre glacier lost an area of 0.41 km^2 and retreated 0.94 km. The Las Vacas glacier retreated at a faster rate, losing an ice area of 4.27 km^2 from 1896 to 2007, and its front retreated 2.92 km. Similarly, Gussfeldt glacier lost 9.22 km^2 of its area and the front retreated 4.99 km between 1896 and 2007. The glacier fluctuations reported in this study are consistent with previously documented fluctuations at similar altitudes in the Andes. While Espizua and Pitte's research has increased the understanding of glacier fluctuations in the Central Andes of Argentina since the 19th century, knowledge of glacier fluctuation in this region is still scarce compared to that in the lower and higher altitudes along the Andes.

Lichenometry and Glacier Dating

Chaujar (2009) investigated the effect of climate change on Himalayan glaciers based on dating lichens that have formed on moraines during various stages of glacier retreat and advance. His findings indicate that maximum advance of the Chorabari glacier in the Himalayas occurred 258 years ago at the peak of the Little Ice Age. Ever since, Chorabari and other glaciers in the southern and northern hemispheres have been in retreat. Chaujar's results suggest that the current climatic changes started during early to mid-eighteenth century rather than mid-fourteenth century.

Four distinct moraines were dated by the lichenometric studies which depend on the assumption that if colonization delay (time taken by the lichen to grow on a surface after its exposure to the atmosphere) and growth rate of lichens are known in a particular area, then a minimum date can be obtained by measuring the maximum diameter of the largest lichen at the site. This method is useful in glacial environments that are mostly above the tree line, where lichens grow slowly and have great longevity. In such conditions, it is possible to date deposits up to thousands of years old, but in most cases, this method is useful for dating deposits just up to 500 years.

The most common lichen growing on the glacial moraines was *Rhizocarpon geographicum*. The longest axes of all the lichens of this species growing on the upper faces of selected boulders were measured with flexible tape and a digital caliper. About 2000 lichens were measured on different moraines and their frequency distribution was plotted to display relative age structure of the population. Seven prominent lichens on different moraines were well marked in the field for future reference. These lichens were then measured again during the first week of November in 2004 through 2007, and a growth rate of 1 mm/year was established.

Since most historical monuments and civil works do not yet have lichen growth on them, the oldest of these, a bridge 85 years old, established a minimum colonization delay of 85 years. Based on the estimated values for colonization delay and growth rate, the largest lichens were estimated to be around 258 years old, suggesting that climatic changes in this part of the world started nearly 258 years ago. After the peak of the Little Ice Age, recession of the glacier was followed by several stages of advance and retreat. Based on these findings, the researchers attempted to confirm the age of the Kedarnath temple, a historical monument that emerged after the melting of Chorabari glacier. They confirmed that the temple is around 3000 years old and that no glacier surrounded the temple until AD 850.

Solar Radiation and its Impact on Glacier Retreat

Global warming may not be the only factor responsible for glacial retreat. Huss *et al.* (2009) investigated the effect of solar radiation on glacier melting at four high elevation sites in the European Alps. They found that snow and ice melt was stronger in the 1940s than in recent years in spite of significantly higher air temperatures in the present decade. An inner Alpine radiation record showed that in the 1940s global shortwave radiation over the summer months was 8% above the long-term average and significantly higher than today, favoring rapid glacier mass loss. Dimming of solar radiation from the 1950s until the 1980s is in line with reduced melt rates and advancing glaciers, suggesting that solar radiation plays a major factor in glacier retreat.

After reviewing 94 years of seasonal mass balance data collected at four different Swiss glaciers, Huss *et al.* concluded that melting conditions have undergone strong temporal variations throughout the last century. During 1942–1952 and 1998–2008 melting was above average (17% and 13% respectively) while from 1971–1981 it was below average (–19%). According to the century-long data series, maximum melting at the study sites occurred in 1947. In fact, melting rates were observed to be substantially higher in 1947 than those in the summer of 2003, which is known for its extreme heat waves in Europe. This phenomenon is intriguing because air temperatures in the 1940s were not as high as they were in 2003.

Huss *et al.* deduced that solar radiation must be a key factor in glacier melting patterns. According to global radiation records collected during the 20th century, maximum global radiation was recorded in the 1940s. During this period, summer radiation was 8% above the long-term average and 18 Wm^{-2} higher than over the last decade. Huss *et al.*'s findings suggest that extreme glacier melt rates in the 1940s were mostly due to radiation changes rather than to air temperature change.

The Unknown Effect of Drought Cycles on Glacier Retreat in the Rocky Mountains

The cause of glacier retreat in the 1850s in the Rocky Mountains and elsewhere still remains unknown. Since the excess of greenhouses gases in the atmosphere at that time was too small to have triggered the process of retreat, some other factor must have started it. Berger (2009) found that the onset of Rocky Mountain glacier recession in Canada and Montana was initiated by drought cycles in the 1830s.

Although glacier retreat is partly due to changes in the brightness of the sun, drought cycles in North America are also linked to changes in the surface temperature of large regions of the ocean. Berger found that winter snow in the Rocky Mountains depends on the ocean climate variability known as the Pacific Decadal Oscillation. Since drought cycles seem to be important in determining the growth and decay of mountain glaciers, Berger investigated the origin of large-scale climate variability in the sea to find cues for the initiation of glacier retreat. According to the author, such ocean-climate oscillations "…have the nature of cycles, although the periods involved are not fixed though time, but vary according to rules that have not been fixed in a satisfactory fashion." Using published data from tree-ring studies, Berger concluded that there was a shift from short climate cycles to long ones in the 1850s. While this shift seems important when attempting to explain glacier retreat, it is not clear what might have caused this shift, unless it was the interaction of different types of oscillations, coinciding and reinforcing each other. In addition, Berger found that Pacific Decadal Oscillation cycles are closely connected to tidal cycles, but they have no apparent connection drought cycles in the region.

The results from scrutinizing the periodicity in drought series and in the Pacific Decadal oscillation are interesting but inconclusive in finding a driver for drought, although it is suspected that the sun had a role the initiation of the retreat of glaciers in the middle of the 19th century.

Glacier Melting and Moraine Dammed Lakes: The Breaking Point

Changes in mountain glaciers are among the best natural indicators of climate change. In the past decade, glaciers in the Dudhi Koshi basin in eastern Nepal have been melting faster than ever. From 1976 to 2000, Lumding and Imja Glaciers retreated 42 and 34 meters per year respectively. Between 2000 and 2007, however, the rate increased to 74 meters per year for both glaciers (Bajracharya and Mool, 2009). As a result of the increased water runoff, existing glacial lakes are expanding and new ones are forming. Understanding the response of glaciers and glacial lakes to rising temperatures is essential for preventing the potential threat of glacial lake outburst floods (GLOFs).

Bajracharya, Pradeep and their colleagues at the Centre for Integrated Mountain Development mapped 264 glaciers in the Dudhi Koshi basin and calculated each of their retreat rates between 1960 and 2007. While some glaciers are melting faster than others, the average minimum retreat rate of all the glaciers was calculated to be 10 meters per year. In addition, the researches measured the growth rate of the 296 existing moraine-dammed lakes. Between 1960 and 2000, the total area of moraine-dammed lakes increased by 21%, and 24 new ones had appeared. After careful study of the largest lakes in the basin, Bajracharya and Pradeep have concluded that 12 of them pose potential threats for glacial lake outburst floods. Due to the rapid accumulation of runoff water, the loose moraine material forming the dams is becoming weaker. Eventually, the dams are expected to break, causing flooding in the surrounding region. The massive Dig Tsho glacial outbreak flood in 1987, for example, resulted in much social, economic, and environmental destruction, wiping out a new hydropower station, 30 houses, 14 bridges, and much cultivated land. Threats of landslides and erosion still exist.

Past research indicates that at least one glacial lake outburst flood occurs every three to ten years in the Himalayan region. With rising temperatures and increased glacial water runoff it is likely that the frequency of GLOFs will increase in coming years, and many of the existing moraine-dammed lakes are already rapidly expanding. Predicting the breaks accurately is difficult, however, and more loss of life and property is to be expected.

Threat of Trace Elements in Glacier Runoff: Eliot Glacier, Oregon Cascades

Because glacier melt feeds downstream ecosystems, the geochemistry of snow and glacier runoff is likely to have an effect on water supply and agriculture. Fortner *et al.* (2009) investigated the relationship between environmentally available elements in fresh and ablation glacier snow and dissolved elements in glacier melt in the Oregon, Cascades at Eliot Glacier, Mount Hood, concluding that environmentally available trace element concentrations occurred in greater median concentrations in shallow ablation snow collected from Eliot Glacier in July 2005 than in nearby fresh snow collected in March 2006.

The researchers chose to undertake their study at Mount Hood because of high winter precipitation rates and rapid spring snowmelt, both of which make it an ideal location for an examination of the processing of natural elements. Snow and melt samples were collected from Eliot Glacier in July 2005 and March 2006 and thirty trace elements and ion samples were obtained in approximately 4–18 cm increments from two snow pits 1 m deep. The samples of fresh and ablation snow were filtered and the Ca^{2+}, Cl^-, Na^+, K^+, Mg^{2+}, SO_4^{2-}, and NO_3^- content in each of the samples was measured. The July 2005 snow samples contained significantly lower concentrations of Ca^{2+}, SO_4^{2-}, and NO_3^- than the March 2006 fresh water samples, likely due to the ongoing loss of soluble ions during early snowmelt. Concentrations of Na^+, K^+, Mg^{2+} were statistically similar between July 2005 and March 2006 snow, although median concentrations of these ions were lower in ablation snow, perhaps a result of the high winter accumulation rate diluting the initial element concentrations.

The greatest trace element concentrations occurred in July 2005 surface snow. While some of these trace elements came from the deposition of atmospheric water particles, most resulted from the fallout of atmospheric aerosols. Dry fallout of heavy metals, including Cu and Pb, is directly related to pollution produced by human activity. The trace elements deposited on the surface snow eventually end up in the water supply after glacial runoff and retreat. Although their present concentrations are well below drinking water standards, and pose no immediate threats to water quality, trace elements could be potentially dangerous if their concentrations increase in the future. As a result, ongoing evaluation of water quality will be especially important in regions with higher reliance on glacier melt for drinking water and agriculture.

Overestimation of Glacier Retreat Rates: How Worried Should We Be?

Due to an increase in global warming in the past few decades, glacier melting has become a serious concern. Scientists, politicians, and environmentally conscious people alike are worried about the consequences of glacial retreat. Using a technique called mass balance, glaciologists have been measuring the yearly retreat rate of 318 glaciers worldwide. Global average mass balance represents the contribution of glaciers to sea level rise during the period of averaging. Although mass balance data clearly indicate a decrease in overall glacial mass and area, it is likely that the rate of retreat has been overestimated. Braithwaite (2009) argues that current mass balance measurements are not representative of global glacier cover for several reasons: "the data are concentrated in a few regions that are well covered (e.g. the Alps) and wide regions with sparse data"; they do not account for the effect of temperature and precipitation on glacier retreat; and they consist of a few long series and many short series.

After reviewing the available mass balance data posted by the World Glacier Monitoring Service, Braithwaite found that glaciers in the Alps and Scandinavia dominated the results. Relatively high amounts of yearly precipitation in these regions have undoubtedly caused average global mass balance measurements to be higher than they should be. Based on the previous studies of Oerlemans and Fortuin in 1992, there is a clear correlation between mass balance amplitude and precipitation; precipitation causes greater glacial runoff and retreat causing mass balance values to increase. In order to mitigate the effect of precipitation on global mass balance data, Braithwaite suggests that glaciologist collect data for more glaciers in drier and cooler environments.

In addition, mass balance data have not been collected consistently for long periods; some have been studied for 5-year periods, others for only two. As a result, the global mass balance average does not necessarily represent long-term trends of glacial retreat. More importantly, Braithwaite asserts, "we must be careful of averages of data that are known to have complex spatial and temporal patterns." Because each glacier varies in location, climate, and time studied, the global average mass balance should not be determined simply by taking the average of all the individual mass balance values. Braithwaite suggests a more mathematically correct approach would be to identify some long and continuous mass balance series measured in different regions so that the analysis is of a complete matrix for different glaciers and different years. The only problem here is that there are few long series and they do not cover the globe in any representative way. As a result, Braithwaite concludes that we urgently need to find better ways of analyzing sparse datasets.

Grace Beck

Conclusions

Based on the conflicting results presented in the previous summaries, it is clear that that the increase of glacier retreat in the 20th century is caused by a variety of factors, including an increase in global temperature, decreased amounts of annual precipitation, and increased exposure to solar radiation. Natural habitats in glacial environments are already at risk, and many ecosystems have already been affected by glacier retreat. If global warming continues, many of the ecological effects of glacier loss will be irreversible.

References Cited

Bajracharya, S., Pradeep, M., 2009. Glaciers, glacial lakes and glacial lake outburst floods in the Mount Everest region, Nepal. Annals of Glaciology 50, 53–81.

Braithwaite, Roger J., 2009. After six decades of monitoring glacier mass balance we still need data but it should be richer data. Annals of Glaciology 50, 191–197.

Berger, W.H., 2009. On glacier retreat and drought cycles in the Rocky Mountains of Montana and Canada. Quaternary International. 30, 1–7.

Chaujar, R., 2009. Climate change and its impact on Himalayan glaciers – a case study on the Chorabari glacier, Garhwal Himalaya, India. Current Science 5, 703–707.

Espizua, L., and Pitte, P., 2009. The Little Ice Age glacier advance in the Central Andes (35°S), Argentina. Paleogeography, Palaeoclimatology, Palaeoecology, 281, 345–350.

Fortner, Sarah K., Lyons, W., Fountain, Andrew G., Welch, Kathleen A., Kehrwald, Natalie M., 2009. Trace element and major ion concentrations and dynamics in glacier snow and melt: Eliot Glacier, Oregon Cascades. Hydrological Processes. 23, 2987–2996.

Huss, M., Funk, M., Ohmura, A., 2009. Strong Alpine glacier melt in the 1940s due to enhanced Solar radiation. Geophysical Research Letters. 36, L23501.

Koch, J., Menounos, B., Clague, J., 2009. Glacier Change in Giribaldo Park, southern Coast Mountain, British Colombia, since the Little Ice Age. Global and Planetary Change 66, 161–178.

Zongxing, L., Yuanqing, H., Tao, P., Wenxiong, J., Xianzhong, H., Hongxi, P., Ningning, Z., Qiao, L., Shijing, W., Guofeng, Z., 2009. Changes of climate, glaciers and runoff in China's monsoonal temperate glacier region during the last several decades. Quaternary International. 30, 1–16.

2. Paleoclimatology: What the Imprints from Past Climates Are Telling Us

Lauren Orme

Paleoclimatology is the study of long term changes in climate throughout Earth's history. It involves collecting data attained from physical traces—imprints from past climates left in natural materials—to reconstruct models of how the surrounding environment was affected over time when these climate changes occurred. The natural materials from which samples are taken include glaciers, ice sheets, tree rings, sediments, corals, shells, and rocks. They often contain physical evidence of trapped air bubbles, pollen, ash, fossils, and ratios of stable atomic isotopes that make it possible to understand trends in climate throughout prehistoric times.

Each source of natural material found in these samples provides specialized data. Pollen found in ice sheets for example, can hint at the amount of precipitation the year the ice was laid down, and the amount of plant growth resulting from it. The ice may also contain ash from volcanic eruptions. The air bubbles trapped in snow that is over time compressed into glaciers provide valuable insight into the composition of the air when the ice sheet was formed. The differential rates of evaporation of isotopes of oxygen and hydrogen in water change during warm and cold periods, and evidence of these changes can be found in the shells of buried marine creatures, fossils, and stalactites. Coral and tree rings respond to their surroundings in response to temperature and other abiotic factors such as precipitation or salinity.

Not only is paleoclimatology useful for understanding past climate and environmental processes and how the environment we know was created, but it is important for understanding the likely ecological reactions to climate change in the present. Unlike prehistoric causes of climate change, many of the present changes are proposed to be anthropogenic in nature, such as increased amounts of CO_2 and greenhouse gases in the atmosphere. Though the present causes are more complex, the reactions of the environment to these changes in temperature will most likely be the same.

By using the existing data taken from the physical evidence found in various natural materials, accurate projections of environmental reactions can be made. These data can be used to construct a model, or projection, of global and hemispheric temperature trends distributed over a long period of time. There are not enough reliable data to reconstruct temperature beyond the past several centuries, so 'proxies'—the data from these natural materials—are used to ascertain temperatures during the past (Mann et al. 2009). Modeling the environmental reactions of climate change in the past makes it possible to predict environmental responses to present climate change. Though modern climate change is influenced by large amounts of atmospheric CO_2 unlike some of the previous climate change, the ecological reactions, like melting ice coverage in the Northern Hemisphere or the expiration of coral reefs in the Southern Hemisphere, are the same.

The results from studying the Medieval Climate Anomaly support the hypothesis that the climate 1500 years ago was consistent with the El Niño Southern Oscillation in a La Niña-influenced climate in the Northern Hemisphere, resulting in warmer and drier temperatures (Mann et al. 2009). Significant amounts of data support the theory of increasing temperatures in the Northern Hemisphere in the present day, resulting in similar conditions. These temperatures are causing changes in the composition of glaciers, sea ice, snow cover, nutrient flux, vegetation assemblies, and the ecological communities they are included in (Brigham-Grette 2009). The West Antarctic Ice Sheet (WAIS) and the Greenland Ice Sheet (GIS) are common subjects of paleoclimatology as their compositions are currently changing. Increases in temperatures, particularly during the winter months, drastically affect the amount of both marine and terrestrial ice cover. Data taken from ice core samples and projected into climate models indicate that total ice cover has waxed and waned throughout time, and if these temperature changes continue, influenced by increased atmospheric CO_2, an Arctic with seasonal ice coverage only is a few decades away (Brigham-Grette).

Elsewhere on the planet, increases in temperature, sea level, and increased nutrients in the water column are causing striking changes in tropical coral reefs. These changes are similar to some that occurred early in the Holocene era, though at a slower pace. Studies of samples taken from fossil reefs have determined that during the last interglacial period approximately 121 thousand years ago, ice sheets in the Northern Hemisphere melted because of increased global temperatures, causing a rise in sea level of 4–6 meters higher than the current sea level (Blanchon et al. 2009). Coral is an organism that requires sunlight for the photosynthesizing organisms that live inside it, and so it grows in clear, shallow waters. As the sea level increased, the corals followed it up, their skeletons remaining as relics when sea levels again declined, showing just how high sea levels had become. These data provide reason to assume that the melting of ice sheets in the Northern Hemisphere occurring presently will have the same effect on coral reefs.

Weather patterns have historically had an effect on global temperatures, and studies of insolation—the amount of sunlight reaching the Earth—are used to predict weather patterns that affected the climate in prehistoric Africa, Asia, and Europe. Prell and Kutzbach (1987) studied paleomonsoons and the effect that changes in insolation had on weather patterns. They supported their hypothesis by numerous proxies including North Atlantic sediment cores and freshwater diatoms.

Global temperature conditions are also affected by changes in earth's orbit. Weather patterns in the tropical Pacific like ENSO respond sensitively and often unpredictably to ocean-atmospheric interactions during earth's rotation around the sun (Chiang 2009). The effect that weather patterns have on local, and often global, temperatures is significant, and their study is central to understanding paleoclimatology.

Paleoclimatology provides two important means of comprehending our planet and its natural processes. First, it allows an understanding of how our familiar environment and its ecosystems were created. Second, it provides information of how they are affected by both natural and human-caused changes in climate. Increases in CO_2 and greenhouse gases in the atmosphere increase the temperature in many parts of the globe. Insolation and orbit also play vital roles in determining the physical conditions of the natural world. Paleoclimatology is a process that uses minute elemental hints and builds models that project across thousands of years of change in order to better understand the processes of our dynamic and fragile planet.

Contemporary Paleoclimatology

Temperatures in the Northern Hemisphere are increasing and are causing changes in the composition of glaciers, sea ice, snow cover, nutrient flux, and vegetation assemblies and the ecological communities they are included in. Increases in the temperatures of the Greenland Ice Sheet (GIS) are most severe in the winter seasons, and summer temperatures are currently less affected. Brigham-Grette (2009) breaks down the present trends of warming in the Nothern Hemisphere by using paleoclimatologic records that employ historical changes in temperature to project future consequences.

The use of physical evidence from paleoclimatology records, including lake sediments, ice cores, and tree rings provide the centuries-long perspective required to assess these changes. Comparing lake sediment from the early Holocene era (approximately 8,000 years ago) which was only slightly warmer on average than present day temperatures, to current sediment from the same region shows that the previous decade was the warmest in over 2,000 years. The increase in temperature caused prehistoric changes in the northern regions; the GIS was reduced and the tree line grew further north.

The projections of the past make it possible to predict environmental responses to future climate change. Though modern climate change is influenced by anthropogenically-emitted atmospheric CO_2 unlike previous climate change, the ecological reactions, like melting ice coverage in the Northern Hemisphere are the same. Unless action is taken to reduce the amounts of CO_2 discharged into the atmosphere, an Arctic with seasonal ice coverage only is a few decades away.

The Last Glacial Maximum

The Last Glacial Maximum (LGM) is known to be the time of the furthest coverage of ice sheets and mountain glaciers, approximately 20,000 years ago (20 ka). Clark *et al.* (2009) found traces of carbon, beryllium, and helium in sediment core samples taken from the West Antarctic Ice Sheet (WAIS) that provide paleontological information of the increase and decrease of ice cover in that area 10–50 ka. It is thought that decreases in the northern summer insolation caused the ice sheets to grow to their maximum levels approximately 33–26 ka, and imminent increases in temperatures in tropical southern regions carried north by ocean conditions caused them to melt and raise the sea level, causing further deglaciation shortly thereafter (approximately 19–20 ka).

The researchers used existing sea level data from the WAIS to project the rise in sea levels that probably occurred 26–19 ka and compared this data with their own previously constrained glaciations to predict the sea level change. The ice models fell within close proximity of each other. The results suggest that while each region within the WAIS had concurrent fluctuations of glaciation, there was considerable regional variability in the timing, however by 26.5 ka it is thought that they had all reached their maximum extents. The C, Be, and He isotopes found in core samples reflected low sea levels during this time, corresponding with the projected glacial maximum.

The resulting data suggest that the ice sheets in the WAIS were in equilibrium with changes in the global climate. Increasing amounts of CO_2 in the atmosphere and consequential increases in temperature caused decreases in ice coverage during the Last Glacial Maximum 50 ka. Reconstructions of these events using paleoclimatological data can give insight into a modern world of rising temperature.

Modeling Fluctuations in the Antarctic Ice Sheet: A Five Million Year History

The West Antarctic ice sheet, or WAIS, has been considered on the verge of severe retreat and collapse. Pollard *et al.* (2009) used a new treatment of grounding-line dynamics and ice shelf buttressing to create an ice sheet/ice shelf model projecting approximately five million years into the past. They compared their simulation to a newly-taken sediment core from the Ross Sea, and the data matched. The paleontological data supported the proxy model in projecting that the melting trends in the Pleistocene were long-winded, and the rapid collapse and breaking of ice was more common. As time progressed and temperatures increased, so did the speed of the ice reduction, until reaching a near modern position three million years ago.

The researchers drove the model with parameterization of surface mass balance, air temperature, and specified sea level. The five-million-year projection indicated that the area of ice cover (the thickness of the ice sheet, the shape of the coastlines, and the distance from ice edge to open ocean) was affected by natural interglacial forcing mechanisms such as temperature and sea level. The variation of each forcing mechanism was determined by examining core samples from the deep sea off shore.

While ocean temperatures and their relationships to Antarctic ice-melting rates are relatively new subjects of study, significant advances in the methods of collecting and projecting data have occurred. Pollard *et al.* divided the interiormelt increase by the current whole ice shelf average and determined that the WAIS began to significantly collapse with a 5°C increase in temperature. By designing accurate models of climate activity alongside existent paleoclimatology data, a realistic and plausible construction of natural processes can be made over an extremely long period of time.

Origins of the Little Ice Age and Medieval Climate Anomalies

The goal of paleoclimatology is to ascertain past fluxes in global climates to gain an understanding of the current and future effects of present climate change. Mann *et al.* (2009) used a global climate proxy network to model temperature patterns over the past 1500 years. This time period includes the Medieval Climate Anomaly (or Medieval Warm Period), approximately 800–1300 AD, and extends into the so called Little Ice Age that occurred afterward, in approximately the 16th to 19th Centuries. To illustrate the gradual shift in climate, the eras were broken down into three specific century-long periods. The conclusions were that although some parts of the Earth during the MCA were as warm as they are currently, the average global temperature is now significantly higher.

There are not enough reliable data to reconstruct temperatures beyond the past several centuries, so 'proxies'—data from ice cores, sediments, and treerings—were used to ascertain temperatures during the past. The results from the Medieval Climate Anomaly supported the hypothesis that the climate 1500 years ago was consistent with the El Niño Southern Oscillation in a La Niña-influenced climate in the Northern Hemisphere, resulting in warmer and drier temperatures. The Little Ice Age (not a true 'Ice Age,' though it had distinctly cooler temperatures from present climates in the same regions by about 1°C) were not considered unusual in those circumstances, though the researchers mentioned that the climate proxy model is most effective for the Northern Hemisphere and the tropics.

These climate changes, most likely instigated by natural factors like solar irradiance and volcanic eruptions, may have had different causes than current climate changes, but the effects can be the same. These paleoclimate reconstructions can predict outcomes of drought and temperature increase that occur from climate change with both natural and anthropogenic initiation. Continued reconstruction of models of past climate change could be expanded with refined methodology to increase the precision of these predictions, to better prepare the world for a climate changed future.

Ice Core Isotopes: Paleoclimatology Projections from the Holocene

Elsig et al. (2009) took measurements of ratios of carbon isotopes in CO_2 in an Antarctic ice core. Using mass-balance inverse model calculations they infer that there was a decrease in atmospheric CO_2 by approximately 5 ppmv in the early Holocene. The increase in carbon intake responsible for the change was most likely an uptake of carbon from the land biosphere and the ocean, evidenced by changes in ratios of stable carbon isotopes from these proxies. From the low point in the Holocene, 7,000 years ago, there was an increase in CO_2 in pre-industrial atmospheric air of roughly 20 ppmv. This carbon contribution is thought to have been due to re-release from past land-biosphere uptake and the formation of coral reefs.

The measurements of carbon isotopes within the ice core samples were taken by placing crushed ice from the original sample under a vacuum which releases gases into a sublimation vessel. The air is dried, and a pressure gauge is used to calculate the CO_2 concentration. The sample is purified and then injected into an isotope ratio mass spectrometer, which allows the characteristics of isotopes and variations within them to be studied.

Interglacial Sea Levels and their Effects on Coral Reefs

Fossil reefs can be used as climate proxies to determine previous climate conditions and provide insight into the resulting reactions of reef ecosystems to changes in temperature. There are data that suggest the existence of a significant increase in sea level during the last interglacial period, approximately 121 thousand years ago, when ice sheet levels were unsustainable and shrunk considerably. Blanchon *et al.* 2009 used samples of fossilized reef from the northeast coast of the Yucatán peninsula, Mexico, to measure reef reactions to increased sea levels. They found that because of the glacial melt, sea level had risen approximately 4–6 meters higher than current levels, and with it, the height of the corals. When sea levels decreased, the reef back stepped in reaction, or essentially died, approximately 6 meters above currfent sea level. These data provide reason to assume that a similar reaction is likely to occur among modern coral reefs with increases in temperature.

The age structure of a well-exposed fossil coral is analyzed through its stratigraphic architecture and palaeoecologic zonation. The northern peninsula of the Yucatán has no neotectonic activity. It's well preserved coral structures date into the Miocene and Pleistocene eras. Global climate change has resulted in dramatic and rapid melting of ice shelves in both Antarctic and Greenland ice sheet areas. The affirmation by this projection of sea level instability has caused concern for the future of coral reefs, which are once again threatened by significant sea level rise due to anthropogenically caused climate change and are already threatened by other anthropogenic activity.

Isotope Evidence of Temperate Climate 3.42 Billion Years Ago

Using a combined analysis of stable oxygen and hydrogen isotopes, a firm and reliable extrapolation of past climates can be made. Hren *et al.* (2009) examined cherts (rocks) composed of 95% microcrystalline quartz from the Buck Reef Chert of the Onverwacht formation in South Africa for these hydrogen and oxygen isotopes. The empirical and theoretical chert-water fractionation data from the isotopes sampled from the 3.42 billion year old sediments are consistent with the formation of waters at low temperatures, estimated at below 40°C. This new method of combined analysis disproves previous paleoclimatology projections that this Palaeoarchaean ocean region was several degrees warmer during the Archaean era.

Cherts are frequently used in studies of paleoceanography. The oxygen composition within the rocks can be used to identify past temperatures by fractionation of the quartz/water ratio. High values are interpreted as cooler temperatures in early oceans. For this study, black and white banded cherts were powdered and sieved through mesh, treated to remove organic material, and oxygen and hydrogen isotopes were measured by infrared laser fluorination. Palaeotemperatures were calculated using the quartz-water oxygen isotope fractionation factor, and had surprisingly high results.

Using these data, Hren *et al.* established that Archaean ocean water was several degrees cooler than previously thought, an outcome consistent with recent paleoclimatology projections of extended hydrogen depletion in both the ancient oceans and the surrounding atmosphere.

Elements and Stable Isotopes in Giant Clams, *Tridacna gigas* provide Paleoclimatology Data

Paleoclimactic reconstructions of temperature can be supplemented by data taken from traces of elements and stable isotopes found in the shells of the bivalve mollusk *Tridacna gigas* or giant clam. The long-lived mollusk is native to the shallow reefs of the South Pacific and Indian oceans and can measure up to four feet across, and weigh as much as 440 pounds; it has been the subject of scientific study since 1825. Elliot *et al.* (2009) measured the growth rates of three individuals taken from locations along the Indo-Pacific, each with different temperature and productivity ranges. It was discovered that the peaks in barium and calcium composition in shell structure are in sync with the peaks in chlorophyll associated with phytoplankton blooms, or increased ocean productivity. By consulting the shell composition of the mollusks, which can live over 100 years, reconstructions of past temperatures and ocean productivity can be made.

The researchers collected the three specimens from the waters of Great Palm Island in the Indo Pacific region, the Great Barrier Reef, and Cocos Island. The specimens were of similar size and age. Traces of the elements Sr, Mg, Ba, and Ca were found using Laser Ablation Inductively Coupled Plasma Mass Spectrometry (LA–ICPMS). The chlorophyll data was measured from each location using a satellite dataset from 1998–2006.

While Mg/Ca and Sr/Ca profiles exhibited little change, or data of value, the Ba/Ca profiles were consistently responsive to surface water chlorophyll measurements. This suggests that barium can be used as an indicator of the timing and intensity of blooms in phytoplankton populations, which depend on specific temperature conditions. Ba is not found in *T. gigas* alone; it is found in the shell composition of many mollusks, however the size of *T. gigas* made it easier to collect samples since all areas of the shells are thick enough to be used in paleoclimatic studies.

Obliquity: Effects on Ice Sheet Oscillations

Naish *et al.* (2009) studied the West Antarctic Ice Sheet (WAIS) during the Pliocene era, a time period 3–5 million years ago with temperatures slightly higher than present day. Understanding ice sheet behavior under these temperatures may shed light on future patterns of ice coverage under global climate change. The authors made projections of ice sheet variations from a core sample taken from the Ross Sea. The data provide evidence in support of oscillations in ice cover as affected by the Earth's axial tilt and patterns in orbit, and show that oscillations in global climate would cause the WAIS to periodically collapse from grounded ice or ice shelves to open waters, and freeze back again in sync with Earth's obliquity.

Geological evidence of obliquity affecting Earth's climate systems is commonly found in oxygen isotopes, ocean circulation and sediments, atmospheric dust, and fluctuations in global sea level. During the Pliocene, climatic changes were regular approximately every 40 thousand years. Significant collapses in ice cover exposing open waters in the Ross embayment would occur when planetary temperatures reached 3–6°C higher than they are today, which at their minimum were under freezing. As a result, sea level is projected to have risen 3–7 meters with the melting of the ice cover. Further climatic conditions during interglacial activity include an elevated amount of atmospheric CO_2. Though influenced by obliquity on Earth's axis, the conditions that arose under the increase in temperature and atmospheric CO_2 are similar to current environmental behavior under global climate change.

Conclusions

Understanding global climate change is important for determining the future of Earth's ecosystems, and how the adjustment to those changing ecosystems should be managed. Paleoclimatology is a valuable insight into the past that few generations have had the privilege to access. The minute imprints left by simple chance are invaluable resources that provide concrete evidence of these past conditions. Changes in temperature and weather patterns cause the immediate environment to react, which affect other natural processes across the globe. The melting of ice sheets and glaciers in the north cause rises in sea level, which destroys coral reefs in the south. When marine systems are less productive the shells of bivalves are slower to grow, and this repose shows in the isotopes that make up their shells. Weather patterns that bring cold air into a consistently warm area cause declines in plant and animal life; likewise when the reverse occurs increased erosion and changes in local biota are among the reactions. These changes are cyclical and natural to our active planet. Regardless of how much, human-caused changes to the climate are occurring in the present. These changes are speeding up the cycles of climate variation on a global scale. They are occurring faster than the environment can adapt. The study of paleoclimatology will not provide answers of how to react to climate change; the answers it supplies are a simple statement of what is to come.

References Cited

Blanchon, P., Eisenhauer, A., Fietzke, J., Liebetrau, V. 2009. Rapid sea-level rise and reef back-stepping at the close of the last interglacial highstand. Nature 458, 881–884.

Brigham-Grette, J. 2009. Contemporary Arctic change: A paleoclimate de´ja` vu? PNAS 106, 18431–18432.

Chiang, J. C. H., 2009. The Tropics in Paleoclimate. Annual Review of Earth and Planetary Sciences. 37, 263–297.

Clark, P. U., Dyke, A. S., Shakun, J. D., Carlson, A. E., Clark, J., Wohlfarth, B., Mitrovica, Jerry X., Hostetler, S. W., McCabe, A. M. 2009. The Last Glacial Maximum. Science 325, 710–714.

Elliot, M., Welsh, K., Chilcott, C., McCulloch, M., Chappell, J., Ayling, B. 2009. Profiles of trace elements and stable isotopes derived from giant long-lived Tridacna gigas bivalves: Potential applications in paleoclimate studies. Palaeogeography, Palaeoclimatology, Palaeoecology 280, 132–142.

Elsig, J. E., Schmitt, J. S., Leuenberger, D., Schneider, R., Eyer, M., Leuenberger, M., Joos, F., Fischer, H., Stocker, T. F. 2009. Stable isotope constraints on Holocene carbon cycle changes from an Antarctic ice core. Nature 461, 507–510.

Hren, M. T., Tice, M. M., Chamberlain, C. P. 2009. Oxygen and hydrogen isotope evidence for a temperature climate 3.42 billion years ago. Nature 462, 205–208.

Mann, M. E., Zhang, Z., Rutherford, S., Bradley R. S., Hughes, M. K., Shindell, D., Ammann, C., Faluvegi, G., Ni, F., 2009. Global Signatures and Dynamical Origins of the Little Ice Age and Medieval Climate Anomaly. Science 326, 1256-1260.

Naish, T., Powell, R., Levy, R., Wilson, G., Scherer, F., Talarico, F., Krissek, L., Niessen, F., Pompilio, M., Wilson, T., Carter, L., DeConto, R., Huybers, P., McKay, R., Pollard, D., Ross, J., Winter, D., Barreth, P., Browne, G., Cody, R., Cowan, E., Crampton, J., Dunban, G., Dunbar, N., Florindo, F., Gebhardt, C., Graham, I., Hannah, M., Hansaraj, D., Harwood, D., Helling, D., Henrys, S., Hinnov, L., Kuhn, G., Kyle, P., La"ufen, A., Maffiolini, P., Magens, D., Mandernack K., McIntoch, W., Millan, C., Morin, R., Ohneiser, C., Paulsen, T., Persico, D., Raine, I., Reed, J., Riesselman, C. 2009. Obliquity-paced Pliocene West Antarctic ice sheet oscillations. Nature 458, 322–328.

Pollard, D., DeConto, R. M. 2009. Modelling West Antarctic ice sheet growth and collapse through the past five million years. Nature 359, 330–333.

Prell WL, Kutzbach JE. 1987. Monsoon variability over the past 150,000 years. Journal of Geophysical Research. 92, 8411–25.

3. Global Effects of ENSO (El Niño Southern Oscillation)

Luisana Hernandez

As a prominent source of inter-annual climate variability, ENSO (El Niño Southern Oscillation) has tremendous effects on our planet (Christie *et al.* 2009). ENSO has two phases in the eastern Pacific Ocean: a warm and dry phase (El Niño) and a cool and wet phase (La Niña) (Leduc *et al.* 2009). The shift in climate during ENSO years causes modifications to occur in affected ecosystems throughout the world. As you will see in this chapter, ENSO affects organisms and areas differently—while some will struggle, others will benefit as a result of the varied climatic conditions (Balbotín *et al.* 2009). This chapter will also present topics related to ENSO chronologies, population growth, species adaptation, and global climate change (GCC).

Cascading effects can also cause damage in social and economic terms because the climate affects where we live and even what we eat. For example, a longer rainy season can cause a larger population of agricultural pests—such as the degu in Chile—which could then potentially harm or lower the annual yield of crops (Previtali *et al.* 2010). The present concern is not that ENSO events will continue to occur, but that they will occur at a faster pace and for longer periods of time.

It is becoming clear that more studies on the effects of ENSO are needed in order to understand the widespread changes that result from GCC. Knowing the direct effects of ENSO, such as drought, on specific areas would help to determine the indirect effects that were triggered, such as low tree growth (Özger *et al.* 2009, Borgaonkar *et al.* 2010). Further development of chronologies and precipitation records will make it easier to compile data and analyze it to find common trends with fewer gaps in the records.

Polylepis tarapacana tree-rings from Central Andes create ENSO chronology

ENSO (El Niño Southern Oscillation) causes weather anomalies all over the world though some areas are not as well researched or documented. For example, there was no ENSO tree-ring chronology for the eastern tropical Pacific to provide a clear climate indicator for the area. Christie *et al.* (2009) analyzed tree-rings of *Polylepis tarapacana* trees of the central Andes and related them to sea surface temperatures (SST), air temperature, and precipitation. The results showed that the growth of *P. tarapacana* is correlated with temperature and precipitation that are in turn connected to ENSO cycles.

Christie *et al.*, from the Universidad Austral de Chile and the Instituto Argentino de Nivología, Glaciología y Ciencias Ambientales, developed an ENSO tree-ring chronology from *P. tarapacana* samples, SST, and precipitation records from two locations in Altiplano, Central Andes—Volcán Guallatiri in the north and Cerro Granada in the south. The relationships between SST, temperature, and precipitation records were analyzed monthly with correlation analysis such as SEA (Superposed Epoch analysis). SEA created a list of ENSO events—five-year windows based on the temperature and precipitation records—which formed a visible pattern of ENSO characteristics.

The results support the idea that variable temperatures and summer precipitation in Altiplano and the tropical Pacific are caused primarily by ENSO. The data show that El Niño causes warm and dry summers, whereas La Niña causes cold and rainy summers, which are reflected in the growth patterns of *P. tarapacana*. ENSO climate anomalies affect the growth of the trees because 85% of the annual precipitation happens during the summer—December, January, and February—and because the peak ENSO season is November through February. This tree-ring chronology provides a much-needed look at the effects of ENSO on an annual basis, which can be compared to other areas of the world.

El Niño Causes Low Teak Tree Growth in Kerala, India

In a similar manner to the Central Andes, a 523 year tree-ring chronology in India showed that El Niño causes low growth years in *Tectona grandis L.F.* (teak trees) (Borgaonkar *et al.* 2010). The area of Kerala in southern India receives the majority of its annual rainfall during the southwest monsoon season and El Niño anomalies seem to be correlated with drought in this area. Many El Niño events coincided with lower precipitation (drought) and low tree growth based on teak samples.

Borgaonkar *et al.,* from the Indian Institute of Tropical Meteorology, collected 74 cores from 44 teak trees from three sites—Narangathara (NAR), Nellikooth (NEL), and Tekkedy (TKD). All the ring series were combined to form the Kerala Tree-Ring Chronology (KTRC) which dates from 1481–2003. Correlation analyses were performed with seasonal rainfall, all India rainfall (AIRF), and mean surface air temperatures.

Out of 46 low growth years (LGY) there were 30 LGYs that were directly associated with El Niño. The climate and tree-ring width from the KTRC revealed that low growth rings were associated with deficient rainfall. The trees showed a dependence on moisture—based on the Palmer Drought Severity Index (PDSI)—since moisture depends on Indian Summer Monsoon Rainfall (ISMR). ISMR is correlated with warm phase of ENSO anomalies (El Niño) but after the mid 1980s the relationship weakened which the authors believe is due to increased winter and spring temperatures across Europe and Asia or changes in the ENSO cycle and influence of the Indian Ocean Dipole. Though trees are being affected by these ENSO anomalies, ENSO is not simply an explanation for everything.

ENSO Not a Cause of Tropical Pacific Climate Change

Based on analyses of marine core samples from the tropics, the change in rainfall has not been caused by ENSO (Leduc *et al.* 2009). Though ENSO is currently a major climatic event that affects many regions, it was not found to control the precipitation during the last glacial period. Thermohaline circulation is a possible power source behind the climate in the tropical Pacific because shifts in the hydrological cycle depend on sea-surface temperatures (SST).

Leduc *et al.* analyzed marine sediment samples from the northwestern tropical Pacific (NWP) and the northeastern tropical Pacific (NEP) and continental sedimentary core samplesfrom the southwestern tropical Pacific (SWP). The samples were used to distinguish between ENSO and ITCZ (Intertropical Convergence Zone)—both possible causes of shifting tropical precipitation. The sediment cores were dated then used to reconstruct a timescale of hydrological changes based on $\delta^{18}O$ of surface water. If rainfall was shifting it would cause the sea-surface salinity (SSS) and $\delta^{18}O$ to shift.

The data did not support the ENSO hypothesis because the precipitation changes observed in the model showed that the SWP region reacted differently than NWP and NEP regions. The NWP and NEP were drier and the SWP was wetter, which is most likely a response to a weakening North Atlantic Deep Water (NADW). The thermohaline circulation hypothesis could then explain the shift in precipitation in the tropical Pacific. The tropical Pacific was not being affected by the climate anomaly, but many areas around the globe continue to experience its effects.

El Niño Causes Drought in Certain Regions of Texas

There exists a positive correlation between El Niño years and drought in certain regions of Texas (Özger *et al.* 2009). Texas contains many climate systems which react differently to climate anomalies like El Niño or La Niña—mostly the sub-tropic semi-humid and continental climate regions are affected by ENSO (El Niño Southern oscillation). Western parts of Texas usually experienced dry conditions after El Niño events, while La Niña produced more moisture. Other countries, like Australia, also suffer a dryer climate because of El Niño since it affects the amount of rainfall an area receives.

Özger *et al.*, from the Department of Biological and Agricultural Engineering at Texas A&M University respectively, observed the possible correlations between drought occurrences in Texas and large scale climate events. The Palmer Drought Severity Index (PDSI) was used to measure drought occurrences from 1895–2007 which was obtained from the National Climate Data Center. Global sea surface temperatures (SSTs) and NINO 3 were used as indices of ENSO activity. The continuous wavelet transform (CWT) and cross-correlation analyses were used to show the relationship between variables—in this case drought and ENSO or PDO (Pacific decadal oscillation).

The data show that the droughts in Texas are related to strong El Niño events on a multi-year or decadal scale. There was a high correlation between semi-arid and continental climate regions with NINO 3 region SSTs, which means that the higher response on the PDSI is due to ENSO events. These results confirm that ENSO is responsible for drought on the annual and decadal time scale. It also means that El Niño years cause droughts because it is cooler and La Niña, because it is warmer, does not have a significant correlation with drought in Texas. Direct effects, like drought, can have lasting effects on the land and on organisms that inhabit or depend on it, especially if they have adapted to specific conditions.

Barn Swallow (*Hirundo rustica*) Populations Affected by Global Climate Patterns

Populations of *Hirundo rustica* (barn swallows) in Denmark and Spain showed that climate change affects populations distinctly because they experience different environmental conditions over a wide area (Balbotín *et al.* 2009). As long-distance migrants, barn swallows can be affected directly or indirectly by climate which may cause a shift in behavioral patterns, or mismatch in insect emergence, resources, or competitors.

Balbotín *et al.*, from the Universidad de Anatomia, Universidad de Extremadura, and the Université Pierre et Marie Curie, captured and studied barn swallows at Badajoz, Spain and Kraghede, Denmark for seventeen years (1991–2007). Weekly captures of adult birds were made during breeding season to tag all the breeding individuals and differentiate between males and females. Adults were identified by a metal ring and a combination of color PVC rings while offspring were just given metal rings. Mean arrival dates were calculated for each year of the study for each adult male and female. Annual survival for yearlings was estimated since barn swallows always return to the same breeding site and partner each year. The authors also observed dispersal rates and environmental variables—Northern Atlantic Oscillation index (NAO), Southern Oscillation index (SOI), and Normalized Difference Vegetation Index (NDVI) in North, West, and South Africa.

Analyses showed that NDVI—a satellite-based measure of aboveground vegetation—increased significantly for Spanish barn swallows during their spring migration. Mean arrival dates got sooner overall during the course of the study, but it was significant only for females from Spain while it was significant for both sexes in Denmark. Spanish barn swallows recruited more when SOI became positive and yearling survival increased when NAO became positive during winter. In contrast, Danish barn swallows recruited more when SOI became negative and yearling survival increased when NAO became negative during winter. Dispersal rate was higher for Spanish barn swallows during El Niño years and lower in La Niña years, while the opposite was true for Danish barn swallows. Though Danish barn swallows will suffer when NAO is positive, some organisms will blossom and prosper, like the degu.

Prolonged El Niño Events Cause Degu Population Growth

Rainfall trends have cascading effects on ecosystems, especially those that are arid or semi-arid. The degu (*Octodon degus*) is a small mammal found in semi-arid Chile whose survival, breeding season, and ability to reproduce is sensitive to changes in rainfall phases (Previtali *et al.* 2010). Analysis showed that degu populations blossom during and after prolonged rain phases.

Previtlali *et al.* studied the degu population in Bosque Fray Jorge National Park in Chile from March 1989–May 2007. The study plots the authors used were in Quebrada de las Vacas where they live-trapped and tagged individuals for four nights per month. Sex, reproductive condition, and weight were recorded for each animal and then it was released. Models of degu population dynamics were created using different variables that the authors believed affected the population, such as density and annual rainfall. Each year was classified as wet or dry depending on the amount of rainfall and was placed in 2-year phases: dry-dry, dry-wet, wet-wet, and wet-dry.

In total, the researchers captured 3,444 individuals, but the population reached the highest density during 2000–2002, which was a 3-year wet period. Data showed that there was above-average rainfall from 1999–2006, which led to longer breeding seasons, and heightened breeding activity. In any case, wet-wet years produced higher juvenile persistence, fertility, and higher chances of survival for adults. It is daunting to find that an increase in ENSO events can cause so many ripples in one ecosystem; an increase in the degu population will affect the Chilean crops which will affect the Chilean human population. Humans are not immune to environmental effects, so it is only natural to wonder if ENSO events caused alterations in our behavior long ago and caused populations to build fortifications.

Fort Construction in the Pacific Not Caused by ENSO

The climate has always led humans to build and plan according to seasonal precipitation which led researchers to question whether the El Niño Southern Oscillation (ENSO) cycles were correlated with the building of fortified settlements on Pacific Islands (Field and Lape 2010). Though many fortifications were built in areas that are affected by drought caused by ENSO they were not actually built at the onset of these climate anomalies.

Field and Lape, from Ohio State University and University of Washington at Seattle, respectively, studied the possible correlation between the dates when climatic events occurred and fortifications in the Pacific were created. The authors used chronologies of ENSO events based on oxygen isotope records and securely dated fortifications to make their analysis. Fortifications were described as settlements or refuges built of stone and earth on steep slopes that would provide some form of protection or barrier to others.

The data did not support the authors' hypothesis about climate-driven construction in the Pacific. The authors found that fortifications were not common before AD 900 but increased after AD 1400 which was after the peak in ENSO frequency. The areas that experienced moderate to severe drought during El Niño had a 99% correlation with fort location—these areas were more likely to have fortifications. There were no positive correlations between El Niño events and fort construction though it was noted that fortifications lagged behind intense ENSO events. The researchers suggest further study of fortifications because there was a lack of securely dated fortifications and regionally-specific climate records. We know that ENSO did not affect our construction in the past, but fast forward to the present and we find that water has become a priority since it is climate-driven and sensitive to human activity.

ENSO-Induced Streamflow connected to Anoxia in Water Reservoirs

Water quality is of great concern for arid areas that rely on reservoirs, so it is important to understand the factors that might affect the water quality. ENSO (El Niño Southern Oscillation) affects the amount of rainfall certain regions receive which could alter the streamflow into reservoirs (Marcé *et al.* 2010). Analyses showed that when streamflow decreased during El Niño, the oxygen content—a measure of water quality—of the reservoir also decreased.

Marcé *et al.* investigated the possible connection between ENSO and reservoir water quality in Sau Reservoir in Spain from 1964–2007. The study consisted of two parts; first the authors tested to see if streamflow—and therefore water quality—was sensitive to ENSO. Water samples were taken almost on a monthly basis since the initial fill of the reservoir in 1964 to measure the oxygen content. The oxygen readings were then expressed as Anoxic Factors (AF)—a standardized appraisal of the absence of oxygen in water (anoxia). After a spectral analysis, the final analysis of coupling time-series was done using continuous wavelet transform (CWT), cross-wavelet transform (XWT), and wavelet coherence (WTC). Secondly, the researchers tried to quantify the effect of the decreasing streamflow on the reservoir. Rainfall-runoff models were used to measure climate variability while another model was built to observe river chloride concentration and mean annual water residence time in the reservoir.

The spectral analysis showed that streamflow, AF, and ENSO occurred on cycles of 5.2 and 2.4 years during 1964–1991. Streamflow also oscillated inter-annually during the spring and autumn, though AF only matched these peaks during 1964–1991 and this trend was most prominent during dry years. These data suggest that anoxia is sensitive to streamflow but loses this sensitivity when waste water entering the rivers has been treated overriding the beneficial effects of streamflow. The wavelet analyses also supported the idea that ENSO affects reservoir water quality through its effect on streamflow.

Conclusions

There is still much to be understood about ENSO because it causes devastation and growth around the world. If these events are becoming longer and more frequent than research must be done to address why that is happening and to further understand its role in global climate change. ENSO is an environmental, social, and economic issue which affects people differently. With more chronologies from areas in the Pacific, common trends can be found which would allow for further awareness on the issue so we can predict what the future will look like for everyone.

References Cited

Balbontín, J., Møller, A., Hermosell, I., Marzal, A., Reviriego, M., De Lope, F., 2009. Divergent patterns of impact of environmental conditions on life history traits in two populations of a long-distance migratory bird. Oecologia 159, 859–872.

Borgaonkar, H.P., Sikder, A.B., Ram, S., Pant, G.B., 2010. El Niño and realted monsoon drought signals in 523-year-long ring width records of teak (*Tectona grandis* L.F.) trees from south India. Paleogeography, Palaeoclimatology, Palaeoecology 285, 74–84.

Christie, D., Lara, A., Barichivich, J., Villalba, R., Morales, M., Cuq, E., 2009. El Niño-Southern Oscillation signal in the world's highest-elevation tree-ring chronologies from the Altiplano, Central Andes. Palaeogeography, Palaeoclimatology, Palaeoecology 281, 309–319.

Field, S., Lape, P., 2010. Paleoclimates and the emergence of fortifications in the tropical Pacific islands. Journal of Anthropological Archaeology 29, 113–124.

Leduc, G., Vidal, L., Tachikawa, K., Bard, E., 2009. ITCZ rather than ENSO signature for abrupt climate changes across the tropical Pacific. Quaternary Research 72, 123–131.

Marcé, R., Rodríguez-Arias, M., Garcia, J., Armengol, J., 2010. El Niño Southern Oscillation and climate trends impact reservoir water quality. Global Change Biology 1–9. DOI: 10.1111/j.1365–2486.2010.02163.x

Özger, M., Mishra, A., Singh, V., 2009. Low frequency drought variability associated with climate indices. Journal of Hydrology 364, 152–162.

Previtali, A., Meserve, P., Kelt, D., Milstead, B., Gutierrez, J., 2010. Effects of more frequent and prolonged El Niño events on life-history parameters of the Degu, a long-lived and slow-reproducing rodent. Conservation Biology 24, 18–28.

4. Current Anthropogenic Emissions and Climate Forcing

Aly Stark

As global climate change becomes a primary concern for both scientists and policy makers, it is increasingly important to understand the intricacies of the direct and indirect effects of emissions on climate forcing—the changes that occur in climate in response to the emissions. The goal is to better explain past temperature trends in light of atmospheric composition, and to predict future warming. Understanding the relationship between anthropogenic emissions and climate forcing will be pivotal in creating policies and actions to help mitigate and minimize increasing temperatures. For example, by examining the links between methane, ozone, and aerosols, Shindell *et al.* (2009) concluded that the amount of one pollutant emitted can significantly affect the properties of other pollutants. Further, the effects of these emissions are altered by gas-aerosol interactions. In this case, the interactions between various emissions were examined for abundance-based forcing and emissions-based forcing. The first technique measured the collective effects of all emissions, while the second measured the individual effects of each specific pollutant on all the others.

While climate forcing attributed to increased anthropogenic emissions is on the rise, natural occurrences can have a similar impact on forcing, for example the interaction between forests and CO_2 results in both warming (through the absorption of solar radiation) and cooling (through carbon sequestration). Rotenberg and Yakir (2010) considered radiative forcing associated with both carbon intake and albedo to find a point at which both forces will be create a surface energy balance.

The causes of climate forcing are broad, which makes it an entirely global phenomenon. Yet, while forcing is a functional means of explaining global climate change, it can also be applied to regional trends. Shindell and Faluvegi (2009) found that examining the susceptibility of individual regions to various climate forcing components can indentify more definite causes. Further, understanding regional trends and forcing impacts can identify certain latitudinal areas which are more prone to temperature change and thus require more immediate attention.

Forcing estimates can assist in creating temperature reconstructions that explain past spatial temperature patterns. Mann *et al.* (2009) employed such a reconstruction to analyze the cooling trend of the Little Ice Age and the warming associated with the Medieval Climate Anomaly, illustrating a "thermostat-like" response to anthropogenic climate forcing.

Future temperature trends can also be predicted by examining climate forcing. By observing the relationship between global CO_2 and temperature, Frank *et al.* (2009) reconstructed temperature from the last millennium and employed forcing trends to forecast anthropogenic warming. Climate forcing models can also illustrate the implications of changing global energy on the environment. Didato *et al.* (2009) coupled forcing with a conceptual erosion technique, to illustrate erosion tendencies and potential for future soil loss. Lastly, climate forcing can be attributed to various economic sectors, as illustrated by Unger *et al.* (2010), who present argue for mitigating anthropogenic forcing economic sector by sector.

This chapter will primarily focus on the various implications of anthropogenic climate forcing. The first sections will examine the characteristics and nature of both natural and anthropogenic climate forcing. Following sections will highlight the span and scope of climate forcing occurrences. The final sections will analyze the consequences of anthropogenic emissions and the conclusions that can be derived from climate forcing mechanisms.

Importance of Gas-Aerosol Interactions in Policy Making

In current emission comparisons, the most cost-effective method is one which employs multi-component climate change mitigation strategies. These strategies involve analyzing both the direct and indirect effects of various linked emissions. However, the information of indirect effects between most gaseous pollutants and aerosols is absent. Shindell *et al.* (2009) took two approaches to calculate the impact of emissions on aerosols and the influence of these on radiative forcing. They found that the global warming potential (GWP) is substantially larger when the direct effects of aerosol interactions are considered and increases further when aerosol-cloud interactions are taken into account. Therefore, as atmospheric chemistry links methane, ozone, and aerosols, the policies regarding multi-gas mitigation should take gas-aerosol interactions into consideration.

Shindell *et al.* relied heavily on averaged radiative forcing (RF) to compare various emissions and to estimate GWP. To find the response of atmospheric composition to both the collective and individual effects of emissions, the researchers calculated abundance-based RF, which measured the effects of all emissions changing concurrently, and emissions-based forcing, which instead measured the responses of all chemical species to changes of a single pollutant. Using these two techniques, Shindell *et al.* estimated several 100-year GWRs. These computations demonstrated that, with the absence of aerosol responses, the results were similar to previous studies. However, once the radiative effects of aerosols are included, the GWP becomes larger, and larger still when aerosol-cloud interactions are included.

Contrasting Climate Effects of Forests through Radiative Forcing

Forests play an important role in global temperature, as their processes involving CO_2 and solar radiation have large impacts on the local and global climate. However, the interactions between forests and these climate changing agents produce contrasting effects on temperature. Rotenberg and Yakir (2010) observed these effects and explained the results by employing climate forcing analysis and examining the differences in climate gradients. As the forest absorbs carbon through CO_2 sequestration, a cooling effect occurs, driven by heavy vegetation during the peak photosynthesis months. However, the forests also absorb solar radiation by suppressing longwave radiation, which results in the opposing warming effect. These findings provide a basis for considering the consequences of surface energy balances when evaluating the success of land-based carbon sequestration.

Rotenberg and Yakir conducted their study in a semi-arid, 2800 ha pine forest located in southern Israel. The characteristics of the forest include high productivity, a mean annual net ecosystem CO_2 exchange (NEE) of 2.3 ton C ha^{-1}, and a mean annual gross primary productivity (GPP) of 820. The ratio of NEE/GPP for this forest was 0.27, higher than the averages for both Europe and the global Fluxnet network, indicating high carbon use efficiency. As a result, there is a range of eco-physiological adjustments in which the global climatic gradient is narrowed due to shifts of peak GPP (demonstrated by peak rates of photosynthesis) in different European regions. The trend is homeostatic and specific to a single vegetation type rather than changes in species composition. Therefore, the trend explains that plasticity of carbon sequestration with regards to a single species.

Vegetation cover is then considered in terms of its effects on surface radiation balance. The specific Israeli forest examined was unique in that its net radiation and sensible heat flux are both higher than those of any other eco-region (35% and 30%, respectively, greater than that of the Sahara). According to Rotenberg and Yakir, one significant implication of those characteristics is that the high global radiation, combined with a decrease in albedo associated with forestation, results in a drastic increase in shortwave surface radiation capacity. Also, as longwave radiation is important to semiarid forests, Rotenberg and Yakir examined its response to the shortwave albedo effect. As the surface cooling in areas of high vegetation suppresses longwave radiation flux, it is found that ecosystems with drier vegetation have increases in surface longwave radiation, which further doubles that shortwave effect.

These results were then synchronized with radiative forcing to gain a more complete knowledge of the consequences of surface radiation associated with carbon sequestration. This was illustrated by combining the observed albedo-derived shortwave radiative forcing with the calculated radiative forcing associated with carbon intake to estimate the number of years until the two forcing values are balanced. Rotenberg and Yakir found that, in the "worst case scenario", a net negative radiative forcing—one which produces cooling—will be found after approximately 80 years of forestation.

Impacts of Regional and Global Radiative Forcing on Regional Climate Change

Although regional climate change is attributable to many variables, the relevance of those variables is not adequately understood for the last century. Shindell and Faluvegi (2009) examined the susceptibility of various regions to changes in forcing. By determining the relationship between forcing and location reaction, and integrating observations of climate change from the twentieth century, Shindell and Faluvegi derived the importance of aerosols and resulting radiative forcing over time and by location. This information showed that the location radiative forcing influences climate response. Aerosols were proven to have great importance for both global and regional climate change. Further, the results demonstrate that, over the past three decades, the Arctic warming trend is influenced by the black carbon and aerosol emissions of the Northern Hemisphere.

Shindell and Faluvegi began by creating latitude bands and finding the response of the surface temperature to various levels of well-mixed greenhouse gases (WMGHG), ozone, and aerosols. Through this modeling, they found that when the forcing occurs within a specific latitude band, the mean temperatures follow the forcing per local unit area. Therefore, when the global mean radiative forcing is considered, the mid-latitude forcing and polar forcing must be greater than the tropical forcing (~ 2.4 and ~7 times, respectively). Higher latitude forcings are thus more sensitive to global forcing when compared to other regions.

Shindell and Faluvegi then compared the results from the modeling to the past patterns of surface temperature over various regions and time periods. These comparisons examined global and gradient responses and found significant implications for Arctic trends. The surface temperatures of the Arctic are warm until 1930, cooler from 1930–1975, and rapidly warmer onwards. Although there were differ-

ences between the observed and the recreated global and gradient responses, Shindell and Faluvegi accredit the discrepancies to internal variability and aerosol forcing. The models demonstrate a necessity for aerosol-provided cooling.

From modeling and comparisons, the results illustrate the prevalence of aerosol presence in both global and regional climate response. Further, forcing in the
northern hemisphere has a particularly strong effect on the Arctic climate. As the
forcing at the mid-latitude northern hemisphere oscillates between positive and
negative, the temperatures of the Arctic transition from warmer to cooler. It is estimated that aerosols are one of the main contributors to the increased Arctic surface temperature; responsible for 1.09 ± 0.81°C of the 1.48 ± 0.28°C increased
warming. As increased aerosol forcing continues, coupled black carbon and tropospheric ozone contributions, Arctic warming will also increase.

Assessing the Role of Natural and Anthropogenic Climate Forcing in Temperature Reconstructions

Despite recent advances in climate proxy data and models, many attempts to
estimate spatially resolved temperature patterns have been limited to periods extending back only a few centuries. Mann *et al.* (2009), however, employ a climate
field reconstruction method to attempt to estimate global and hemispheric trends
for the past 1500 years. The proxy-based temperature reconstruction was derived by
using both global proxy data and surface temperature information that is created by
the annual mean surface temperature field over a recent overlap of proxy and instrumental data. Mann *et al.* highlighted the Little Ice Age (1400–1700 C.E.) and
the Medieval Climate Anomaly (950–1250 C.E.) as two periods which have some
climatological interest. The one period is found to have a La Niña-like nature,
while the other follows an opposite trend. The difference between these two periods
has a consistent pattern of surface temperature and atmospheric circulation for the
North Atlantic Oscillation (NAO) and the Arctic Oscillation (AO). Mann *et al.*
conclude that these findings provide evidence for a thermostat-like response of
anthropogenic climate forcing.

The reconstruction of Mann *et al.* not only greatly extended temperature responses further into the past, but also includes multiple degrees of freedom, allowing
for a more telling estimate. By observing patterns of variation, it was determined
that the climate 1000 years ago (the time of the Medieval Climate Anomaly) dis-
plays La Niña conditions. The Medieval Climate Anomaly (MCA) was then characterized with warmer hemispheric conditions, while the Little Ice Age (LIA) corresponds to colder conditions. In nature of La Niña, the MCA had a warmer
northern hemisphere and a colder southern hemisphere, while the LIA had a cold
north and a warmer south.

To make meaningful comparisons with current climate stimulations, Mann *et al.* examined their findings against two coupled models. While the estimates of the global mean temperature difference for these periods is consistent with other climate models, the spatial patterns of response for the two comparison models varies distinctly. Mann *et al.* attribute these differences to the tropical Pacific "thermostat", which is not present in either comparison model. The thermostat mechanism is also linked to the surface temperature changes in the MCA positive phase of the NAO-AO pattern. Therefore, it is possible that the tropical Pacific thermostat reaction may be indicative of forced climate changes.

Estimating Sensitivity of the Global Climate System using Reconstructed Temperature and CO_2 Records

As concerns about the global climate system increase, it is becoming increasingly important that projected warming be accurate. However, there are many uncertainties associated with such predictions, most of which can be attributed to a general lack of understanding of the behavioral trends of the carbon cycle. Frank *et al.* (2009) attempted to reduce these uncertainties by constraining the variable associated with global CO_2/temperature feedback, γ. This particular attempt to constrain γ was unique because it considered numerous data sets and analysis periods, which resulted in 229,761 estimates and therefore facilitated distributions and confidence intervals that were previously unavailable. This also made it possible to assign likelihoods and create a benchmark for future simulations. The mean γ was found to be 7.7 ppmv CO_2 per °C, and the range (80% of estimates), excluding upper tail sensitivities, was estimated to be between 1.7 and 21.4 ppmv CO_2 per °C. Further, it was found that it was found that γ was likely to fall in the lowermost quartiles of estimates. These predictions are key to understanding the global climate system and the impacts of amplifies anthropogenic warming.

Frank *et al.* begin by examining the variability of reconstructed temperature and atmospheric CO_2 from the past millennium. Long-term decreases in CO_2 were attributed to the cooling that is associated with the shift from the Medieval Warm Period (MWP) to the Little Ice Age (LIA), characterized by changes in both atmospheric and oceanic carbon circulation. These two climate anomalies demonstrate that the amplitude of hemispheric to global-scale temperature change is significant. To further illustrate this notion, Frank *et al.* noted that peak LIA conditions (1601–1630) were 0.3–1.0°C cooler than present day temperatures. Additionally, after deriving and analyzing ensembles of past temperature changes, it was determined that the most recent evaluated period (1971–2000) was, on average, 0.7°C warmer that the coldest LIA period, and 80% of the estimates yielding between 0.52 and 0.99°C . These results may be explained by increased anthropogenic influences, which are predicted to have widened the temperature range by approximately 75% over the last millennium.

The data for reconstructed temperature and CO_2 records were then regressed to derive γ estimates. Three different time periods were analyzed with respect to γ: 1050–1800, 1050–1549, and 1550–1800. The mean for all γ values was found to be 7.7 ppmv CO_2 per °C. The values for the earlier period were found to have a lower mean that the later period, with median γ values of 4.3 and 16.1 ppmv CO_2 per °C, respectively. The higher γ values in the later period are recognized as a result of an influential CO_2 drop during the LIA (1600). This drop was not solely a consequence of large-scale temperature, and it is possible that changes in atmospheric or oceanic CO_2 states contributed to the carbon decrease. When the γ estimates are subjected to a range of carbon-cycle climate models, the average γ increases and is estimated to be 8.5 ppmv CO_2 per °C. Empirically, the estimates are twice as likely to be in the lower bound quartile (between 2.1 and 8.5 ppmv CO_2 per °C). However, the empirical findings cannot be compared with the model-derived estimates due to the internal variability of the model. Nonetheless, the estimates of γ values are informative and assist in reducing uncertainties associated with projected warming and climate responses.

Using Climate Forcing to Model Erosion for Various Time Scales in Southern Italy

In the Sele River Basin, farm soil fertility is severely limited by sediment that comes from tillage erosion. The erosion events can further perpetuate soil loss and essential ecological functions. Although it has been demonstrated that climate change influences the relationship between erosive rainfall and decreased soil quality, Didato et al. (2009) attempt to expand current models by quantifying the past interactions between climate change and erosion to produce a model which incorporates various erosion situations at different time periods. This process began by constructing a Net Erosion Model (NER), which examined monthly sediments and attempted to evolve erosion processes from monthly to annual time scales. The NER model was used in conjunction with other equations to derive monthly, seasonal, and annual erosion rates. An adapted conceptual erosion technique, Climate Forcing and Erosion Modelling (CliFEM) was also considered throughout the study. Didato et al. found that the potential for future average soil erosion was high, although the more hazardous concern was the estimate of monthly soil loss. The monthly soil erosion from August to November is the most devastating as these months follow the soil tillage process, which promote soil erodibility and decreased soil coverage.

Didato *et al.* conducted this study in the Sele River Basin, which serves many land uses including spaces for crops and mixed-deciduous woods. However, much of the forests have been cleared for agricultural use, increasing the potential erosion and placing soil quality at risk. With a volatile average annual precipitation, of 700–2000 mm, weather has considerable influence over erosion and agriculture. This study therefore considered historical water and land use records to present a more comprehensive knowledge of the climate drivers behind erosion.

The main model employed was the NER, which calculated the amount of sediment in the basin and presented the information at different time scales. These data were then converted to gross soil loss by dividing NER by the fraction of eroded soil that is delivered outside of the basin, or sediment delivery ratio (SDR). This basic model was altered and combined with other data to derive a monthly NER model, a gross erosion evaluation, and an estimation of tolerable soil loss. The models demonstrated many essential details about erosion and erosion patterns in the Sele River Basin. First, between 1973 and 2007, only 10 years exceeded the long-term average of soil loss, and soil erosion comprised 60% of total loss, indicating that long-term erosion can be heavily influenced by a small number of short-term events. Also, it was shown that human activities, such as landscaping and irrigation, increased the erosion of soil during the considered time period. Lastly, the most important conclusion was that soil was most vulnerable to erosion following tillage (from August to November) suggesting the benefits of minimizing tillage and increasing the use of perennial cover crops.

An Analysis of Radiative Forcing by Economic Sector

Unger *et al.* (2010) argue that industry, power, and biomass burning, on-road transportation, household biofuel use, and animal husbandry are the economic sectors most responsible for emissions leading to climate change specifically because of their emissions of CO_2, ozone (O_3), and aerosol particles. Of those three, O_3 emissions are especially worrisome as the pollutant is mainly responsible for the warming that occurs in the atmosphere. Aerosols can also contribute to climate change by affecting the properties of clouds, increasing the number of cloud droplets and resulting in smaller droplet sizes, which in turn can result in decreased precipitation and evaporation of clouds. The authors think that the main focus of mitigation policy should be these anthropogenic emissions.

Unger *et al.* argue that the IPCC's traditional method of examining radiative forcing is ineffective. This method examines individual pollutants and their changes over various time periods, but does not consider possible interactions between chemicals or the potential for effects caused by multiple pollutants. Therefore, to ensure smart climate policy, a complete evaluation that is sector-based is required.

This study presented a comprehensive look at the total climate forcing, with emissions broken down into 13 components of the economic sector. Also included was an analysis of short-lived pollutants and aerosol radiative forcing. Unger *et al.* found that aerosols from industry, power, and biomass burning are contributing to larger quantities of cloud droplets, which in turn increases total cloud cover and cloud optical depth. These effects amplify reflectivity. However, aerosol effects from other sectors were found to be insignificant. Additionally, positive radiative forcing was found in the power and industry sectors, suggesting that these sectors are major sources of SO_2 emissions and contribute greatly to anthropogenic sulfate accumulation. The biomass burning and industry sectors were found to have the greatest amount of negative radiative forcing, driving cooling. On the other end of the spectrum, the aviation sector was found to have the smallest amount of radiative forcing, likely due to less fuel use compared to other anthropogenic activities. Looking ahead at 2100, Unger *et al.* found that the change in radiative effects and positive forcing is significantly perpetuated by the power industry.

Conclusions

Increases in anthropogenic emissions are significantly impacting the global climate. The environmental and economic consequences of these changes are likely to be considerable and adverse to many regions, and it is important to understand exactly how the radiative forcing works and what causes it. For example, employing forcing in temperature reconstructions not only clarifies past warming and cooling, but also aids in predicting future temperature movement.

Further, an understanding of climate forcing is essential to creating policies that will assist in mitigating the impacts of climate change. By recognizing the relationship between emissions and forcing, governments can aim to reduce pollutants that cause fluxes in global energy. Also, policy makers can identify which economic sectors are perpetuating climate forcing and attempt to scale back those areas. While the environmental and economical ramifications of anthropogenic emissions are significant, understanding the processes of climate forcing can encourage action that will minimize the consequences of climate change.

References Cited

Didato, N., Fagnano, M., Alberico, I., 2009. ClimFEM- Climate forcing and erosion modeling in the Sele River Basin (Southern Italy). Natural Hazards Earth System Science 9, 1693–1702.

Frank, D., Esper, J., Raible, C., Buntgen, U., Trouet, V., Stocker, B., Joos, F., 2010. Ensemble reconstruction constraints on the global carbon cycle sensitivity to climate. Nature 463, 527–530.

Mann, M., Zhang, Z., Rutherford, S., Bradley, R., Hughes, M., Shindell, D., Ammann, C., Faluvegi, G., Ni, F., 2009. Global Signatures and Dynamical Origins of the Little Ice Age and Medieval Climate Anomaly. Science 326, 1256–1260.

Rotenberg, E. and Yakir, D., 2010. Contribution of Semi-Arid forests to the climate system. Science 327, 451–454.

Shindell, D., Faluvegi, G., Koch, D., Schmidt, G., Unger, N., Bauer, S., 2009. Improved Attribution of Climate Forcing to Emissions. Science 326, 716–718.

Shindell, D. and Faluvegi, G., 2009. Climate response to regional radiative forcing during the twentieth century. Nature Geoscience 2, 294–300.

Unger, N., Bond, T., Wang, J., Koch, D., Menon, S., Shindell, D., Bauer, S., 2010. Attribution of climate forcing to economic sectors. PNAS 107, 3382–3387

Section II—Fossil Fuels and their Legacy

5. Fossil Fuel: How Much is Left?

Caitrin O'Brien

Human beings are heavily dependant on fossil fuels to provide the electricity and mechanical energy used to power practically every aspect of daily life. From the petroleum used in cars and plastics to the coal used for electricity generation, the world runs on hydrocarbons. The United States Energy Information Administration estimates that in 2003, 86% of worldwide energy consumption was from fossil fuels such as oil, coal, and natural gas (US EIA 2003). Fossil fuels are nonrenewable resources because they take millions of years to form, and as the world's population and energy consumption grow, oil, coal, and natural gas reserves are being depleted at unsustainable rates. Fossil fuel dependency raises environmental issues because the burning of fossil fuels releases CO_2 into the air and contributes to global climate change. Equally pressing, however, is the question of what will happen as supplies of nonrenewable fuels dwindle and, eventually, cease to be available in useful quantities.

Several scientists have projected the dates at which different fossil fuels will reach their peak production levels, after which point these fuel reserves will decline and new production will not sufficiently offset depletion. It is estimated that worldwide coal production will peak in 2034, and by 2100 the world will have all but exhausted its coal supplies (Mohr and Evans 2009). In spite of a 2009 study suggesting that "large endowments of oil, natural gas and natural gas liquids exist in North, Central, and South America" (Aguilera and Aguilera 2009), peak oil is estimated to occur between 2015 and 2025. Petroleum is the most common fuel used for the movement of goods, and it has been predicted that the combination of climate change and oil depletion will result in "peak globalization," after which point the volume of world exports will decline. The current policy responses to climate change and oil depletion are most likely too late and too costly to prevent this peak globalization (Curtis 2009).

New technologies and types of fuel have a limited capacity to delay the onset of fossil fuel declines. Several types of unconventional fossil fuels exist and can be extracted using cutting-edge technologies and new production methods. Alternative methods of oil and gas production may have the potential to mitigate the effects of peaking worldwide fossil fuel production. In particular, extra heavy oil, tar sand oil, and fossil fuels trapped in shale fields can be retrieved through unconventional mining techniques. Unconventional oil production is expected to peak between 2076 and 2084 (Mohr and Evans 2010).

Recoverable unconventional hydrocarbons far exceed current industrial reserves of oil and gas, and recent advances in tar sand oil and coalbed methane extraction have great potential as methods of extracting unconventional fossil fuels. Unconventional oil is primarily found in Canada, Venezuela, and the United States, and shale oil has the largest production potential (Lakatos and Lakatos-Szabó 2009). One promising but controversial method of unconventional hydrocarbon extraction is hydraulic fracturing. This technique releases oil and natural gas trapped deep in shale beds by propagating fractures in rock through high hydraulic pressure. Several scientific studies have proposed new hydraulic fracturing methodologies, including more effective production prediction technologies (Hoffman and Chang 2009) and optimal fracturing fluids (Gupta *et al.* 2009). Hydraulic fracturing techniques are currently being used in the newly-discovered Marcellus Shale field in the eastern United States, where by evaluating and capturing the best practices of hydraulic fracturing tests, scientists hope to develop standing operating procedures that can be put towards full-scale development of natural gas extraction in this region (Houston *et al.* 2009). The development of unconventional domestic sources of oil and gas using hydraulic fracturing techniques has the capacity to reduce America's dependency on foreign oil, although the effects of unconventional oil on worldwide fossil fuel peaks are predicted to be negligible.

Estimating Coal Production Until 2100

Several different models have been devised to predict total remaining worldwide coal yield. Projections of mineral resources are often made using the Hubbert linearization model, a method invented in 1976 that has been quite accurate in estimating oil production in the United States. Coal reserves have also been estimated using a method that sums estimates of current reserves with estimates of cumulative production. S.H. Mohr and G.M. Evans devised a new methodology for estimating coal production that takes into account supply and demand interactions in different countries and for different types of coal (Mohr and Evans 2009). These three models are compared based on the predicted amounts of coal production by country, production levels by type of coal, and energy produced by the estimated amounts of coal. The "Best Guess" method devised by Mohr and Evans predicts that overall worldwide coal production will last much longer and provide more energy than the predictions of the Hubbert linearization model, but the model that sums reserves and cumulative production predicts higher coal production than the Best Guess and the Hubbert methods. Based on the Best Guess methodology, worldwide coal yield will be between 700 and 1,243 gigatonnes, and worldwide coal production will peak in 2034 on a tonnage basis, and in 2026 on an energy basis. The Best Guess model indicates that the notion that coal is widely abundant appears to be unjustified.

S.M. Mohr and G.M. Evans created a model for estimating coal production that takes into account more than 400 constants for 132 countries and many different coal types. This new model includes data from external disruptions, such as wars and depressions, and can be used for any resource where production is derived from mining. Mohr and Evans compared their new model to two more traditional models used to estimate coal production. The Hubbert linearization method was devised in 1976 to plot production data for the US oil industry, and this method has also been used to predict the depletion of other finite mineral resources. The Hubbert model assumes production to be a symmetric bell curve, and does not take into account estimated reserves of coal. The second method that Mohr and Evans compare is denoted as the "R+C" model, which is the summation of current estimates of coal reserves and cumulative production worldwide. The authors used these three methods to compare the coal production for each country or region of the world, in gigatonnes. The three models were also compared based on their estimates of production based on type of coal, and the amount of energy produced by each type of coal.

The scientists found large discrepancies between the three models of coal production. When comparing the scenarios based on coal production predictions, the R+C scenario predicted much higher overall coal production than the other two, and the Best Guess scenario predicted a level of coal production in between the Hubbert estimate and the R+C estimate. All three of the models estimate that China will run out of coal around 2100, but the R+C scenario and the Best Guess scenario both predict a huge increase in coal production in the Former Soviet Union around 2110. The Hubbert method shows very little production in any region past 2100, whereas the other two scenarios estimate that coal production will last beyond 2200, especially in the United States. All of the scenarios show that Western Europe is the only continent where coal production has already peaked and is declining, and study data indicates that European coal production peaked in 1988 and is declining at a rate of 3% per year. All of the models indicate that world coal production in tonnes will peak between 2010 and 2048.

Mohr and Evans compared worldwide coal production for each of the three models based on the amounts of coal estimated for each model. Four different types of coal were considered: anthracite, bituminous, sub-bituminous, and lignite. For all three scenarios, bituminous coal is the most prevalent, because bituminous coal is the world's most abundant type of coal. Anthracite estimates are very low and approximately the same for each scenario. The Hubbert method estimates that the coal that is produced worldwide will be primarily bituminous, whereas the Best Guess and the R+C methods predict a huge spike in lignite extraction. This is presumably because as bituminous coal begins to run out, the energy industry will increase production of less efficient types of coal such as lignite and sub-bituminous.

Finally, the authors compared the three models based on the energy values of the predicted coal extraction. All models predicted that anthracite will produce high amounts of energy compared to its mass, although bituminous coal will produce the most overall energy because it is the world's most abundant coal. The Hubbert method estimated that by the year 2100, less than 30 exajoules per year will be produced by coal worldwide, whereas the R+C scenario's estimate for the same year is about 60 exajoules per year. The Best Guess methodology predicts that by 2100, over 90 exajoules per year will be produced by coal. The author's Best Guess scenario indicates that the amount of worldwide energy produced by coal will peak between 2011 and 2047. Mohr and Evans conclude that the worldwide coal yield is between 700 and 1,243 gigatonnes, and that worldwide coal production will peak in 2034 on a tonnage basis and 2026 on an energy basis. According to the research by Mohr and Evans, the world has almost reached its maximum levels of coal production, and by 2100 will have all but exhausted worldwide coal supplies.

Fossil Fuel Endowments in North, Central, and South America

Several scientific studies, including a 2000 United States Geological Survey study, estimate that there exist large volumes of hydrocarbons that "can be recovered given sufficient research and development and appropriate public policies" (Aguilera and Aguilera 2009). Two scientists from the Society of Petroleum Engineers used data from this USGS survey to create a model specifically designed to estimate regional oil endowments of North, Central, and South America, as well as the natural gas and natural gas liquids that exist in these regions. The scientists concluded that North, Central and South America have large petroleum endowments that will last for several decades, and these fossil fuel reserves have the capacity to "contribute significantly" to the energy needs of these regions.

Roberto Aguilera and Roberto F. Aguilera of the Society of Petroleum Engineers combined data from a 2000 US Geological Survey (USGS) estimation of world petroleum supplies and a variable shape distribution model to estimate the endowments of natural gas, oil, and natural gas liquids (NGL) throughout North, Central, and South America. The USGS survey estimated average global oil endowments by assessing conventional petroleum reserves for 409 of the world's 937 different petroleum provinces. Unconventional oil was not assessed. The survey also estimated the world's natural gas endowment, but again did not include unconventional sources of natural gas. In 2006, Aguilera developed a variable shape distribution (VSD) model, which has been used to forecast conventional oil, natural gas, and natural gas liquid endowments in the petroleum provinces evaluated by the USGS. The authors used this model to determine oil, natural gas and natural gas liquid endowments for North, Central, and South America.

Aguilera and Aguilera used the VSD model to estimate Central and South American oil endowments of 367 billion barrels of oil equivalent (boe), which is significantly higher than the USGS estimate of 219 billion boe. The natural gas endowment for these regions was nearly the same, with the USGS estimating 759 trillion cubic feet (tcf) of natural gas in Central and South America, and the VSD model generating an estimate of 756 tcf. The VSD model estimated that natural gas liquid endowments in Central and South America are approximately 22,674 million boe, which is very similar to the USGS estimate of 22,698 million boe. For North America, the USGS and the VSD models generated the same estimate of 434 billion boe of oil and natural gas liquids. The natural gas for this region was estimated at 1,787 tcf for the USGS model, which compares well to the 1,772 tcf calculated by the VSD model. The composite conventional oil endowment in North, Central, and South America was found to be 882 billion stock tank barrels of oil, and the cumulative conventional natural gas endowment was estimated to be 3,440 tcf. Overall, the authors determined that the VSD model accurately estimates the amounts of hydrocarbons available in different regions, and determined that large endowments of oil, natural gas, and natural gas liquids exist in North, Central, and South America. If scientists and policymakers actively pursue research and development of petroleum reserves, these endowments have the capacity to last for decades.

Effects of Climate Change and Oil Depletion on Global Trade

The global market depends on reliable, inexpensive transport of goods along long-distance supply chains. Global warming and oil depletion have the potential to dramatically alter transportation costs and freight movement. Fred Curtis argues that climate change and oil depletion will result in "peak globalization," after which point the volume of world exports will decline (Curtis 2009). By examining scholarly literature on the pathways of the effects of global climate change and oil consumption on global trade, Curtis takes a unique look at the effects of climate change and natural resource management on human goods and transportation, and concludes that current policies designed to mitigate climate change and oil deple-tion will be ineffective in halting the onset of "peak globalization."

Fred Curtis examined existing scholarly literature on globalization and the en-vironment in tandem with data on peak oil and climate change. While most exist-ing scientific literature has focused on "the impact trade treaties and increased glob-al trade flows have on the ecosystem," Curtis examines how environmental changes have the capacity to alter human trade. Curtis particularly focuses on oil depletion, as oil is heavily used in global transportation, and on the effects that global warm-ing will have on oil use and transportation infrastructure. Finally, Curtis examines both real and proposed policies designed to mitigate climate change and oil deple-tion, and concludes that these policies are "too little and too late" to prevent peak globalization, and will not be able to protect global supply chains.

Globalization, or the liberalization of international trade among nations, has caused a rapid increase in global economic growth and international trade. This growth in global exports has been supported by the creation of a massive global transportation infrastructure which transports goods worldwide via roads, railways, ports, and airports. In order for this long-distance trade to be efficient, transporta-tion must be cost-efficient, rapid, and predictable. The physical impacts of global warming will reduce this efficiency, simultaneously increasing the cost of transpor-tation. Melting arctic ice is expected to cause sea levels to rise by three to six feet by the end of the century, which will threaten coastal roads, railways, seaports, and airport facilities. Greater evaporation due to rising temperatures is predicted to low-er water levels in intercontinental lakes and rivers, which will reduce the amount of goods that can pass through these waterways, slowing transportation and increasing costs. Climate change is expected to cause an increase in catastrophic natural disas-ters similar to Hurricane Katrina, which can have devastating impacts on transpor-tation infrastructure. Climate change is also predicted to negatively impact agricul-ture and manufacturing, as higher temperatures and changes in precipitation will decrease crop output and make the transportation of manufactured goods less pre-dictable and more expensive. Overall, Curtis argues that climate change will dam-age physical infrastructure, cause delays in freight transit, and increase costs to the extent that global warming will "undermine the economic logic of current supply chains."

The effects of climate change on globalization will be reinforced by the effects of oil depletion. Petroleum is the most common fuel used for the movement of goods, and it has been predicted that peak oil will occur prior to the year 2015. After this point, world oil production will begin to decline, and the price of crude oil will rise significantly and become much more volatile. Shortages and interrup-tions in oil supply will be common as world oil continues to decline. Oil depletion will have a huge effect on the global trade of goods. Air freight uses the most fuel per ton-mile of all transportation modes, so it will be the most adversely effected by increased oil prices. Air speeds can be slowed to conserve fuel, but this would decrease the efficiency of the supply chain. Container ships use bunker fuel oil, which is untaxed on international journeys and therefore will not be as impacted by oil price jumps as air travel. However, Curtis notes that "it is possible for ocean shipping costs to rise high enough to impact the global sourcing of production." High oil prices also destroy global supply chains by impacting goods production, as higher oil prices result in increased food production costs. The current global trade market will be greatly impacted by higher fuel costs, slower movement of freight, and potential fuel supply interruptions as a result of peak oil.

Curtis argues that the current policy responses to climate change and oil depletion are too late and too costly to prevent peak globalization. Climate change policies designed to reduce greenhouse gas emissions could have direct impacts on globalization, but these policies have not been effectively implemented. These policies, which would involve taxes, regulations and/or cap-and-trade systems, would not prevent the shrinking of global supply chains. Policies intended to slow the onset of peak oil primarily include fuel taxes, and regulations that increase vehicle fuel efficiency or promote technological improvements in oil recovery techniques. The author argues that even if the most ambitious of these policies were implemented, the impending worldwide oil crisis would not be avoided. Curtis concludes that globalization will be threatened as long as climate change and oil depletion continue, and the only solution would be for production and trade to become more local or regionally-based.

Effects of Unconventional Oil Production on Peak Oil

It is estimated that conventional oil production will reach its peak prior to 2025. Unconventional methods of oil production may have the potential to mitigate the effects of peaking worldwide oil production (Mohr and Evans 2010). Extra heavy oil and oil that is trapped in tar sands and shale can be retrieved through mining and through *in situ* techniques. The efficacy of *in situ* and mining techniques in extracting this unconventional oil was projected under three different models, which were used to estimate when unconventional oil production will peak, and whether alternative methods of production can delay the onset of peak oil. The authors determined that unconventional oil production will peak between 2076 and 2084, and that unconventional methods alone cannot mitigate the onset of peak oil.

S.H. Mohr and G.M. Evans developed a model to project unconventional oil production, including *in situ* and mining extraction techniques. Unconventional types of oil include extra heavy oil, natural bitumen from oil sands and tar sands, and oil shale. *In situ* techniques involve injecting steam into the well to heat the oil, forcing the hot oil towards the surface. Steam Assisted Gravity Drainage (SAGD) is a type of *in situ* technology that extracts the oil through horizontal drilling. Using the Cyclic Steam Stimulation (CSS) method, the well is put through cycles of steam injection, soak, and oil production until the hot oil can be pumped out of the well. The model developed by the authors was calibrated based on Canadian data of historic bitumen production. Mohr and Evans developed the unconventional oil production model based on their previous model for worldwide coal production. Production for mining is determined by the sum of the individual mines in the basin. Production from *in situ* is identical to the mining model, but the data is from a SAGD/CSS plant rather than a mine. Three scenarios were determined from the model, providing "pessimistic," "optimistic," and "best guess" estimates of ultimately recoverable resources from unconventional oil production. Finally, the data extracted from the model were combined with conventional oil analysis and literature to obtain composite oil production projections. The authors compared these results to estimates of worldwide peak oil, to determine whether unconventional oil production can provide a smooth transition when conventional oil peaks.

Unconventional oil is primarily found in 3 countries: Canada, Venezuela and the United States. The Former Soviet Union is also predicted to contribute considerable amounts of unconventional oil in the future. Mohr and Evans used the *in situ* model to model *in situ* natural bitumen and extra heavy oil production, whereas the mining model was used to predict production from mined natural bitumen and shale oil production. Based on the three scenarios, unconventional oil production will peak between 18 billion barrels per year (Gb/year) in 2076 and 32 Gb/year in 2084. The best guess scenario estimates that production will peak at 22 Gb/year in the 2077. Shale oil has the biggest production potential, although it also has the greatest uncertainty regarding its extraction methods and economic viability. Mohr and Evans's total unconventional oil production projections are higher than the estimates from most scientific literature on the subject, and the authors theorize that this is because their scenarios do not consider economic constraints. In spite of the overall optimistic nature of the assumptions in these scenarios, both the pessimistic and the best guess scenario forecast that total oil production will decline within 5 years. The authors estimate that unconventional oil will only delay the peak of world oil production by twenty-five years at the most. After combining the three scenarios developed in this model with literature projections of oil production, only the optimistic scenario estimates that unconventional oil could partially mitigate the peak of conventional oil production, extending the worldwide oil production peak to 2050. The pessimistic and the best guess scenarios both estimate that total oil production will peak within the next 5 years, and unconventional oil production will not significantly offset this peak.

Role of Conventional and Unconventional Hydrocarbons in the 21st Century

Energy demand is expected to quadruple in the 21st century, whereas worldwide oil production is predicted to peak prior to the year 2015. Increasing production of unconventional hydrocarbons has been suggested as a potential method of meeting rising global energy demands. Lakatos and Lakatos-Szabó (2009) estimated the availability of these unconventional sources of oil and gas by evaluating and comparing existing data, including approximations of recovery rates based on present average values and probable technological progress. *In situ* and *ex situ* techniques, as well as chemical methods, were considered. Overall, the scientists estimated that recoverable unconventional hydrocarbons far exceed current industrial reserves of oil and gas, and that recent advances in tar sand oil and coalbed methane extraction have made many types of unconventional hydrocarbons competitive with crude oils and natural gases. This study proposes that research, development and utilization of new recovery technologies for unconventional oils and gas will be of critical importance in the 21st century, as production of conventional sources of oil and gas begin to decline.

I. Lakatos and J. Lakatos-Szabó of the University of Miskolc evaluated and compared data from "reliable organizations" to determine the potential of worldwide unconventional oils and gases. The authors classify unconventional oils as oil shale, oil and tar sands, and pyrobitumen, while unconventional gases include gas shale, gas sand, tight gas sand, basin-concentrated gas accumulation, and coalbed methane. Lakatos and Lakatos-Szabó compared historical production of unconventional sources of oil with estimates by the UN Energy Map of the World (1995) and the US Geological Survey. The potential of unconventional gases was found by comparing forecasts from the British Petroleum Statistical Review and the US Geological Survey. After comparing projected estimates of ultimately recoverable unconventional gas and oil resources, the authors estimated the production costs of these hydrocarbons for different recovery methods. The final data were used to determine the effects that unconventional hydrocarbons could have on global oil and gas demand.

The authors determined that while "it seems very probable that natural hydrocarbons will remain the mainstay of energy supply until the middle of the 21st century," unconventional hydrocarbons will be critically important in the future. Global reserves of unconventional gases and oils "significantly exceed" the estimated availability of conventional hydrocarbons. Production of several of these unconventional hydrocarbons has already started in several countries. In particular, shale oil, sand oil, and coalbed methane resources are already being tapped using alternative extraction methods such as hydraulic fracturing. Recent increases in

Caitrin O'Brien

hydrocarbon prices may further accelerate the production of unconventional sources of oil and gas, especially because production cost of tar sand oil and coalbed methane gas are now competitive with recovery costs of conventional hydrocarbons. Overall, more research and development activities are needed to allow for wider application of new, sophisticated recovery technologies that could be key to increasing extraction of unconventional hydrocarbons.

Proposed Method of Modeling Productivity of Hydraulic Fractures

Hydraulic fracturing is a technique that employs hydraulic pressure to initiate a fracture in coalbed wells to better enable the extraction of oil or methane gas. This method is often used to improve production efficiency in low permeability gas reservoirs. Hydraulic fracturing often creates multiple fractures in a single well, but because current production modeling software does not adequately capture the complexity of interconnecting fractures, a proposed new methodology treats each fracture as an interconnected series of fractures, enabling a more accurate representation of the production value of the fractures (Hoffman and Chang 2009).

B. Todd Hoffman and Wui Min Chang of Montana Tech have proposed a method of fracture modeling which utilizes existing commercial simulator software to treat fractures as interconnected. Under current production modeling techniques, the productivity of a single fracture is compared to the well's unfractured state, using models that assume a uniformly porous rockbed as well as a steady flow of gas. Hoffman and Chang assert that this modeling technique oversimplifies the characteristics of both the fracture and the gas reservoirs. Instead, the authors propose that each fracture can be represented in commercial production simulators as a "discrete connection of nodes" or a well, thus placing no limitations on the fracture's geometry or size. Hoffman and Chang use this technique to model four hydraulically-fractured wells from a low-permeability gas reservoir in Montana.

The Bowdoin gas field in north-central Montana is a low permeability gas field accessible primarily through hydraulic fracturing, and the rockbed contains a mixture of several types of stone and shale. Hoffman and Chang compared the real production rates of the four study wells to the predicted rates from both the traditional simplified production model and their well model. The well model was determined to be an acceptable method of modeling the productivity of hydraulic fractures.

By treating each hydraulic fracture as an interconnected series of fractures in a well, current modeling technology can more accurately represent the productive value of the fracture. Under this technique, the production value of fractures of different shapes can be calculated, and variabilities such as reservoir properties and

68

the conductivity of the fractures can be captured. Additionally, multiple fractures can be modeled in a single well. This method can be particularly useful for wells that do not have uniform conductivity, such as those found in the Bowdoin gas field. Hoffman and Chang focused their case study on a tight gas reservoir, but their methodology could potentially be applied to any type of hydraulically-fractured well. This tool will allow fractures of different geometries and permeabilities to easily be tested in the production simulator, potentially allowing oil and gas companies to be more selective in well placement and extract oil and gas more efficiently.

Development of a New Hydraulic Fracturing Fluid

Hydraulic fracturing pumps fluid into fractures in rock bed in order to extract oil or gas. The chemical composition of fracturing fluids is dependent on the type of rock, the size of the fracture, and the fuel being extracted. Scientists with the Society of Petroleum Engineers developed a new hydraulic fracturing fluid designed to be used in low permeability tight gas wells (Gupta *et al.* 2009). After evaluating the chemical mixture based on its viscosity, foam generation, fluid loss, and conductivity, the scientists tested the fluid's efficiency in a field study in the Greater Green River Basin, Wyoming. The results were compared to similar treatments using conventional fluid; the new fluid was found to have better initial and cumulative field production than standard hydraulic fracturing fluids.

D.V.S. Gupta and his colleagues with the Society of Petroleum Engineers developed a new, low-pH fracturing fluid that is best suited for tight gas formations. Low-pH fluids have been shown to cause less permeability damage and better fracture cleanup in these formations than fluids with a higher pH. The newly developed hydraulic fracturing fluid is energized with N_2 to create foam that can enhance the fluid recovery. This fluid also has a crosslink system, which is used to minimize friction and reduce the energy necessary to pump the highly viscous fluid. Gupta and his colleagues studied the new fluid's viscosity by measuring how quickly the fluid traveled at different temperatures. The fluid's foam capabilities were tested using a foam generator, and the fluid loss was tested at various temperatures. The scientists determined the fluid's conductivity by measuring the time it took for a test proppant to move through a fake hydraulic fracture. After thoroughly testing the properties of the newly developed fracturing fluid, 20 wells in the Frontier formation in southwest Wyoming were stimulated with the new fluid. The productivity of these test wells was compared to that of other wells in the formation that utilize various conventional fracturing fluids.

The new low-pH, high yield fracturing fluid developed by Gupta and his colleagues is designed for optimal production in low permeability gas reservoirs. The fluid was found to have adequate viscosity to initiate and propagate the fracture, and the fluid effectively transported the proppant in the fracture. The foam produced by the fluid has reasonable stability compared to other types of fracturing fluid, and the lower polymer loadings in this fluid inflict less damage on the rock formation. The newly designed fluid was found to be very conductive and did not cause obvious damage to the fracture. The fluid was tested in the Frontier formation, a shale formation in southwest Wyoming, where the results were favorable. Wells stimulated with the new fluid were found to produce more gas than conventional low-pH and high-pH efficient fluid systems.

Lessons Learned from Hydraulic Fracturing in the Marcellus Shale

The Marcellus Formation is a shale reservoir in eastern North America the natural gas reserves of which are accessible primarily through hydraulic fracturing. Over 100 fracture wells have been stimulated in the shale's Pennsylvania region, "resulting in an in-depth understanding of details needed to achieve optimal frac performance" (Houston *et al.* 2009). Type and concentration of fracturing fluid, drill cutting placement, geochemical controls, proppant and perforation strategies have all varied significantly from the beginning of Marcellus Shale extraction to the present. These important factors of hydraulic fracturing have been tested and evaluated in order to capture the best hydraulic fracturing practices for the Marcellus Shale formation. By studying the effects of fracturing strategies and technologies used for these test wells, more rapid advancement towards full-scale natural gas extraction in the Marcellus Shale region can be achieved.

Nathan Houston and colleagues from the Society of Petroleum Engineers reviewed methods and technologies used in the Marcellus Shale from early development of the field to the present. By evaluating and capturing the best practices of hydraulic fracturing in this reservoir, the scientists hope to develop standing operating procedures that can be put towards full-scale development of natural gas extraction in the Marcellus Shale. Houston and his colleagues considered practices from hydraulic fracturing in other shale reservoirs, as well as several new techniques that have been developed specifically for the Marcellus. The scientists reviewed the best type of fluids used to stimulate fractures while minimizing runoff and leaks, as well as the best methods of analyzing fracture placement for drill cuttings. Houston and his colleagues also analyzed types of geochemical controls that are used in the fracturing fluid in the Marcellus Shale, such as biocides, scale control and iron control, as well as the results of using different types of surfactant, sand, and perforating and fracture techniques. After reviewing the results of different methodologies, the scientists determined how these each factor interacts with the unique geologic composition of the Marcellus Shale, and made decisions as to which technology or fluid composition was best suited to hydraulic fracturing in this region.

The Marcellus Shale formation is characterized by low permeability rock that has high amounts of organic matter and clay, very fine grain size, and extremely fine porosity. This combination of traits has required hydraulic fracture stimulation fluids with low viscosities, high rates of flow, and large quantities of proppant to hold fractures open. Houston and his colleagues determined that the most effective fracturing fluids for the Marcellus Shale region are slickwater stimulation fluids pumped at high rates, with low sand concentrations. This combination minimizes leakoff, and when combined with a liquid-polymer additive, the slickwater reduces friction in the shale fractures. Analysis of drill cuttings is an important technology to optimize fluid design and fracture placement, and X-ray technology was found to be the best method of identifying the unique mineralogy and fracture geometry of fracture in the reservoir. The scientists found that including several geochemical controls in fracturing fluids is crucial to optimize fracture production and minimize damage to the shale. In particular, "environmentally responsible" biocides that kill sulfate-reducing and slime-forming bacteria are useful to inhibit any potential damage to the shale. Similarly, geochemical precipitants and scale control are useful to protect against carbonate, sulfate and iron-based scale build up in fractures, which can reduce productivity. Houston and his colleagues also determined the most useful concentration of surfactant and proppant, as well as the most effective rate of proppant to be used in the Marcellus Shale. The use of surfactant in the Marcellus Shale fractures has been found to reduce surface tension and lower the pressure in the fractures, resulting in increased recovery of natural gas. White sand has evolved to be the proppant of choice in the Marcellus reservoir, and sand concentrations between 0.25 to 2.5 lb/gallon of fluid have been proven, through trial and error, to be the best concentrations to prop fractures open. Finally, Houston and his colleagues determined the best perforation and fractures for the Marcellus Shale to be those made using deep-penetrating and cleaner-hole technologies, to reduce fracture initiation and breakdown pressures. A mixture of 7.5% hydrochloric acid has proven most effective in reducing friction in the fractures and enhancing performance. By reviewing the lessons learned from the stimulation of more than 100 shale gas wells, Nathan Houston and colleagues from the Society of Petroleum Engineers were able to outline the most effective methodologies for natural gas extraction in the Marcellus Shale region.

Conclusions

The world is running out of fossil fuels. Exploring unconventional sources of fossil fuels is extremely costly and highly controversial. Chemicals used in hydraulic fracturing have the potential to contaminate critical groundwater supplies or induce dangerous seismic activity. As energy companies search for new places to drill for unconventional oil they will get closer to populations centers, where drilling techniques have the potential to affect millions of people, yet, the impending fossil fuel crisis is a very real threat that needs to be addressed by governments worldwide. While unconventional sources of hydrocarbons may delay the crisis for a few years, they are not a permanent solution. Instead, more research and development activities need to focus on finding alternative sources of renewable energy and developing new technologies to reduce worldwide dependency on dwindling fossil fuel supplies.

References Cited

Aguilera, R.F. and Aguilera, R., 2009. Oil, Natural Gas and NGL Endowment in North, Central, and South America. Society of Petroleum Engineers Technical Conference 2009, 1–8.

Curtis, F., 2009. Peak Globalization: Climate change, oil depletion and global trade. Ecological Economics 69, 427–434.

Gupta, D, Jackson, T, Hlavinka, G, Evans, J, Le, H, Batrashkin, A, Shaefer, 2009, M. Development and Field Application of a Low-pH, Efficient Fracturing Fluid for Tight Gas Fields in the Greater Green River Basin, Wyoming. Society of Petroleum Engineers, SPE Paper 116191, 602–610.

Hoffman, B, Chang, W, 2009. Modeling hydraulic fractures in finite difference simulators: Application to tight gas sands in Montana. Journal of Petroleum Science and Engineering 69, 107–116.

Houston, N, Blauch, M, Weaver, D, Miller, D, O'Hara, D. Fracture-Stimulation in the Marcellus Shale- Lessons Learned in Fluid Selection and Execution. Society of Petroleum Engineers Eastern Regional Meeting 2009, 1–11.

Lakatos, I., Lakatos-Szabó, J., 2009. Role of Conventional and Unconventional Hydrocarbons in the 21st Century: Comparison of Resources, Reserves, Recovery Factors and Technologies. 71st EAGE Conference and Exhibition 2009, 1–13.

Mohr, S., Evans, G., 2009. Forecasting coal production until 2100. Fuel 88, 2059–2067.

Mohr, S., Evans, G., 2010. Long term predictions of unconventional oil production. Energy Policy 38, 265–276.

6. Ocean Acidification and Deoxygenation, Part I

Matt Stjernholm

The potential risks associated with anthropogenic burning of fossil fuels and CO_2 emissions have encouraged countless initiatives to mitigate atmospheric carbon in order to avoid the potentially bleak outcomes of global climate change. While CO_2 is highly publicized as a greenhouse gas responsible for global warming, it is also known for altering many oceanic processes that seem to regularly go overlooked by the general public. Almost half of the CO_2 that has been emitted into the atmosphere since the Industrial Revolution has been absorbed into our oceans. This large uptake of CO_2 is responsible for measureable decreases in carbonate saturation and increased seawater acidity. As global warming, ocean acidification, and carbonate saturation are all processes that directly affect one-another, they each have their own specific impacts that threaten marine life. While the discoveries of these phenomena are fairly recent, a great deal of research has gone towards understanding and being able to predict how the oceans and the planet will respond to increased CO_2 conditions.

Ocean acidification is a term that has been coined for the combination of two processes resulting from CO_2 uptake into oceans: decreasing ocean pH and alterations in carbonate chemistry. Our oceans are the largest sink for anthropogenically emitted CO_2 by automobiles, power plants, and the combustion of fossil fuels that don't end up in the atmosphere. Decreased ocean pH is caused by CO_2 dissolving in water to produce carbonic acid; releasing hydrogen ions. The release of hydrogen ions in solution corresponds to a decrease in pH of the water, which means that it becomes more acidic. These conditions can have many negative effects on marine life, however, the extent of marine sensitivity to such events are still largely unknown. The pH of our oceans has decreased by 0.1 pH units since pre-industrial times and they are expected to drop another 0.3–0.4 units lower by the end of

Matt Stjernholm

2100. At face value, these numbers seem to be small and insignificant, however, pH is measured on a logarithmic scale and 0.1 units correspond to a 30% change in acidity. These predictions are largely responsible for driving current research on how decreased pH will affect current oceanic processes.

The second effect of CO_2 uptake into ocean waters is the increased propensity for the water to become undersaturated with respect to carbonate ions. When carbonic acid is created in oceans, it decreases the amount of dissolved inorganic carbon (DIC) by shifting the normal equilibrium conditions. DIC is oftentimes found in carbonate ions which are primarily used to construct shells and skeletal structures for calcifying organisms. Coral reefs, shellfish, and forminifera are examples of some calcifying organisms that rely on the presence of carbonate ions in sufficient amounts, such that the concentration is high enough to build their shells. The concentration of carbonate ions must be sufficient enough in water to maintain a saturation state that permits calcification. When the saturation state of calcium carbonate is too low, meaning there are not enough free carbonate ions available in solution for calcification to occur, then the environment becomes corrosive and shells/skeleton formation becomes inadequate. Recent research by Yamamoto et al. (2009) indicate that previously unseen undersaturation in large bodies of water is currently occurring in the Arctic ocean and could be a precursor to what the future may hold for many other waters throughout the world if preventative action isn't taken.

Along with acidification, the oceans are also susceptible to significant amounts of oxygen loss as a byproduct of CO_2-induced climate change. Ocean deoxygenation is an issue that we face today, which could develop into a major problem for coastal ecosystems and economies in the future. Ocean warming as a result of climate change causes decreased oxygen solubility and is responsible for creating large regions of low oxygen content known as hypoxic zones. These areas of low oxygen content are defined as regions where oxygen concentrations are below 60–120 μmol kg^{-1}, which cause added stress and increased mortality of organisms that are unable to adapt or escape these large regions. The definition of a hypoxic zone varies between such a large range of oxygen concentrations, because various organisms have different susceptibilities to decreased oxygen. One area that is particularly susceptible to small changes in global temperature is the oxygen minimum zone (OMZ), which is a region between 200–1000 m below the surface where oxygen saturation is lowest. The actual depth and extent of hypoxia in the OMZ's around the world vary depending on ocean circulation and oxygen consumption, which makes some areas more sensitive to deoxygenation than others. Recently, Stramma et al. (2010) found that hypoxic regions around the world are on the rise, and have been growing throughout our oceans over the past 50 years. Moreover, climate modeling predicts that dissolved oxygen in the oceans will decrease for many years to come and will increase in severity as our earth becomes warmer. Large-scale decreases in oxygen content places a great deal of stress on marine organisms and are responsible for compressing fish species into smaller habitats. This compression of habitats leads to increased competition for resources and decreased oceanic biodiversity.

Taken together, ocean acidification and deoxygenation are relatively new environmental issues at hand that require great attention. The following chapter is a compilation of current literature that outlines some of the newest research regarding oceanic studies pertaining to these phenomena.

Physical and Biogeochemical Modulation of Ocean Acidification in the Central North Pacific

The physical and chemical principles that cause ocean acidification are well-understood, however, there are very few data sets that have been sufficient in duration and resolution to thoroughly characterize the factors that contribute to acidification intensity and variability. Using 20 years of ocean data from the ALOHA station in the North Pacific Ocean near Hawaii, Dore *et al.* 2009 were able to observe a significant trend of decreasing surface pH while monitoring dissolved inorganic carbon (DIC), pH, total alkalinity (TA), and the partial pressure of CO_2. The findings show that over the past 20 years, a rise in ocean CO_2 concentration has been coupled with a decrease in ocean surface pH. Additionally, the results suggested a strong seasonal pH cycle that is driven by temperature, mixing, and gas exchange between marine organisms. The authors also found interesting interannual increases and decreases in pH due to mixing with lower, phosphate-rich waters. They observed decreases in surface pH up to 600 m with the largest decline in ocean pH at 250 m below the surface. This is attributed to large amounts of freshening and increased dissolved inorganic carbon from microbe respiration.

Dore *et al.* used *in situ* data of atmospheric and ocean CO_2 concentrations, DIC, and TA collected at the ALOHA site to make measurements and calculations regarding ocean pH. While DIC and TA can be used to calculate pH Dore *et al.* found that when calculating the pH, compared to the actual measured values, the results occasionally disagreed. They found a decreasing linear regression when plotting pH vs year for 0–30 m and 235–265 m from 1988 to 2008. When plotting the rate of pH change over time versus ocean depth, they found that the upper 600 m shows significant decreasing pH while waters 1000–5000 m below the surface aren't experiencing measurable acidification. When looking at the temporal variability of surface pH they found that the seasonal temperature cycle causes changes in the carbonic acid equilibria, such that greater sea surface temperatures correspond to decreased pH. A yearly plot of carbon fluxes and surface layer pH anomaly shows interannual variability in surface pH due to deep turbulent mixing. This mixing causes an upward movement of DIC that ultimately lowers the pH of the surface waters and creates sea surface pH anomalies.

The interannual variations in surface water show unexpectedly large increases in pH which the authors attribute to deep mixing with phosphates that sequester DIC. These reversals in surface layer acidification events are only temporary, however they provide information that suggests that the North Pacific could begin to see increases in pH over time. They propose that fertilizing the ocean with phosphates could mimic this natural process and possibly halt the effects of ocean acidification. Furthermore, they urge future researchers to monitor entire water columns as they have in this study, because the deep water that mixes with upper layers can have far-reaching effects on the water pH.

What Acidification and Undersaturation in the Arctic Ocean means for Calcifying Organisms

Ocean acidification is largely attributed to excessive anthropogenic emissions of CO_2. A third of this emitted CO_2 is absorbed by the oceans, which not only decreases the pH of the waters, but also changes the carbonate chemistry that plankton and invertebrates rely on for survival. This process reduces the availability of carbonate ions required by many organisms to construct shells and skeletons, mostly consisting of calcium carbonate or aragonite. Present research indicates that aragonite, a more soluble form of calcium carbonate, is being diluted by global warming-induced ice sheet melting and altering ocean carbonate chemistry which decreases the free carbonate ions in the Canada Basin of the Arctic Ocean. (Yamamoto *et al.* 2009) The authors quantified the saturation state of aragonite from 1997 to 2008 from 0–300 m below the surface. A saturation state greater than 1.0 is conducive to shell formation whereas a saturation state less than 1.0 is corrosive to shelled organisms. The literature indicates that the Arctic Ocean is the first deep ocean to become a corrosive habitat with significant aragonite undersaturation over the past decade (Yamamoto *et al.* 2009).

Yamamoto *et al.* suggest that decreased aragonite concentrations are due to anthropogenic burning of fossil fuels that cause melting of sea ice and increased carbonic acid as a result of CO_2 uptake which decreases the amount of free carbonate ions. They came to this conclusion after comparing the differences between aragonite saturation states, total alkalinity, salinity, and changes in sea ice melt in the Canada Basin between 1997 and 2008. By creating vertical profiles of aragonite saturation they were able to make the observation that the saturation state of aragonite had significantly decreased in the upper 50 m of water since 1997. A strong correlation between increased sea ice melt and decreased aragonite saturation state indicates that global warming is partly responsible for this undersaturation in the

Arctic Sea. Not only does melted sea ice dilute aragonite concentrations, but the loss of ice causes a decrease in a physical barrier between the water and the atmosphere that typically blocks CO_2 absorption. Computer models suggest that this trend of sea ice melting will continue and could possible carry on until 2030, when it could be completely gone. The authors also found that the changes in sea ice have caused significant upwelling of Pacific Winter Water which is highly undersaturated with aragonite, further decreasing the amount of free carbonate ions within 50 m of the sea surface.

Large-scale ocean acidification or undersaturation have not been observed prior to the recent discovery in the Canada Basin, and therefore scientists can only speculate on the potential problems that such an issue poses to aquatic life. Based on computer models and laboratory experiments, researchers are fairly certain that if nothing is done to combat this event then waters will only become increasingly corrosive due to undersaturation.

Ocean Acidification and Marine Trace Gas Emissions

Recent studies regarding ocean acidification have primarily focused on decreased ocean pH and altered carbonate chemistry due to the uptake of anthropogenic CO_2. Increased CO_2 concentrations in ocean systems also have a significant effect on gasses emitted by marine biota; another danger of ocean acidification. Iodocarbons, bromocarbons, and dimethylsulfide (DMS) are trace gases emitted by phytoplankton that play important roles in the chemistry of our atmosphere. Using small-scale marine communities, researchers found that iodocarbons and DMS gases that are produced by phytoplankton were significantly reduced under high CO_2 concentrations (Hopkins *et al.* 2009). Phytoplankton play a large role in the DMS cycle, which affects the global radiative budget by altering ocean's albedo. Computer models show that a 50% decrease in atmospheric DMS could result in a 1.6 °C increase in air temperatures. Additionally, five out of the six phytoplankton species tested showed significant biomass decline in the presence of high CO_2 concentrations. This poses a significant threat to gas-producing phytoplankton that are sensitive to increased ocean CO_2. Bromocarbon emissions increased in the presence of high CO_2 concentration while iodocarbons and DMS decreased. The data suggest that the reduction in iodocarbon concentrations is likely due to decreased pH rather than biological activity, and further tests will need to be performed to fully understand these processes. The findings here are important to take note of because these trace gases can heavily influence environments around the world.

Hopkins *et al.* used chlorophyll *a* concentrations as an indicator of phytoplankton growth which corresponded to bloom and postbloom phases, allowing them to record marine trace gas concentrations at various stages of life and respiration. The gases were measured in mesocosms, small biological communities, with various species of phytoplankton floating in a fjord in Norway. A total of six mesocosms were analyzed at present-day CO_2 concentrations and CO_2 levels predicted for 2100. By 2100 CO_2 levels are predicted to double and scientists are highly uncertain as to how this doubling will affect current global systems. Hopkins *et al.* note that these mesocosms cannot be extrapolated to oceans throughout the world, but suggest that their analyses are relevant to areas of high productivity in high-latitude oceans and costal waters. Although the results aren't indicative how worldwide waters will be affected, the high-latitude oceans account for an important amount of global water that cannot be overlooked.

The decrease found in DMS could have a direct and significant affect on global climate change if enough ocean water albedo becomes altered. Likewise, since iodo and bromo-carbons are major sources of atmospheric halogens, plankton play integral roles in mediating the transfer between the hydrosphere and the atmosphere. Although halogens act as greenhouse gases in the atmosphere they have beneficial properties that reduce harmful, tropospheric ozone. The work done by Hopkins *et al.* provide quality information regarding trace gas emissions and ocean acidification, however, the topic is far from being well-understood and requires a great deal of further attention.

Effect of Ocean Acidification on Iron Availability to Marine Phytoplankton

Uptake of CO_2 into the world's oceans is known to have numerous affects on the chemical processes that govern the successful survival of marine life. Recent studies suggest that ocean acidification decreases the bioavailability of iron (Fe) for phytoplankton. Iron is an essential element for marine organisms and its availability is very susceptible to fluctuations in pH. In the ocean, Fe is often found formed in complexes with various ligands and chelating agents. As water becomes increasingly acidic, iron's bioavailability for marine organisms decreases when it is complexed with ligands that release significant amounts of hydrogen ions upon dissociation. Shi *et al.* 2010 reported that a decrease in ocean pH from 8.6–7.8 results in a reduction of the rate at which phytoplankton uptake Fe. In the Fe(III) species that are strongly chelated by ligands which release protons upon dissociation, the authors found large reductions in Fe uptake; most notably when using EDTA as a chelating agent.

Shi *et al.* 2010 looked into the effects of lowered pH on iron uptake in various scenarios using diatoms and coccolithophores. Iron typically forms strong complexes with ligands in surface waters and previous research shows that iron in the form of Fe(III) determines its bioavailability in phytoplankton. Thus, Shi *et al.*

analyzed Fe uptake in these marine organisms using various chelating agents to simulate different quantities of usable Fe(III) in waters at a pH of 8.4, 8.0, and 7.6. The chelating agents used spanned a wide range of Fe binding abilities and therefore was their presence one of the determining factors that allowed the researchers to observe changes in bioavailability. The results indicated that there was a downward, decreasing trend of short-term Fe uptake as the water became more acidic; depending on the number of protons released upon dissociation of Fe from its complex. By plotting the rate of Fe uptake using various chelating agents versus pH and phytoplankton growth as a function of cellular Fe content compared to surrounding pH, Shi *et al.* determined that the changes in uptake that they observed were due to alterations in Fe chemistry and not changes in physiological changes.

If ocean acidification continues, based on their laboratory results, Shi *et al.* foresee decreases in iron availability for phytoplankton. The acid-base chemistry of the Fe and its chelating ligands dictates the amount of usable Fe(III) in the waters and the present levels are expected to diminish if anthropogenic CO_2 continues to be taken up by the oceans. This research is one of only few experiments regarding Fe uptake as a function of ocean pH, however, the results suggest that further studies must be performed for a more complete understanding of Fe chemistry in water and how its bioavailability is altered.

Ocean Acidification Affects Iron Speciation in Seawater

Previous studies indicate that physiology of phytoplankton is highly dependent on the pH of the surrounding ocean water. As phytoplankton blooms are affected by various species of iron, alterations in the ocean's pH due to anthropogenic introductions of CO_2 have the potential to significantly alter the bioavailability of iron and the biological productivity of phytoplankton. As stated in the previous summary, Fe(III) bioavailibiliity was found to decrease with increased ocean acidity for various marine organisms. Different species of iron have been shown to impact the CO_2 production by phytoplankton, which in turn provides a mechanism for a negative feedback mechanism as the forms of iron in the ocean change. The results of a recent study by Breitbarth *et al.* (2009) indicate that as CO_2 concentrations increase in ocean water the quantity of dissolved iron also increases. This alteration in ocean iron chemistry opposes what was found by Shi *et al.* (2009) and suggests that an increase in the amount of bioavailable iron in coastal waters will largely dictate the phytoplankton activity and ultimately the amount of CO_2 that is present into the ocean.

Breitbarth *et al.* used data from 9 mesocosms in which they controlled the event of phytoplankton blooms in the presence of varying CO_2 concentrations. They measured the phytoplankton blooms by quantifying the chlorophyll-a concentrations and monitored the mesocoms for 24 days, calculating the corresponding pH values from total alkalinity and dissolved inorganic carbon. Chemiluminescence flow injection analysis was performed to determine the total and dissolved quantities of iron during the days of the most prominent phytoplankton blooms, which correspond to days 7–13 of the experiment. When plotting the dissolved iron at varying CO_2 concentrations on a graph that was overlayed with the phytoplankton bloom, it is apparent that higher CO_2 concentrations correspond to lower Fe concentrations. On the other hand, concentrations of the Fe(II) species were consistently higher for high CO_2 environments, however, the quantities were dependent upon light intensity. Breitbarth et al. were able to show that half life duration of Fe^{2+} in the mesocoms decreased as the environments became less acidic.

Breitbarth et al. believe that their results warrant further analyses of iron chemistry pertaining to ocean acidification and its potential ecological implications. If Fe bioavailability is significantly altered by ocean acidification, it could effect the biological productivity of phytoplankton and other organisms throughout the ocean. Furthermore, this change in biological productivity as a byproduct of more readily available oceanic Fe(II) is expected to become more dramatic as time goes on, and more CO_2 is absorbed by the oceans. Fe(II) is a factor that figures into processes of carbon cycling in ocean waters, and can have a significant effect on atmospheric CO_2 quantities. With this in mind, it will be important to further analyze how Fe speciation affects marine organisms and the large-scale affects that they may have on global carbon levels.

Modeling Ocean Deoxygenation

Fossil fuel emissions and global warming are slowly causing oxygen loss in oceans. A recent study indicates that this trend poses a severe long-term threat to marine environments that must be considered as another dangerous factor of global warming. Using the Danish Center for Earth System Science model to test two IPCC scenarios of varying climate sensitivities with climate forcing models researchers were able to observe global changes in ocean oxygen concentration as a result of CO_2 emissions (Shaffer et al. 2009). The model indicates that once fossil fuels have been exhausted, their presence in the atmosphere will have a long-lasting affect on the oceans for nearly 100,000 years. Ocean temperatures are predicted to rise due to global warming, and the model predicts that ocean temperatures will be highest 1500–2000 years following the global warming maximum in the atmosphere. As the temperature of water increases, its oxygen content decreases. Since oxygen's solubility decreases as the water temperature rises, global climate change will be responsible to altering vast areas of marine environments. The upper 500 m of ocean water will be largely affected by this warming, and it has been hypothesized that ocean overturning and convection could extend this depletion to deep ocean areas as well. Furthermore, the projections indicate that the increased water temperatures will cause an enhancement of hypoxic zones. The simulations show large expansions of these oxygen poor regions throughout the oceans, which in turn presents great danger for marine life in these areas.

Shaffer and colleagues obtained the 100,000 year projections using a low-resolution computer model that incorporated many variables, notably: the atmosphere, ocean, ocean-sediment, and the land biosphere. Climate sensitivity scenarios of 3.0 ºC and 4.8 ºC were used for the 100,000 year projections using historical forcing and multiple emission scenarios (A2 and B1) as prescribed by the IPCC. Assuming that fossil fuel use will end in 2100, Shaffer *et al.* determined that the atmosphere would first increase by 2–8°C followed by 2–5°C increase in ocean temperature up to 2000 years later. Moreover, the temperature and oxygen content was not predicted to return to present levels until 100,000 years later.

Carbon dioxide is a greenhouse gas that allows incoming short-wave solar radiation from the sun, but blocks reflected long-wave radiation. This radiation acts as trapped heat that is unable to escape the atmosphere and increases the earth's temperature. As the projections suggest, if anthropogenic fossil fuel emissions continue as planned, marine life will be in serious danger throughout the world. Increased hypoxic zones will make large expanses of ocean water uninhabitable for marine life and will increase the number or mortality events in marine organisms. With these points considered, the long-lasting effects of oxygen depletion in oceans is an important factor to be discussed in-hand with global climate change. .

Ocean Oxygen Minima Expansions and their Biological Impacts

One previously noted concern regarding global warming is the loss of oxygen in oceans, known as deoxygenation. Recently, Stramma *et al.* 2010 analyzed oxygen content in oxygen minimum zones (OMZ) between 1960–1974 and 1990–2008 in the tropical regions of the Pacific, Atlantic, and Indian Oceans. OMZ's are areas in the ocean that naturally occur with low oxygen saturation that generally exist between 200–1000 meters below the surface or at pressures between 200–700 dbar. Stramma *et al.* found that large areas of these subsurface tropical oceans showed significant decline over the past three decades and regions where oxygen levels are uninhabitable for larger organisms, $O_2 < 70$ μmol/kg, have increased by 4.5 million km². These changes in oxygenation can cause critical shifts in nutrient cycling, habitat compression of entire ecosystems, and many other adverse affects which the authors advise should be further studied.

Stramma *et al.* looked at numerous datasets to create depth profiles of 100 dbar intervals between 200–700 dbar. The dissolved oxygen anomalies were then calculated according World Ocean Atlas 2005. These values were incorporated into a model with a 1° x 1° resolution between 40°S and 40°N. Stramma *et al.* also used apparent oxygen utilization (AOU) as an estimate of oxygen taken up by subsurface waters, because this calculation removes factors other than temperature that effect oxygen solubility. By doing so, they were able to directly examine the temperature influence on the datasets that they analyzed. They constructed maps of ocean oxygen differences in vertical and horizontal regions and found a general trend of decline in oxygen concentration over time. Contrarily, some areas indicated anomalous oxygen increases during these periods. Stramma *et al.* also observed that the area of the hypoxic regions, which don't have sufficient O_2 concentration to support certain species of macro-organism survival, are expanding westward in the equatorial Pacific and Indian and South Atlantic. Models predict further deoxygenation due to global warming because oxygen solubility decreases with surface-layer warming, which poses considerable threats to marine life.

It is predicted that this deoxygenation will have the greatest effect on larger organisms between 200–300 m because it is common for upwelling of oxygen-poor water to occur in this layer near shelf breaks. Furthermore, with increasing areas of OMZ's they believe that tropical pelagic fish (those that live in the upper layers of the ocean) will be compressed into smaller habitats where competition for resources will cause decreased bio-diversity in these zones. On a similar note, the expansion of hypoxic regions have already been shown to increase the prevalence of jellyfish population in various ecosystems, because they are able to tolerate lower levels of oxygen than most other marine organisms. Increased jellyfish populations pose a threat to further increasing the amount of hypoxic regions, because they feed primarily on zooplankton, which maintain the ocean-oxygen balance by releasing O_2 into the water during photosynthesis. Overall, the authors were able to make many observation based on their models, however, they concede that the lack of complete ocean data limits their scope on gaining a full and accurate understanding of deoxygenation trends into the future. They suggest that more complete data sets, along with long-term monitoring will allow for better modeling of these deoxygenation events.

The 20th-Century Development and Expansion of Louisiana Shelf Hypoxia, Gulf of Mexico

The previous summaries indicate that many areas of ocean water throughout the world are becoming increasingly hypoxic today. Some of these hypoxic regions are termed "Dead Zones" and the largest one in the United States is found in the Northern Gulf of Mexico. This is also the second largest dead zone in the world, and has been monitored since 1985. To determine oxygen content prior to these measurements in order to gain a better understanding of this hypoxic phenomenon, Osterman *et al.* used forminiferal analysis of protists in the area along with lead-dating to serve as a proxy for oxygen content in the Lousiana shelf since 1900. The proxy was based on the percentage benthic-forminifers capable of surviving in low oxygen conditions, which correlates to the amount of oxygen in the water at any given point in time. Evidently, around the 1950's the Northern Gulf of Mexico faced a great decline in oxygen content that is continuing today.

Ostermann *et al.* previously created an index using the bethic formanifers as a proxy for hypoxic events called PEB (*% Protononion atlanticum* + *% Epistominella vitrea* + *% Buliminella morgani*). Since these organisms are capable of surviving in low-oxygen environments, an increase in the PEB value corresponds to a decline in less-tolerant species, and therefore is an index of hypoxia. Once the PEB analysis was completed, Ostermann *et al.* used lead (^{210}Pb) dating to determine the sedimentation rate from where formanifera samples were taken to indicate to which year each PEB value corresponded. They found in nearly all sampling sites that there was an event of sharp oxygen content decline around the 1950s based on the percent of PEB organisms present. Previous studies indicate that hypoxia in this area is largely due to anthropogenic inputs of fertilizer, sewage, and livestock runoff. When large quantities of these materials enter the Gulf from upstream sources on the Mississippi and Atchafalaya rivers, large blooms of phytoplankton release organic carbon into the surrounding waters. The release of carbon leads to eutrophication, which is the presence of high quantities of nutrients, which in turn increases the productivity of the ecosystem to a point that and much of the oxygen content is consumed.

The data presented the study indicate that many regions in the hypoxic zone have risen to PEB values above 80%. When compared to the 1,000 year mean PEB that was determined as background data at 12%, these high PEB's indicate a large deviation from the natural amount of oxygen content of the last millennium. Additionally, Osterman *et al.* determined that in the early 1900s, hypoxic regions were present only near the mouth of the Mississippi River, whereas the entire Lousiana Shelf is now deemed a hypoxic zone. Based on the number of hypoxic events per year, Osterman *et al.* concluded that over the past 50 years, hypoxic conditions have become much more frequent and occur over more extensive periods of time. As the proxy data indicate a southern expansion of the hypoxic zone, it is will be necessary to continue extensive monitoring in the area.

Conclusions

The summarized analyses of the studies reported in this chapter indicate that ocean acidification and deoxygenation are events clearly could pose dramatic threats to marine life and a large network of natural processes. The implications of ocean acidification are far-reaching and range from changing the composition of marine ecosystems to other processes such as altering the planet's albedo. On the same token, ocean deoxygenation poses long-term threats of habitat compression and loss of biodiversity if ocean temperatures become too high. These changes are not only expected to impact only biological processes, but will also have economic effects related to fishing industries. The over-arching message from the articles presented in this chapter is that we proceed with caution and mitigate CO_2 emissions as much as possible. However, most of the studies concede that much further testing and analyses are required, as the current understanding of these oceanic mechanisms are only in their infancy. Although proxies are available to make conjectures about previous ocean conditions, direct analysis and longer datasets are needed to solidify the basis of these claims.

Undoubtedly, many of the articles in this chapter are at the forefront of their field in oceanic research and will likely serve as springboards for future studies to come. As more attention is given to these increasingly pressing issues, better understanding of the mechanisms that drive these complex systems will be forthcoming. It will be necessary for more data, more sophisticated computer models, and a better comprehension of the variables involved in ocean acidification and deoxygenation to gain a better idea of how urgent these issues may really be.

References Cited

Breitbarth, E. Bellerby, R., Neill, C.,Ardelan, M., Meyerhofer, M., Zollner, E. Croot, P., Riebesell, U. 2009. Ocean Acidification Affects Iron Speciation in Seawater. Biogeoscience Discussions 6, 6781–6802.

Dore, J., Lukas, R., Sadler, D., Church, M., Karl, D., 2009. Physical and Biogeochemical Modulation of Ocean Acidification in the Central North Pacific. PNAS 106, 12235–12240.

Hopkins, F., Turner, S., Nightingale, P., Steinke, M., Bakker, D., Liss, P., 2010. Ocean Acidification and Marine Trace Gas Emissions. PNAS 107, 760–765.

Osterman L., Poore R., Swarzenski P., Senn D., DiMarco S., 2009. The 20th-Century Development and Expansion of Louisiana Shelf Hypoxia, Gulf of Mexico. US Geological Survey 29, 405–414.

Shaffer, G., Olsen, S., Pedersen, J., 2009. Long-term Ocean Oxygen Depletion in Response to Carbon Dioxide Forcing to Emissions. Science 326, 716.

Shi D., Xu Y., Hopkinson B., Morel F., 2010. Effect of Ocean Acidification on Iron Availability to Marine Phytoplankton. Science 327, 676–679.

Stramma, L., Schmidtko, S., Levin, L., Johnson, G., 2010. Ocean Oxygen Minima Expansions and their Biological Impacts. Deep-Sea Research I. DOI:10.1016/j.dsr.2010.01.005

Yamamoto-Kawai, M., McLaughlin, F., Carmack, E., Nishino, S., Shimada, K., 2009. Aragonite undersaturation in the arctic ocean: Effects of Ocean Acidification and Sea Ice Melt. Science 326, 1098–1100.

.

7. Ocean Acidification and Deoxygenation, Part II

Julia Levy

Anthropogenic carbon emissions and global warming have significantly impacted the Earth's oceans since the beginning of the industrial revolution, and will probably continue to affect them even after carbon emissions have decreased. As CO_2 is released into the atmosphere, it dissolves into the ocean, triggering a chemical reaction that results in an increase in the concentration of H^+ ions, lowering pH. Already, pH has dropped by 0.1 and is likely to continue to drop to as low as 7.8 by the end of this century (Feely *et al.* 2009).

The wellbeing of calcifying organisms is the main concern that scientists have expressed when it comes to ocean acidification. Elevated CO_2 concentrations cause an increase in the solubility of calcite and aragonite, forms of calcium carbonate that marine organisms use to create hard shells (Cohen and Holcolmb 2009). The calcification process depends on a low solubility of aragonite, which enabling an organism to create a pocket of water with a great enough concentration of calcium that calcium carbonate can precipitate. It is through this process that calcifying organisms form their protective shells. Lower concentrations of aragonite may decrease shell size in the animals, making them much less healthy and more prone to predation.

Further implications of ocean acidification involve the loss of the relationship that humans have evolved with marine ecosystems. These complications include provisioning, regulation, culture, and support—especially for coastline communities in developing nations (Cooley *et al.* 2009). These coastal communities tend to rely on coral reefs for income (through tourism) and on shellfish as their main source of protein. Thus, the loss of these organisms and the natural beauty of the ocean's reefs could have devastating economical effects.

Now that ocean acidification is recognized as a serious threat to the ocean's ecosystems, various organizations have devoted their time to researching the problem, including the European Project on Ocean Acidification (EPOCA). Though studying the problems caused by ocean acidification is difficult to do in a laboratory setting, the organization hopes to make predictions about the effects of ocean acidification with respect to marine organisms and ecosystems, and to evaluate any major "tipping points" (Gattuso and Hansson 2009). Another source that may be a promising possibility for evaluating ocean acidification is satellite technology (Gledhill *et al.* 2009). Because collecting data via on-site methods is time consuming and sometimes impossible, the ability to evaluate the carbonate chemistry of the oceans from space is useful, but cannot yet be used in areas that have complex currents.

Despite the wide array of research being done, the effects of ocean acidification are not something that can easily be studied in a lab. The geological record provides scientists with a better idea of what the implications of a changing climate may mean for calcifying organisms. In recent history, changes in ocean acidity have occurred in conjunction with huge releases in carbon dioxide. The record shows that most calcifying plankton were able to adapt to the new climate. However, it is the calcifying organisms living in the benthic regions of the ocean that are the most endangered by climate change (Cooley *et al.* 2009). Studying the geological record could very well be the best way to learn about ocean acidification, even with all of the advanced research that is currently underway.

The release of carbon into the atmosphere is not only causing the oceans to increase in acidity, it is also causing deoxygenation, particularly in areas called oxygen minimum zones. The solubility of oxygen in water depends, among other things, on water temperature. As the temperature of the earth rises, the waters warm, meaning that oxygen is less soluble, and less concentrated. Only over the last few decades has this decrease in oxygen been observed. Oxygen concentrations in the tropical North Atlantic have dipped below 40 μmol/kg, lower than any previously recorded concentrations since at least 1993 (Stramma *et al.* 2009). Oxygen concentration data indicate that the world's oceans are becoming depleted in oxygen by about 0.5 μmol/kg per year. If deoxygenation were to continue at this rate, many of the oxygen minimum zones would be completely devoid of oxygen in the next 100 years.

Because records on deoxygenation are sparse, a new system for measuring oxygen concentration would be a helpful technology for future predictions and studies. The joint Argo-Oxygen program has proposed an implementation of dissolved oxygen sensors to be used worldwide, in order to make ocean deoxygenation an easier problem to evaluate in the future (Gruber *et al.* 2010). However, these sensors are difficult to calibrate and are not always accurate, problems that must be addressed before implementation can occur.

Dissolved CO_2 in Oceans Lowers pH and Decreases Aragonite Concentrations

The consumption of fossil fuels since the industrial revolution has dramatically increased the amount of CO_2 dissolved in the oceans, the effects of which have only recently fallen under the lens of scientific research. The Earth's oceanic ecosystems are dependent on the balance between pH levels and dissolved carbonic compounds such as CO_3^{2-}, aragonite, and calcite, all of which are drastically effected by CO_2 dissolution. Studies indicate that pH levels have dropped by about 0.1 (Feely *et al.* 2009) since the industrial era and will continue to drop in conjunction with a decrease in carbonic compounds in the decades to come. This change may eventually disable marine organisms' ability to produce calcium carbonate shells.

Richard A. Feely and associates at the World Ocean Circulation Experiment/Joint Global Ocean Flux Study spent nine years conducting cruises to measure different carbon parameters in oceans throughout the world. Carbonate ion, aragonite, calcite, and pH are among the parameters that the researchers measured. They then predicted future changes in the aforementioned parameters using data from the National Center for Atmospheric Research.

Their findings indicate that the current pH of the oceans is 8.1 but will drop to 7.8 by the end of this century. Concentrations of CO_3^{2-} are also projected to decrease drastically before the turn of the century, low enough that aragonite and calcite will become undersaturated (anticipated to occur 2020 and 2050 respectively). It is this decrease in calcium compounds that will make it difficult if not completely impossible for aquatic creatures to form calcium carbonate shells.

The mechanism by which carbonate shell production decreases occurs through a series of chemical reactions. After CO_2 in the atmosphere is dissolved into the ocean, it reacts with water to produces more H^+ ions (decreasing the pH of the ocean). The newly available H^+ ions react with CO_3^{2-}, decreasing the concentration of CO_3^{2-}, which decreases aragonite and calcite concentrations, inhibiting the formation of calcium carbonate shells. The projections made by Feely and his colleagues indicate that this century is a pivotal time for humankind to decrease its CO_2 emissions, or else marine ecosystems will be in danger as early as the year 2020.

Corals Struggle to Build Skeletons in a High CO_2 World

The wellbeing of coral reefs is of great concern as CO_2 emissions increase and pH levels of the oceans decrease. As concentrations of CO_2 in the oceans increase, the concentrations of aragonite and calcite decrease, which is likely to cause coral skeletons to be less healthy as well as less developed (Cohen and Holcolmb 2009).

An unhealthy coral reef could have a devastating effect on the ocean's ecosystem, as reefs provide shelter, nesting grounds, and foods for a variety of marine organisms.

Anne Cohen and Michael Holcomb studied the impact that ocean acidification has on biological calcification. The study shows that when aragonite concentrations are supersaturated, corals are able to accrete enough calcium carbonate to form healthy skeletons. However, with each slight decrease in concentration, the skeletons become both smaller and poorly structured, and when aragonite concentrations are around saturation level, skeletons are severely underdeveloped.

To fully comprehend the effects of decreased aragonite, the paper stresses the importance of understanding the calcification process. The exact mechanism for calcification remains unknown but the most widely accepted hypothesis for the process is that the coral accretes seawater into special pockets underneath its tissue. It then uses proton pumps to discard protons and take in Ca^{2+}. After some time, calcium carbonate is formed from the supersaturation of calcium and carbonate ions.

Unfortunately, this process is a taxing one for the coral. It is estimated that calcification expels about 20–30% of the organism's total energy. The amount of energy the process consumes is dependent on the acidity of the water; the more acidic it is, the harder the proton pump must work to create calcium carbonate. At a certain point, the coral can no longer spend its energy on skeleton production, as it must focus on other functions such as feeding. Once this point is reached, the health of a coral reef is at risk.

Relationship between Humans and Marine Ecosystems likely to Change due to Ocean Acidification

The examination of the effects of anthropogenic CO_2 emissions on oceanic ecosystems includes investigating how the oceans' uptake of CO_2 may drastically alter the relationship that humans have with their environment. In other words, humans should expect to feel the effect of oceanic climate change. The provisioning, regulation, culture, and support provided by marine resources are four categories that will undergo change in the decades to come (Cooley *et al.* 2009).

Data from the Food and Agriculture Organization and the United Nations were used to interpret the provisional effects of ocean acidification on marine harvests. A current estimate suggests that marine fisheries provide 143.7 metric tons of products per year, most of which is food. The annual income for these fisheries will probably suffer from ocean acidification because of its effects on calcifying organisms (like mussels, clams, and crabs). These species may decline, and because they are reliable prey for many predator species, a ripple effect may take place throughout oceanic ecosystems. This would, in all likelihood, diminish the income and food these organisms provide for humans.

Regulation of shorelines is another beneficial effect of marine ecosystems. Coral reefs provide physical protection for the nearby shore from waves and tsunamis. Unfortunately, reefs are one of the ecological zones that may be negatively affected by ocean acidification. Without this buffer zone, the coasts may become harsher environments more prone to damage from storms. This could cause an increase in the cost of living in these targeted areas.

Culture is another factor affected by the changing ocean chemistry. Coral reefs, for example, provide tourism, recreation, and income for coastal communities. As oceanic organisms suffer, so will these sources of income, producing lasting effects on the economies of many small countries that depend on such tourism. Developing nations are expected to be especially effected by ocean acidification, because they tend to depend more heavily on calcifying species for their source of protein. The decrease in marine produce coupled with an increase in world population could pose a serious threat to developing coastal countries.

Objectives and Current Research of the European Project on Ocean Acidification

The European Project on Ocean Acidification (EPOCA) is a four-year project that is working toward four main objectives regarding the research and understanding of ocean acidification (Gattuso and Hansson 2009). The project's first objective is to study past data regarding ocean chemistry and biogeography. The hope is that these data will offer insight into future predictions on the effects of ocean acidification. Its second objective is to assess the reaction of marine organisms and ecosystems to the changing chemistry of the oceans. The third goal of EPOCA is to determine the response of the oceanic ecosystems as a whole to ocean acidification and the final goal is to predict any major "tipping points," and to successfully communicate the importance of ocean acidification to the public in an attempt to raise the awareness of this issue.

The EPOCA consortium is working towards its first goal by studying past pH fluctuations and how they have affected oceanic ecosystems. Thus far, the consortium has begun determining past pH levels by studying Boron, an element whose isotopic composition shifts depending on acidity. Scientists hope to soon determine how past fluctuations in pH have effected the ecosystems of calcifying organisms.

The consortium presents a variety of research methods to study the effect that increasing acidity has on marine organisms and on marine ecosystems, each with its own advantages and disadvantages. The most controlled of these methods are bottle experiments, which are conducted in a contained environment, with most variables controlled for. Unfortunately, this method is difficult to use when studying interactions among species. On the other end of the spectrum, the consortium employs field experiments and observations, which are very realistic and provide insight into the relationship between species, but are not controlled.

The final goal—communicating ocean acidification issues—is being carried out in the education system, focusing on a young audience. Among other methods, the EPOCA has created a movie for young audiences about ocean acidification, and has also set up a program called CarboSchools. This program connects teachers with scientists in order to collaborate in informing students about the effects of climate change. The EPOCA plans to continue gathering and assessing data, and promoting communication until 2012.

Advancements in Satellite Technology provide Data on Ocean Acidification

Evaluating ocean acidification from space may be a more effective method of research than assessing data gathered by ships from on-site locations. Satellite observations can help assess the carbonate chemistry of areas of the ocean where on-site data are not available, providing information such as the sea surface temperature, wind speed, productivity estimates, and upwelling estimates. From these data, extrapolations can be made on the concentration of aragonite, an important parameter for organisms with calcium carbonate shells such as coral (Gledhill *et al.* 2009).

The Experimental Ocean Acidification Product Suite combines data from various satellite sources—such as the National Oceanic and Atmospheric Administration (NOAA) and NASA—in an effort to extrapolate regional mean aragonite saturation in the Greater Caribbean Region (GCR). Thus far, the GCR is the only ocean studied by satellite due to its relatively low amount of upwelling. This factor allows scientists to use simpler and more reliable formulas when extrapolating predictions.

The organization has used previous satellite data to show the decrease in ocean aragonite concentration from the beginning of the industrial era to the present. The results indicate that current aragonite conditions in the summer (when aragonite concentrations are highest) are lower than the wintertime minimums from only about 20 years ago. With satellite data, The Experimental Ocean Acidification Product Suite made comparisons of aragonite concentration by latitude using the years 1988 and 2007. The results show the effects of seasonal variability on aragonite concentration, indicating that the higher the latitude, the more the annual fluctuation. This variation in high latitudes probably correlates with an increase in coral productivity during summer months.

Though satellite predictions could be instrumental in making predictions about the wellbeing of the oceans, they are not yet advanced enough to use outside of the GCR. Other areas of the ocean have much more complicated upwelling patterns, making the algorithms used to extrapolate meaningful information too complicated to be statistically viable. In other words, there is no single equation that can model the complicated chemistry of the Earth's oceans on a global scale.

Ocean Acidification may have Extreme Effects on Benthic Calcifiers

Most studies on ocean acidification remark on the negative effect that a lower pH level will have on calcifying organisms, however, these effects are highly species specific, and do not account for adaptation, making the effect of pH on calcifying organisms impossible to test with complete accuracy in a laboratory setting (Ridgwell and Schmidt 2007). The best possibility for understanding the effect of pH on calcifying organisms is to look at the geological record, which indicates that organisms living in the deep benthic ocean may be the most at risk when it comes to climate change.

Ridgwell and colleagues observed past geological records, and noted that the pH of the world's oceans may have been lower by 0.6–0.7 pH units during the Cretaceous and Jurassic periods. These data imply that a change in pH in the coming century may not mean the end for calcifying organisms, because of their ability to adapt to climate and ocean geochemistry.

Changes in the pH of the world's ocean pose a threat only if they occur at a rate so rapid that organisms cannot adapt. The geological record from 55.5 million years ago when a large amount of carbon was released, rapidly lowering ocean pH, shows that calcifying plankton did not become extinct, but rather, they adapted.

The ability of an organism to adapt in a rapidly changing environment is enhanced by a fast reproductive cycle. Most plankton have very short life spans, which makes for good adaptive abilities. However, benthic foraminifers live for several years, making them more prone to extinction due to climate change. Furthermore, because they live in the deep sea—a very stable environment not conducive to high genetic variability—they may be even more at risk of extinction.

Oxygen Minimum Zones Decrease in Oxygen from 1993 to Present

Oxygen minimum zones (OMZ), areas of the ocean that have low concentrations of dissolved oxygen, have been increasing over the last two decades. Not only have these zones been increasing, but the total amount of dissolved oxygen in these zones has reached an all time low. Recent data have been collected indicating that oxygen concentrations in the eastern tropical North Atlantic are down to a low of 40 μmol/kg (Stramma *et al.* 2009). It is postulated that this increase in OMZs will result in a serious decrease in the habitat of some fishes and will reduce biodiversity overall.

Lothar Stramma and associates conducted research on a German ship RV Merian in the tropical eastern Atlantic Ocean. They collected data for temperature, conductivity and oxygen levels, mostly between 300 m and 600 m in depth comparing them with data gathered in the past two decades. In March 1993 the lowest dissolved oxygen concentration was 60 μmol/kg. The lowest concentration of oxygen according to the most recent research is around 40 μmol/kg, a drastic decrease.

Despite these oxygen depletions in the oxygen minimum zones, oxygen levels have increased in areas of the upper central water. Researchers believe, however, that this increase could be a reflection of seasonal trends rather than a true indication of average oxygen levels. Previous data on oxygen levels are patchy, so it is hard to chart a definitive trend.

The researchers estimate that the recorded change in oxygen concentration is approximately –0.5 μmol/kg per year. If this amount of oxygen depletion were to continue, the oceans would be completely devoid of oxygen within the next 100 years. However, a scenario such as this is extremely unrealistic. The purpose of such a hypothetical situation is to help recognize the sensitivity of the oceans due to climate change.

Argo to Implement Dissolved Oxygen Sensors Globally

The joint Argo-Oxygen program plans to implement a global system of dissolved oxygen sensors to measure the decrease of ocean oxygen concentrations (Gruber *et al.* 2010). Dissolved ocean oxygen sensors mounted on free-floating buoys are a new technology that will be more accurate and consistent than current technologies because of the large spatial distribution of the buoys and ability to take recordings at regular intervals. The sensors will be added to floats around the globe, and will provide data to determine seasonal and long-term variability in ocean oxygen concentrations.

A small-scale pilot project will be run initially to determine accuracy, precision, and speed of data transfer, before the oxygen sensors are distributed globally. This pilot phase will provide a cost estimate, and will work out other issues. After the pilot test, global implementation of the sensors will provide the first data on ocean oxygen concentrations at a global level.

Another issue the project is taking into consideration is the lowered lifetime of the floats by about 10% to 30% due to the addition of oxygen sensors. The cost of implementing the devices is estimated to be between $2,000 and $10,000 per float per year, a price range that Argo expects to fund independently. The oxygen sensors will be important in measuring hypoxic and anoxic zones—areas of great or minimal oxygen abundance that may be highly affected by oceanic warming. Currently, testing of oxygen sensors has begun, but their accuracy and calibration efficiency has not yet reached the standards that Argo hopes to meet.

Conclusions

Though ocean acidification and deoxygenation are major sources of concern for the wellbeing of the Earth's oceans in the coming century, the implications of these issues are yet unknown. Many current studies, based on laboratory data, appear pessimistic about the future of calcifying organisms. Studies carried out in a lab show the negative effects that low aragonite concentrations can have on marine calcifiers; these effects appear drastic and irreversible when looked at in a small, contained experiment.

However, a laboratory model can never account for all of the intricacies of nature. The ability of organisms to adapt and evolve has been proven time and time again in the geologic record. The question is whether or not marine organisms are capable of adapting to the fast pace of current climate change.

References Cited

Cohen, A., Holcomb, M., 2009. Why corals care about ocean acidification; uncovering the mechanism. Oceanography 22, 118–127.

Cooley, S., Kite-Powell, H., Doney, S., 2009. Ocean acidification's potential to alter global marine ecosystem services. Oceanography 22, 172–181.

Feely, R., Doney, S., Cooley, S., 2009. Present Conditions and Future Changes in a High-CO_2 World. Oceanography 22, 36–47.

Gattuso, J., Hansson, L., and the EPOCA consortium, 2009. European Project on Ocean Acidification (EPOCA): Objectives, Projects, and Scientific Highlights. Oceanography 22, 190–201.

Gledhill, D., Wanninkhof, R., Eakin, M., 2009. Observing Ocean Acidification from Space. Oceanography 22, 48–59.

Gruber, N., Doney, S., Emerson, S., Gilbert, D., Kobayashi, T., Körtzinger, A., Johnson, K., Johnson, G., Johnson, K., Riser, S., Ulloa, O., 2010. Adding Oxygen to Argo: Developing a Global in-situ Observatory for Ocean Deox-

Julia Levy

ygenation and Biogeochemistry. OceanObs'09: Sustained Ocean Observations and Information for Society 2, WPP–306.

Ridgwell, A., Schmidt, D., 2010. Past constraints on the vulnerability of marine calcifiers to massive carbon dioxide releases. Nature Geoscience 3, 196–200.

Stramma, L., Visbeck, M., Brandt P., Tanhua, T., Wallace, D., 2009. Deoxygenation in the oxygen minimum zone of the eastern tropical North Atlantic. Geophysical Research Letters 36, DOI:10.1029/2009GL039593.

.

8. Carbon Capture and Storage: a Practical Option for Short-Term Climate Change Mitigation

Shanna Hoversten and Jake Bauch

Carbon capture and storage (CCS) technology is a promising technique for mitigating emissions from coal-fired power plants. Scientists and politicians alike argue that we will be reliant on fossil fuels for energy many years into the future, thus CCS represents an opportunity for us to continue using cheap and readily available energy while at the same time keeping that CO_2 from entering the atmosphere and contributing to climate change. Although CCS does not represent the only feasible mitigation for climate change, it could be used effectively in concert with other technologies to transition to a carbon-neutral economy. The effectiveness of CCS technology has been largely proven through years of Enhanced Oil Recovery (EOR) projects and a series of pure CCS demonstration projects around the world, however there are still debates about its safety and cost-effectiveness.

The CCS process can be viewed as three distinct processes: capture, transport, and storage. The capture process arguably has the most potential for improvement from current techniques. Scientists are still experimenting with three different methods of capture, including pre-combustion, post-combustion, and oxyfuel. Amine scrubbing is a form of post-combustion capture that has been used by power plants in the past, and thus may present an economically viable option for carbon capture. It has yet to be determined which form of capture technology will predominate, but in the mean time, new coal-fueled power plants need to be outfitted with capture equipment if CCS can be widely deployed in the near future.

Transport of the CO_2 from the source of the emissions to the storage site is the second element that must be considered in any large-scale CCS scheme. Transport of CO_2 via pipeline has been used in EOR projects for decades; thus safe and efficient CO_2 transport is not a significant concern. The primary consideration for the CCS transport system comes in planning out the network of pipelines. Policymakers and scientists in various countries and regions are working together to out-line a theoretical branching of pipelines from clusters of capture-equipped power plants—the CO_2 source—to corresponding storage basins—the CO_2 sink—using as little pipeline as possible. These decisions also must take into account the overall storage potential of the region, allocating CO_2 in a way that will take full advantage of the finite number viable basins.

Storage of the captured CO_2 is the final component in the CCS chain. Injec-tion of CO_2 into saline aquifers has been performed effectively for decades in EOR projects, thus the oil industry can offer considerable knowledge about this tech-nique. Most scientists believe that subsurface basins will provide an effective and safe sink for CO_2, however there is some debate over how long the CO_2 will remain there, and what an appropriate time horizon for storage is, given the costs of the process.

Safety is the foremost consideration associated with storage of CO_2, and one of the potential pitfalls in the court of public opinion. CO_2 has the potential to leak from storage basins either in mass quantities due to a catastrophic event such as an earthquake, or more likely, it could leak gradually through fractures in the basin. Gradual leakage can become a health and safety hazard should it leak into a con-fined building or into a source of potable water. Although current research does not suggest any significant risk associated with CCS projects, scientists are in the process of determining health and safety standards to accompany storage sites. Ad-ditionally, a series of monitoring and verification technologies are currently under development that will serve to enforce these standards.

CO_2 storage also represents a challenge for carbon accounting, given that a certain amount of CO_2 will inevitably leak back into the atmosphere over time. However, scientists predict that most basins have the potential to store their in-jected CO_2 on the order of 10,000 years. This suggests that at the very least, CCS provides a viable opportunity for short-term climate change mitigation.

One of the most pressing concerns about the efficacy of the CCS process in its entirety is the potential for it to be economically viable. The combined cost of cap-ture, transport, injection, and monitoring, leads to a very high price per ton of CO_2 stored. Arguably, this price will decline as capture technology, the most expensive and least established element, improves. CCS could also become cost effective if legislation imposes a significant price on carbon emissions. Another promising op-tion for making CCS affordable, and even lucrative, would be to sell captured CO_2 to oil companies executing EOR projects. This suggests that CCS could very possi-bly become economically viable in the near future.

CCS processes as applied to coal burning power plants are currently being demonstrated on a worldwide level. These pilot projects suggest that the technology can be successfully applied, and that the major hurdles now are political and economic rather than scientific. Scientists are beginning looking at how the CCS chain can be applied more widely, and are experimenting with processes such as ambient air capture. Should this technology ever be practically executed, capture units will be able to remove CO_2 directly from the atmosphere, allowing for it to be stored permanently underground. This chapter reviews a selection of literature detailing current progress in developing and deploying CCS systems.

Amine Scrubbing could be Useful On-site CO_2 Capture Technique for Coal Fired Power Plants

Coal fired power plants provide roughly half of the power generated in the United States each year. Since these plants will inevitably keep operating, amine scrubbing to capture CO_2 from the plants could be the most effective way to reduce emissions. A technique patented in the 1930s and currently the most common method for removing sulfur from flue gas at power plants, amine scrubbing has seen technological improvements in the last decade amounting to a cost reduction from $77 to $52/ton of CO_2 removed (Rochelle 2009). Strong legislation in the form of a cap-and-trade system, or a carbon tax could provide the necessary incentives for the first major amine scrubbing project.

Gary Rochelle of the Department of Chemical Engineering at University of Texas at Austin looked at ways that current process and solvent improvements could reduce costs of amine scrubbing. His basis for the economics of amine scrubbing was a 2007 study by the US Department of Energy that showed cost reductions from 2001 to 2006. The process of amine scrubbing is as follows: CO_2 from gas exiting the power plant is absorbed at a high temperature into an amine solution, water vapor is used to strip the amine from the CO_2, the water in the vapor is condensed leaving pure CO_2, and then the CO_2 is compressed to between 100 and 150 bar for transportation and storage.

Costs can be divided into power used (half is steam to heat the vapor and half to compress the CO_2), capital costs, and operating and maintenance cost. Improvements in the process such as stripping at multiple pressures could reduce power used but would increase capital costs. Solvents with higher rates of absorption, or greater capacity can reduce power costs. The theoretical minimum amount of energy used the chemical reactions for amine scrubbing is 12% of the power plant capacity, but even with all known improvements in solvents and process, the amount used could only be reduced to 20%. Amine scrubbing technology can be added on to existing plants, and can be shut off during times of peak electricity demand.

Shanna Hoversten and Jake Bauch

Steps to Implementing an Effective CO_2 Transport System in the European Union

CCS technology will be an important component of the European Union's strategy to reduce CO_2 emissions, however, the EU faces a series of challenges to building the necessary pipeline infrastructure to transport CO_2 from source to sink (Coleman 2009). The first task is to identify source and sink locations and match them based on capacity. CO_2 transport will likely occur across national borders, and potentially across regions outside of the EU, thus there is an imminent need for coordinated administrative and legislative frameworks. The estimated pipeline capacity required is very large—400 million tonnes per year by 2030 to meet the EU interim targets for emissions reductions. Although this network will likely require infrastructure as intensive as the existing infrastructure for natural gas pipelines, it is unlikely to be as physically invasive because the pipelines will carry CO_2 from many source locations that will then be tied to large trunk lines that feed into large storage sites. Because the EU is extremely urbanized, there are numerous health and safety concerns that come along with these massive installments. In his paper, Coleman seeks to describe these transport infrastructure hurdles in detail and outline the way by which they can be resolved.

D. Coleman of Shell Future Fuels & CO_2, sought to base his series of recommendations on an investigation into the pattern of emission sources and storage sites across the EU Generally, he found that large population centers contained the majority of large-scale single-source points of CO_2 that will ultimately be captured. Europe has numerous locations that can accommodate CO_2 storage, and thus it can be assumed that captured CO_2 would only have to be transported 200–250 miles, on average, to its designated storage location. Coleman went on to preliminarily coordinate point sources and sinks throughout Europe.

Based on Coleman's analysis, it is clear that matching sources and sinks will frequently straddle national borders, thus Coleman outlines the need for EU-wide regulatory standards. A completely new permitting and safety regime is not necessary, as CO_2 transportation can be regulated under many of the same mechanisms existing today for the pipeline transport of natural gas. However, there are a few distinctions between CO_2 and natural gas transport that will need to be considered, including the need to bury transport pipelines deeper underground to ensure that the pressure is great enough to keep the CO_2 at its supercritical phase level, and the addition of crack arrestors to ensure that if a puncture in the line does occur, an uncontained longitudinal explosion will not occur. CO_2 pipelines have historically been built in rural areas, and thus in the highly urbanized environment that predominates in the EU, a reasonable distance between the pipelines and buildings or dwellings must be maintained. In addition to these regulatory requirements, the next important consideration is to design the most effective and rational transport network given the location of sources and sinks; for the development of this Coleman recommends a flagship program to kick-start the EU CCS industry implementation.

Using CO_2-EOR Project Experience to Improve the Design of Injection Equipment for CCS

Several decades of experience with CO_2-EOR projects provide invaluable lessons about how to conduct CCS operations in a safe and technically sound way (Parker *et al.* 2009). Public perception of the safety risks associated with CCS is one of the major hurdles to wide scale deployment of this technology; CO_2-EOR projects have stored over 600 million tons of CO_2 without any significant safety endangerment events, thus the technologies and procedures employed in CO_2-EOR ought to be emulated. In the CO_2-EOR industry, improvements in the design of injection infrastructure can be applied to the design of the standard equipment used in CCS sites.

M. E. Parker from ExxonMobil and his partners at Contek Solutions, LLC. and the American Petroleum Institute, provide a synthesis of information on technical design improvements that have been made over years of CO_2-EOR projects. An important caveat to these recommendations stems from the heightened potential for corrosion that takes place in CO_2-EOR projects due to the use of the WAG (water alternating gas) process; because CCS uses CO_2 that is essentially in a dry state, there is a smaller incidence for problems with corrosion as compared to CO_2-EOR projects. Thus, Parker *et al.* proceed to detail recommendations based on CO_2-EOR experience while recognizing that these measures are relatively conservative.

Parker *et al.* detail specific designs that should be employed to the wellbore and completion equipment to ensure safe injection of CO_2. Wellbore elements include the casing, cement, and casing heads, and the completion includes the packer, tubing, and wellhead valves assembly. Casing should be made out of carbon steel, which is both economically feasible and technically sound, provided that it is coated in corrosive resistant material. Tubing strings exposed to wet CO_2 can also be subject to corrosion, and thus should be coated with a protective liner of plastic, epoxy, or glass reinforced epoxy. Cement is important in anchoring the casing to the formation and providing a seal as well as structural stability. CO_2-EOR suggests that Portland cement can be used effectively in spite of some presence of carbonic acid, despite laboratory data suggesting that the carbonic acid will compromise the integrity of the cement. However, in cases where carbonic acid is a more significant threat, adding materials such as fly ash, silica flour or other resistant materials can

101

mitigate the risk of corrosion.

To control corrosion that can potentially occur in the completion equipment, wellhead valve trims and wetted parts of packers should be made of stainless steel, nickel, or Monel. Experiences with injection of supercritical CO_2 have demonstrated the need for elastomers and seals resistant to swelling. Additionally, CO_2 as a solvent will dissolve any hydrocarbon-based material, therefore Teflon, nylon, and hardened rubber are effective materials for use in packing and sealing elements. These refinements made in the design of injection equipment for CO_2-EOR can be applied to CCS such that these projects are technically safe and reliable.

The US May not have as much Economically Underground CO_2 Storage Space as Previously Thought

A new model to predict the economic viability of CO_2 geosequestration in sandstone saline aquifers indicates that previous estimates for storage potential in the US may be overly optimistic (Eccles *et al.* 2009). The model identifies an estimated minimum for storage costs in a typical basin in the range of $2–7 per ton CO_2 sequestered, based on estimates of a maximum CO_2 storage potential and a maximum CO_2 injection rate. Eccles *et al.* use data from carbon capture and storage pilot projects to explain that many assumptions in their model lead to artificially high estimates for the maximum storage potential and the maximum injection rate, and as a result, they conclude that geosequestration will be even more expensive than their model conservatively indicates. However, Eccles *et al.* proceed to apply the model to identifying economically optimal storage basins in the US.

J. K. Eccles and colleagues at the Nicholas School of the Environment, Duke University, begin building their model by estimating maximum storage potential as a function of the optimal injection depth and the available void space in the formation. However, this estimate does not account for the reality of most pilot projects, during which the CO_2 has bypassed the majority of the available pore space. The maximum injection rate is calculated based on a determination of the injection-induced pressure that would cause hydraulic fracturing beyond the perforated zone around the well. However, comparison of the modeled results with the pilot project at Nagaoka, Japan indicates that lower injection rates are probably more realistic due to engineering constraints and actual reservoir conditions. The cost per ton of CO_2 sequestered is generated based on the total cost of drilling, injection, equipment, and operation and maintenance, notably excluding the costs that would arise from capture and transport of the CO_2. Finally, the cost for storage in a typical basin in the United States was computed using estimates for storage potential and the cost per ton of CO_2 stored.

Results from the modeling indicate that although depth is an important determinant of storage potential, it is not the most important factor in storage cost. While increased depth can increase the cost by a factor of two, layer thickness and permeability of the storage reservoir can increase cost by a factor of fifty. This hints at the myriad of basin characteristics that need to be assessed before arriving at a viable cost estimate. Additionally, costs within a single basin are likely to differ considerably due to the extreme variability in aquifer characteristics. The most important conclusion that can be drawn from this analysis is that the amount of CO_2 storage provided by low-cost regions within saline aquifers in the US is considerably lower than the estimates reported by previous studies. The study by Eccles *et al.* suggests that there are only perhaps ten storage reservoirs in the US that would have an average storage cost of below $10 per ton CO_2. If more basins are to become economically viable for CO_2 storage, then policymakers will need to devise a regime that imposes a rather significant cost on carbon.

How Much CO_2 can Leak from an Underground Storage Site before it poses a Health and Safety Concern?

Although there is a substantial amount of research into the propensity of storage sites to leak CO_2 over time, there is currently an insufficient number of studies addressing the health, safety and environmental (HSE) impacts of these unmitigated leaks (Stenhouse *et al.* 2009). The study done by Stenhouse *et al.* attempts to quantify the impacts of CO_2 leakage on human health and safety by examining a scenario in which CO_2 leaks directly into an enclosed dwelling, causing increased indoor CO_2 concentration, and a scenario whereby CO_2 leaks into a source of potable water, thereby causing lead mobilization. The model predicts that to meet Health Canada's recommendation for indoor air CO_2 concentrations, CO_2 leakages into an enclosed house should not exceed 5.4 kg d^{-1}. Further modelling indicates that aquifers containing unpolluted groundwater can tolerate a leakage rate of 1.7e-4 kg CO_2 d^{-1} without mobilizing enough lead to exceed regulatory limits on lead concentrations in drinking water. A comparison of the two scenarios reveals that the health risks associated with leakage into drinking water occur with a lower level of CO_2 leakage than do health risks associated with elevated CO_2 levels in the home; thus regulators need to set limits on CO_2 leakage using the numbers derived from the water scenario.

M. Stenhouse and colleagues at Monitor Scientific LLC generate their models determining maximum allowable CO_2 leakage based on data from the Weyburn Midale CO_2 Storage Project. To assess acceptable leakage rates into a dwelling, the model is based on a small one-story house with a ventilation rate of 3.1 exchanges per day, and conservatively assumes that the entire quantity of leaked CO_2 enters the dwelling as opposed to some of it getting stuck in the soil due to mass transport resistance. To identify the effects of CO_2 leakage on groundwater, a model was used to simulate the acidification that would gradually occur with the addition of CO_2 and the resultant mobilization of lead. Several simulations were performed to assess the varying impacts of the CO_2 given the presence of a combination of minerals in the sediments, including calcite, goethite, and cerrusite.

The results derived for levels of CO_2 leakage rates into houses allowable before health and safety becomes a concern were conservative, but relatively straightforward. The model for the water scenario was able to generate a number for how much additional CO_2 could be leaked into the water supply, however, this figure was largely dependent on the variety and concentrations of minerals assumed to be in the aquifer sediments. The model demonstrates that with the addition of 0.01 mol calcite to the water, the change in concentration of lead over time is dramatically affected. Thus safe levels of CO_2 leakage into potable water will be rather disparate across a range of sediment geology. Stenhouse *et al.* conclude that their analysis should be used to provide regulatory bounding limits on CO_2 leakage rates, but that there should be a strong site-specific component to guard against over-reliance on the model. Further, the paper goes on to suggest a number of areas that require additional research in order to gain a fuller understanding of the health, safety and environmental impacts of CO_2 leakage from storage sites. Some of these topics include: the propensity of high CO_2 concentrations to cause tree kills, the effect of intermediate CO_2 concentrations over long periods of exposure, and the effect of heightened CO_2 concentrations on underground microbial populations and the subsequent ecological consequences.

Developing New and Effective Monitoring and Verification Technology

Developing effective technology for surface monitoring of CO_2 leakage is an instrumental part of ensuring the wide-scale deployment of CCS technology (Madsen *et al.* 2009). The primary methods used to monitor surface CO_2 flux as the gas is released from the soil into the atmosphere include the micrometeorological method and the chamber method. Although there are many methods that fall under these two broad categories, this paper focuses specifically on the closed-chamber method (a chamber method) and the Eddy Covariance method (a micrometeorological method). Madsen *et al.* argue that two new designs for monitoring equipment have made surface monitoring far more effective and reliable. The study considers the LI–8100 Automated Soil CO_2 Flux System (closed-chamber method) and the LI–7500 Open Path CO_2/H_2O Analyzer (Eddy Covariance method), details the advantages of each, and outlines the importance of employing their use in CCS projects so as to build public confidence in the safety of this technology.

R. Madsen and colleagues at LI–COR Biosciences, estimate the capacity of this surface monitoring equipment to pick up CO_2 fluxes using mathematical models combining elements of the new technology with environmental variables that effect flux measurements. The paper also provides details on new design features that allow for additional accuracy in flux measurements, such as the LI–8100's vent design to minimize the effect of wind on the flux data. The efficacy of this new technology is assessed by looking at its use in the monitoring and verification regimes at several pilot CCS plants around the world.

In discussions about the closed-chamber method, Madsen *et al.* identify several key difficulties with getting accurate flux readings. Maintaining pressure equilibrium between the inside of the chamber and the ambient air is one of the greatest challenges, and it can be especially problematic under windy conditions. Ensuring good mixing within the chamber is also necessary, but if a fan is installed to do this it can oftentimes alter the pressure equilibrium. The LI–8100 factors in these concerns by having a unique chamber geometry that allows mixing without a fan, thereby maintaining the pressure equilibrium. It also has a new feature in which the chambers all open and close automatically and slowly so that fresh ambient air is not pushed into the soil or removed from the soil, thereby distorting the data.

The Eddy Covariance method measures fluxes by taking measurements of the deviation of vertical wind velocity and of an associated scalar from their mean values. The sensors for Eddy Covariance are usually mounted on a tower and they then measure the average CO_2 flux over an integrated area that can extend to an area about 100 times the height of the sensors to the up-wind direction. For this monitoring technique to be effective, it is necessary that the instruments be able to correct for density perturbations caused by sensible heat and latent heat flux; they must be set up over a relatively large and flat field site. Both the LI–7500 and the LI–8100 have been used in CCS projects all over the world, and have so far been effective, however it is still not known how these technologies will perform over the long lifespan of a project.

Predictions of the Efficacy of CCS Technology: Short-term Storage may be a Solution

The potential of CCS to mitigate global climate change is still widely contested; in this study the potential benefits are quantified and the efficacy is examined under several different scenarios (Stone *et al.* 2009). When estimating the possible benefits of CCS, the most important variables are the storage retention time of the reservoirs used, the energy penalty of the operation, the extent that CCS technology will be deployed, future emissions scenarios, and the degree of climate sensitivity. The study finds that CCS technology is worthwhile, and has the potential to significantly curb rising temperatures, especially in the short term.

E.J. Stone and colleagues analyzed the potential benefits of CCS under a variety of circumstances by combining a model of the carbon cycle with a model for CCS storage potential and propensity for leakages. One of the strengths of this study is that Stone *et al.* took into account the atmospheric sensitivity to increased CO_2, which had previously been ignored in similar models. The study modeled climate change reductions under two IPCC scenarios—the A1F1 which constitutes a fossil fuel intensive world, and the B1 which represents a world driven by clean, resource-efficient technology. The effects of variable retention times, energy penalties, fractions of fossil fuel emissions released from a single plant, and the fraction of global fossil fuels emissions subject to CCS are then modeled.

The result is that there are considerable benefits to deploying CCS technology, especially in the short term. It is much easier to achieve a break-even point for shorter time spans than longer time spans due to the small but constant leakage that will occur from the storage site. Even so, it may be beneficial to apply this technology in the short term while we are still looking for alternative energy sources that do not emit such high concentrations of CO_2. The importance of these short-term measures will also depend on climate sensitivity, as the maximum temperature reduction benefits of CCS will increase with heightened climate sensitivities.

Retention time was found to have a significantly greater effect on the efficacy of CCS projects than did other factors such as energy penalty. Even large energy penalties can be tolerated provided that the retention time of the storage site is adequate. However that does not mean that storage sites should only be considered if they have the ability to store the CO_2 for a 10,000 year duration; one of the most interesting findings of this study was that the use of storage reservoirs previously considered to have insufficiently low leakage rates may still have the potential to confer climate benefits. Storing the CO_2 for even a short period of time may allow for stabilization of atmospheric CO_2 concentrations which would in turn reduce climate sensitivity and mitigate substantial rises in temperatures.

CO_2-EOR Projects can help Launch CCS Technology on a Large Scale

Economic viability is one of the greatest challenges to the effective deployment of CCS technology on a wide-scale; but by using captured CO_2 in Enhanced Oil Recovery (EOR) projects, some of this economic burden may be alleviated (Ferguson *et al.* 2009). EOR projects have been underway since the 1970s, and entail the injection of CO_2 into largely depleted oil wells, whereby the CO_2 lowers the oil viscosity and allows this residual oil to be removed from areas where it was once trapped between pore spaces. It is estimated that 87.1 billion additional barrels of oil may become recoverable in the United States with the use of CO_2-EOR. The added advantage of this procedure is the storage of injected CO_2 in the newly depleted oil field. Coal burning power plants equipped with CO_2 capture technology could sell their CO_2 to EOR project operators at a price of approximately $25 to $35 per metric ton, which would offset the cost of generating power with CCS by approximately $17 to $24 per MWh, thereby facilitating a more widespread installation of this technology across America's power plants.

R. C. Ferguson and colleagues at Advanced Resources International and the U.S. Department of Energy, used a base case scenario to model the propensity for coordination between EOR activities and CO_2 capture activities. First they looked at the conventionally recoverable versus the "stranded" crude oil resources in the US; then they further broke this down by estimating what proportion of the stranded reserves could be recovered using EOR. Ferguson *et al.* used a base case to evaluate CO_2-EOR potential using an oil price of $70 per barrel and a CO_2 cost of $45 per metric ton, differentiating between oil that is technically recoverable and oil that is economically recoverable. Based on these numbers, the amount of CO_2 that could be purchased from capture technology equipped power generating plants was calculated, and the potential economic gain of these plants was estimated. Finally, Ferguson *et al.* calculated that oil produced by CO_2-EOR would be approximately 70% "carbon free" given the trade-off between CO_2 sequestered and CO_2 released by burning the oil.

The potential for extensive use of CO_2-EOR technology has many positive implications for CCS deployment. The revenue offsets and the value for carbon abatement could allow for 40% of the new coal-fuelled power capacity built between now and 2030 to install CCS. In real terms, this means that sales of captured CO_2 emissions by power plants build after 2020 would support the installation of 33 additional CCS equipped plants by 2030. CO_2-EOR projects provide a considerable "value added" market for the sale of CO_2 emissions, thereby defraying some of the costs of installing and operating CCS technology. Although the CO_2 would be used to facilitate the extraction and continued use of oil, a CO_2 intensive energy source, the storage of the CO_2 within the oil field would help offset some of the oil's emissions, and even more importantly, using CCS in this economically lucrative industry would help support early market entry of CCS technology in the coal-fuelled power sector, providing a foundation for future emissions reductions. Additionally, storing CO_2 with EOR would help bypass two present legal barriers to geologic sequestration: establishing mineral (pore space) rights, and assigning long-term liability for the injected CO_2. The promotion of CO_2-EOR is a promising avenue for advancing the development and deployment of CCS technology.

Shanna Hoversten and Jake Bauch

Ambient Air Capture Technologies: Progress So Far

Technology to capture CO_2 directly from ambient air has the potential to significantly reduce emissions from non-point sources and to capture historic emissions (Lackner 2009). Sorbents used in flue gas scrubbing can be used much to the same effect in free standing CO_2 capture units, which can be designed to compensate for the lower CO_2 concentration in the air stream. It is important to carefully choose a sorbent material that will maximize capture, and to consider a practical and marketable unit design and size. Lackner proposes that capture units be made on the scale of capturing one ton of CO_2 per day. Given this, and the energy tradeoff associated with the operation and manufacturing of these units, Lackner determines that it would take approximately ten million capture units to make a significant impact on the world's CO_2 emissions. At present, prototypes for these units could break even at \$200/ton of CO_2 captured, but Lackner predicts that over time this price could drop to \$30/ton; ambient air capture is at this time technologically feasible, and may in time be economically feasible with the improvement of sorbent materials and as the need for retroactively capturing emissions grows.

K.S. Lackner from Columbia University presents a comprehensive review of the progress towards implementing ambient air capture units, and focuses more deeply on capture sorbent development. Lackner discards the notion of using an aqueous sorbent due to the large binding energy required and the corrosiveness of a strong sodium hydroxide solution. Experiments were thus carried out to identify a sorbent with lower binding energy that could still maintain an uptake rate equal or better to that of a sodium hydroxide solution. Ultimately a solid strong-base ion-exchange resin was deemed to be the best sorbent option. Experiments showed that this resin could be loaded with absorbed CO_2, and upon exposure to moisture the CO_2 would be driven off and the resin would be ready to recommence CO_2 uptake after dried. Based on this, Lackner goes on to describe a modular unit that could be easily deployed and could be expected to capture one ton of CO_2 per day.

Lackner's summary of ambient air capture technology exposes both the potential for further innovation and development of this technology, and the great promise for this technology to significantly reduce CO_2 emissions. At present, 70% of the cost of the device derives from the development of the resin and the regeneration chamber; a reduction in these costs is essential in order to make the technology viable. Although changes in the filter thickness can compensate for regional differences in CO_2 composition of the air stream, and air flow rate over the filter, current technology excludes the deployment of these modules from locations with extremely cold temperatures or locations with high humidity. However, in places where the units would work effectively, large air capture parks could be established directly on top of the designated storage site, eliminating the need for transfer networks. Ambient air capture units would collect CO_2 from power plants and transportation sources alike, in addition to capturing past emissions at a rate far exceeding collection rates by trees, thus providing a promising technique for CO_2 emission mitigation in the future.

Conclusions

Current research suggests the real and relatively immediate possibility for deployment of CCS technology. The scientific research behind the concept has been demonstrated to be sound in a number of pilot projects, and the major hurdles that remain are largely political and economic. However, CCS will only progress beyond the demonstration stage if public perception surrounding the technology is positively influenced and the price of carbon increases via some policy mechanism. CCS has principally been viewed as a remedy for high emissions from dirty fossil fuels, providing us with a way to neutralize their emissions; new technology such as ambient air capture is exciting in that it goes a step further by neutralizing historic emissions. By employing CCS technology in concert with the gradual proliferation of renewable energy technologies, meaningful CO_2 emissions reductions can commence at an accelerated pace.

References Cited

Coleman, D., 2009. Transport Infrastructure Rationale for Carbon Dioxide Capture & Storage in the European Union to 2050. Energy Procedia 1, 1673–1681.

Eccles, J., Pratson, L., Newell, R., Jackson, R., 2009. Physical and Economic Potential of Geological CO_2 Storage in Saline Aquifers. Environmental Science & Technology 43, 1962–1969.

Ferguson, R., Nichols, C., Van Leeuwen, T., Kuuskraa, V., 2009. Storing CO_2 with Enhanced Oil Recovery. Energy Procedia 1, 1989–1996.

Lackner, K., 2009. Capture of carbon dioxide from ambient air. The European Physical Journal 176, 93–106.

Madsen, R., Xu, L., Claassen, B., McDermitt, D., 2009. Surface Monitoring Method for Carbon Capture and Storage Projects. Energy Procedia 1, 2161–2168.

Parker, M., Meyer, J., Meadows, S., 2009. Carbon Dioxide Enhanced Oil Recovery Injection Operations Technologies. Energy Procedia 1, 3141–3148.

Rochelle, Gary T., 2009. Amine Scrubbing for CO2 Capture. Science 325, 1652–1654.

Stenhouse, M., Arthur, R., Zhou, W., 2009. Assessing environmental impacts from geological CO_2 storage. Energy Procedia 1, 1895–1902.

Stone, E., Lowe, J., Shine, K., 2009. The impact of carbon capture and storage on climate. Energy & Environmental Science 2, 81–91.

9. Terrestrial Carbon Sequestration

Jake Bauch

There are three ways to achieve carbon reductions in the atmosphere: (1) Efficient use and conservation of energy to reach the same levels of production with lower emissions, (2) use of sources such as wind, solar, or nuclear energy that emit less carbon, or (3) sequestration of carbon (Litynski 2006). Carbon Sequestration refers to the process by which carbon in the atmosphere is transferred into a carbon sink. In efforts to mitigate the effects of global warming, society has turned to sequestering carbon in higher amounts through many different methods. Since coal accounts for 50% of the energy used in the US and 30 percent of national CO_2 emissions (Rochelle 2009), one strategy is to capture CO_2 at the sources of the emissions: flue gas from coal and gas fired power plants. On site capture at coal fired power plants, however, is expensive (Rochelle 2009) so many other avenues of carbon sequestration are being explored.

Through photosynthesis, plants convert CO_2 to carbohydrates and most of the carbon eventually returns to the atmosphere when the plant material decomposes, but a portion remains in the ground (Litynski *et al.* 2006). Terrestrial carbon sequestration refers to increasing the portion of carbon stored in natural sinks such as trees, soil, and wetlands. The scope of terrestrial carbon sequestration extends from the main areas of forestry and agriculture, to developing techniques like biochar (Spokas *et al.* 2009) and currently impractical techniques sequestration through mineral carbonation (Krevor and Klaus 2009).

Forestry, including deforestation, is responsible for 17.4% of global GHG emissions and up to a quarter of the world's carbon is stored in tropical rainforests (Van der Werf *et al.* 2009). When forests are destroyed for logging or agriculture, the carbon stored in the forest is released. The Kyoto Protocol to the United Nations Framework Convention on Climate Change rewards GHG offsets for projects that rejuvenate destroyed forests (reforestation) or create new forests (aforrestation)

(Ramachandran Nair *et al.* 2009). These projects qualify as a Clean Development Mechanism under the Kyoto Protocol, so developed countries can achieve GHG offsets with projects in developing countries. Agroforestry which consists of integrating trees into agricultural areas is believed to create more complex ecosystems which will use nutrients, light, and water more efficiently and create a synergistic carbon sequestration effect whereby agroforests will sequester more carbon than the sum of the trees and the crops would if separate (Ramachandran Nair *et al.* 2009). Sequestration in forests has a finite limit since trees and vegetation can become saturated with carbon and the sequestered carbon can be returned to the atmosphere if the forests are burned. Nonetheless, sequestering carbon in forests can be an immediate, low cost method.

Agriculture can be managed to sequester more carbon by increasing the amount of CO_2 absorbed by vegetation, facilitating the transfer of carbon from plants into the soil, and increasing the duration of retention in the soil. Ancillary benefits of carbon sequestration for agriculture are more fertile and stabile soil that holds more water and reduces effects of toxic substances present (Morgan *et al.* 2010). Switching from conventional to conservation tillage—leaving twice as much crop residue on the soil—sequesters 0.1–0.3 metric tons of carbon per acre per year (West and Post 2002). However, carbon is not the only greenhouse gas affected by agriculture: methane is released from livestock and decomposition in wetlands and nitrous oxide results from fertilizer. Addition of biochar (biomass burned in the absence of oxygen) to soil sequesters carbon and suppresses nitrous oxide release, but suppresses methane oxidation, which increases the levels released to the atmosphere (Spokas *et al.* 2009). Biochar has been proposed as an offset mechanism in Africa where afforrestation and reforestation projects have not attracted investors (Whitman and Lehmann 2009). Though agriculture only accounts for 7% of the carbon emissions in the US, maintaining the soil as a carbon sink will be important as other sequestration technologies are developed (Morgan *et al.* 2010).

Carbon Capture and Storage at Power Plants could Substantially Reduce GHG Emissions

Capturing carbon promptly after it is emitted from gas or coal fired power plants, called carbon capture and storage (CCS) could be responsible for reducing global carbon emissions by up to 20%. To date there are no existing CCS power plants but experiments exist in the form of 1/10th-scale plants with 100% of emissions captured, and full size plants with 0.001% of emissions captured (Haszeldine 2009). Since commercial CCS plants will not be built until several example plants are built, immediate funding of projects may be necessary or commercial plants are unlikely to be up and running by 2020.

Stuart Haszeldine reviews the existing literature on CCS to find the issues to be resolved before construction can take place. There are unresolved issues with the capture, transport and storage of carbon. Barriers to entry for CCS are lack of legal standing in the form of performance standards and lack of economic incentive in the form of carbon being priced. Technological improvements are expected to increase efficiency by 20–60% and pipe sharing by multiple plants could reduce costs. These expected improvements may be delaying investment in CCS projects now. After departing the power plant, captured carbon can be sent through pipes from power plants to the storage sites in aquifers, oil fields or gas fields. The risks associated with storage are a deterrent from CCS projects.

The three capture techniques, postcombustion, precombustion, and oxyfuel combustion, are all comparable in terms of cost and efficiency; all would produce energy that is 10% more expensive. The postcombustion method uses a chemical solvent to remove CO_2 from the gas exiting the power plant. Postcombustion capture can be added onto existing plants but is limited by the high costs for equiptment and chemicals. Oxyfuel, likewise, can be added onto existing plants but is limited by the costs of the process of separating oxygen from air. The precombustion method can work on a larger scale but it requires integration with the entire power plant at the time of intial construction. Since all three technologies are receiving attention, no individual one has developed to full potential.

Estuarine Wetlands can be Rehabilitated to Provide Carbon Sequestration Benefits

Wetlands are vital sinks of carbon but the positive carbon sequestering effect on the environment is partially offset in most wetlands by the methane released from biomass decomposition. Wetlands in areas where a river reaches the sea, called estuarine wetlands, contain sulfates that minimize methane release so they are potentially the most beneficial in terms of effects on climate. Estuarine wetlands have also been shown to store carbon for longer than other wetlands. This study showed that if tidal flows are reintroduced to drained wetlands, the carbon sequestration potential can be higher than undisturbed wetlands because of higher rates of vertical accretion in the soil. Wetlands make up 5% of the Earth's surface and contain 40% of the planet's soil organic carbon (Howe *et al.* 2009). In Australia where this study takes place, 50% of the wetlands have been converted to other uses. As land use decisions are being made around the world, it is critical to examine the characteristics that benefit a wetland's carbon sequestration potential.

Howe and colleagues at the University of Newcastle in Australia looked at carbon sequestration in an undisturbed and a rehabilitated estuarine wetland, and predicted the effects of rising water levels. This study was the first to look at carbon sequestration in estuarine wetlands in temperate conditions with saltmarsh and mangrove habitats. The study is one of the first on the topic in Australia, and the modern method of measuring soil surface evolution provides useful data for future research.

The rates of carbon sequestration were relatively low because there were low rates of vertical accretion and low amounts of suspended sediment in the estuary. Since most carbon in wetlands is stored in peats, biomass, or sediment, lower rates of sediment accretion reduces the carbon sequestration potential. Vertical accretion is a process by which the wetland adapts to changes in the water level. Failure to adapt may create a completely submerged wetland which sequesters far less carbon. Since there is a relative elevation defecit (the surface elevation is not rising as much as the water levels), there must be sufficient "buffer zones" surrounding the estuary for the water to move to, or else wetlands will become submerged. Saltmarsh wetlands are already shrinking as a result of failure to occupy the buffer zones fast enough

Agroforestry may have High Carbon Sequestration Potential, but Methodological Difficulties still Loom Large

The principle behind agroforestry is that carbon sequestration is highest and resource utilization higher when trees and crops are combined to form a more complex ecosystem. An estimated 1,023 million hectares of land are already under agroforestry, but the knowledge of agroforests are inadequate so agroforestry is underutilized as a type of Clean Development mechanism (CDM) for polluters to earn carbon credits under the Kyoto Protocol (Ramachandran Nair et al. 2009). Only when the research is trusted, and the projects are more profitable than alternative CDM carbon mitigation projects, will agroforestry become a common strategy.

P.K. Ramachandran Nair and colleagues at the University of Florida and Kerala Agricultural University in India, review the state of agroforestry research and the associated methological inconsistencies precluding agroforesty from reaching its full potential. The authors propose a calculation for the global area under agroforestry, a number whose uncertainty is one of the major unknowns about agroforestry. Estimates of carbon sequestration potential (CSP) are calculated by a composite of aboveground and soil sequestration plus a time-averaged measurement of carbon stocks. The main limitation is that most of the existing studies used only carbon stocks rather than measurements of carbon per area over a certain time. Aboveground sequestration is calculated assuming that 45–50% of branches and 30% of foliage is comprised of carbon, but estimates of the volume of each is done by inaccurate general models. The trend revealed in soil carbon sequestration is that forests sequester the most carbon followed by agroforests, tree plantations and arable crops.

However, the data reviewed was not uniform and other critical physical characteristics of the sites were not recorded. Belowground sequestration is the least understood component of the measurements.

If the measurement techniques were refined, would agroforestry see a rise in popularity? The price of carbon reductions in the international markets will need to be high and the cost of monitoring carbon sequestration must remain low. Supplementary revenue for the farmers from increased production will make the farmers more willing to take on the projects. Since sequestration from agroforestry is equally beneficial to the environment regardless of location, remote farmers with little access to markets will be inclined to undertake projects.

Landuse Practices are a Cheaper and More Accurate Way to Model Carbon Sequestration for Awarding Carbon Credits

If best management practices were implemented for the entire agricultural sector of the US, the carbon sequestered in the soil would account for 10% of all national emissions (Yadav *et al.* 2009). With voluntary greenhouse gas emissions trading emerging and trading for compliance on the horizon, the accuracy of measuring carbon sequestration is of great importance. Since the amount of erosion is so strongly linked to soil organic carbon (SOC) concentrations, upstream farmers are not rewarded for their practices and downstream farmers are over rewarded. Awarding carbon credits based on practices rather than SOC concentrations, which also eliminates the monitoring costs, is an advantageous method.

Yadav and colleagues calculated the carbon sequestration potential of crop rotation sequences in sub-basins of the Big Creek watershed in Southern Illinois. The area covered was roughly four fifths crop land, one fifth and deciduous forest, and a small amount that was urban or used for transportation. Since tillage and land use are the strongest determinants of soil organic carbon concentrations, the SWAT model was used to divide up the land into sub-basins which were then labeled with their dominant land use and soil type. Using the sub-basins examined, SOC concentrations of all possible three year crop rotations were predicted. Since deforestation was more common upstream, the downstream soil was more fertile so the WEPP model accounted for the varying levels of erosion. The CENTURY model was used to come up with the final carbon sequestration predictions.

Overwhelmingly, crop based rotations sequester less carbon than perennial crops such as tall fescue, hay, pasture and forrests. Only when crop soil has undergone no tillage and little erosion, and is used for pasture, hay, or forest does the sub-basin exhibit carbon sink properties. Awarding carbon credits based on land use practices rather than measured amount of carbon stored drastically reduces costs because no monitoring is required. Therefore, accurate models can be used to open possibilities for land use that limits carbon levels in the atmosphere.

Arbuscular Mycorrhizal Fungi Linked to Higher Soil Aggregation and Carbon Sequestration

The presence of Arbuscular mycorrhizal fungi (AMF) in ecosystems is believed to increase carbon sequestration through two mechanisms: directly through translocating carbon from the roots to the soil (from the extrametrical mycorrhizal hyphae (EMH)), and by forming soil macroaggregates from microaggregates (Wilson *et al.* 2009). The results of the study show that AMF levels are positively correlated with soil aggregation and carbon and nitrogen levels in soil. Since increases in nitrogen deposition, soil temperatures, and CO_2 levels all reduce the quantity of AMF in ecosystems, humans are steadily contributing to decreases in this type of carbon sequestration. Furthermore, the study indicates that land use practices such as tillage, over fertilization, and overgrazing must be mindful of reductions to AMF.

Gail W.T. Wilson and colleagues tested the effects of 17 years of annual burning and addition of Nitrogen on EMH production, soil aggregation, total soil carbon and nitrogen, and production of biomass. The second part of the study involved 6 years of fungicide application to measure the same variables. While previous studies have used potted plants, and focused on agriculturally relevant plants, this study was the first to look at soil aggregation in native ecosystems.

The decreases in soil aggregation from fungicide treatment displayed a linear relationship, with no suggestion of any type of threshold. Though the mechanism is not fully understood, it may be that the microaggregates form macroaggregates which are linked with increased carbon and nitrogen sequestration. The mass of EMH, which is a network of fungus filaments coming off of the roots, showed a strong positive correlation to both the soil aggregation and carbon and nitrogen sequestration. Mass levels of roots, above ground biomass, and grass also showed positive correlations to carbon and nitrogen sequestration but not to soil aggregation, and not as strongly as EMH. Existing studies had shown linkage between high levels of AMF and soil aggregation, but this study showed that the trend remains for decreased levels of AMF which were artificially created in the experiment but may result from continued human action.

Placement of Biochar in Soil to Sequester Carbon has Potential to Provide Secondary Benefits to Soil

Burning biomass in an oxygen free setting, a process called pyrolysis, and putting the resulting biochar back into soil is an emerging method of carbon sequestration and it may have ancillary benefits in the form of GHG reductions of nitrous oxide. The environmental benefits from suppression of nitrous production could outweigh negative effects of suppression of CH4 oxidation (Spokas *et al.* 2009). The herbicides atrazine and acetochlor are absorbed and retained at higher rates by soil with biochar added. The effect of this increase is twofold: less of the herbicide is lost due to leaching and runoff, but more herbicide may be required to achieve the same effect. What remains to be seen is how long lasting the effects are of biochar on soil.

K.A. Spokas and colleagues at the USDA- Agricultural Research Service added biochar to soil samples and calculated the resulting reductions in carbon dioxide and nitrous oxide production, reductions of methane oxidation, and increased sorption of two herbicides. There are apparent increases in CO_2 production, but once the CO_2 in the biochar material is subtracted the effect is negative. One sample of biochar was added fresh, one was placed under a vacuum, and one sample was rinsed with hexane.

Though the amount of biochar was correlated with the magnitude of each of the effects, the processes involved in soil with biochar are still unknown. Since the hexane soaked biochar and the vacuum treated biochar both reduced CO_2 production, while added moisture increased CO_2 production, the CO_2 production is believed to come from a reaction between water and O_2. Because biochar makeup depends on the input material and the design of the pyrolysis conditions, the effects could vary greatly on soil. The ph balance of biochar can be anywhere from 4 to 12 which results in radically different effects on soil. Since pyrolysis converts carbon into a form that stays in soil for hundreds to thousands of years, the long term potential of biochar could be high, but the long term effects on soil must be determined and considered before biochar becomes a widely used method.

Use of Certain Sodium Salts can increase Effectiveness of Carbon Sequestration by Mineral Carbonation

Mineral CO_2 sequestration is a chemical method of sequestering CO_2 that produces an environmentally harmless substance with minimal efforts required to monitor or verify the results (Krevor and Klaus 2009). The method, which has only been around as a CO_2 sequestration technique since the 1990s consists of adding magnesium silicate or calcium silicate with supercritical CO_2 to form a carbonate. Unfortunately, high amounts of energy are required in the process compared to other methods of carbon sequestration. Three quarters of the energy is from the process of grinding the particles down to a small enough size. Though the addition of sodium citrate, sodium oxalate and sodium EDTA increase dissolution; the costs of chemicals and energy use preclude the commercial success of this form of carbon sequestration.

Krevor and researchers at Columbia University tested the effect of adding different inorganic salts and sodium salts to the carbonate forming reaction. In all cases the CO_2 was supercritical, at 120°C and 20 bars of pressure. Of the salts added, sodium citrate, sodium oxalate and sodium EDTA showed highest initial dissolution and within 10 to 20 hours, dissolution reached almost 100%. Measurements ended after 24 hours, so the long term dissolution of the other salts was not measured.

The chemical process involves two steps: dissolution and then precipitation. The dissolution is more efficient in more acidic solutions, but precipitation is impossible in an acidic solution. A complicated process could change the pH balance during the process, but has not been developed. Consequently, researchers typically add sodium bicarbonate to the reaction to create a neutral solution so that both dissolution and precipitation can happen simultaneously. Since neutral solutions yield low amounts of carbonate, the dissolution is the limiting part of the reaction. Hence, the particles are ground into finer particles to increase the dissolution.

Conclusions

Voluntary greenhouse gas emissions in the US are traded on the Chicago Carbon Exchange because companies are under increasing pressure to offset carbon emissions, and expectations of a legally binding compliance standard has motivated polluters to begin finding the best way to offset emissions. Carbon trading on the CCX and international markets could be the focus of future research. If the US Congress passes a bill to cap greenhouse gas emissions with the option to offset emissions, research will be directed towards the guidelines of the offsets allowed.

In Agriculture, the research still lacks effective measurements for soil organic carbon levels because variability even across small areas is very high. Yadav and colleagues suggest that modeling carbon sequestration with land use practices instead of soil carbon measurements would be a more accurate and less expensive method (Yadav et al. 2009). Future research will likely develop best management practices for soil organic carbon levels, taking into account the effects on methane and nitrous oxide to create a set of best practices with regard to all greenhouse gasses.

Older forests are more complex and are thus better at adapting to different climatic conditions. However, carbon sequestration decreases with age of forests, so forestry research will have to address the conflict between these two objectives (Bradford and Kastendick 2010). Creating a standard for measurement of carbon sequestration will be the focus of future research, especially as any certified offsets will require proof of additionality—that the reductions would not have been achieved otherwise.

References Cited

Bradford, John B., Kastendick, Douglas N., 2010. Age-related patterns of forest complexity and carbon storage in pine and aspen–birch ecosystems of northern Minnesota, USA. Can. J. For. Res 40, 401–409.

Haszeldine, R. Stuart, 2009. Carbon Capture and Storage: How Green Can Black Be? Science 325, 1647–1652.

Howe, A.J., Rodriguez, J.F., Saco, P.M., 2009. Surface Evolution and Carbon Sequestration in disturbed and undisturbed wetland soils of the Hunter Estuary, southeast Australia. Estuarine, Costal and Shelf Science 84, 75–83.

Krevor, Samuel C., Lackner, Klaus S., 2009. Enhancing Process Kinetics for Mineral Carbon Sequestration. Energy Procedia 1, 4867–4871.

Litynski, John T., Klara, Scott M., McIlvried, Howard G., Srivastava, Rameshwar D, 2006. An Overview of the Terrestrial Sequestration of Carbon Dioxide: The United States Department of Energy's Fossil Energy R&D Program. Climatic Change 74, 81–95.

Morgan, Jack A., Follett, Ronald F., Allen, Leon Hartwell Jr., Del Grosso, Stephen, Derner, Justin D., Dijkstra, Feike, Franzluebbers, Alan, Fry, Robert, Paustian, Keith, Schoeneberger, Michelle M., 2010. Carbon Sequestration in Agricultural Lands of the United States. Journal of Soil and Water Conservation 61, DOI: 10.2489/jswc.65.1.6A.

Ramachandran Nair, P.K., Mohan Kumar, B., Nair, Vimala D., 2009. Agroforestry as a strategy for carbon sequestration. J. Plant Nutr. Soil Sci. 172, 10–23.

Rochelle, Gary T., 2009. Amine Scrubbing for CO_2 Capture. Science. 325, 1652–1654.

Spokas, K.A., Koskinen, W.C., Baker, J.M., Reicosky, D.C., 2009. Impacts of woodchip biochar additions on greenhouse gas production and sorption/degradation of two herbicides in a Minnesota soil. Chemosphere 77, 574–581.

Van der Werf, G. R., Morton, D. C., DeFries, R. S., Olivier, J. G. J., Kasibhatla, P. S., Jackson, R. B., Collatz, G. J., Randerson, J. T., 2009. CO_2 emissions from forest loss. Nature Geoscience 2, 737–738.

West, Tristram O., Post, Wilfred M., 2002. Soil Organic Carbon Sequestration Rates by Tillage and Crop Rotation: A Global Data Analysis. Soil Sci. Soc. Am. J. 66, 1930–1946.

Whitman, Thea, Lehmann, Johannes, 2009. Biochar—one way forward for soil carbon in offset mechanisms in Africa. Environmental Science and Policy 12, 1024–1027.

Wilson, W.T. Gail, Rice, Charles W., Rillig, Matthias C., Springer, Adam, and Hartnett, David C, 2009. Soil aggregation and carbon sequestration are tightly correlated with the abundance of arbuscular mycorrhizal fungi: results from long-term field experiments. Ecology Letters 12, 452–461.

Yadav, Vineet, Malanson, George P., Beleke, Elias, Lant, Christopher, 2009. Modeling watershed-scale sequestration of soil organic carbon for carbon credit programs. Applied Geography 29, 488–500.

10. Geoengineering

Ellie Pickrell

Geoengineering, or climate engineering, is the concept of manipulating the Earth's climate to offset the negative effects of global warming and greenhouse gas emissions. The first two articles in this chapter show us the general outcome of a world exposed to climate engineering. The articles are rather general and don't offer the specific strategies of geoengineering, but they show us what a manipulated climate could do for our planet.

There are many different geoengineering mechanisms, but the most promising involve solar radiation management and carbon sequestration. Solar radiation management is the concept of reducing the amount of sunlight that hits the Earth's surface and increasing the amount of sunlight that is reflected back into space. This would not reduce the greenhouse gas concentrations in the atmosphere, but could cool the Earth's surface and air temperatures. But solar radiation management through geoengineering isn't a remedy for adding CO_2 to the atmosphere by fossil fuel burning. Researchers tend to think of it as a strategy that could buy the planet some time by cooling it off in the short term while projects which can reduce the amount of atmospheric CO_2 are developed and put into effect. Solar radiation management is relatively inexpensive, however, and could create a world where we don't have to change our emissions levels; where CO_2, values could double, and the planet would remain cool and suitable for most life. The two most researched and most popular strategies for managing the Earth's solar radiation are the injection of sulfate aerosol particles into the clouds and the engineering of cropland plants to increase their albedo (reflectivity). There are definite advantages and disadvantages that accompany each strategy, and the following article summaries will show that. The first articles written about solar radiation management argue that crop albedo manipulation and seeding of clouds are promising strategies with minimal negative consequences and substantial benefits for the Earth's climate.

Climate engineering involving carbon sequestration is the concept of removing greenhouse gases, mainly CO_2, from the atmosphere. This strategy is a long-term fix to this problem and is essential if we are to offset the negative effects of global climate change. The article in this chapter associated with carbon sequestration involves fertilization of the oceans, which would then increase populations of phytoplankton and algae and in turn remove CO_2 from the atmosphere.

The final articles in this chapter suggest an alternate ending to a world exposed to climate engineering, especially engineering through solar radiation management. They suggest that although these strategies may help the Earth's surface temperature, they do not make a very significant difference, and the negative side effects they create are not worth it. The authors of these articles suggest that the root of the problem needs to be addressed directly. That emissions must be cut, removal of the greenhouse gases from the atmosphere must occur, and alternative sources of energy must be explored.

Solar Radiation Management Geoengineering: Possible Solution for the Shrinking Greenland Ice Sheet

The effects that climate change has on polar ice sheets, particularly in Greenland, are important for many reasons. The two most important considerations discussed in this article involve rising sea levels and decreased planetary albedo as the globe's ice sheets melt. Solar radiation management has been suggested to reduce the warming of the globe and buy some time while engineers and scientists address the larger problem of removing CO_2 from the atmosphere. The installation of a solar "sunshade" or the injection of sulfate aerosols into the clouds are the two most promising methods of geoengineering. Previous studies have shown that a world exposed to climate engineering would experience warming at the poles, cooling in the tropics, and a decreased precipitation rate, which may adversely affect the Greenland ice sheet (Irvine *et al.* 2009). In this study, the melting of the Greenland ice sheet was prevented at levels of partial climate manipulation, which suggests that the level of geoengineering required to cool the planet and reduce the impacts of greenhouse warming may not be as intensive as geoengineers originally believed.

Irvine *et al.* conducted twelve 400-year simulations on a computer climate model. The first model run was a control simulation that modeled a climate similar to that of a pre-industrial world, and wasn't exposed to climate engineering. The second has atmospheric CO_2 concentrations of 1120 ppmv, four times the pre-industrial amount, and 0% climate manipulation. The last ten simulations have 1120 ppmv CO_2 concentrations and range from 10% to 100% climate engineering in intervals of 10%. In each simulation, Irvine *et al.* measured the temperature and precipitation anomalies in comparison to the control simulation. The results were then combined with an observed climatology to create an ice-sheet model— Glimmer. Glimmer is a three-dimensional ice sheet model representing the Greenland region, and provided results showing the impact of solar radiation management on the ice sheet.

In the simulation with 0% climate engineering, the center of the Greenland ice sheet had an annual temperature increase of 8°C, and an average summer temperature that increased by 6°C when compared to the pre-industrial simulation. This 0% geoengineering simulation also showed an increase in annual precipitation of over 6 meters a year, which would increase the amount of annual snowfall, which could potentially cause the ice sheet to grow.

For simulations experiencing 100% engineering, the annual average surface air temperature was significantly lower than simulations with lower climate manipulation, although Greenland remained warmer than it was in the pre-industrial period. The island showed an increase of at least 0.5°C, with its northern and southern coasts undergoing an increase of 0.75°C, and a 1°C increase at the southern tip. For simulations experiencing 50% engineering, the model predicted a warming of 3°C across the majority of Greenland. Both 100% and 50% simulations showed an increase in precipitation rates, although it was lower than the 0% engineering simulation. A 100% simulation resulted in a precipitation rate of 21 mm per year.

The results from the Glimmer test were then used to predict the change in sea level of the Greenland region. In the pre-industrial control simulation, the sea levels were at 8.6 m. In the 0% simulation, only 12.8% of the original ice sheet remained, which could result in a sea level rise of 6.4 m. The remaining 12.8% of the ice sheet is located at the high altitude regions on the southern tip and on the eastern coastline. In the 100% simulation, there was a sea level increase of 0.1 cm. These results show that as the climate engineering percentage came closer to 100%, the volume of the ice sheet increased.

The Glimmer test also showed that instead of a linear relationship, there was a step-like behavior between increases in climate engineering and increases in height and coverage of the ice sheet. The 20% simulation showed an ice sheet that was slightly larger than the 0% simulation, but the remaining ice sheet was more interconnected. The 30% and 40% simulations show slight increases from the previous simulation, with a partial ice sheet in the north that wasn't present in the 20% simulation. The ice sheet at the 60% simulation was at full height and coverage, and the pre-industrial ice sheet was maintained.

For all of the simulations that include geoengineering, Greenland experiences a warmer and wetter climate in comparison to the pre-industrial period. On average, the temperature and precipitation rates of Greenland decrease relatively linearly with increases in the level of climate manipulation.

Ellie Pickrell

Positive Effects of Geoengineering on Ocean Acidification and Aragonite Saturation Levels

In the past, geoengineering has been considered a promising strategy for global cooling, although it has had some drawbacks. One of these drawbacks was the common belief that engineering the climate would not have any beneficial effects on ocean acidification, which is a negative component of raised atmospheric CO_2 levels. Matthews *et al.* (2009), however, proposed that geoengineering could have a beneficial impact on ocean acidification and offset some of the impacts that greenhouse gas emissions have had on our planet's oceans, specifically pH levels. Aquatic organisms that rely on shells for survival can only build these shells in waters with high aragonite saturation levels; as the ocean becomes more acidic, the aragonite saturation levels go down, and these organisms cannot survive. Climate engineering could potentially slow the ocean's current pH decreases, which would ideally slow the rapid reduction of aragonite saturation in the oceans. But, although simulations from this experiment do show an increase in oceanic pH values, they are not significant enough to stop the rapid decline in aragonite saturation levels.

Matthews *et al.* conducted a series of experiments on an earth system model that resembled a world exposed to climate engineering. They performed five simulations which all began at a preindustrial climate equilibrium, and compared the model's results at what represented conditions in the year 2100. The control group, A2, lacked climate engineering and consisted of prescribed SRES CO_2 emissions. The next simulation, A2+eng consisted of prescribed CO_2 emissions and climate engineering, which began after 2010. Next was the A2A+ eng, which consisted of the same CO_2 emissions as simulation A2, but again was exposed to climate engineering after 2010. The first three simulations represented a world with an active biosphere, providing carbon sinks for atmospheric CO_2 and thus partially offsetting its increases. The fourth simulation, A2nb, consisted of a neutral biosphere (in which the land biosphere does not exchange carbon with the atmosphere after 2010), prescribed CO_2 emissions, and no geoengineering. The final simulation, A2nb+eng was the same as the previous simulation, but was exposed to climate engineering.

After all of the simulations were tested, Matthews *et al.* compared the results of the pH and the aragonite tests between the different scenarios. In both the A2 and A2+ eng simulations, pH values were reduced (7.6 and 7.85), compared to the control group with a pH value of 8.05, and aragonite concentrations of 1.85. A model with climate engineering showed a slightly higher pH value at the 2100 mark in comparison to the A2 non-engineered simulation, but a lower aragonite saturation value (1.80 to 1.90). Climate engineering was also effective at reducing the average atmospheric temperatures, as well as lower atmospheric CO_2 concentrations, due to an increase in carbon uptake by natural carbon sinks as a result of the cooler temperatures.

In the A2A+eng simulation, the change in ocean pH was smaller and was extremely close to the control simulation's pH, but the aragonite saturation decreased more rapidly as a result of climate engineering. An increase in dissolved inorganic carbon and colder temperatures lead to aragonite saturation values that were 9% lower than the values in the A2 simulation (from 1.72 in A2 to 1.58 in A2A+eng), because colder temperatures lead to slightly higher pH values, but result in lower aragonite saturation values.

Next, A2nb+eng and A2nb were compared. In A2nb+eng, surface temperatures were colder, and ocean dissolved inorganic carbon values were higher than in A2nb, which created unaffected pH values and a further decrease in aragonite saturation relative to the non-engineered simulation. The A2nb+eng simulation had a pH value of 7.75, and aragonite saturation values of 1.7, while the A2nb simulation had a pH value of 7.25 and aragonite saturation values of 1.85.

These effects and results are dependent on the enhanced accumulation of carbon in the land biosphere. Without this accumulation of carbon, climate engineering will have little effect on ocean pH levels, which would then lead to accelerated declines in aragonite saturation.

Solar Reflectivity by Plants Could Reduce Global Surface Temperature

Some plants reflect more solar energy back into space than others, and could be used to cool the planet. This solar reflectivity, or albedo, depends primarily on the glossiness of the leaves. By replacing current crops with maximum albedo crops, the planet could experience a cooling by 1°C across central North America and midlatitude Eurasia (Ridgwell *et al.* 2009). Further development of this new bio-geoengineering could result in advanced genetic manipulation of plant leaves, which could eventually result in greater temperature reductions. This method of global cooling appears to be much more affective than other proposed strategies (such as the injection of sulfate aerosols into the atmosphere or the creation of a sunshade), since it doesn't require the construction of infrastructure and industry.

Andy Ridgwell and the Bristol Research Initiative for the Dynamic Global Environment conducted a set of climate-model-sensitivity experiments and examined the albedo levels of different plants. Five different models were set up, simulating different climates. Atmospheric CO_2 concentration and maximum albedo were altered between each experiment, and the global mean surface area temperature (SAT) was compared among the different conditions. Four of the five conditions experienced climates with elevated CO_2 concentrations of 700 ppm, and higher vegetation albedo values of 0.2, 0.22, 0.24 and 0.28. The fifth condition, the control group, represented current CO_2 concentrations of 350 ppm and an unadjusted cropland albedo of 0.2.

After the SAT values were calculated for each condition, it became very clear that higher albedo values resulted in cooler global surface air temperatures. Each condition experienced an increase maximum albedo (by values of +0.02, +0.04, and +0.08), and as these values increased, the mean SAT showed a consistent cooling of the planet. The effects of a +0.04 maximum albedo change are primarily focused on in the results and analysis of this experiment. It was estimated that with a +0.04 change, the SATs would be 0.11° C lower than the control experiment. The results clearly show that in a climate with increased CO_2 concentrations, the planet will be much cooler with a higher maximum albedo value.

It is important to notice, however, that the small reduction in the global SAT for a +0.04 change misrepresents the reality of a larger regional cooling. During the summer, temperatures drop by over 1°C across central North America and Eurasia, which is most likely due to the dense cropland that covered these regions in the model.

With this approach we can achieve geoengineering by manipulating the crops of the existing global agriculture industry rather than starting from scratch. It is also a more realistic and practical method since it doesn't require separate maintenance. The annual replanting of crop plants is guaranteed since they are primarily grown as a food source. This plan is much less costly and much more efficient than other proposed strategies of geoengineering.

One drawback to this strategy is the amount of available arable land. If this method were implemented, these crops would mostly be localized to an area spanning central North America through midlatitude Eurasia. Places like Africa and South America would not be used to plant this modified vegetation, as the land isn't as easily cultivated and wouldn't really contribute to global cooling. It is also important to realize that this process is not only affected by physical boundaries but by seasons as well. This means that bio-geoengineering of croplands may be most effective if used simultaneously with other geoengineering strategies.

Cloud Seeding: A Promising Strategy for Cooling the Planet and Rebuilding the Polar Ice Caps

Cloud seeding has been seen as a possible method of decreasing the overall surface temperature of the globe. Seeding our planet's maritime boundary layer clouds would increase the number of raindrops released from these clouds and reduce the average droplet size, thus increasing their albedo (Rasch *et al.* 2009). This could result in the cooling of the planet and compensation for some of the negative effects of climate change. The effects of cloud seeding were looked at in a model that represented a globe whose atmospheric CO_2 concentrations were twice as high as they are today. Global surface temperature, polar sea ice cover, and the global precipitation rate would experience drastic changes if this cloud seeding strategy were put into action. We would see an overall cooling of the planet, a halt in the rapid shrinking of the polar ice caps, and an overall decrease in the global rate of precipitation.

Philip J. Rasch and the Pacific Northwest National Laboratory conducted an experiment in which they examined the effects of cloud seeding on an "Earth" with atmospheric CO_2 concentrations that were twice as high as present day values. They used a Community Climate System Model and set up four different geoengineering situations, with a control system that consisted of zero climate engineering. The four cases were 20%, 30%, 40%, and 70% cloud seeding of the areal extent of the ocean surface. They then examined the effects that these four situations had on global surface temperature, polar sea ice, and global precipitation.

The test showing effects of cloud seeding on the Earth's surface temperature produced promising results. The control group showed an increase in surface temperature of 1.8 K (equivalent to 1.8°C) compared to the Earth's current conditions, but the models that included cloud seeding show much more positive results. In the 20% case, the warming is reduced to 0.8 K more than the current temperatures, which is almost half as much heating if we were to dismiss the idea of cloud seeding. The 70% case actually produced a cooling of 0.4 K *less* than the current temperatures, which would result in an overcooling of the planet. Based on the results, it is clear that the maximum amount of cloud seeding isn't necessary, and even the minimum amount of 20% would make a 50% difference in the surface temperature.

Next, Rasch *et al.* compared the results regarding the polar sea ice cover and its reaction to cloud seeding. In this experiment they looked at the effects that cloud seeding would have on the Northern Hemisphere and the Southern Hemisphere separately, because the clouds in the Southern Hemisphere require less seeding than the clouds in the Northern Hemisphere (they are more susceptible to brightening). The control group shows a 20% decrease in the Northern Hemisphere and a 36% decrease in the Southern Hemisphere from the current sea ice levels. In the 40% case the sea ice is 9% smaller than the control group in the Northern Hemisphere, and 8% smaller in the Southern Hemisphere. To really make a difference in the polar ice caps, the Earth requires a 70% cloud seeding strategy, which is almost impossible as it may overcool the Earth. Regardless, in the 70% case the sea ice is restored to within 2% of the present day level.

Finally, Rasch *et al.* looked at the effect that cloud seeding could have on the global precipitation rate. As the percentage of cloud seeding increases, the global precipitation rate decreases. The control group shows an increase of 0.1 mm of rain per day, compared to the current precipitation rate. The 20% case shows an increase by 0.01 mm, while the 70% case shows a decrease by 0.08 mm. These reductions in precipitation occur along the equator between the eastern Pacific and the maritime subcontinent, especially across South America. For all the cases there is, however, an increase in precipitation in the South Pacific convergence zone.

This study shows how difficult it is to address multiple changes resulting from climate change. If the atmospheric CO_2 concentrations were to double, it would be impossible to simultaneously cool the planet and return sea ice and global precipitation to the present day amounts.

Climate Engineering through Ocean Upwelling could Cool the Planet and Simultaneously Remove CO_2 from the Atmosphere

Ocean fertilization through oceanic pipe upwelling has been proposed as a possible strategy for removing CO_2 from the atmosphere and cooling the planet. The model in this experiment shows that artificial upwelling by oceanic pipes may be able to sequester atmospheric CO_2 at a rate of 0.9 PgC per year, storing 80% of the sequestered carbon on land (Oschlies *et al.* 2010). Like many other methods of geoengineering, the removal of these oceanic pipes would result in a rapid increase in surface temperature and atmospheric CO_2 concentrations, which makes it a risky option for solving the climate crisis.

Oschlies *et al.* used an earth system climate model from the University of Victoria to test the effects of geoengineering through ocean upwelling. The model's ocean depths range from 50 to 500 m and consist of a basic marine ecosystem with the two major nutrients, nitrate and phosphate, and two phytoplankton classes. The model is run under fossil fuel and land-use carbon emissions representing conditions from the year 1850 to 2000. Then, from the year 2000–2100, the model is exposed to CO_2 emissions following the SRES A2 scenario, which involves an increase from today's emissions of roughly 8 PgC per year to roughly 29 PgC per year in 2100.

The proposed method of creating ocean upwelling is through flap-valve ocean pipes, but for the model, Oschlies *et al.* simulated these pipes by using artificial transport terms that move water from the lower end of the pipe to the ocean surface. The model was exposed to three different scenarios. The first was the control group, which simply consisted of the SRES 92A emissions scenario. The second was the pipe minus control situation in the year 2100, which had different maximum pipe extensions. The last group was the pipe minus control group in the year 2100 with different upwelling velocities. Atmospheric, oceanic, and terrestrial carbon inventories were recorded in each scenario, as well as partial pressure of CO_2, export of organic carbon, pipe-induced upwelling, nitrogen fixation, and global mean surface area temperature. For the scenarios including the pipe engineering, the pipes were installed in 2010, and their maximum vertical extensions are limited to 1000 m.

For the standard pipe situation with 1 cm per day of artificial upwelling from the maximum depth of 1000 m, the simulated upwelling of all the pipes is roughly 20 Sv (Sv= 10^6 m^3/s) in year 2010. As CO_2 concentrations increase, the amount of area suitable for upwelling also increases, reaching global values of roughly 26 Sv in 2100. When comparing the two results from the geoengineered simulations to the control, there is an obvious increase in the overall strength in the overturning circulation by 30%, whereas there is a 20% decline in overturning strength in the control simulation. When comparing the annual export of organic matter across a depth level of 125 m, we see a more than 50% increase from the control to the engineering experiment from 6.3 PgC per year to 9.7 PgC per year. This includes the contribution from nitrogen fixation, which almost doubles from 129 Tmol N per year to 251 Tmol N per year after the insertion of these oceanic pipes. This results in an additional carbon fixation of 0.7 PgC per year. Although we see a great increase in the export of organic carbon, only 7% of oceanic carbon is sequestered, as about 70% of the carbon returns to the atmosphere on a centennial time scale.

One result that surprised the researchers was a reduction in atmospheric CO_2 concentrations that was much larger than the increase in the oceanic carbon inventory. By 2100, the reduction in CO_2 concentration was at 83 PgC, which is more than four times the oceanic sequestration. The model also showed global surface air temperatures decreasing by up to 1°C. A major risk involved with this method of geoengineering, along with many other climate-engineering strategies, is that if the pipes failed or had to be removed, a rapid increase in surface area temperature and CO_2 concentrations would be inevitable. In 2010, simulated temperatures were higher than the control group by 0.3°C, 0.07°C, and 0.23°C with artificial upwelling stopping at 10, 20, and 50 years, respectively.

Although Sulfate Aerosol Injections may Cool the Planet, they still Reduce the Amount of Ozone in the Earth's Atmosphere

Injecting sulfate aerosol particles into the Earth's atmosphere is one of the most popular strategies of geoengineering, as it would increase the albedo of the planet and reflect more light back into space. These sulfate aerosols, however, have to be a certain size to be effective in increasing the planet's albedo, and particles with a radii of roughly 0.1 μm are the most efficient in cooling the planet. Heckendorn *et al.* (2009) show which injection strategies will produce the smallest and most efficient aerosol particles, and how long these particles will stay in the atmosphere. This is of large concern since there is speculation regarding aerosol injection, and if it ends up having negative impacts it would be even worse if the particles remained in the atmosphere for long periods of time. This paper also explains how risky injecting sulfate aerosols into the atmosphere can be, as increased aerosols reduce the amount of ozone in the atmosphere.

Heckendorn *et al.* ran a series of experiments on a global model. These calculations were carried out with two types of sulfur injection methods. The first was a continuous pumping of sulfur into the clouds with fluxes of 1,2,5 and 10 Mt/a, while the other simulations were pulsed injections with periods of one month and six months with fluxes of 5 Mt/a. The control group consisted of zero sulfur injections. All simulations were run for 20 years with present day concentrations of ozone depleting substances, green house gas, carbon dioxide emissions, sea ice, and sea surface temperatures.

The results of the simulations show that the surface area density of the aerosol particles increases as concentration increases. In simulation GEO5 (continuous injection with fluxes of 5 MT/a) the surface area density is larger than 40 μm^2 cm^{-3}. In the simulation where the injection takes place twice a year (GEO5p2), the surface area density is larger than 100 μm^2 cm^{-3}.

Next, Heckendorn *et al.* looked at how the injection strategies affected the stratospheric residence time of the aerosols. They found that smaller particles have a longer residence time. For the GEO1 simulation (continuous injection with fluxes of 1 Mt/a), the residence time, referred to as aerosol burden, is 1.4 Mt S. For all the other simulations, the aerosol burden is less than one year with 3.7 Mt S for the GEO5 simulation and 6.0 Mt S for the GEO10 simulation (continuous injections with fluxes of 10 Mt/a). They also found that if the sulfur injection occurs at a higher altitude, the residence time increases.

Finally, Heckendorn *et al.* looked at how the injection strategies would affect the mean O_3 column. For the GEO5 simulation, the O_3 column is predicted to decrease by 4.5%, and the GEO10 model predicted a decrease by 5.3%. These values are greater than the O_3 loss due to the emission of greenhouse gases from 2002 to 2005, a decrease by 3.5%.

Although geoengineering by injection of sulfur aerosols into the Earth's clouds has shown promise in cooling the planet and decrease levels of atmospheric CO_2 concentrations, it also has the negative impact of reducing the Earth's ozone layer.

Removal or Failure of Climate Engineering by Sulfate Aerosol Injection Threatens Dangerously Abrupt Temperature Increases

Sulfate aerosol injection as a method of geoengineering and cooling the planet has been showing great promise and growing in popularity as a fix for the climate crisis. It has long been suggested that geoengineering could function independently and provide researchers with more time to create and improve methods of removing CO_2 from the atmosphere, which is the real fix. Ross *et al.* (2009), however, claim that if we rely on geoengineering and do not implement it alongside the removal of CO_2, there will be drastic temperature changes if the geoengineering strategy is removed or fails. If CO_2 emissions do not decrease, the failure or removal of climate engineering methods would result in a large temperature spike, increasing global temperatures by a maximum of 4.5°C, which would have catastrophic impacts on the planet's ecosystems and possibly result in mass species extinctions.

In this study, Ross *et al.* used a climate model to predict the effects of the implementation and subsequent removal of climate engineering by injection of sulfate aerosols with the A1B emissions scenario. The control group consisted of a business as usual emissions scenario. The second simulation consisted of a model exposed to climate engineering that started in the year 2020 and was removed in 2060. These two simulations were repeated 40 times each, varying with climate sensitivity of the model from 0.5 to 10°C. Climate sensitivity is the response of global mean surface air temperature to a doubling of atmospheric CO_2 concentrations. An estimated climate sensitivity probability density function was used from another paper (Hegerl *et al.* 2006) to identify the likelihood of each set of model situations.

In the control group where climate engineering was not applied, temperatures increased consistently from 1990 to 2100, ranging from 0.6 to 5.1°C for climate sensitivities ranging from 0.5 to 10°C. Atmospheric CO_2 concentrations at the year 2100 ranged from 690 to 739 ppmv, with higher climate sensitivities containing the higher concentrations. In the climate engineered simulations, temperatures dropped to values very similar to the temperatures in 1990 between 2020 and 2059, with respect to the control scenario. As soon as the engineering was removed, however, temperatures increased rapidly, ranging from 0.15 to 4.5°C between 2060 and 2100. The temperature change after the removal of the engineering was higher with higher values of climate sensitivity. The final CO_2 concentrations in the geoengineering runs were similar to those in the control simulations (between 689 and 722 ppmv).

Next, Ross *et al.* looked at the annual rate of temperature change between 1990 and 2100 for each simulation. In the control scenario, the annual rate of temperature change increased until 2060, when greenhouse gas emissions decline with the A1B emissions scenario. This resulted in a decreased rate of temperature change. In the climate engineering scenarios, the rate of temperature change was relatively small up until 2020, when geoengineering was implemented and temperatures dropped. From 2020 to 2060 the rate of temperature change was insignificant, until temperatures abruptly increased after the removal of geoengineering. The maximum rate of warming ranged from 0.13 to 0.76°C/year. These high rates of warming, however, only lasted for a few years and within a decade, the rates decreased to less than 0.1°C/year. The maximum rate of sea level rise was also higher in the geoengineering simulations than in the controls.

Finally, Ross *et al.* looked at the probability density functions between 1990 and 2100, which measures the likelihood that these temperatures will change. For the control group, the most likely maximum annual temperate change was 0.031°/year. The geoengineering simulation showed a likely maximum rate of temperature change just under 0.5°C/year, which occurred in 2060 at the high temperature spike.

Increasing Plant Albedo to Reduce Surface Air Temperature may not Cause a Significant Temperature Change

Croplands cover over 10% of the land surface, with concentrated agricultural regions in Europe, South Asia, and the Eastern United States. Singarayer *et al.* 2009 ran simulations on a climate model to estimate what would happen to the global surface area temperature if the plants in these croplands were replaced by different varieties with higher albedo. The crop canopy albedo was increased by 0.04, and although this geoengineering showed regional and season cooling, the global temperature change of 0.1°C was insignificant. Europe and Southern Asia, which have intensive agriculture regions, were generally the only regions that benefited from this bio-geoengineering.

Singarayer *et al.* ran a series of different scenarios on the Hadley Centre climate model to test the effects of modified cropland albedo on the average surface temperature in three atmospheres with different CO_2 concentrations; 350 ppmv, 700 ppmv (x2) and 1400 ppmv (x4). They set up six different situations for the climate model. The first was the control group, which consisted of atmospheric CO_2 concentrations of 350 ppmv and no geoengineering. Next were simulations consisting of doubled and quadrupled CO_2 concentrations with geoengineering, and finally simulations consisting of doubled and quadrupled CO_2 concentrations without geoengineering. In the geoengineered cases, the plant albedo was increased by an average of 0.4.

Singarayer *et al.* primarily looked at the effects that plant geoengineering had on the planet's surface air temperature. The results generally confirmed a relatively small impact on a global scale. In the model, a doubling of CO_2 leads to an increase of about 3.0°C, yet the mitigation from increasing the crop albedo is only roughly 0.1 °C. The results did show, however, a strong regional and seasonal impact on the globe's temperatures. For all three CO_2 scenarios, geoengineering produced a reduction by 0.5 to 2°C within Europe during northern hemisphere summer. The results show that the maximum mitigation of climate change is in Western Europe during the summer, with a cooling effect of 20% of the surface air temperature. After the harvest season is over in the winter, however, the impacts of plant geoengineering are minimal. Singarayer *et al.* also found significant increases in winter temperatures in Southern Asia, as a result of increased CO_2 levels and monsoonal circulation.

The regions that will benefit the most from this type of geoengineering are Southern Asia and Europe, with a regional summer-time cooling of 1°C across Europe, and a regional winter-time cooling of 1°C of Southern Asia. Although this method of geoengineering is less expensive, less risky, and more practical than other methods, it only shows a significant reduction in surface air temperature on a regional scale, and not on the preferred global scale.

Conclusions

Geoengineering is an appealing concept when it comes to offsetting the negative results of global climate change. Although there are negative consequences that accompany any method of geoengineering, it seems that this is the case for most effective methods of reducing the impacts of global warming. Geoengineering is a promising field, but there is more research that needs to be done. The major piece that needs to be focused on is creating positive impacts on a global level. When it comes to climate engineering it seems that not everyone benefits, and those that don't, experience extremely negative impacts. Climate engineering needs to be further researched and altered so that it makes a more significant impact on the overall global temperature, really addresses the root of the climate problem, and impacts all countries in a positive way.

References Cited

Heckendorn, P., Weisenstein, D., Fueglistaler, S., Luo, B., Rozanov, E., Schraner, M., Thomason, L., Peter, T., 2009. The impact of geoengineering aerosols on stratospheric temperature and ozone. Environmental Resolution Letters 4, 045108.

Irvine, P., Lunt, D., Stone, E., Ridgwell, A., 2009. The fate of the Greenland Ice Sheet in a geoengineered, high CO_2 world. Environmental Research Letters 4, 045109.

Matthews, H., Cao, L., Caldeira, K., 2009. Sensitivity of ocean acidification to geoengineered climate stabilization. Geophysical Research Letters 36, 10706.

Oschlies, A., Pahlow, M., Yool, A., Matear, R., 2010. Climate engineering by artificial ocean upwelling: channeling the sorcerer's apprentice. Geophysical Research Letters 37, 04701.

Rasch, Philip J., Latham, John, Chen, Jack, 2009. Geoengineering by Cloud Seeding: Influence on Sea Ice and Climate System. Environmental Research Letters 4, 045112.

Ridgwell, A., Singarayer, J., Hetherington, A., Valdes, P., 2009. Tackling Regional Climate Change By Leaf Albedo Bio-geoengineering. Current Biology 19, 146–150.

Ross, A., Matthews, H., 2009. Climate engineering and the risk of rapid climate change. Environmental Resolution Letters 4, 045103.

Singarayer, J., Ridgwell, A., Irvine, P., 2009. Assessing the Benefits of Crop Albedo Bio-Geoengineering. Environmental Resolution Letters 4, 045110.

Section III—Biofuels

11. Biofuels: Which Alternative is 'Fueling' Us into the Future?

Alec Faggen

The modern world is at a critical stage in its development. Without new technologies and drastic reforms, economic and population growth will no longer be sustainable (Ayhan 2007). The major source of this crisis is the use of fossil feed stock—petroleum, coal, and natural gas. These substances are not sustainable or environmentally friendly (Naik *et al.* 2010). Burning of fossil fuel adds enormous amounts of CO_2 to the atmosphere, subsequently worsening the effects of global warming that have already been felt in recent decades. In addition, it is estimated that petroleum reserves will only last a few more decades (Ayhan 2007). Consequently, substantial efforts have been initiated to decrease dependence on foreign energy and oil, assist agriculture industries, and lessen harm to the environment (Sims *et al.* 2010).

Solutions must be economically, technologically, and environmentally feasible to meet high-energy demands in the industrialized world (Meher *et al.* 2006). Biofuels produced from renewable resources have shown great promise in their ability to fulfill these demands. The term biofuel refers to a liquid or gaseous fuel manufactured from biomass. Biomass is a biological material from living or recently dead organisms (Demirbas 2006). Thus, fossil fuels, which are normally millions of years old, are not considered biomass.

Biomass used for biofuel production is most commonly plant material. Biofuels originating from plant-derived biomass could potentially reduce greenhouse gas (GHG) emissions as the CO_2 released from burning the fuel might be offset by the CO_2 absorbed during photosynthesis (Osamu and Carl 1989). These biofuels would therefore diminish the consequences of global warming (Naik *et al.* 2010). However, production of these biofuels must be carefully considered while evaluat-

137

ing their carbon cost. Debate remains as to the net GHG savings if direct and indirect land-use transformations are considered (Sims *et al.* 2010).

Biofuels are divided into two distinct categories: first generation and second-generation biofuels. First generation biofuel such as biodiesel (or bioesters), bioethanol, and biogas is defined by its ability to use previously established technologies such as internal combustion engines, distribution infrastructure, or alternative vehicle technology such as FFVs (Flexible Fuel Vehicle) or natural gas vehicles (Naik *et al.* 2010). These fuels are characteristically produced from raw materials such as sugar, starch, vegetable oil, and animal fats that are also used for food. Corn, wheat, and sugar beets are the most common forms of bioethanol feedstock, whereas sunflower and oil seeds are generally used as biodiesel feedstock (Demirbas 2009).

About 50 billion liters of first generation biofuels are produced each year (Naik *et al.* 2010). Students and staff at the University of Cincinnati are current contributors to this figure through their efforts converting used fryer oil from campus dining halls into biodiesel via a transesterification process. The successful production serves as a microcosm to oppose global warming by means of an otherwise disposed of raw material (Agnew *et al.* 2009).

Biodiesel is produced by the transesterification of vegetable oils, residual oils, and fats in the presence of a catalyst. The fuel can be effective as a diesel substitute after a few minor engine adaptations. The transesterification reaction simultaneously produces glycerol, currently creating a waste problem as biodiesel production rates increase, but methods for recycling glycerol into a useful product such as hydrogen (Sabourin-Provost and Hallenbeck 2009) are being investigated. This investigation has led to the discovery of bacteria capable of converting glycerol into hydrogen at fairly high yields, which can subsequently be processed as a fuel source itself.

Bioethanol is produced as a gasoline substitute by sugar or starch fermentation. Fermentation refers to the metabolic process in which enzymes that are secreted by yeast, bacteria, or mold chemically convert organic substrates into ethanol. Bioethanol can be mixed with gasoline, optimally via an initial conversion into ethyl tertiary butyl ether (ETBE), or it can be fully functional in flexi-fuel vehicles (Naik *et al.* 2010)

Lastly, the third first generation biofuel—biogas or biomethane—can also function equivalently to gasoline in modified vehicles. Although many of the specific processes and raw materials differ, bioethanol, biodiesel, and biogas can also be produced as second-generation biofuels.

Unfortunately, first generation biofuels have been met with resistance, especially with respect to competition with food. First generation feedstock is normally cultivated on high-quality agricultural land (Demirbas 2009); as such this biofuel production has been blamed for the escalating cost of food (Laursen 2006), perhaps as much as 15–25% (Chakrabortty 2008). In reality, crops cultivated for first generation biomass occupy less than 2% of the world's arable land (WWI 2007) and food costs have recently decreased without a corresponding decrease in biofuel production (Sims *et al.* 2010). Regardless, competition with food is perceived as causing major technical and economic hurdles to deployment of biofuels on a large scale. In reality, production is not economically viable without government subsidies to cover the costly raw materials and processing machineries (Ma and Hanna 1999).

Geographic locations of cultivation, processing, storage, and delivery steps need to be carefully assessed, as site placements could drastically inhibit or enhance biofuel production (Sims *et al.* 2010). As there are many factors affecting production, progress towards renewable resources is sensibly occurring in small steps (Eisberg 2006). Currently, manufacturers are balancing the ecological benefits with the economic drawbacks by supplementing conventional techniques with the first generation biofuel production (Eisberg 2006). Further progress seeks to slowly eliminate this dependence on conventional techniques.

In contrast, second generation biofuels are still in the stages of research before commercial use. These fuels tend to be manufactured using non-edible plant biomass from lignocellulosic feedstock, which can produce bioethanol via hydrolysis and fermentation or biodiesel via gasification. Biochemical methods using enzymes and other micro-organisms convert cellulose and hemicellulose components of feedstocks to sugars before their fermentation into ethanol. In contrast, thermochemical process using pyrolysis or gasification techniques create a synthesis gas (carbon monoxide and hydrogen gas), which can undergo the Fischer-Tropsch conversion to produce synthetic diesel, aviation fuel, or ethanol (Sims *et al.* 2010)

Lignocellulosic feedstocks for biofuels include non-edible oilseeds, high erucic— monounsaturated, omega–9 fatty acid—mustard, Indian beech, green seeds canola, micro algae, and aquatic biomass (Naik *et al.* 2010). Micro algae have been found to be 10–20 times more effective than vegetable oils in producing biofuels, especially under nitrogen depletion conditions. They also benefit the environment by fixing CO_2 in the atmosphere and thus lower GHGs. Following oil extraction, waste products can be further utilized to make fertilizer, feed, biogas, or high value chemical compounds (Gouveia and Oliveira 2009).

Another non-food, renewable carbon source for biofuel production is methyl halides. Unfortunately, methyl halides are not produced in high enough quantities to qualify as a practical source for biofuel. To address this problem, researchers employed genetic engineering to manufacture yeast capable of producing methyl halides. The genetically modified yeast was then co-cultured with cellulolytic bacterium. The end product was successful at producing methyl halides from switchgrass, corn stover, sugar cane bagasse, and poplar (Bayer *et al.* 2009). Research capacity of biofuel production is greatly expanding, as new technologies such as genetic engineering allow for the synthetic manipulation of useful variables.

Feedstocks for bioethanol include forestry crops, perennial grasses (miscanthus and switchgrass), and also wood, forestry, and agriculture residues. As these materials are cheaply and commonly available, land requirements are minimal (Sims *et al.* 2010). In addition to not competing with food productions, these second generation fuels have been estimated to be more economically comparable to standard petrol and diesel (Naik *et al.* 2010). In terms of ecology, switchgrass can be produced under conditions that both decrease GHG emissions and save nonrenewable energy by about 80%. A large percentage of this carbon intake was attributable to soil sequestration during the first 20 years, before a new equilibrium was reached. All environmentally-related measurements decreased during these years, except for acidification and eutrophication. Variables such as soil type, climate, and tillage methods had demonstrated effects on measurements, underscoring the need for meticulous analysis of methodology before conclusions can be accurately made (Cherubini and Jungmeier 2009).

A study comparing two of these perennial grasses— switchgrass and miscanthus— found miscanthus to be more than twice as productive as switchgrass. The study accredited this finding mainly to miscanthus's higher leaf photosynthetic rates. The biological basis for differences in feedstock productivity will help elucidate the most advantageous criteria for development of biofuels (Dohleman *et al.* 2009).

Nonetheless, second generation biofuels are not commercially available for many reasons. Effectiveness of the enzymes and overall processes during pretreatment, production, and integration need to be improved (Sheehan *et al.* 2004). Specifically, the rate-limiting step is often the exposure of the cellulose and hemicellulose for consequent enzymatic hydrolysis (Sims *et al.* 2010). Previous chemical and physical treatments to address this limitation were costly and inefficient. Electron beam irradiation (EBI) of lignocelluloses was tested due to its low yields of harmful byproducts and its ability to function without extreme temperatures. Although glucose yields from rice straw, (another lignocellulose crop), did improve after EBI, previous literature recorded higher levels of glucose production via preparatory techniques such as dilute-acid, ammonia fiber explosion, and presoaking in aqueous ammonia (Bak *et al.* 2009).

Overall enhancement of the biorefinery system is essential to current research. The concept of a biorefinery was first coined in the 1990s as a collective term for biomass production, processing, and final use. Since its establishment, a significant amount of literature has been written documenting various biorefinery concepts generating multiple bio-based products (Haung *et al.* 2008, Mabee *et al.* 2005).

These systems utilize a number of different methods including physical, chemical, biological, and thermal means, some utilizing multiple processes.

One such study used a two-phase process in which algae were first grown in a photobioreactor and later converted into methane using a catalytic hydrothermal gasification process in supercritical water. Supercritical fluid is a liquid held at a temperature and pressure above its vapor liquid critical point such that it is neither liquid nor gas (Naik *et al.* 2010). Supercritical water is especially useful as a solvent for biomass production, exhibiting special properties including very low solubility for salts. The methane produced during the gasification process was pipeline quality, synthetic natural gas. The photobioreactor used recycled CO_2 and nutrients from subsequent biofuel processes in order to optimize sustainable growth of the algal biomass (Stucki *et al.* 2009). More research is currently needed to resolve some of the infrastructure deterrents before successful marketing of this biorefinery system is possible. Success of the biorefinery technologies in general will depend largely on how well current infrastructure can acclimate to new technological advances (Sim *et al.* 2010).

Gas Stations of the Future: Biodiesel Production from Used Cooking Oil on a College Campus

Biodiesel production has the potential to both reduce foreign dependence and environmental damage (Agnew *et al.* 2007). Biodiesel is non-toxic, biodegradable, and has lower emissions of carbon monoxide, particulate matter, and unburned hydrocarbons than petroleum-based fuels. It also has health benefits because it has no sulfur or carcinogenic components. Despite the environmental and health-related advantages, biodiesel from fresh oil is not economical in the short-term. Raw materials alone account for approximately 70–95% of total manufacturing costs. Thus, studies are being conducted to evaluate the feasibility of converting used cooking oil into biodiesel.

Agnew and colleagues working in the Department of Civil and Environmental Engineering of the University of Cincinnati participated in one such study using a transesterification methodology to convert methanol and fryer oil from campus dining halls into biodiesel (or methyl esters) and glycerol. They began by using an acid-base titration in order to determine the amount of catalyst (sodium hydroxide) needed for their oil supply and discovered a higher content of free fatty acids compared to the majority of waste oils described in the literature, a result of the hydrolysis of triglycerides during heating. Later, they varied the catalyst in small-scale pilot tests to determine optimal catalyst usage for each batch of recycled oil. Recycled oil requires more catalyst and higher gelling temperatures than fresh oil because frying produces free fatty acids. Filtration is also necessary to remove any remaining food debris. The catalyst (NaOH) is dissolved into the methanol and mixed for over an hour with heated cooking oil. After settling for eight hours, the glycerin's higher density separates it from the biodiesel, and it can be drained from the bottom of the reactor. After multiple washings with water to remove the catalyst and a final filtration using hairnets, the biodiesel is ready for use in a diesel engine.

Since the start of the project in 2007, the University of Cincinnati has produced hundreds of gallons of biodiesel. The fuel has been successfully tested in a Jeep's diesel engine, and it is in the process of being used by both delivery fleets and shuttle services. The University has also signed an agreement to use 2% biodiesel in its utility plant plants, providing an example to both its own community and other universities by demonstrating the viability of a more environmental and economical means for energy production. Unfortunately, the byproduct, glycerol, remained as a waste product and drawback in an otherwise sustainable process.

When Life Gives You Lemons: How Waste from Biofuel Production can be Converted into a Possible Energy Source

As biodiesel manufacturing continues to skyrocket, glycerol, previously a sought-after by-product has caused an increasingly threatening waste crisis (Sabourin-Provost and Hallenbeck 2009). The most commercially-used process in biodiesel production is the base-catalyzed trans-esterification of oil, which produces about 10 kg of glycerol per 100 kg of biodiesel. As demands for biodiesel multiply in order to reduce petroleum dependence and greenhouse gas emissions, the development of a feasible method to convert glycerol into a usable resource becomes increasingly critical. Fuel is one of the only viable resources that fulfills this long-term demand. Therefore, conversion of glycerol into either ethanol or hydrogen has been deemed the most apt solution. Ethanol production from crude glycerol has been met with many setbacks such as low yields and impracticality. Thus, current research looks to hydrogen, which is currently being investigated as a future fuel, to resolve the glycerol crisis.

Sabourin-Provost and Hallenbeck working in the Department of Microbiology and Immunology at the University of Montreal found that the purple non-sulfur photosynthetic bacterium, *Rhodopseudomonas palustris* photoferments glycerol to hydrogen via an active nitrogenase. The authors of the paper were able to collect 6 moles of hydrogen gas/mole of glycerol, (almost 75% of theoretical maximum yield). Although not required for synthesis, the addition of a nitrogen source maximized hydrogen formation. Crude glycerol and pure glycerol had about the same yields of hydrogen production.

A number of benefits to hydrogen manufacturing exist. Hydrogen is a water insoluble product; thus, it is relatively easy to collect in comparison to water-soluble products such as ethanol. Furthermore, necessary dilutions, in order to counter possible contaminant complications, are not as consequential if producing a gaseous product like hydrogen.

Nonetheless, many obstacles remain before hydrogen synthesis from glycerol can be efficient. An economic photobioreactor where the reactions can take place is yet to be constructed. The photobioreactor must be transparent so light can catalyze the reactions and also hydrogen-impermeable so the hydrogen gas can ultimately be collected. In addition, *R. palustris* is inefficient at utilizing light, and future research should investigate optimal light intensity for these organisms.

Microalgae: Potentially the Most Efficient Raw Material for Biofuel Production

Alternatives to fossil fuels such as biofuels have shown promise in not only reducing harmful gaseous emissions, but in facilitating the return of the Earth's atmosphere to equilibrium (Gouveia and Oliveira 2009). Although oleaginous crops are normally used to produce biofuels, recent research has concluded that microalgae can be 10–20 times more efficient than oleaginous seeds or vegetable oils. In addition, microalgae fix carbon dioxide and thus help to decrease greenhouse gases in the atmosphere. After oil is extracted from the algae, the remaining product can be further processed to create fertilizer, feed, biogas, or high value chemical compounds.

Gouveia and Oliveira at the Instituto Nacional de Engenharia compared six species of microalgae to determine the algae with the fastest growth rate and highest oil content with adequate composition. *Nannochloropsis sp.* and *Neochloris oleabundans* have high oil contents and under nitrogen depletion, increase oil quantity by about 50%. The oil content is characterized by iodine value. Careful comparisons of these values demonstrate that these microalgae have better quality oil than some vegetable oils. Although neither *Nannochloropsis sp.* nor *Neochloris oleabundans* alone can produce biodiesel, when used in conjunction with other microalgal oils or vegetable oils, they are viable. Although its oil quantity is smaller, *Scenesdesmus obliquus* has the best fatty acid profile and is feasible without other algae or oils.

Microalgae are especially promising sources for biofuel due to their fast growth rate, their high photosynthetic efficiency, their high biomass productivities, their ability to be harvested daily, their minimal need for water, and their capacity to grow in infertile land. However, cell lipid content must be monitored during production, which, in addition to being time consuming, produces harmful wastes if not properly distilled. Advances in biorefinery and photobioreactor engineering will help to resolve these limitations. As the biodiesel market speedily expands, microalgae are arguably the only potential source of renewable biodiesel that does not disrupt food production.

Engineering the Perfect Combination: Methyl Halide Production from Renewable Carbon Sources in Engineered Yeast

As previously mentioned, an attractive method to satisfy the growing demand for fuel is the conversion of non-food agricultural resources into liquid fuels (Bayer *et al.* 2009). Specifically, methyl halides are useful reactants for gasoline production via a catalyst called Zeolite. Methyl halides show promise as a petroleum substitute because the compounds can be derived from renewable carbon sources. However, the feasibility of producing methyl halides remains a problem. Methyl halides are naturally produced from many organisms, including marine algae, fungi, and halophytic plants, but it is time-consuming to harvest them and the yields are low. The enzyme responsible for this process is methyl halide transferase (MHT). Current research is exploring ways to transport MHTs into more industrially sound organisms for faster, more effective methyl halide production. Researchers are now employing a special technique called "synthetic metagenomics" to construct genetic sequences from DNA libraries based on functional similarities. The identified genetic sequences are then cloned into a vector for replication by *Escherichia coli (E. coli)* or yeast.

Bayer and colleagues working at the University of San Francisco combined naturally producing MHT yeast and cellulolytic bacteria in order to effectively convert lignocellulosic biomass (such as switchgrass, poplar, corn stover, and sugar cane bagasse) to methyl halides. Eighty-nine MHT genes were initially selected after multiple BLAST searches on all putative MHT genes from the NCBI sequence database. These genes came from diverse sources of plants, fungi, bacteria, and unidentified organisms. New chemical synthesis techniques obviated the need for host organisms for cloning, which is especially beneficial because some of these genes are from unknown organisms.

Methyl halide production, using the synthesized MHT genes, was then tested on three ions in *E. coli*. The MHT from the halophytic plant, *B. maritime,* presented with the highest activity of all genes on each ion. The *B. maritime* MHT was then transferred to the yeast *S. cerevisiae*. Yeast is especially useful as a host organism for its natural resistance to the toxic effects of methyl halides up to high levels. Its productivity from glucose was found to be 12,000 times better than the best production rate from a culturable organism. A co-culture using this newly engineered yeast and the cellulolytic bacterium *Actinotalea fermentans* attained successful methyl halide production from unprocessed switchgrass (*Panicum virgatum*), corn stover, sugar cane bagasse, and poplar (*Populus* sp.). These results demonstrate the potential of producing methyl halides from non-food agricultural resources.

The Total Picture: The Benefits of a Switchgrass Biorefinery System after Analysis using Life Cycle Assessment

Switchgrass (*Panicum virgatum*) is a type of prairie grass that has been proposed as a valuable crop for bioenergy, bioethanol, and biochemical (phenol) manufacturing (Cherubini and Jungmeier 2009). The grass's attractiveness arises from its minimal nutrient intake, its high overall energy production, its habitat diversity, and its ability to sequester carbon. Biomass energy has been considered most efficient while using a biorefinery approach in which multiple technological approaches are used conjointly.

Cherubini and Jungmeier working at the Norwegian University of Science and Technology and at the Institute of Energy Research used a Life Cycle Assessment (LCA) methodology to compare a biorefinery system to a fossil reference system. The biorefinery approach used switchgrass to produce bioethanol (instead of gasoline), heat from biomethane (instead of natural gas), electricity, heat, and phenols. The LCA calculates the total magnitude of contributions from all inputs and outputs throughout production. The authors were especially focused on GHG emissions and fossil energy usage because high demands for sustainable energy and climate change mitigation are the primary dictators of biorefinery progression.

The biorefinery technique for switchgrass decreased GHG emissions by 79% and saved about 80% of non-renewable energy. The energy output of the system is 3.6 times the non-renewable energy input. During the first 20 years, the soil sequesters a large amount of atmospheric carbon before it reaches a new equilibrium. These years contribute heavily to the decrease in GHG emissions for both carbon dioxide and methane. After these first years, the GHG emissions were produced mainly from switchgrass pellet production (85%). The biorefinery system also decreased all other investigated environmental impacts during the first 20 years, except for the impacts in the areas of acidification and eutrophication, which increased.

Nitrous oxide (N_2O) has a 298 times greater global warming potential than carbon dioxide, making N_2O an important variable to study in terms of nitrogen fertilizer use and organic matter decomposition in soil. Although the biorefinery system released more N_2O into the atmosphere, the emissions varied considerably depending on variables such as soil type, climate, and tillage methods.

Alec Faggen

Transforming a Demanding Goal into an Attainable Destiny: Use of Miscanthus as A Raw Material for Biomass

The United State's Department of Energy and Department of Agriculture have recently focused their efforts on increasing biofuel production from biomass (Dohleman *et al.* 2009). The Departments' goal to increase biomass production (and consequent biofuel production) will be more successful if an investigation first determines the most efficient raw material for the manufacturing of biomass. C4 grasses such as *Miscanthus x giganteus* (miscanthus) and *Panicum virgatum* (switchgrass) have particularly been targeted for their low anthropogenic inputs, higher net energy gains, and lower greenhouse gas emissions. The low anthropogenic inputs are partly attributable to the species' symbiotic relationship with bacteria capable of nitrogen fixation, which diminishes needs for nitrogen fertilizer, decreasing fossil fuel usage. Previous studies comparing miscanthus and switchgrass have found that miscanthus is more than two times as productive as switchgrass.

Dohleman and colleagues working at the University of Illinois and Iowa State University researched the hypothesis that this disparity in production can be attributed to miscanthus's higher leaf photosynthetic rates compared to switchgrass. investigated (1) leaf photosynthetic CO_2 uptake under varying growing conditions; (2) the effectiveness of the plants' water and nitrogen usage; and (3) energy loss during photosynthesis. This multi-phase study took place in central Illinois over 20 different days during 2005 and 2006, resulting in over 3300 recordings. The authors found that miscanthus has a 33% higher leaf photosynthetic rate. In order to achieve this higher photosynthetic rate, miscanthus must absorb higher levels of CO_2 by opening its stomata more frequently and/or for longer durations of time. This increase in stomatal conduction, unfortunately, costs the miscanthus a 25% loss of water.

The study explained the species' higher leaf photosynthetic rate using various tests. The authors measured a 23% increase in whole-chain electron transport rate in miscanthus compared to switchgrass. During transduction into whole chain electron transport, the authors found that light energy loss was significantly lower in miscanthus. They also observed that leaf nitrogen and water use were significantly higher in miscanthus. These findings all yield additional understanding as to the species' higher photosynthetic rate.

These results, however, do not fully explain the higher productivity of miscanthus. Other factors such as smaller root partitioning, decreased respiration, more extensive leaf canopy, and/or higher leaf area index must also contribute. Increased understanding as to the factors behind the greater productivity of miscanthus will elucidate appropriate selection criterion for more successful biomass production.

Irradiating the Future of Biofuel: Using Electron Beam Irradiation Pretreatment to Improve Cellulosic Biofuel Production

Cellulose's abundance makes it an obvious choice as a raw material for biofuel production (Bak *et al.* 2009). Specifically, enzymatic hydrolysis of lignocellulose, which is composed of cellulose, hemicelluloses, and lignin, has been studied to satisfy the demanding ambitions to reduce gasoline usage from groups like the United State's Department of Energy. Unfortunately, complications arise during cellulosic biofuel manufacturing because the cellulose in lignocellulose is not normally accessible to hydrolytic enzymes. Many physical and chemical pretreatments have been suggested to improve access to the cellulose in order to produce higher glucose yields. The majority of the proposed chemical processes generate byproducts that inhibit enzymatic hydrolysis of the cellulose, establishing a need for costly, resistant enzymes.

Many physical pretreatments, such as the milling process, have been deemed inefficient and energetically costly. Instead, electron beam irradiation (EBI) of lignocelluloses was proposed for its low yields of harmful byproducts and for its functionality in the absence of extreme temperatures.

Bak and colleagues working at the Korea University and Korea Atomic Energy Research Institute evaluated the efficacy of EBI to improve enzymatic hydrolysis of cellulose for biofuel production. The authors pretreated a type of lignocellulose called rice straw with EBI and determined its subsequent enzymatic digestibility and physical composition. Multiple trials were performed using varying crystallinity indexes of cellulose, EBI currents, and EBI dosage to determine optimal levels for pretreatment. The authors also varied the concentration of hydrolytic enzymes, resolving that no concentration of enzymes could effectively hydrolyze the lignocellulose without proper pretreatment. Scanning electron microscopy and X-ray diffraction verified that the EBI was causing the physical changes in the rice straw.

Compared to the control samples of untreated rice straw, EBI-treated rice straw increased glucose yields from 5.1% to 43.1% after hydrolysis for 24 hours, and from 22.6% to 52.1% after hydrolysis for 132 hours. However, these yields were lower than other physical and chemical pretreatment methods such as dilute-acid, ammonia fiber explosion, and soaking in aqueous ammonia, documented in previous literature.

Alec Faggen

Revolutionizing Methane Production and Carbon Capture via Algal Biomass

Biomass production from food sources has been shown to increase greenhouse gas emissions and other pollutants through land use changes (Stucki *et al.* 2009). In order to provide a sustainable source of biofuel in the future, biomass production must be enacted that does not exacerbate climate problems or compete with food production. Microalgae have recently been targeted as great potential sources for biofuel. The two main problems for this type of production are an efficient means to grow the algae and an efficient means to convert the algae into useful energy. One potential clean energy source is methane. New technologies are currently being explored to make methane production from algae more efficient.

Stucki and colleagues working at the Laboratory for Energy and Materials Cycles in Switzerland have revolutionized biofuel production via algal biomass. The authors employ a two-phase process in which they first grow the algae in a photo-bioreactor and later convert it into methane. The methane produced is pipeline quality synthetic natural gas.

The authors' first process ameliorates the issue of climate change by using carbon dioxide emissions for algae cultivation. The subsequent process converts these algae into biofuel via a catalytic hydrothermal gasification process in supercritical water. The hydrothermal process also succeeds in recycling the algal organic matter back into nutrients for algae growth. These processes are experimentally designed to be sustainable whereby all heat demands are satisfied by heat recovery or by combustion of some of the methane gas product.

This methodology successfully lessens fossil fuel dependence, without disturbing food production. It is especially useful because the yields do not depend on algal products such as lipids, which are limited. A challenge to the procedure and area for future study is the protection of the catalyst from the toxic effects of the heteroatoms present in the algal biomass.

Conclusions

Unfortunately due to certain negative aspects of first generation biofuels, the entire biofuel industry is being heavily resisted, especially in small, environmentally friendly countries (Naik *et al.* 2010). Although there are certainly challenges and impediments to successful production, first generation biofuels are nevertheless necessary to prepare infrastructure that will later assist in the transition to second-generation biofuels. Although current investments of second generation fuels are encouraging, technology seems to be developing at a steady enough rate such that the disadvantages of first generation biofuels will not be passed over, but used in combination biorefineries until second generation fuel problems are more effectively resolved.

References Cited

Agnew, R., Ming, C., Lu, M., 2009. Making Biodiesel from Recycled Cooking Oil Generatd in Campus Dining Facilities. Mary Ann Liebert, Inc. 2, 303–307.

Bak, J., Ko, J., Han, Y., Lee, B., Choi, I., Kim, K., 2009. Improved enzymatic hydrolysis yield of rice straw using electron beam irradiation pretreatment. Bioresource Technology 100, 1285–1290.

Bayer, T., Widmaier, D., Temme, K., Mirsky, E., Santi, D., Voigt, C., 2009. Synthesis of Methyl Halides from Biomass Using Engineered Microbes. Journal of The American Chemical Society 131, 6508–8615.

Chakrabortty, A., 2008. Internal World Bank study – biomass caused food crisis. http://www.guardian.co.uk/environment/2008/jul/03/biofuels.renewableenergy.

Cherubini, F., Jungmeier, G., 2009. LCA of a biorefinery concept producing bioethanol, bioenergy, and chemicals from switchgrass. The International Journal of Life Cycle Assessment 15, 53–66.

Demirbas, M., 2006. Current technologies for biomass conversion into chemicals and fuels. Energy Sour Part A 28, 1181–8.

Demirbas, A., 2009. Political, economic and environmental impacts of biofuels: A review. Applied Energy 86, S108–S117.

Dohleman, F., Heaton, E., Leakey, A., Long, S., 2009. Does greater leaf-level photosynthesis explain the larger solar energy conversion efficiency of miscanthus relative to switchgrass? Plant, Cell and Environment 32, 1525–1537.

Eisberg, N., 2006. Harvesting energy. Chem Ind 17, 24–25.

Gouveia, L., Oliveira, A., 2009. Microalgae as a raw material for biofuels production. Journal of Industrial Microbiology & Biotechnology 36, 269–274.

Haung, H., Ramaswamy, S., Tschirner, U., Ramarao, B., 2008. A review of separation technologies in current and future biorefineries. Sep Purif Technol 62, 1–21.

Laursen, W., 2006. Students take a green initiative. Chem Eng, 32–4.

Ma, F., Hanna, M., 1999. Biodiesel production: a review. Bioresource Technology 70, 1–15.

Mabee, W., Gregg, D., Saddler, J., 2005. Assessing the emerging biorefinery sector in Canada. Appl Biochem Biotechnol 121, 765–78.

Alec Faggen

Meher, L., Vidyasagar, D., Naik, S., 2006. Technical aspects of biodiesel production by transesterification—a review. Renewable Sustain Energy Rev 10, 248–68.
Naik, S., Goud, V., Rout, P., Dalai, A., 2010. Production of first and second generation biofuels: A comprehensive review. Renewable & Sustainable Energy 14, 578–597.
Osamu, K., Carl, H., 1989. Biomass Handbook. Gordon Breach Science Publisher.
Sabourin-Provost, G., Hallenbeck, P., 2009. High yield conversion of a crude glycerol fraction from biodiesel production to hydrogen by photofermentation. Bioresource Technology 100, 3513–3517.
Sims, R., Mabee, W., Saddler, J., Taylor, M., 2010. An overview of second generation biofuel technologies. Bioresource Technology 101, 1570-1580.
Sheehan, J., Aden, A., Paustian, K., Killian, K., Brenner, J., Walsh, M., Nelson, R., 2004. Energy and environmental aspects of using corn stover for fuel ethanol. J. Indust. Ecol. 7, 117–146.
Stucki, S., Vogel, F., Ludwig, C., Haiduc, A., Brandenberger, M., 2009. Catalytic gasification of algae in supercritical water for biofuel production and carbon capture. Energy Environmental Science 2, 535–541.
WWI, 2007. Biofuels for transport: global potential and implications for agriculture, Worldwatch Institute, Report Prepared for the German Federal Ministry of Food, Agriculture and Consumer Protection.

12. A Sustainable Approach to Biofuels

Jenny Ward

Cellulosic biofuels production is an increasingly popular, although controversial, alternative solution to finding a sustainable fuel source. Researchers have already uncovered many of the costs and benefits, both environmental and economic, of substituting conventional gasoline and diesel with plant-based fuels. The various advantages and disadvantages of producing biofuels become apparent at all stages of production; plant growth, processing, transformation into fuel, transportation, and actual usage of biofuels in vehicles. Because of the range of possibilities for biofuels to exhibit their beneficial and detrimental effects, researchers have found that the best way to determine the sustainability of biofuels is to employ a life cycle analysis (LCA) approach when studying their production. An LCA approach means taking into account the entire system involved in creating and using biofuels. All stages of biofuel existence are examined, from growth and harvest, to oil extraction, to fuel processing, to vehicle emissions. Among the factors considered are land use practices, fertilizer composition, carbon sequestration rates, net energy and water usage, logistics emissions, and the implications of biofuels production on local communities and global food prices. Depending on the unique combination of these factors, a thorough LCA of biofuels may or may not prove their incorporation into the global fuel market to be sustainable.

Scientists have experimentally altered different stages of biofuels production in attempts to improve its sustainability. For example, researchers have compared different land sources for cultivating feedstock used to produce biofuels, various plant species and non-plant sources used for feedstock, and a range of fuel blends that incorporate varying levels of biofuels. Different studies have also examined the impact biofuels trade will have on global food markets and the social effects of biofuels production on less-developed countries, which currently cultivate the majority of feedstock used for biofuels production. The findings of these studies vary in their conclusions because biofuels have only recently been examined in significant detail. There are not yet uniformly accepted scientific processes for determining the most sustainable life cycle of biofuels production. Conducting a true LCA for biofuels is a complex and sometimes unachievable task; it is difficult to consider every indirect contribution to climate change that the production of biofuels might invoke. Overall however, most researchers agree that to label biofuels as a sustainable source of energy, their economic, social, and environmental implications must be investigated.

Cellulosic Biofuel Production is Cost-Effective when Indirect Greenhouse Gas Emissions are Minimized

Cellulosic biofuel is increasingly considered as a solution to meeting low carbon fuel standards in the 21st century, but there are costs and benefits, both economic and environmental, of biofuels production. Melillo *et al.* (2009) assess the life cycle costs of using biofuel as an energy source, including the effects of land-use changes, net fluctuations in both direct and indirect greenhouse gas (GHG) emissions, and measures of carbon intensity (CI), or according to the authors, the "simultaneous consideration of the potential of net carbon intake through enhanced management of poor or degraded lands, nitrous oxide (N_2O) emissions that would accompany increased use of fertilizer, environmental effects on terrestrial carbon storage, and consideration of the economics of land conversion." Based on indirect emissions and CI data from different scenarios of biofuels production, the process is beneficial only if existing managed land, rather than natural land, is used for the process as much as possible, and if N_2O fertilizer use is managed properly.

Jerry M. Melillo and colleagues compared two different cases of biofuel production. The first case provided for the economically sound conversion of natural lands into biofuel growth sources; the second relied on existing managed land for biofuels production. Using a computable general equilibrium (CGE) model and a processed-based terrestrial biogeochemistry model, Melillo *et al.* estimated the projected changes in global land cover, the direct and indirect effects on projected cumulative land carbon flux, and the partitioning of greenhouse gas balance among fossil fuel abatement and fertilizer N_2O emissions for each case. In addition, they created a CI index that measured the accumulation and emission of direct land carbon, indirect land carbon, and fertilizer N_2O during increasing time periods from 2000 to 2100.

Each observation revealed the benefits of producing biofuels using existing managed land rather than converting natural land to biofuel harvest. Through this practice, less depletion of natural forests will occur, which in turn will increase the carbon sequestration from the air by trees. Furthermore, preventing deforestation coupled with an increased use of pastures, shrubland, and savannah for biofuels production will decrease the initial carbon accumulation and increase the eventual carbon sequestration.

Although initial increases in GHG emissions and carbon accumulation will occur in each cellulosic biofuel production land-use case, these negative effects precede eventual reductions in atmospheric carbon during the latter part of the century. This occurs most significantly when existing managed land is reused, which minimizes the indirect emissions gains associated with more environmentally detrimental land-use changes.

A Sustainable Approach to Biomass Feedstock Production in Nebraska

Biomass growth for biofuel use can be an economic and environmentally sustainable production if land and water resources are used efficiently. The available marginal land and degraded water sources in Nebraska can be used to improve the productivity of biomass growth (Gopalakrishnan *et al.* 2009). Utilizing marginal land prevents land allotted for food production from being converted to biofuel growth, making biofuels production more economically and socially feasible. Incorporating degraded water resources into the irrigation of biomass feedstock will improve the productivity of biofuel growth and contribute to the decontamination of the Nebraska watershed. After a spatial analysis of Nebraska's landscape, Gopalakrishnan *et al.* concluded that an approach to biomass feedstock growth that considers the energy, agricultural, and environmental sectors as part of an overall system is the way to achieve sustainable biofuels production.

Gayathri Gopalakrishnan and colleagues used geographic information software to develop a map displaying the marginal land and degraded water sources in Nebraska. Road and river networks and two sample biorefinery locations (one where marginal land is a significant resource and one where it is not) were included in the map. Four types of marginal land were observed in this study: 1) agricultural land that has been abandoned or set aside for conservation purposes; 2) buffer strips along roads; 3) buffer strips along rivers or riparian buffers; and 4) brownfield sites. The degraded water resources studied were groundwater sources contaminated by nitrate and wastewater from livestock farms and municipal treatment facilities. The purpose of this study was to determine which combination of resources provided the most economically and environmentally sustainable process for growing feedstock for biofuels.

After analysis, Gopalakrishnan *et al.* concluded that for the sample biorefinery located near significant marginal land resources, marginal agricultural land provided the greatest percentage of feedstock requirements, but both roadway and riparian sites also contributed percentages. The sample biorefinery located far from marginal land resources obtained the highest percentage of feedstock requirements from minor roadway and riparian buffer sites, and very little from marginal agricultural land. In both cases, using degraded water resources as irrigation significantly increased the percent yield of feedstock. These results indicated that a systems approach to biofuels production can enable more croplands to be used for food production, reduce energy used for transportation by intensifying the biofuel potential of buffer sites, and reduce need for nitrate fertilizers by using degraded water as irrigation. It was speculated that a decrease in net greenhouse gas emissions would accompany a systems approach to biofuels production due to the reductions in nitrous oxide emissions from fertilizer and from the increased carbon sequestration by biomass feedstock grown. Further investigations in these areas need to be conducted, however Gopalakrishnan *et al.* concluded that a systems approach has the potential to improve the economic, social, and environmental sustainability of biofuels.

Sustainability of Biodiesel Production using Palm Oil versus Jatropha Oil for Feedstock

Palm oil and oil from *Jatropha curcas L.* can be mass produced in Malaysia and used for biofuels production. Lam *et al.* (2009) used a life cycle assessment (LCA) process to compare the sustainability of this process using each oil for feedstock. During the LCA, they considered the plantation and cultivation of each crop, the milling (extraction) of each oil, and the conversion of each oil into biodiesel. The sustainability measures were based on land area required, net energy consumption, greenhouse gas (GHG) emissions, and CO_2 sequestration. The debate over whether jatropha oil (a non-food crop) should be used instead of palm oil (a food crop) to prevent food prices from rising was also considered. After the LCA for each case was conducted, the authors found that palm oil required less land, produced a higher output to input energy ratio, and enabled larger amounts of CO_2 to be sequestered. Thus palm oil is a much more environmentally efficient feedstock for biodiesel production than jatropha oil (Lam *et al.* 2009).

The authors collected data from recent literature reviews and statistics from the Malaysian Palm Oil Board (MPOB), the Indonesian Palm Oil Board (IPOB), and various previous studies. For the plantation stage of the LCA, they analyzed yields of oil per tonne of fresh fruit bunch harvested, fertilizer components, energy and water requirements, peatland use, and CO_2 emissions. For the milling stage, the authors compared oil yields from extraction, energy and water requirements, and GHG emissions. For the conversion of oil to biodiesel, they compared methanol to oil ratios, percentage yields of biodiesel and glycerol, electricity and steam usage, and CO_2 emissions from production and transportation of biodiesel.

The Malaysian government is interested in using jatropha oil to supplement palm oil as a feedstock for biofuels production because jatropha is drought-resistant, able to grow on wasteland, and is not cultivated for food use, thus it would settle the "food versus fuel debate." Despite the advantages it may seem to have, Lam *et al.* found that jatropha oil is less efficient than palm oil when cultivated as feedstock for biodiesel production. Using palm oil as feedstock for the production of 1 tonne of biodiesel would require 0.28 ha of land per year, while using jatropha oil as feedstock would require 0.61 ha per year, a 118% increase. Agroforestry techniques and livestock crop integrations cannot be applied to jatropha plantations like they can to palm oil plantations, making jatropha less sustainable. Production of 1 tonne of palm oil biodiesel has an output to input energy ratio of 2.27, while jatropha oil biodiesel has a ratio of 1.92. These data indicate that 1 tonne of palm oil biofuel would provide 43% more energy than 1 tonne of jatropha oil biofuel. Finally, after comparing emissions from fertilizers, energy usage, land usage, and logistics, both palm oil biodiesel production and jatropha oil biodiesel production processes were found to emit about 11,000 kg CO_2 eq/tonne biodiesel each. When using palm oil however, the amount of CO_2 sequestered was almost 20 times more than when using jatropha oil.

Overall, palm oil was significantly more sustainable than jatropha oil as a feedstock source for biodiesel production in Malaysia. To determine the true sustainability of biodiesel, a life cycle analysis of the feedstock-to-fuel process must be considered in addition to the immediate social and environmental effects of biofuels production.

Sustainable Biofuels Production using Composted Urban Waste as Fertilizer

Biofuels production is a sustainable source of renewable energy, however the use of nitrogen-heavy fertilizers greatly increases its net energy consumption and CO_2 emissions. This study revealed that by using composted waste from urban, municipal, and industrial sources as fertilizer for biomass feedstock, the environmental and economic sustainability of biofuels production could be greatly improved (Butterworth 2009).

The author uses the Bates family farm, a member of the Land Network group, as an example of a farm that relies on photosynthetic carbon capture and storage (PCCS) to reduce its net carbon emissions to almost zero by using urban 'wastes' as fertilizer for oilseed rape. This crop is harvested using noninvasive practices and then converted into biodiesel, producing enough biofuel to satisfy all the energy needs of the farm. The article compares the closed energy loops for different methods of turning crops into biofuels: using mineral fertilizers, using wastes, and using PCCS in soils. Finally, nitrogen leakage levels from 'controlled waste' fertilizers were measured and compared among several other farm sites within the Land Network.

PCCS is a practical, economically feasible way to sustainably produce both biofuels and cash crops on a farm. Ten percent of the Bates' farm is dedicated to oilseed growth for biofuels production, and the other 90% of the land is used to harvest food crops. About 300 tpa of 'waste' from local municipal and industrial sources can make 250 tonnes of compost, which is enough to fertilize 1 ha of oilseed rape. In turn, this 1 ha of land can produce 1 tonne of biofuel, which when burned, emits 5 tonnes of CO_2. The PCCS process in the soil however, sequesters 70 tonnes of CO_2, resulting in a net storage of 65 tonnes of CO_2 in the ground, forming a carbon sink called a 'humus'. This facilitated process used on the farm mimics the naturally occurring process in the soil between hyphae and plant roots.

The waste sources are in close proximity to the farm, reducing logistics expenses and making this process more economic. Also, the harvest produces all the biofuel the Bates' need to power all their other processes on the farm, making the system environmentally sustainable. Furthermore, at most farms the amount of nitrogen that leaks into the ground from the compost is negligible, especially when compared to the amounts leaked by mineral fertilizers.

Overall, the use of urban wastes as compost for sustainable biofuels production should explode as an environmentally friendly fertilizer source, once restrictive environmental legislations are overcome and techniques to monitor the land onto which wastes are recycle are improved.

Varying Emissions from Buses using Biodiesel in Madrid, Spain

Lopéz et al. (2009) compared two types of emissions after-treatments on urban buses in Madrid. The first treatment utilizes selective catalytic reduction (SCR) combined with urea, and the second uses exhaust gas recirculation (EGR) with a particulate filter. The effects on greenhouse gas emissions of these two treatments were studied on buses using diesel fuel, fuel that is 20% biodiesel (B20), and 100% biodiesel fuel (B100). Reductions in carbon monoxide (CO), CO_2, unburned hydrocarbon (THC), nitrogen oxides (NO_x), and particulate matter (PM) emissions, and decreases in fuel consumption varied according to treatment technology and fuel type.

The authors used a driving cycle, designed by the Madrid Municipal Transit Company, which was developed for fuel economy and emission testing with onboard equipment. The Horiba OBS 2200 measurement device used collected data under real driving conditions. PM emissions data were measured using laser technology. Measurements for each fuel type were obtained from five test runs within the driving cycle.

Lopéz *et al.* observed that between the two after-treatment technologies, SCR produced greater reductions in CO_2 and NO_x emissions, while EGR performed better according to CO and PM emissions reductions. More importantly, varying trends were seen when diesel and biodiesel powered buses were compared. Both the B20 and B100 fuels caused greater NO_x and CO_2 emissions and consumed more fuel than regular diesel buses, but the biodiesel buses did have a greater reduction in particulate matter emissions. Despite increases in some greenhouse gas emissions, the authors recommend that biodiesel still be used as an alternative fuel source because "it is non-fossil, biodegradable, CO_2-neutral, and its combustion is sulphur oxide free".

Carbon Emissions from Biodiesel Engines in Brazil compared to Other Fuels

Coronado *et al.* (2009) examined the greenhouse gas (GHG) emissions from engines running on biodiesel, derived from both soybean and frying oil, as compared to the GHG emissions from gasoline, diesel, and anhydrous ethanol engines in Brazil. The latter three are currently the predominantly used fuels in the Brazilian transportation market. Pure biodiesel and mixtures of biodiesel and conventional diesel were considered.

The authors used data from the Brazilian Association of Automotive Vehicle Manufacturers and the Brazilian Department of Transit to develop an idea of the transportation system in the nation. CO_2 emissions for each fuel were reported in tons of CO_2 per m^3 of fuel. The emissions for various blends of biodiesel and biodiesel from various sources were also compared. Using the vehicle data from the last five years, the tons of CO_2 emitted per year for Brazil were calculated. Finally, Coronado *et al.* projected the GHG emissions for pure diesel, 20% biodiesel (B20), and 100% biodiesel (B100) vehicles in Brazil for the next fifteen years.

Ethanol fuel emitted the least amount of carbon (1.511 ton CO_2 per m^3 fuel), followed by gasoline (2.316 ton CO_2 per m^3 fuel), soybean-derived biodiesel (2.480 ton CO_2 per m^3 fuel), and frying oil-derived biodiesel (2.492 ton CO_2 per m^3 fuel); diesel fuel was the worst contributor to GHG emissions (2.683 ton CO_2 per m^3 fuel). Although when considering just vehicle emissions, biofuels seem to have higher carbon footprints, the authors explain that biomass-derived fuels reduce the net atmospheric carbon content because, unlike fossil fuels, they rapidly recycle carbon from the atmosphere into fuel. Photosynthetic biomass draws CO_2 from the atmosphere, then the combustion of biofuels releases CO_2 back into the air. This rapid turnaround is much more carbon efficient than burning fossil fuels, which

Jenny Ward

releases carbon that took millions of years to sequester from the atmosphere.

Coronado and colleagues also show that as the percentage of biofuels in diesel/biodiesel blends increases, the CO_2 emissions caused by using these fuels decreases. They predict that by phasing out diesel and other main fuels, and phasing in biodiesel use in Brazil's vehicular fleet, the nation will improve its environmental and economic state.

Comparison Between Biofuels and Hydrogen as Alternative Energy Sources

The European Union (EU) considers both biofuels and hydrogen as viable sources of energy to replace fossil fuels. Sobrino *et al.* (2010) examined, from an economic perspective, the advantages and disadvantages of replacing fossil fuels with biofuels or hydrogen in European vehicles. Although each alternative source of energy has different reasons for being a plausible fuel replacement, the authors found more reasons for hydrogen to be the more environmentally friendly and economically sound choice.

The authors first discussed the different reasons for promoting the use of biofuels and hydrogen, which include: reducing the EU's reliance on foreign oil, constraining the price growth of petroleum, cutting down greenhouse gas emissions, and generating income for the agricultural sector. Current EU policies in place to mandate the use of alternative fuels were also identified. Finally, the benefits and difficulties of using hydrogen to power vehicles was analyzed and compared to biofuels and fossil fuels.

Sobriono *et al.* found that the best way to compare efficiency of alternative fuels to gasoline and gasoil was to study the price per unit of energy on the lower heating value (LHV) of each source. This figure indicated that hydrogen was a more efficient source of alternative fuel than biofuels and gasoline. Although biofuels may boost the agriculture industry and decrease CO_2 emissions form cars, their production still requires raw materials to be imported from non-EU nations, consumes energy and releases greenhouse gases, and is not cost effective yet.

Hydrogen, produced by electrolysis of seawater, can be used in internal combustion engines or in fuel cells. This process does require an input of energy, and the authors discovered a wide range of efficiency when using hydrogen as an alternative source of energy. Its use is most cost effective and least environmentally harmful when wind generators and hydraulic or nuclear power plants provide the energy needed for electrolysis.

Finally, the authors identify the policies in the EU such as Directive 2003/30/EC, which calls for 5.75% of fuels used for transportation to be biofuels by the end of 2010 (Sobrino *et al.* 2010). Some of these policies seem too ambitious because the production of biofuels and hydrogen fuel is more expensive than current methods for obtaining fossil fuels. Gas prices however, are heavily taxed, and these taxes could be removed from alternative sources of energy, making them not only a better environmental choice, but also a more affordable option.

Globalization of Biofuels Market Requires New Forms of Environmental Regulation

P. J. Mol (2010) identifies the advantages and controversies of biofuels production and consumption throughout the world. While growing concerns over fossil fuel use and climate change have boosted the biofuels market, issues of sustainability, agricultural competition, and food insecurity for less developed nations have sparked debate over the negative effects of biofuels. Mol discusses how biofuels trade crosses geographical borders and poverty lines, thus individual state authority over the environmental and social impacts of biofuels use is no longer substantial. He concludes that this globalization of biofuels must be regulated by a combination of private market authorities, moral and scientific authorities, and other forms of hybrid, non-state environmental authorities.

After dedscribing the current trends and controversies surrounding biofuels, Mol reviews the changing nature of authority, both at the state level and the global level. Globalization has transitioned environmental authority away from nation or state-based power, to authorities that cover larger areas, such as the European Union. Also, non-political forms of environmental authority have begun to rise, such as scientific research consensuses and the moral authorities of environmental non-governmental organizations.

Mol concludes that all these authorities must collaborate to effectively regulate biofuels to ensure that they are a "fair fuel." Fair fuels "are fuels that fulfill social and environmental conditionalities throughout the production chain" (Mol 2010). More inquiries are needed to discover the most effective methods for regulating sustainable biofuels. Developing environmental authorities must integrate "representation, deliberative interactions, transparency, and accountability measures" (Mol 2010) to establish effective control in the globalized biofuels market.

Conclusions

Although it may not be clear what is the most successful method of producing biofuels, their promise as a way to mitigate climate change while maintaining our current transportation habits is apparent. Researchers have established that it is important to employ a life cycle analysis approach in determining the sustainability of biofuels production. Prevailing science has proven that preventing destruction of

Jenny Ward

natural land and carbon rich land, such as dense forests, is important when growing and harvesting biomass used for feedstock. Studies have also shown that there are many sources of feedstock that can be used in biofuels production; some are more environmentally sustainable, such as palm oil, while others are more socially sustainable, for example jatropha oil or composted urban wastes, because they do not impact food prices or disrupt local agricultural communities. Finally, by applying universal standards for biofuels trade and consumption, global political leaders can enhance their potential for success. Further investigation is necessary before biofuels can be adopted as a mainstream fuel source and used by the general population. Additional research will reveal the most sustainable methods of biofuels production; currently we only know that they have the potential to reduce greenhouse gas emissions and prevent further increases in climate change.

References Cited

Butterworth, W. R., 2009. Sustainable biofuel production derived from urban waste using PSCC. Biofuels, Bioproducts, and Biorefining 3, 299–304

Coronado, Christian Rodriguez, Andrade de Carvalho, João, Silveira, José Luz., 2009. Biodiesel CO_2 emissions: A comparison with the main fuels in the Brazilian market. Fuel Processing Technology. 90, 204–211

Fernando Hernández Sobrino, Carlos Rodríguez Monroy, José Luís Hernández Pérez., 2010. Critical analysis on hydrogen as an alternative to fossil fuels and biofuels for vehicles in Europe. Renewable and Sustainably Energy Reviews 14, 772–780

Gopalakrishnan, G., Negri, M., Wang, M., Wu, M., Snyder, S., LaFreniere, L., 2009. Biofuels, Land, and Water: A Systems Approach to Sustainability. Environmental Science and Technology 43, 6094–6100

Lam, Man K., Lee, Keat T., Mohamed, Abdul R., 2009. Life Cycle Assessmet for the Production of Biodiesel: A Case Study in Malaysia for Palm Oil versus Jatropha Oil. Biofuels, Bioproducts, and Biorefining 3, 601–612

Lopéz, José María, and Felipe Jiménez, Francisco Aparicio, and Nuria Flores., 2009. On-road emissions from urban buses with SCR + Urea and EGR + DPF systems using diesel and biodiesel. Transportation Research Part D: Transport and Environment 14, 1–5

Melillo, J., Reilly, J., Kicklighter, D., Gurgel, A., Cronin, T., Paltsev, S., Felzer, B., Wang, X., Sokolov, A., Schlosser, C., 2009. Indirect Emissions from Biofuels: How Important? Science 326, 1397–1399

Mol, P. J., 2010. Environmental authorities and biofuel controversies. Environmental Politics 19, 61–79

13. Re-evaulating the Implications of Expanding the Biofuels Industry

Elena Davert

As the world continues to face changes in climate, population, and international relations, global energy use will be forced to adapt accordingly. Because a continued reliance on fossil fuels has been deemed unsustainable due to the dwindling sources and taxing effects on the environment, new scientific focus has been directed to investigating the possibility of biofuels as a viable supplement or replacement for fossil fuels in the future. However, expanding the biofuel industry to accommodate global fuel demands is a complex goal because it will augment several preexisting environmental challenges associated with industrialized farming; the resources required for growing and processing many biofuel feedstocks will place extra pressure on agricultural issues such as water resource allocation, land use, pesticide use, implementation of genetically modified organisms, crop biodiversity, food security, and livestock grazing. Because the extent of these pressures directly impacts the cost-benefit analysis of the biofuel industry, accurately evaluating the economic, social, and environmental costs of biofuels is crucial to determining their sustainability.

Although most mass agricultural operating systems function solely on a 'bottom-line' economic basis, socioeconomic concerns such as pollution, lowered nutritional content in food, increasing numbers of 'superfarms', and reduced biodiversity are all negative externalities absorbed by society and thus are not accounted for as losses in economic models (Hanson and Hendrickson 2009). Without accounting for these socioeconomic costs, evaluations of the agricultural industry portray economic growth and increased productivity as having few negative consequences. In order for agricultural practices to be sustainable, more emphasis must be placed on preservation of the natural productivity and quality of land, as well as individual farm-level management and integrated onsite energy uses, such as biofuels, that will promote agricultural stewardship instead of exploitation.

In addition to changing general agricultural practices involved in the biofuel industry, region-specific effects of biofuel crops must be calculated to understand the feasibility of biofuels in different locations. Initial studies of the biofuel industry have used incomplete or narrow-scoped data to make wide-sweeping generalizations about the possibilities of global biofuel use (Johnston *et al.* 2009). In order to combat both over- and under-estimations of costs and viability, new geographically-specific models are necessary for accurately appraising biofuels. In a Brazilian case study, a new spatially explicit model projects the effects on the Amazon due to increased biofuel production that accounts for land-use changes as well as local government subsidies that clarify the actual costs of converting crop and grazing land to biofuel production areas (Lapola *et al.* 2009). By considering geographically specific characteristics of the biofuel industry, Lapola *et al.* were able to identify the need for institutional environmental enforcement between biofuel growers and other agricultural sectors strengthened by the Brazilian government. In a study in South Dakota, geographically considerate models have also highlighted the importance of tailored regional analysis in order to account for soil quality in a number of climates and environmental conditions that would affect the overall sustainability of a potential biofuel production site.

Not only are geographically-specific models an important step in evaluating the biofuel industry, but so is defining the costs and benefits considered within those specific system boundaries. Although there has been a large effort to perform fully comprehensive Life Cycle Analysis (LCA) of the costs and benefits associated with the entire biofuel production process, inconsistencies among various LCA data have led to a wide range of inaccurate results. Davis *et al.* (2009) suggest that because the biofuel industry involves aspects of science, economics, politics, and engineering, that future LCA should not only include input from experts from all these fields but should also have standardized terminology through which they can all easily communicate. Many recent biofuel appraisals have begun to use this combination of interdisciplinary information to increase the accuracy of their results. By combining the efforts of engineers and plant scientists, a Malaysian study was able to examine several different meathods of biofuel combustion that work most efficiently with the banana plant's physical makeup (Tock *et al.* 2009); this type of coordination would not be possible without expert input. Similarly, DeHaan *et al.* (2009) combined socioeconomic information—data regarding the US's reliance on the Grain Belt—as well as horticultural expertise—data regarding soil quality and grassland biodiversity—to determine combinations of switchgrass that would efficiently yield the most biomass for biofuel feedstock. Finally, one of the newer areas of biofuel research includes complex insights into microbiological systems of organisms that can break down organic matter more efficiently than man-made processes (Rude and Schirmer 2009).

Whether it be rethinking agricultural land use to encompass new space for biofuels, creating geographically explicit models to account for diverse topography and soil quality, or working to include information about biological systems at a microbial level, the new movement in the biofuel industry is pushing for the most inclusive analyses possible.

Bottom-line Economics No Longer the Most Efficient Means of Making Decisions in the Agricultural Industry

Because of current trends in population growth and climate change, the agricultural industry faces competing needs for both higher production capacities as well as more environmentally sustainable practices. These population and environmental transformations have presented new challenges in animal and crop agriculture, industrialization, globalization, fossil-fuel energy use, development of biofuels, and water availability (Hanson and Hendrickson 2009). While productivity will continue to be a major factor in food production systems, bottom-line agricultural production does not benefit the US in a rapidly changing global marketplace that calls for more sustainable agricultural systems.

Within the last century in the US, the agricultural industry's drastic reduction in its workforce as well as in its contribution to the GDP have led to increased farm size and land degradation. This industrialization of agriculture has led to farm consolidation into fewer individual operations, and given rise to new 'super-farms.' Although large farm corporations are more efficient by combining all stages of production, processing, and distribution of products, many of their resource-intensive systems are characterized by an increasing lack of biodiversity, declining soil organic carbon, high levels of pollution, and heavy reliance on fossil fuels.

The use of fossil fuels has been a primary impact in the agriculture industry because of rising fuel prices. High fuel costs increase costs of transportation, fertilizer, and animal feed production. If future agricultural production aims to be sustainable, it will no longer be focused solely on food and feed markets, but will include other outlets like energy and industrial uses. For example, developing a farm-based bioenergy program not only helps environmentally sustainable community efforts, but also enhances the local economy by providing jobs and lowering energy costs.

In addition to environmental concerns, socioeconomic and health effects have also increased. Socioeconomic concerns such as federal regulation, disparate farmer incomes, disappearance of the midsized farm, and urban sprawl are all negative externalities that are not absorbed as direct costs into the agricultural systems, and thus are not calculated as losses in current economic models. Trends of overuse of antibiotics in animal production, nitrate and pesticide contamination of water and food, and release of toxic residues into our food supply are also results of industrialized farming. Unfortunately, health consequences are usually handled by reactive rather than proactive approaches because they require less initial effort.

All of these problems have been overlooked because agricultural industrialization in the US has focused almost entirely on the economic bottom line. As the authors note, however, that bottom-line economics do not always favor US producers because other countries can often produce agricultural commodities more cheaply. The authors argue that if bottom-line economics are neither economically nor environmentally beneficial, then sustainable methods are the best investments at this point.

Sustainable agriculture can be defined as implementing methods that manage on-farm resources efficiently in order to minimize adverse effects on the environment and people. It also encompasses the preservation of the natural productivity and quality of land, water, and overall rural communities. With economic growth and industry mergers no longer the focus, sustainable agriculture aims to achieve marginal profits while still conserving the natural resource base, minimizing negative externalities, improving farm-level management, and enhancing socioeconomic viability of rural communities. In order for this to work, agricultural producers need to respond to environmental changes by reducing risk through management flexibility. Holistic management and integrated agricultural systems are approaches in which whole-farm strategies and technologies are organized to help producers manage enterprises in a synergistic manner for greater profitability and natural resource stewardship.

New Geographically-Explicit Agricultural Dataset Provides Most Accurate Estimates of Potential Production of Biofuels Worldwide

Although aggressive renewable energy policies have allowed for the immense growth of the biofuel industry, they have also exhausted surplus agricultural feedstocks and subsequently contributed to rapid commodity price increases in crops such as corn, soybeans, and rapeseed. The rapid expansion without heed to negative consequences can be attributed to simplistic yield tables frequently used to project the success of biofuel feedstocks that fail to consider geographic location and have overestimated yields by up to 100% (Johnston et al. 2009). With new spatially-explicit global agricultural datasets—M3 cropland datasets—as well as more accurate yield conversion methods, scientists are able to better describe total global biofuel production, and thus more accurately predict its potential as a sustainable energy source.

While some non-food-based biofuels such as algae-biodiesel and cellulosic ethanol are under consideration, at the moment the food-based biofuels are the only profitable alternatives to liquid fossil fuels currently being produced at an economic scale. In order to make the information about biofuels more accessible, yield tables have become crucial in translating complex differences between chemical analysis of multiple crops into understandable illustrations of their potential fuel volumes. It is often the case, however, that single yield estimates for a unique location are applied to global models, and specific units are not always appropriate for comparing different crops. Unfortunately, despite these shortcomings, the yield figures are so heavily relied on in scientific journals, policy reports, and even media articles, that many assume that the frequency with which the values are cited corresponds to their accuracy.

Johnston *et al.* address these issues by producing the most comprehensive report to date of global biofuel production potential, including crop area and yield statistics drawn from over 22,000 agricultural surveys, censuses, and statistical databases. Statistical datasets for ten ethanol crops (barley, cassava, maize, potato, rice, sorghum, sugarbeet, sugarcane, sweet potato, and wheat) and ten biodiesel crops (castor, coconut, cotton, mustard, oil palm, peanut, rapeseed, sesame, soybean, sunflower) were analyzed across 238 countries, territories, and protectorates, then converted to standardized units of liters-per-hectare. This standardization was achieved by multiplying current agricultural yields, percent oil content, and oil densities for each crop, as well as factoring in constant processing ratios and refining factors specific to different regions.

This detailed agricultural analysis shows that barley, cassava, castor, maize, rapeseed, and sunflower global biofuel yields were overestimated in some earlier studies by at least 100%, with wheat-ethanol and groundnut-biodiesel yields overestimated by 150% or more. By establishing that previously accepted biofuel yield estimates are highly unrealistic, the study illustrates the actual cost-benefit consequences of expanding cropland dedicated to its production. Resetting the expectations for global agricultural biofuel production and the required technology is important from an environmental standpoint because it will help more accurately frame the allocation of funding for alternative energy research.

Holistic Approach to Life Cycle Analysis for Accurate Appraisal of Biofuel Feedstocks

As research and development in the biofuel industry continue to increase, so does the necessity for accurate comparisons and appraisals of the fuels themselves. Although second-generation biofuels hold great promise as a supplemental energy supply, the ecological and environmental consequences cannot be fully understood without enhancing and standardizing life cycle analysis (LCA) (Davis *et al.* 2009). Because the currently incomplete datasets can cause significant variation in the estimates for both the energy yields and the greenhouse gasses (GHG) associated with biofuel production, including more ecological data and establishing uniform units of comparison are both key components of furthering the accuracy of comparable fuel analysis.

LCA is an all-inclusive account of the inputs and outputs of a production system, likened to a food web that traces the fluxes of energy throughout an ecosystem. In the case of biofuel production, the major inputs and outputs are energy requirements and net yields, economic costs and surpluses, and ecological feedstocks and environmental consequences. More specifically, the life-cycle inventory is a list of components assessed within an LCA for each step of the production chain; for biofuel LCA, the life-cycle inventory could include components such as manufacture and transport of fertilizers, pesticides, herbicides and seeds, to represent the inputs for step of feedstock production. However, not all life-cycle inventories include the same components even when the boundary for the analyzed system is same. The life-cycle inventory thereby influences the outcome of an LCA and can be manipulated in order to understand which components have the greatest effect on the calculation of GHG balances for various fuels. LCA results are also frequently used in political and economic applications such as cost-benefit analysis, so accurate and comprehensive scientific data are crucial to evaluating the ecological and economic sustainability of biofuel crops.

Davis *et al.* compared published biofuel studies that analyzed corn, switchgrass, miscanthus, and mixed temperate grasses using various methods LCA, and found that the reported net energy values (NEV) and fuel energy ratios (FER) had highly disparate ranges in the different studies. The authors also realized that even within reports regarding the same species, inconsistencies developed due to conflicting initial data. Not only did variation in life-cycle inventories produce discrepancies among the LCA reports, but only three studies included uncertainty estimates of inventory item values and many of the inventories were incomplete. The authors also found an alarming lack of actual plant science incorporated into the analysis, which had been ignored since many LCA applications are used for engineering and mathematical applications.

In addition, although topography, soil and climate variability within a region prevent the direct application of small-scale LCA data to larger areas, this was ignored in many of the reports and yielded inaccurate assessments. The authors also noted that many LCA analyses ignored the fact that fuel energy production is so closely influenced by economic and political interactions, and failed to communicate in common terminology to the professionals (engineers, economists, and policymakers) who work within other branches of the biofuel production system.

Second-generation biofuels have potential as alternate forms of energy, but the consequences of increasing the use of biofuels cannot be communicated without a transparent and standardized approach to LCA. By increasing collaboration among ecologists, economists, and engineers, a more holistic approach to constructing the inventories will lead to more accurate appraisals of biofuel potential.

New Comprehensive Estimates of Consequences of Direct and Indirect Land Use Changes in Brazilian Biofuel Industry More Accurately Highlight Necessary Policy Change

With the new increases in biofuel production around the world, attention must turn to the potential negative environmental impacts due to altered land use. Previous estimates of these consequences used models that were not geographically or ecologically specific and led to gross miscalculations. This case study in Brazil uses a spatially-explicit model to project the effects on the Amazon due to increased biofuel production and the resulting land-use changes caused by that expansion in 2020 (Lapola *et al.* 2009). New estimates reveal that current methods of land use allocation may create a carbon debt that would take up to 250 years to be repaid, an amount which overcomes the carbon sequestering benefits of biofuels over fossil fuels.

Currently, Brazil's government, in conjunction with the biofuel industry, is planning a large increase in the production of biofuels over the next 10 years. With the potential ethanol production increase of 35 x 10^9 liters in the 2003–2020 period, which equates to a projected indirect deforestation of 121,970 km^2 by 2020 there are clear concerns about measuring the consequences of the land-use changes (LUC) associated with this increase. Some previous studies focused on the direct land-use changes (DLUC) and the resulting "carbon debt" caused by replacing native habitats with biofuel crops, while others pointed to the probable indirect land-use changes (ILUC) in Brazil caused by future expansion of food and biofuel croplands in other countries such as the US. Although these studies showed that potential LUC must be taken into account to assess the efficacy of a given biofuel, they were neither spatially explicit, nor did they specifically consider competition between different land uses in view of concurrent food and biofuel demands. Because of this, calculations of the effects of LUC in previous studies are mostly underestimated or incomplete.

In order to create a fully comprehensive estimate of effects due to LUC, Lapola *et al.* used a new spatially explicit modeling framework to project the complete DLUC and ILUC resulting from Brazil's biofuel production targets for 2020. In addition to being spatially explicit, the new model also considers increasing food and livestock demands and their demands for land as well. The modeling framework comprises 3 major components: (1) a land-use/land-cover change model for land-use suitability assessment and allocation; (2) a partial equilibrium model of the Brazilian economy of the agricultural sector for future food demands, livestock demands, and advancement of crop yields due to improved technology; and (3) a dynamic global vegetation model for varying crop and grassland potential productivity driven by climate changes. The competition for land resources is also incorporated into the model based on an evaluation of suitability, hierarchical dominance of major land-use activities (settlement, crop

Elena Davert

cultivation, livestock grazing), and a land allocation algorithm which looks for land-use pattern stability over multiple land use objectives.

According to the new model, 88% of the DLUC (145,700 km²) due to sugarcane cropland increasing by 57,200 km² and soybean cropland increasing by 108,100 km² will take place in areas previously used as rangeland, and the amount of cropland area replaced by biofuels would reach 14,300 km². The resulting deforestation amounts to only 1,800 km² of forest and 2,000 km² of woody savanna; the required payback time for sugarcane DLUC emissions would be 4 years, while the DLUC carbon emissions for soybean biodiesel would not be paid back for at least 35 years. While these numbers are not overly daunting, the model revealed that ILUC could compromise the GHG savings from growing biofuels, mainly by pushing rangeland frontier into the Amazon forest and Brazilian Cerrado savanna. With an expansion of 121,970 km² of rangeland into forest areas, and 46,000 km² into other native habitats owing to the expansion of biofuel croplands, the required payback time for GHG emissions increases to 44 years for sugarcane crops and 246 years for soybean crops.

Ultimately, the dramatic costs of ILUC in this study raise the question of whether the common practice of reallocating all displaced rangeland should continue. Changes in current practices will be difficult because not only is animal acquisition heavily subsidized in Brazilian cattle ranching, especially in the Amazon region, but very few incentives are provided for the recovery of degraded pastures. Socioeconomic surveys also suggest that technological innovation and the intensification of livestock use inside the Amazon region may increase the attractiveness of cattle ranching and thus further deforestation. The authors argue that in order to avoid the undesired ILUC caused by biofuels, strategies for increased cooperation between the cattle ranching and biofuel-growing sectors should be implemented by the biofuel sector, and institutional links between these two sectors should be strengthened by the Brazilian government.

South Dakota Analysis Highlights the Importance of Geography in Biofuel Production

With the potential development of biorefineries that can utilize lignocellulosic feedstock, it is anticipated that South Dakota may be one of the leading producers of biofuel. In addition to examining historic trends of South Dakota crop production in order to calculate maximum yields, Rosentrater et al. (2009) also accounted for the level of residues that must remain in each field in order to reduce wind and water erosion, as well as maintain soil nutrients and carbon levels. While this paper specifically calculates and discusses South Dakota's potential biomass supplies, it also highlights the importance of tailored regional analysis for each geographic area of interest in the global biofuel industry. Responsibly examining biomass availability worldwide will require environmental and economic sustainability as a cooperative, rather than competitive venture.

South Dakota has become an area of interest in the biofuel industry because such a large percentage of the state is used for agriculture. As of 2007, the Economic Research Service within the United States Department of Agriculture reported that 90.2% of the total land area of the state (approximately 43.8 million acres) is dedicated to farmland, and of this land, approximately 50.3% is utilized as pastureland, while nearly 46.4% is dedicated to cropland. Currently, the three major row crops grown are corn, soybeans, and wheat—all of which have increased significantly in the last two decades—followed by smaller volume grains such as rye, oats, barley, sorghum, flax, sunflower, and hay.

In order to create a comprehensive understanding of the state's historic trends in crop production, yield data from each crop for the years 1950 through 2005 were compiled using the National Agricultural Statistics Service from the USDA. A prediction equation was crafted from the resulting historical trends in order to better estimate South Dakota's potential biofuel growth in the future. According to the model, the resulting projections of annual biomass yield show an increase from approximately 22 million tons in 2005 to nearly 38.9 million tons by 2025. However, these estimates quantify the total amount of biomass theoretically available if 100% of the biomass from each crop were harvested and removed, and there are many questions about how much can be sustainably removed. In order to provide a wide range of estimates in addressing this issue, the authors also examined the total biomass available for removal rates of 75%, 50%, and 25%.

Concerns have arisen because excessive biomass removal can lead to a reduction in organic soil matter and additional soil erosion losses. This decrease the overall productivity of the soil varies depending on initial soil quality as well as the crop removed, but soil compaction due to additional harvest operations needs to be considered across the board. When factoring in environmental implications of each crop in addition to potential yield projections for each county, sustainable annual biomass collection in South Dakota should vary between 20–50% of what is produced. By refining the analysis of feedstock production to examine biomass availability on a county-by-county basis, the authors have begun to account for the fact that biofuel feedstock production and its environmental consequences is a geographic-dependent quantity that ranges not only within a single state or country, but on a global scale as well.

Banana Biomass Proven to be a Feasible Source of Renewable Energy

Renewable energy is gaining popularity in Malaysia because of the country's new environmental policy and greater understanding of the possibilities of green energy

(Tock *et al.* 2009). Because Malaysia has many natural resources in agriculture and forestry, it has several sources for new carbon neutral biofuel feedstocks, such as banana biomass, which has been proven sufficient enough to produce more than half of the renewable energy requirement in the new national policy.

The nature of a banana plant's cultivation and structure make it an excellent candidate as a source of green energy. Because it can only produce fruit once during its lifetime, it loses its agricultural value after one season and leaves farmers with large quantities of biomass waste. Banana biomass is also ideal because of its widespread availability and high growth rates. Not only does its rapid growth and harvest rate of 10–12 months allow for a relatively constant supply of energy feedstock, but its sturdy, fibrous stalk structure—its pseudostem—and dense planting allow for a high yield of biomass per plant as well as per hectare. Currently, small percentages of banana pseudostems are either used as organic fertilizer, animal feed, or temporary plates and food storage; current methods of extracting banana fiber for textiles are far from economical. In addition to the banana pseudostems, rejected fruits make up about 30% of the total derived feedstock and are easy both to handle and to store. The fruit's peels are also a feedstock; a consideration in countries where bananas are a major food crop. When disposed of indiscriminately, rejected fruits and peels produce noxious gasses such as hydrogen sulphide and ammonia as they decompose, both of which are environmental hazards.

Currently there are two feasible methods for conversion of banana biomass into energy: thermal conversion (gasification), and biological conversion (anaerobic digestion). Gasification, or supercritical water gasification (SCWG), utilizes water that supercedes its critical temperature (647 K) and pressure (22.1 Mpa), exhibiting density and viscosity characteristics between water and steam, in order to create rapid reactions of organic compounds. Although SCWG avoids high processing costs associated with drying processes by using wet biomass, it is still a relatively expensive technology. Instead, anaerobic digestion is preferable because it can also directly process wet biomass, but at much lower temperatures and costs. This is accomplished by the fermentation of chopped and ground banana residue and waste that yields CO_2 (that has been fixed during the plant's lifetime), and larger amounts of methane than are produced by the fermentation of other fruits. Using these technologies, Malaysia has been able to produce 4.6% its total energy needs, just short of its 5% goal.

Because bananas produce a very clean form of biogas, and because the waste is normally dumped in landfills or nearby bodies of water, companies have access to virtually free feedstock for energy production. As the current technologies become more widespread for commercial use, the combustion of banana biomass may be able to meet the growing demand of energy from Malaysia as well as other developing tropical nations.

Biodiversity in Biofuel Cropland Responsible for Increasing Aboveground Biomass

In previous studies, high plant diversity systems have been more effective than fertilized monocultures in achieving carbon-negative biofuel feedstock, not only because of the low-input rates of fertilizer and pesticides, but also because of their high biomass yields. However, bicultures including nitrogen-fixing legumes have been found to be just as effective in increasing aboveground biomass as high-diversity grasslands in this most recent 11-year study (DeHaan *et al.* 2009). Therefore, these bicultures could be an adequate starting point for biofuel plant breeding programs and might later be combined into more species-diverse systems in order to rejuvenate natural ecosystem functions.

Two established approaches to perennial biofuel crop production are fertilized grass monocultures and low-input high-diversity grasslands. While high-yielding perennial grass varieties can be developed in controlled fertilized monocultures, breeding for yield in more natural high-diversity environments is much more difficult because of variation in planting densities, harvest dates, and genotype interactions among species. The initiation of biofuel crop breeding programs in low-input systems could be very successful, but the feasibility hinges on the level of plant species diversity required in the system. Because monocultures have been proven inadequate to achieve maximum sustained yield in low-input systems, agricultural scientists have been concerned with defining the minimum species number required to achieve aboveground high biomass production and yield stability, as well as if the presence of any particular species or functional groups aids in achieving maximum biomass yield with low input comparable to that of high diversity systems.

In order to mimic natural high-diversity systems, scientists monitored the number of perennial grassland species in 168 plots in Minnesota, in which species were selected at random from a pool of 18, and 1, 2, 4, 8, or 16 of these were planted in each plot. Initially, they found a strongly positive log-linear relationship between the number of species planted and average annual aboveground biomass, but there was also a large amount of unexplained variability between plots.

With additional analysis, it became evident that the presence of specific legume species had large effects on yield in the diversity experiments. Among the 168 plots, three main categories proved to have strong correlations: plots with no legumes, plots with the legume species *Lupinus perennis*, and plots with any legume other than *L. perennis*. It was found that in the plots with *L. perennis* in particular, variation in number of species had no effect in increasing average annual biomass yield. On average, over 11 years the yields of *L. perennis* and grass bicultures were similar to those of maximum-diversity 16-species plots, and both of these yields were more than 200 percent greater than the average of monocultures.

171

In addition to biofuel crops, there is potential to develop low-input perennial cropping systems that sustainably yield harvestable, storable, transportable grains suitable for human consumption. If these systems with relatively low plant species diversity can be bred to require few inputs while maintaining high yields comparable to those of naturally high-diversity systems, plant breeders may be able to develop controlled perennial crops that can meet not only the world's energy needs, but basic needs for food as well.

New Microbial Biofuels Could Increase Commercial Viability of Renewable Energy

Although bioethanol and plant oil-derived biodiesel have comprised the first generation of the biofuel industry, their relatively low energy content and incompatibility with existing fuel distribution and storage infrastructure limits their economic use in the future. However, scientists and engineers are now able to develop more sustainable and economically feasible microbial biofuels through means of metabolic engineering and synthetic biology. Exploiting the diverse metabolic pathways in organisms such as *Saccharomyces cerevisiae* and *Escherichia coli* produces biofuels that have physical properties closely resembling petroleum-derived fuels without requiring additional chemical conversion, which suggests that investigating these new microbial fuels may provide insight into more efficient and commercially viable renewable energy (Rude and Schirmer 2009).

All biofuel production involves accessing the energy of the sun stored as chemical energy in the bonds of biologically produced materials through photosynthesis. Three major pathways to convert renewable resources into energy-rich fuel-like molecules currently exist: 1) direct production by photosynthetic organisms, such as plants or algae; 2) chemical conversion of biomass into fuels; and 3) the fermentative or non-fermentative production by heterotrophic microorganisms such as yeast, fungi, or bacteria. Although the first two options can rely on expensive feedstocks and timely processes, research on key biocatalysts responsible for converting metabolic intermediates into fuel-like molecules hope to increase the economic viability of the third option.

Microbiologists have started this research process by investigating the metabolic pathways of microorganisms that produce all four types of microbial fuels, which are divided into classes depending on the biological pathway from which they are derived: non-fermentative alcohols, fermentative alcohols, isoprenoid-derived hydrocarbons, and fatty acid-derived hydrocarbons. As is the case with non-microbial biofuel production processes, the organic feedstocks involved in microbial fuel production still represent the largest cost component. Because of this, the overall production cost is directly related to the efficiency of the metabolic pathway in converting sugar to fuels.

In order to effectively examine these efficiencies, the metabolic mass yield, gallon of product per ton of glucose, enthalpy of combustion, and enthalpy of combustion yield was calculated and compared for each microbial fuel pathway and characteristic. Although ethanol had the highest metabolic mass yield within the microbial gasoline fuels (ethanol, butanol, isobutanol, and 3-methyl-1-butanol), butanol had the highest enthalpy of combustion, making ethanol and butanol equally efficient with enthalpy of combustion yields of 97% and 95%. Although the microbial diesel fuels had slightly lower enthalpies of combustion yields ranging between 75 and 88%, the fatty acid-derived hydrocarbons have the advantage of low solubility in water. This means that centrifugation can be used to separate these compounds from fermentation broth, as opposed to distillation, which requires much more energy.

Understanding these metabolic pathways will allow for the expansion of the renewable fuel industry as greater knowledge of biocatalysts leads to a greater variety of hydrocarbon product discoveries. Because the specific metabolic efficiency of any given pathway has a significant impact on the economics of fuel production in a microbial host, investing in further research is crucial. Because microbial biofuels are easy to recover and do not require additional chemical conversion, the biofuel production process has the potential to develop into a cost-effective and unsubsidized commercial processes.

Conclusions

Because continuing to consume fossil fuels at their current rates is neither economically nor environmentally feasible, the expansion of the energy market into alternate fuel sources is inevitable. Although biofuels have been designated for further research investment, the methods through which they have been evaluated have been inconsistent and incomplete, leading scientists to inaccurate appraisals of biofuel sustainability. Newer studies that have been able to incorporate multidisciplinary expertise as well as narrow-scope evaluations of specific geographic areas have been able to deliver more accurate evaluations of biofuel use in varying regions of the world without wasting research resources on inconclusive data. While the cooperation amongst experts from the fields of biology, engineering, mathematics, economics, and politics are all required for the most inclusive analysis of the implications of expanding the biofuel industry, the next step would be to work for more extensive global cooperation. Because climate and energy are inherently global problems, cooperation and collaboration among world scientists and collective resources is the next step in enhancing the biofuel industry.

Elena Davert

References Cited

Davis, S., Anderson-Teixeira, K., DeLucia, E., 2009. Life cycle analysis and the ecology of biofuels. Trends in Plant Science 14, 140–146.

DeHaan, L.R., Weisberg, S., Tilman, D. Fornara, D., 2009. Agricultural and biofuel implications of a species diversity experiment with native perennial grassland plants. Agriculture, Ecosystems and Environment, DOI: 10.1016/j.agee.2009.10.017.

Hanson, J. D., Hendrickson, J. R., 2009. Toward a sustainable agriculture. Farming with Grass: Achieving Sustainable Mixed Agricultural Landscapes. Ankeny, IA: Soil and Water Conservation Society. 26–36.

Johnston, M., Foley, J.A., Holloway, T., Kucharik, C. Monfreda, C., 2009. Resetting global expectations from agricultural biofuels. Environmental Research Letters, 4014004, 1–9.

Lapola, D.M., Schaldach, R., Alcamo, J., Bondeau, A., Koch, J., Koelking, C., Priess, J.A., 2009. Indirect land-use changes can overcome carbon savings from biofuels in Brazil. Proceedings of the National Academy of Science 107, 3388–3393.

Rosentrater, K., Todey, D., Persyn, R., 2009. "Quantifying Total and Sustainable Agricultural Biomass Resources in South Dakota – A Preliminary Assessment". Agricultural Engineering International: the CIGR Journal of Scientific Research and Development 11, 1–14.

Rude, A. M., Schirmer, A., 2009. New microbial fuels: a biotech perspective. Current Opinion in Microbiology 12, 274–281.

Tock, J.A., Lai, C.L., Lee, K.T., Tan, K.T., Bhatia, S., 2009. Banana biomass as potential renewable enrgy resource: A Malaysian case study. Renewable and Sustainable Energy Reviews 14, 798–805.

Section IV—Wind and Solar Power

14. Wind Power

Noah Proser

Developing renewable energy production is one of the keys to the long-term success of the United States and the global community. Most conventional energy technologies are simply not sustainable in the long run since they are dependent on limited fuel supplies. Coal, for instance, is likely to reach peak production by 2030 (Höök and Aleklett 2009). Other fuel sources are concentrated in regions that have volatile relationships with the US. Conventional energy production is also responsible for pollution and greenhouse gas emissions, which contribute to global climate change.

Recently, there has been great political pressure to reduce CO_2 emissions and achieve energy independence. Accordingly, there is a lot of research in renewable energy sources like wind power. There are many challenges associated with replacing conventional energy sources with wind power; however, the scientific literature suggests that it will be an important part of our future energy portfolio. If we are to develop wind power on a larger scale it is important to understand all aspects of this technology. This chapter will focus on the problems associated with wind power and the solutions available according to current scientific research.

Though wind power theoretically does not emit greenhouse gases, it can be harmful to the environment. The manufacture and transport of wind turbines can emit large amounts of CO_2 depending on the type of electricity being used and the method of transport. Though these emissions are not directly related to wind power, they should be taken into account. More directly, collisions with turbine blades are responsible for the deaths of thousands of birds and bats (Smallwood and Karas 2009). Wind farms can also affect avian breeding grounds, reducing the avian population density in some areas (Pearce-Higgins *et al.* 2009). Finally, the installation of offshore turbines can destroy ocean-floor habitats. While this may sometimes be a problem, Wilson and Elliott (2009) found that offshore wind farms, when properly designed, could actually create new, productive marine habitats while limiting harmful bottom trawling.

In addition to its environmental problems, wind power is often criticized for its undependability. Since it depends an intermittent source of energy, utilities cannot fully rely upon wind power. Thus, wind farms are typically only given credit for roughly 20% of their actual capacity. Fortunately, there is an array of methods to reduce the variability of wind power output. For instance, when wind farms are coupled with other renewable sources like wave power, energy production is much more consistent (Fusco *et al.* 2009). Simply moving the turbines offshore can also greatly reduce variability according to Dvorak *et al.* (2009). Similarly, high-altitude wind power reduces intermittence, while greatly increasing power output (Archer and Caldeira 2009).

Along with these reductions in variability, utilities can also take advantage of pumped hydroelectric and compressed air energy storage. These methods store energy during times of excess production and provide electricity to the grid when the wind dies down. As energy storage, renewable power integration and high-altitude wind power technologies progress, wind capacity credits should increase.

The transition to large-scale use of renewable energies is likely to occur rapidly, both by necessity and in response to public demand. Yoo and Kwak (2009) demonstrated that there is already a significant portion of the population willing to pay extra for clean sources of energy, suggesting that this transition may already be taking place. As the clean energy movement gains momentum, it is imperative that policy makers and the general public be well informed about renewable energy. After all, the solutions to problems like wind intermittence could come from relatively unknown technologies like high altitude wind generators. Furthermore, Yoo and Kwak found that people were more likely to support renewable energies when they were well informed. The eight papers reviewed in this chapter are only a sample of the wide variety of research and innovation occurring in the field of wind power.

New High-Capacity Wind Turbines Significantly Reduce Collision-Related Avian Mortality

While wind power has received great support as a carbon-neutral, renewable energy source, it is not without ecological problems. Smallwood and Karas (2009) found that wind turbines in the Altamont Pass Wind Resource Area in Central California were responsible for the deaths of thousands of birds from 1998 to 2003. Many of the birds that were killed were endangered or otherwise protected species.

Fortunately, as outdated wind turbines are replaced with newer, more efficient ones avian mortality decreases by 66%. Nonetheless, it is important to consider migratory pathways and avian habitats when constructing new wind farms in order to best mitigate the environmental impacts of such projects.

Smallwood and Karas counted the number of birds killed by wind turbines in the Altamont Pass from 1998 to 2003. In 2005, the Diablo Winds Energy Project replaced 126 inefficient turbines with 31 higher capacity turbines. With a higher surface area and lower rotor speed these turbines were expected to be less dangerous for birds flying through the pass. Subsequently, the researchers conducted another survey from 2005 to 2007 to determine whether the new turbines significantly reduced avian mortality. In order to avoid complications from differing bird populations over time, both old and new turbines were included and compared in the later survey.

The authors found that the new turbines killed 66% fewer birds than the old generation of turbines. Furthermore, since the new turbines have a much higher capacity, modern wind farms can be more sparsely populated or smaller while still producing the same amount of power. This reduction in size or density can further reduce the risk for birds. Despite the advantages of the new generation of turbines, these levels of avian mortality may still be unacceptable. For this reason, future wind power proposals should be carefully evaluated to avoid the migratory patterns of endangered birds.

Unfortunately, some level of bird kills may be inevitable when it comes to wind power regardless of the precautions taken. With that said, wind power should not be abandoned. After all, turbines are not the only anthropogenic causes of avian mortality. Untold numbers of birds are killed each year from collisions with windows, television and radio broadcasting towers, and power lines (Drewett and Langston 2008). In all likelihood, wind turbines are responsible for a minute amount of overall avian mortality. Moreover, wind farms can replace steam power plants, which pollute the habitats these birds depend on. We should make efforts to minimize bird kills from wind turbines; however, avian mortality is not likely to be a vital issue in the future of wind power.

Marine Habitat Creation from Offshore Wind Power

Offshore wind farms are a relatively new source of power that has gained tremendous popularity in Europe. Offshore turbines are often preferable to onshore projects since winds are typically steadier at sea; however, environmentalists have raised concerns about the impact they could have on marine life. In particular, the construction of monopiles to support turbines could destroy important seabed habitats. Surprisingly, Wilson and Elliott (2009) discovered that offshore wind farms can actually create thriving new habitats that far outweigh the amount of seabed disturbed by their construction.

The researchers examined the effects of existing wind farms in the United Kingdom on colonization and fish use. In particular, they focused on the habitat creating potentials of different types of scour protection. Monopile scour occurs when the sediment around the base of a monopile is washed away, compromising the integrity of its foundation. In order to prevent scouring, monopiles are surrounded with gravel, boulders, or synthetic fronds.

Though such protection disturbs the original seabed habitat, it also increases the surface area and complexity of the area around the monopile. Wilson and Elliott found that both boulder and gravel protection create more than double the habitat lost to their construction. While synthetic frond protection does not perform as well as the other methods, it still almost entirely makes up for the habitat lost. The habitat created by the scour protection is different from what is lost; however, Wilson and Elliott contend that, since turbines are likely to be placed in areas with relatively sparse seabed, the added complexity from the scour protection will raise the carrying capacity of the surrounding environment. Further improvements can be made by using a blend of different scour protection methods on different turbines to promote diversity. 'Reef balls' (boulders with holes bored into them to maximize surface area used to create artificial reefs) can also be used in place of other scour protection materials. Furthermore, the authors suggest that wind farms could act as *de facto* marine sanctuaries because bottom trawling would not be allowed near them to prevent damage to the turbines.

Despite the concerns over the environmental impact of offshore wind projects, Wilson and Elliott assert that wind farms have a largely beneficial impact on marine life. They expect that the new habitats created by the turbines will boost fish populations and thus benefit fishermen as well. It seems as though productive, complex marine habitats may just be yet another benefit of wind power.

The Potential for Offshore Wind Farms in California

In order to take advantage of the many benefits of wind power, the regions that can harness the technology must be identified. Without a clear picture of the extent of wind resources it would be impossible to know their potential impact on the grid, and therefore, the environment. Dvorak *et al.* (2009) modeled the average wind speeds off the coast of California to measure the total available offshore wind power for the state. Remarkably, 17–31% of California's electricity demand could be met using current offshore turbine technology. Factoring in floating turbines (which are still in prototype stages, but could be constructed in deeper waters) offshore wind power could provide 174–224% of the state's energy needs. Clearly, not all of this energy capacity can be harnessed; however, there is still an enormous renewable energy resource to be developed off the coast of California.

In order to measure the total wind power available, Dvorak *et al.* used data from offshore buoys to create a weather model. It was not possible to create a useful map of wind speed from just the data from the buoys since there are too few of them, but when the buoy data were compared to the results of the weather model, the variance between the two was relatively low, justifying the use of the model. The researchers also examined bathymetry (water depth) data to determine the type of turbine foundation that could be constructed in each area. Typically, monopile foundations can be used in waters up to 20 m in depth; multi-leg foundations are used up to 50 m in depth, and floating turbines would be used in deeper waters.

Though the authors discounted the power available in deeper waters somewhat, floating turbine technology will soon be a reality as demonstrated by a 2.3 MW floating turbine currently operating in the North Sea off the coast of Norway. As more research is conducted on this technology, the wind resources available to California and many other coastal states will greatly increase.

Overall, California has an abundant wind power resource that should not be ignored. The offshore wind capacity in Northern California is particularly impressive, potentially providing 2.2 GW of average output. Offshore wind is also relatively consistent throughout the day unlike land-based wind power. Though only a fraction of this resource is likely to be utilized, it can still have a substantial impact on California's energy independence and greenhouse gas emissions.

Using Wave Power with Wind Power Alleviates Intermittency Problems

The intermittence that both on and offshore wind farms face weaken their potential as baseload power sources. Pumped hydroelectric energy storage can mitigate the variability associated with wind power; however, it is not available everywhere. When energy storage is not an option and wind conditions are sub-optimal, conventional power plants are used to supply the grid. These conventional power plants run less efficiently when they are forced to change output on the basis of wind intermittency, creating decreasing marginal reductions of CO_2 emissions (ESB 2004). In order to avoid the problems associated with intermittency, Fusco *et al.* (2009) propose using wind power in combination with wave energy. Since these two resources have an inverse correspondence in some areas, together they could reduce the need for energy storage and CO_2 emitting, backup power plants.

The researchers focused on the ability to combine wind and wave power in Ireland in order to meet the country's new goal of 33% renewable energy. They used data on wind speeds, wave periods, and wave heights collected from weather buoys by the Irish Marine Institute. Energy potentials were calculated based on 3.5 MW offshore wind turbines and the 750 kW Pelamis wave energy converter. The researchers considered the West, Southwest, South, and East coasts of Ireland separately since wind/wave correlations differ geographically.

Fusco *et al.* found that the West and South coasts of Ireland experienced winds and waves that were not highly correlated, while there was a high correlation on the East coast. Since the East coast is protected from the Atlantic, wave energy is largely dependent on local winds, thus creating a high correspondence. On the other hand, the West and Southern coastlines can utilize wave energy created in the open ocean. These higher energy swells provide power when local wind power is insufficient.

In combination, wave and wind power can significantly reduce renewable power variability. Though more dependable power sources will still be necessary without significant energy storage options, this reduced variability will allow these plants to run more efficiently. Fusco *et al.* also emphasize that wave power is relatively predictable, making grid management easier. Though more research is needed in order to identify the best arrangements of wind and wave power systems, it is clear that grouping these technologies will make Ireland's energy goals more feasible and efficient.

High-Altitude Wind Power May Solve Future Energy Needs

Conventional wind farms are often criticized for their intermittence and lack of overall power. While using other forms of energy—like wave power—in combination with wind power can reduce the variability of energy production, it does not entirely eliminate it. Furthermore, such combinations do nothing to address the relative weakness of land-based wind power production. Harnessing wind power from higher altitudes (500–12,000 m) could mitigate both of these problems by making use of the jet streams' abundant and relatively persistent wind energy (Archer and Caldeira 2009). Though it will still require large energy storage capabilities if it is to become a reliable source of electricity, high altitude wind power is promising because it can provide clean energy to areas where it might have otherwise been unfeasible.

Archer and Caldeira assessed the availability of high-altitude wind power using data collected from the National Centers for Environmental Prediction and the Department of Energy from 1979 to 2006. They focused on wind speed and density in order to determine the optimal elevations and geographic regions for high-altitude wind power. Wind power densities were then divided into percentiles representing the density that was exceeded 50, 68, and 95% of the time as a measure of dependability. For the purposes of this assessment, they considered two means of high-altitude wind power. The first system, KiteGen, uses kites connected to generators on the ground that create electricity when the kites are pulled by the wind. KiteGen is designed for altitudes of 1,000 m and can produce 620 kW per unit. Alternatively, Flying Electric Generators produced by Sky Windpower use rotors to generate electricity, which is transmitted back to the ground. These generators are designed to fly at 10,000 m and produce 40 MW each.

Archer and Caldeira found that cities like Tokyo, Seoul, and New York, which are affected by polar jet streams, could harvest more than 10 kW/m^2 at high altitudes (8,000 m) at least 50% of the time. Furthermore, since wind speed increases with altitude, most regions considering wind power would be greatly benefitted by using high-altitude generators rather than conventional turbines. Ideally, these high-altitude generators would be able to adjust their altitudes as winds shift with weather conditions.

Even with all of the advantages of high-altitude wind power, intermittency can still be a problem. To deal with this problem, wind farms can store energy in batteries, pumped hydro, and other forms during non-peak hours. This stored energy can then be supplied to the grid when the wind farm is not at optimal production. Another way to deal with the intermittency of wind power is to have several farms in different locations. When the wind isn't blowing in one area, farms in other areas can still provide electricity to the grid.

It is still unclear whether wind can provide reliable baseload power for our growing energy demands; however, high-altitude wind power seems like a serious contender among renewable energies. At high altitudes reliability and overall power production are greatly increased. Furthermore, high-altitude wind power is available where ground-level wind power may not be feasible. Nonetheless, before widespread wind power can become a reality, improvements must be made in energy storage technologies, as well as large-scale transmission grids.

Urban Wind Power: Another Source of Renewable Energy

Wind power can also be used on a small scale to reduce greenhouse gas emissions and household energy costs. While roof-top wind turbines are not as efficient as those used for large-scale wind farms, they have the advantage of not being subject to energy losses from transmission and distribution. Nalanie Mithraratne (2009) performed a life cycle assessment of 1.5 kW Swift wind turbines in New Zealand to determine their net energy savings and emissions reductions. She found that, for households in New Zealand, a roof-top turbine would take 7–11 years to make returns on energy, and 10–16 years to compensate for the CO_2 emitted in its manufacture, transport, and maintenance.

First, Mithraratne had to determine what locations and turbines would be viable for micro-scale wind power production. In the urban environments being considered, wind resources are affected by nearby buildings and trees as well as the architecture of the building the turbine is mounted on. These obstacles can significantly reduce wind energy production. Additionally, the turbines cannot exceed community noise standards and must be light enough to be installed on an average household's roof. The inherent difficulties involved with urban wind power effectively limit turbines to areas with average wind speeds of at least 5.5 m/s. Mithraratne also suggests that turbines should only be installed on buildings that are 50% higher than the surrounding structures.

The life cycle analysis of the turbines revealed that the manufacturing process accounts for nearly 80% of the energy used and roughly 70% of the greenhouse gases emitted in the turbine's life. The author also evaluated the energy costs of transporting, installing, maintaining, and, finally, decommissioning the turbines. Overall, one turbine can be expected to emit 2312 kg of CO_2, while generating 10520–16820 kWh of electricity during its 20-year lifespan. Thus, using urban wind power can create a net reduction of 539–2246 kg of CO2. The wide range of this statistic is due to the different scenarios Mithraratne considered, which involved different maintenance regimes and disposal techniques.

The life cycle analysis presented here was focused on urban wind power in New Zealand. Transportation of the turbines from the UK was a large factor in the energy costs and emissions in this scenario (roughly 18%). Clearly, less remote locations would have lesser transportation costs, and correspondingly higher net CO_2 reductions with quicker returns on investments. Though urban wind power is unlikely to make up any large portion of worldwide energy production, it could be a useful and practical addition to the grid.

Public Demand for Green Energy May Eliminate the Need for Renewable Energy Price-Equivalency

The relatively high cost of renewable energy sources, like wind and solar power, is a major hurdle to reducing greenhouse gas emissions and meeting green energy goals. While wind power has relatively low operating costs, the initial costs of wind projects are quite high. This is especially true when new transmission lines are required in order to connect wind farms to the grid. Though other sources of power may be cheaper, Yoo and Kwak (2009) suggest that consumers are willing to pay more for clean energy. This willingness to pay (WTP) is enough to foster investments in renewable energy that can increase green energy production while reducing future costs. Consequently, the current high cost of wind power may not be a problem for the industry.

The researchers performed a dichotomous choice contingent valuation survey to determine the WTP for green energy of individual households in South Korea. Participants in the survey were first given information about renewable energy sources, as well as governmental policies on green energy. They were then asked whether they would accept a specified surcharge on their monthly energy bill in order to increase South Korea's renewable energy from 0.2% to 7% of total energy consumption (a goal that has been set by the South Korean Government). Following a 'yes' or 'no' answer the researchers would offer another bid to arrive at a more specific WTP. They used a total sample of eight hundred households with varying starting bids to insure the amount originally specified did not affect the responses.

On average, households offered a monthly WTP of about ₩1681 (South Korean Won), or roughly $1.8. Though this amount may seem small, when multiplied by the number of households it translates to about $160 million per month. This amount should provide a large incentive for energy corporations and governments alike to supply renewable power.

This result is an average of the responses offered. In reality, the large majority of participants showed no willingness to pay whatsoever. There are many reasons for this outcome. Contingent valuations are often criticized for depending on abstract responses rather than actual behavior, which can be studied through revealed preference valuation. Furthermore, Yoo and Kwak found that only 19.5% of participants were well acquainted with renewable energy. Though the survey included basic information on the subject, it is unlikely that this information alone would be enough to sway a response. With a more educated public there may have been a higher WTP.

Nonetheless, a significant amount of the population was willing to pay extra for renewable energy. Even if a surcharge like the one described in the survey was purely voluntary, it seems a substantial amount of money could be raised for green energy sources. Governments and energy providers should take note of this WTP when creating energy policies and building new power plants. Essentially, the price disparity between renewables and cheaper sources may not matter if the public is willing to pay for cleaner energy.

Climate Change Can Affect Local Wind Power Resources

As wind power becomes a more important part of electricity production around the world there will be increased efforts to locate suitable regions with high wind power density where wind farms can be developed. Normally, wind farm sites are selected based on the proximity of transmission lines, the environmental impact of installing turbines, and the abundance of wind resources in the area. This process fails to take into account possible future changes in wind availability due to variations in surrounding vegetation, or even global climate change. De Lucena *et al.* (2009) project that wind conditions in Brazil may improve as the climate changes, making investment in new wind farms an attractive prospect.

In this study, researchers examined the A2 (high future CO_2 emissions) and B2 (low future CO_2 emissions) IPCC scenarios using a downscaled, regional HadCM3 general circulation model (GCM). They focused on Brazil, which has a flourishing market for renewable energies, especially wind power. Though wind power density is affected by both wind speed and wind shear, they were only able to project the average wind speeds for the region due to the limitations of the GCM. Furthermore, there is no way to account for factors such as future changes in vegetation and land use that can also affect wind power density.

Overall, De Lucena *et al.* demonstrate very little certainty regarding their predictions. Even with advanced climate models, it is impossible to account for all of the factors affecting wind power density in an area. Matters are further complicated by man-made changes in vegetation like deforestation. Such changes can have huge effects on wind patterns; however, they cannot be effectively modeled.

Nonetheless, the study does provide some important insights. Unlike conventional power plants, which have a quantifiable supply of fuel, renewable sources depend on resources that are in constant flux. Just as hydroelectric power plants are dependent on rain to renew their water sources, wind farms are subject to changing wind patterns. Brazil may, in fact, gain better wind resources due to climate change. Though this projection is relatively uncertain, it highlights the dependence of wind power on climate conditions and it is important that energy investors and regulators are aware of this dependence when planning for renewable energies.

Conclusions

Overall, wind power is a promising technology for our future. Though, in its most basic form, it may seem outdated and rural, recent developments have made wind power a realistic means of powering modern cities. Through the use of offshore, high-altitude, and land-based turbines in combination with other renewable sources it is possible to achieve energy independence while eliminating greenhouse gas emissions. Intermittence, and interference with wildlife, are serious concerns; however, these are problems that can be either minimized or entirely resolved. At the same time, it is clear that wind power has numerous benefits. While it is uncertain how long the transition between conventional and renewable energies will take, the scientific literature, especially regarding wind power, suggests it will be sooner rather than later.

References Cited

Archer, C., Caldeira, K., 2009. Global assessment of high-altitude wind power. Energies 2, 307–319.

De Lucena, A.F.P., Szklo, A.S., Schaeffer, R., Dutra, R.M., 2009. The vulnerability of wind power to climate change in Brazil. Renewable Energy 35, 904–912.

Drewitt, A.L., Langston, R.H.W., 2008. Collision effects of wind-power generators and other obstacles on birds. N.Y. Acad. Sci. 1134, 233–266.

Dvorak, M.J., Archer, C.L., Jacobson, M.Z., 2009. California offshore wind energy potential. Renewable Energy 35, 1244–1254.

ESB National Grid. Impact of wind power generation in Ireland on the operation of conventional plant and economic implications. February 2004.

Fusco, F., Nolan, G., Ringwood, J.V., 2009. Variability reduction through optimal combination of wind/wave resources – An Irish case study. Energy 35, 314–325.

Hööke, M., Aleklett, K., 2009. Historical trends in American coal production and a possible future outlook. International Journal of Coal Ecology 78, 201–216.

Mithraratne, N., 2009. Roof-top wind turbines for microgeneration in urban house in New Zealand. Energy and Buildings 41, 1013–1018.

Pearce-Higgins, J.W., Stephen, L., Langston, R.H.W., Bainbridge, I.P., Bullman, R., 2009. The distribution of breeding birds around upland wind farms. Journal of Applied Ecology 46, 1323–1331.

Smallwood, K.S., Karas, B., 2009. Avian and bat fatality rates at old-generation and repowered wind turbines in California. Journal of Wildlife Management 73, 1062–1071.

Wilson, J.C., Elliott, M., 2009. The habitat-creation potential of offshore wind farms. Wind Energy 12, 203–212.

Yoo, S.H., Kwak, S.Y, 2009. Willingness to pay for green electricity in Korea: a contingent valuation study. Energy Policy 37, 5408–5416.

15. Solar Thermal Decomposition: Clean Fossil Fuel?

Tim Fine

The developed world depends on fossil fuels to maintain its way of life. Fossil fuels are the primary source of the world's power and fossil fuel derivatives, such as plastic, are commonly used throughout the developed world. However, the greenhouse gases generated from burning fossil fuels are thought to be the primary cause of global warming. As greenhouse gases accumulate in the upper atmosphere, they trap heat causing an increase in global temperature. The increasing global temperature associated with global warming melts the ice sheets at the Earth's poles, causing sea levels to rise. Global warming affects weather patterns, increasing the frequency of hurricanes and altering rainfall patterns. Rising sea levels threaten to put large amounts of the world's coast and low lying areas under water while hurricanes cause millions of dollars worth of damage each year. Changing rainfall patterns may make it difficult to continue to grow crops and could result in decreased food availability; farmers use the past to predict weather patterns and will be slow to react to changes in rainfall pattern. The aggregate effects of fossil fuel emissions pose a significant threat to the welfare of the human race. Furthermore, fossil fuels are a finite resource that will eventually run out. As the rest of the world develops, the demand for fossil fuel has been steadily increasing for what is already scarce and non-replenishable resource. Concern about the adverse affects of fossil fuel emissions and world energy security has significantly increased research aimed at discovering alternative energy sources.

Solar thermal decomposition technology may help reduce the worldwide CO_2 emissions from fossil fuel and natural gas consumption while simultaneously prolonging the lifespan of the world's fossil fuel supply, effectively buying time for the development of alternative energy sources (Ozalp *et al.* 2009). Solar thermal decomposition uses solar radiation to heat feedstocks such as methanol and methane, causing them to break down into their elemental components: hydrogen gas (H_2)

and carbon-black (elemental carbon). The carbon-black produced by the reaction can be used in many manufacturing processes. The H_2 produced can be used as a substitute for fossil fuels in either a combustion reaction or with other technologies to produce power without generating CO_2. The use of solar thermal decomposition technology can drastically reduce and even eliminate the CO_2 emissions that would be generated from the conventional use of fossil fuels. Solar thermal decomposition technology is remarkable in that it uses carbon-based fuels while producing little to no CO_2. The principle feedstocks currently being tested, methane and methanol, can be produced from renewable sources as well as fossil fuels, giving solar thermal decomposition technology the potential to create a carbon sink (Cherubini *et al.* 2010). Cellulosic biomass absorbs CO_2 from the atmosphere during its life cycle. Typically the CO_2 is returned to the atmosphere when the biomass is burned as an energy source. The use of solar thermal decomposition technology creates a net loss of CO_2 from the atmosphere since little to no CO_2 is emitted depending on the type of technology used.

There are two different types of solar thermal decomposition technologies: solar thermal cracking and solar thermal reforming. Solar thermal cracking uses concentrated solar energy to heat the feedstock temperatures between 1000 and 2000°C, at which point the feedstock will decompose into it's elemental components: H_2 and carbon-black. Solar thermal reforming, also known as solar thermal steam reforming, mixes a carbon-based feedstock with water at a specified ratio. The resulting mixture is vaporized and injected into the reactor where it is heated until both the carbon-based feedstock and the water decompose. Since solar thermal reforming also decomposes water, it produces a small quantity of CO_2, as well as more H_2 per mol of the carbon-based feedstock. Each technology has advantages and disadvantages; solar thermal cracking produces H_2 with no CO_2 emissions but requires higher temperatures relative to solar thermal reforming, which produces more H_2 at lower temperatures but emits some CO_2.

The high temperatures required by solar thermal decomposition reactors greatly increase the costs of operating on a large scale. Large solar collecting plants are needed to collect enough solar radiation to generate the high temperatures necessary to drive decomposition reactions. However, adding catalysts to solar decomposition reactors can dramatically reduce the required temperatures, reducing the required temperature to near 1000°C; adding catalysts to solar thermal reforming reactors can reduce the temperature required for decomposition to as low as 150°C (Hong *et al.* 2009).

As with all solar technologies, both solar thermal reforming and solar thermal cracking are adversely affected by the intermittent availability of solar radiation; even short interruptions in the availability of solar radiation can greatly decrease the efficiency of solar thermal reactors which are most efficient with constant internal reactor temperatures to drive the decomposition reaction. Even short interruptions of solar radiation can cause a reactor's internal temperature to fluctuate significantly, affecting its feedstock conversion rate. One way to eliminate the problem posed by the intermittent availability of solar radiation is to use doubled-walled reactor tubes lined with salts. The salts have a high specific heat, and when molten can absorb and lose large amounts of energy without their temperatures being significantly altered (Gokon *et al.*2009). This setup has been shown to allow the reactor to continue operating at above a 90% feedstock conversion rate after 30 minutes without solar radiation (Kodama *et al.* 2009). Another proposed solution uses the concentrated solar radiation to heat molten salt to a desired temperature rather than irradiating the reactor directly.

The versatility of solar thermal decomposition technology means that it can be used both to augment existing technologies and infrastructures and used as a stand-alone technology. Reformers powered by fossil fuels are already operational and can retrofitted to partially power the reaction with solar energy, thereby reducing the emissions from fossil fuels. At a time when emissions standards are becoming more stringent, the option to both reduce CO_2 emissions and save money by reducing fossil fuel consumption will become steadily more appealing to consumers. Fitting natural gas facilities with solar reformers will allow them to produce hydrogen-enriched methane, which can be pumped into existing infrastructure and will produce less CO_2 per unit of energy. Solar thermal decomposition technology can also be implemented on a large scale to build fields of solar concentrators and reactors.

Solar Decomposition Technology could prolong the Lifespan of Fossil Fuel Reserves

Hydrogen was once touted as the alternative energy source that would end the civilized world's dependence on greenhouse gas-emitting fossil fuels. However, while hydrogen is the most abundant element on earth, it is almost always bonded to other elements and large amount of energy is required to obtain elemental hydrogen. This energy requirement has made using hydrogen as a fuel prohibitively expensive. Solar decomposition technology puts hydrogen back on the table as a potential alternative fuel. Solar decomposition technology can take a variety of feedstocks, including fossil fuels, water, and biomass, and release hydrogen and commercially usable carbon-black without producing any harmful greenhouse gases. The resulting hydrogen can be used in internal combustion engines and fuel cells. Additionally, using solar decomposition with a fossil fuel feedstock would prolong the lifespan of the fossil fuels, which would give more time for new alternative power sources to be developed (Ozalp *et al.* 2009).

Tim Fine

Nesrin Ozalp at Texas A&M University at Qatar, and his colleges at the Solar Research Facilities Unit at the Weizmann Institute of Science in Israel did a study examining the different solar decomposition processes currently available to produce hydrogen. Solar decomposition technologies are an interesting fusion of conventional and alternative power sources. Using the hydrogen generated by the decomposition reactions would eliminate greenhouse gases from the fuel life cycle, resulting in a huge step towards a carbon neutral economy. However, depending on which solar decomposition technology is used, some CO_2 will be produced. The solar decomposition technologies that produce CO_2 also produce more hydrogen than those that do not produce CO_2. Producing hydrogen without simultaneously producing CO_2 represents a tradeoff, less hydrogen for no CO_2. The carbon-black—pure carbon—generated by solar decomposition of fossil fuels and biomass is used in the manufacture of rubber, batteries, nanotubes, polymers, cars, and many other consumer items. Because the carbon produced by solar decomposition is marketable, the hydrogen produced has the potential to compete profitably on a per unit basis with gasoline, and the sale of the carbon can offset the costs of using solar decomposition technology. Used in combination with fossil fuels, solar decomposition technology has the potential to prolong the lifespan of fossil fuels—buying time to find a permanent sustainable energy source.

Increasing Temperature and Residence Time Increases the Efficiency of a Solar Chemical Reactor

Decarbonizing energy will help avoid further CO_2 emissions and provide a more sustainable energy solution in the near to medium-term future. Solar decomposition technology takes carbon based energy sources such as natural gas and fossil fuels and converts them to carbon-black and H_2. There is a variety of different types of solar decomposition reactors in development; Rodat et al. (2009) examined the effects of temperature, methane concentration, and residence time on methane decomposition in a 10 kW solar chemical reactor prototype. They found that temperature and residence time significantly affect both methane conversion and H_2 yield. Higher temperatures cause the decomposition reaction to go to completion, eliminating the ethane, butane, and acetylene byproducts. An increase in residence time—the amount of time the methane spent in the reactor—also resulted in a higher methane conversion and H_2 yield.

Sylvain Rodat and colleagues at the Processes, Materials and Solar Energy Laboratory calculated the effects of temperature, methane concentration, and residence time on methane decomposition in a 10 kW solar chemical reactor prototype. The reactor was insulated with three layers of different insulation materials to retain heat. The functional parts of the prototype consisted of three double graphite tubes. Each tube consisted of two tubes, one inside the other, through which a mixture of argon and methane gases was pumped. The gas entered through the inner tube and exited through the outer tube, and because of the way the solar reactor was designed, the outer tube is slightly hotter. This prevents the carbon generated by methane decomposition from depositing on the pipe. The reactor retained 60% of the solar energy as ambient heat to drive the reaction. Thirty-five percent of the energy was lost through the walls of the reactor and the remaining 5% was lost through the gas flow.

Increasing the concentration of methane pumped into the reactor was found to have no significant effect on either the percent decomposition of methane or the H_2 yield. This indicates that the efficiency of the reactor can be greatly increased by increasing the concentration of methane present in the gas source. The temperature inside the reactor was found to have positive correlation with the efficiency of the reactor. Increasing the temperature from 1670 K to 1740 K resulted in a 22% increase in methane conversion and a 3% increase in the H_2 yield. Increasing residence time of the gas also increased the efficiency of the reactor. Increasing the residence time from 12 ms to 35 ms increased the methane conversion by 36% and the H_2 yield by 40%. The three aspects examined—residence time, methane concentration, and temperature—are basic components of a solar thermal decomposition reaction suggesting that these results may be useful in the development of other solar reactors.

Testing a 5 kW Solar Thermal Cracking Reactor

Possibly the biggest obstacle to stopping climate change is the world's fossil fuel based economy. Economic growth means increased fossil fuel consumption and the accompanying rise in greenhouse gas emissions. Solar cracking presents a way to continue to use fossil fuels without generating the greenhouse gases such as CO_2 and CO that cause global warming. While solar cracking reactors are still in their prototype phase, the results generated by the 5 kW reactor tested in this study show great promise; the reactor had a methane conversion ratio of 98.8% and a hydrogen yield of 99.1% (Maag et al. 2009). Furthermore, the results indicate that increasing the amount of methane pumped into a reactor as a fraction of the total gas could increase the energy efficiency of the reactor beyond the maximum 16.1% solar-to-chemical energy conversion rate observed.

G. Maag and colleges at the Department of Mechanical and Process Engineering in Zurich tested a 5 kW solar partial-flow solar chemical reactor in a solar furnace over a 1300–1600 K range. The reactor was equipped with a continuous flow of methane laced with μm sized carbon black particles. The effect of flow rate on reactor efficiency was examined.

The key to solar thermal cracking is the heating of the target feedstock. This study found that the carbon-black particles injected into the methane acted as a catalyst, amplifying the conversion of the light striking the reactor into heat that is absorbed by the methane, increasing the rate at which the reaction proceeded, and improving the efficiency of the reactor. Higher concentrations of methane led to increased gas temperature and cooler reactor walls because the higher concentration of methane absorbed more light before it reached the reactor walls. There appears to be a trade-off between reaction completion—how much methane is converted— and the efficiency of the reactor. The reaction completion decreases when the concentration of methane is increased. While the temperature of the gas increased with a higher concentration, the energy per molecule went down, resulting in a lower conversion ratio. The solar-to-chemical energy conversion efficiency increases with an increase in methane concentration: more energy is being absorbed by the gas instead of the reactor walls, resulting in a higher energy conversion efficiency. Modeling simulations suggest that using pure methane could increase the efficiency of the reactor by a factor of 2–4.

Steam Reforming of Methanol May Provide an Economical Way to Produce Hydrogen

With the impending shortage of fossil fuels and the concerns over climate change, many new alternative sources of power are being considered. Solar hydrogen technologies promise to help alleviate the world economy's dependence on fossil fuels; many of the new solar hydrogen technologies currently being tested use very high temperatures to obtain hydrogen. A new study demonstrates the potential feasibility of solar hydrogen production at temperatures as low as 150–300°C (Hong et al. 2009). The study examined a new process involving the steam reforming of methanol using light as the energy source. Methanol conversion ratios of 90% and 98% were achieved with a reactor temperature of 220–280°C. The hydrogen obtained with the process reached purities of 99.99% with hydrogen recovery rates between 80% and 90%.

Hui Hong and colleagues at the Chinese Academy of Sciences tested a new process for producing hydrogen using low temperature steam reforming of methanol. The process was made up of three parts: a tracking parabolic trough concentrator with a concentration ratio of about 30–100, middle and low temperature solar reformers laden with $Cu/ZnO/Al_2O_3$ catalysts, and a pressure swing adsorption (PSA) unit. The PSA unit was used to extract the hydrogen from the products of the solar reformer. However because the PSA unit works at 35–40°C the product gases need to be cooled. The heated cooling water used to cool the product gas was fed into the preheater—the feedstocks are heated before being injected into the reformer—thus increasing the efficiency of the process.

The conversion of methanol increased with an increase in the average solar energy, reaching a conversion rate of more than 90% at 580 W/m^2. The heat to chemical conversion efficiency peaked at 45%, and a heat to chemical conversion efficiency of over 40% was achieved with the average solar energy ranging from 580 W/m^2 to 720 W/m^2. At average solar energy values above 720 W/m^2, the heat to chemical conversion efficiency started to decrease, indicating a higher radiance heat loss from the reactor. The 35–46% energy conversion efficiency obtained in this study is competitive with the 30% energy conversion efficiency found in high-temperature solar reforming of natural gas.

Because the process investigated in this study uses a solar reformer, it has a higher H_2 yield than conventional methane reformation: H_2 is obtained from H_2O in addition to the feedstock. Both methanol and water are decomposed to produce H_2 and GHGs, the majority of which were CO_2. Because of the high efficiency of the PSA at extracting pure H_2 from the product gas, the CO_2 produced can easily be captured for sequestration.

The low heat requirement of this process greatly reduces one of the largest obstacles to the large-scale implementation of solar hydrogen decomposition technologies. The low heat requirement lowers the energy required to obtain the hydrogen, which means that any power plants built using this process can be smaller than their high-temperature counterparts. Smaller plants will cost less and several can be built on the area required a single high temperature reactor. The decrease in reactor costs and size associated with low temperature methanol reformation may help hydrogen become a viable power source.

Hydrogen Production Using Middle-Temperature Solar Thermal Reforming

Middle temperature solar thermal methanol steam reforming reactors have been shown to be very effective at efficiently producing hydrogen (Liu *et al.* 2009). Higher solar flux values lead to an increase in methanol conversion as more energy is available to drive the reaction. The reactors decomposed over 90% of the injected methanol at a solar flux of 580 W/m^2 with an injection rate of 3.0 kg/h and 750 W/m^2 with an injection rate of 4.3 kg/h. The volumetric concentration of hydrogen found in the product gas was between 66–74%: within 1% of the theoretical maximum hydrogen concentration. Hydrogen was produced in a 3:1 ratio with CO_2, with trace amounts of CO, CH_3OH and H_2O also found in the product gas. The maximum hydrogen yield produced per mole of methanol was 2.90 mole, which was 0.10 mol less than the maximum theoretical yield of 3.00 mol per mol of methanol. The observed thermochemical efficiency of 30–50% is competitive with other high-temperature thermochemical processes.

Lui and colleges at the Chinese Academy of Sciences' Institute of Engineering Thermophysics examined the effect of solar radiation and mole ratio of water/methanol on the reactivity and hydrogen yield in a methanol steam reformer. The mole ratio of water to liquid methanol was set from 1 to 2.5. The reactor laden with $Cu/ZnO/Al_2O_3$ was driven by solar energy at 150–300°C.

The study showed that increased solar flux values raised the reactor temperature and increased methanol conversion. Methanol conversion rates were found to be higher than 90% for solar flux values of 580 W/m^2 and 750 W/m^2. More than 40% thermochemical efficiency can be achieved with two different mass flow rates. The observed 3.0 kg/k injection rate had a maximum thermochemical efficiency of 46%; the 4.3 kg/h injection rate was had a maximum thermochemical efficiency of 50%. However, the thermochemical efficiency of the reactors decreased above 580–630 W/m^2, indicating that more solar energy was being lost through heat radiation from the reactor. The study found that hydrogen concentrations of up to 66–74% were found using solar driven methanol steam reforming, which is larger than the 58–63% concentrations produced by methanol decomposition. It is important to note that the maximum theoretical hydrogen concentrations obtainable for each technology are 75% and 66% respectively. With a solar flux of about 600 W/m^2, the hydrogen yield ranged from 2.56–2.90 mol per mol of methanol, which is very close to the maximum theoretical hydrogen yield of 3.0 mol per mol methanol. Solar thermal methanol reforming can produce a hydrogen yield 70% greater than solar methanol decomposition because hydrogen is obtained from the water as well as the methanol.

Using Molten Salts may help Solve Solar Thermal Reforming's Intermittency

As with many other alternative energy sources, solar thermal reforming suffers from intermittency problems. Tatsuya Kodama and his colleges (2009) have come up with a new way to reduce the impact temporary disruptions—such as clouds drifting across the sun—have on the efficiency of a solar thermal reformer. They lined the outer tube of a double-walled tubular reformer with a mixture of the salt Na_2CO, and MgO. While molten salt has a high heat and latent heat capacity, it conducts heat poorly. Mixing it with Mg, which has high conductivity, allows the heat from the salt to transfer to the methane in the reactor efficiently. The integration of Na_2CO_3 and MgO into a solar thermal reformer allowed it to continue running at high efficiency with a methane conversion of 90% or more for 22 minutes longer than without the salts.

Kodama and colleges at Niigata University's Department of Chemistry and Chemical Engineering tested the effects of integrating Na_2CO_3 and MgO into a reformer. The intent of the experiment was to examine the feasibility of this approach for solar thermal reforming. The experiment used a conventional reformer reactor. The tubes were heated until the catalyst bed reached 920°C. After 100% methane conversion was observed the power to the reactor was intermittently turned on and off to simulate clouds drifting over the sun.

Clouds drifting over the reactor cause a greater decrease in the efficiency in solar thermal reforming than in traditional photovoltaic panels because to work, thermal reformers must be maintained at the temperature necessary to break down their feedstock. Using molten Na_2CO_3 as an energy reservoir can circumvent this problem by providing heat when the solar energy is temporarily disrupted. This study tested double walled tubes lined with Na_2CO_3, 90% Na_2CO_3 and 10% MgO, and 80% Na_2CO_3 and 20% MgO. All three combinations retained heat more efficiently when the power was off than did tubes without Na_2CO_3. The tube containing 90% Na_2CO_3 and 10% MgO proved most effective at maintaining the reactor temperature after the power supply had been interrupted. Thirty minutes after powering off the reactor, the temperature had dropped to 770°C: the methane conversion rate had only marginally decreased to 95%. The findings presented in this study could greatly reduce the problems caused by intermittent solar radiation in solar reformers, so long as they can be replicated in field tests.

Using Small-Scale Solar Thermal Reforming in Conjunction with a Hydrogen Fuel Cell

Solar steam reforming of bioethanol offers a sustainable way to domestically produce hydrogen for use in a hydrogen fuel cell. However, intermittency of solar energy prevents the solar reformer from always operating at full efficiency, affecting the rate of hydrogen production. Shin'ya (2009) found that even with intermittent solar energy, a domestic hydrogen reformer—running on a combination of solar and electrical power—operated at above 40% on both cloudy and sunny days. The GHGs emitted during the reformers' operation were found to be 19% lower than conventional commercial power generation. Furthermore, the percent utilization of solar energy by the 2 m^2 collecting area of solar reformer was superior to that of photovoltaic cells.

Shin'ya Obara at the Kitami Institute of Technology's Department of Electrical and Electronic Engineering studied the efficiency of a domestic bioethanol reformer used in conjunction with a hydrogen fuel cell. Two solar collectors measuring 1 m^2 were used to collect the solar energy for vaporizing the bioethanol feedstock and operating the solar reformer. Gaps between the solar energy available and the energy required for reforming were met with power from the grid. The results were obtained using the meteorological data from March 1 and August 23, 2007.

The uneven heating of the catalyst in the solar reformer leads to a drop in the efficiency of the reactor, as it prevents the decomposition reaction from reaching completion. Consequently, the changes in solar energy available due to cloud coverage can have a significant effect on the efficiency of a solar reformer. The study looked at the theoretical operating results of both a cloudy and sunny day in Sapporo, Japan by using the meteorological data from March 1 and August 23 of 2007. The reforming component operated with an efficiency of 47% on the cloudy day, March 1, and 42% on the sunny day, August 23. While efficiency of the reactor was lower for the sunny day, the longer daylight hours—there were nearly 2 more hours of sunlight on the 23rd—meant that the reactor produced 17g hydrogen and 0.5 kWh more than it did on the cloudy day. Considered as a fraction of the power demand for each day, the reactor produced 21.4% and 25.3% of the energy required to run the reactor for March 1 and August 23rd respectively.

While running, the reforming component required a significant portion of energy from the grid; adding a solar thermal component to the reformer was found to be a more efficient way to capture solar energy—thereby reducing the energy needed from the grid—than adding a photovoltaic cell array of the same size. Domestic implementation of solar thermal reforming, in conjunction with a hydrogen fuel cell, presents a possible way to reduce GHG emissions; the emissions per unit of power from the reforming process are less than those generated by conventional power production.

Using Solar Energy to Enrich Methane and Generate Electricity

Solar thermal decomposition technology may eventually help rid the world of its dependence on fossil fuels. In the meantime, some of these technologies could be integrated with existing infrastructure to help lower CO_2 emissions. Scientists at the University of Rome proposed and modeled integrating solar steam reforming technology with a steam turbine and existing natural gas (NG) infrastructure to create a tube and shell reactor (De Falco *et al. 2009*). Following decompression, natural gas with a volumetric hydrogen concentration of 17% (HCNG-17) can be fed straight into a low or medium pressure NG grid. This hydrogen-enriched NG will produce less CO_2 when burned and CO_2 per unit of energy produced since hydrogen produces only water as a byproduct when burned. The model found that a concentrating solar plant with an area of 16,000 m^2 coupled with a tube and shell reactor with 4 reformers is capable of supplying the enriched methane and electricity demands of about 2930 domestic users.

Marcello De Falco and colleagues at the University of Rome and the ENEA Research Center modeled the integration of solar thermal methane reforming to enrich natural gas with a steam turbine to generate electricity.

In the model, a field of solar collectors concentrates sunlight onto solar receivers filled with molten salt. The molten salt is used as a heat transfer fluid and is transferred into a storage tank. From the tank, the salt is pumped to either a steam reformer where it heats the feedstock and drives the reformer or to a steam turbine to generate electricity. The model assumed an exit temperature of 550°C for the molten salt; the flow rate would be adjusted to meet this depending on the intermittency of solar radiation. The salt storage tank allows for the flow of salt to the reformers to be kept constant at 4 kg/s. Allowing longer residency times in the reformers and steam turbine increased their thermal efficiency but reduced the rate at which enriched methane was produced. The residence time would need to be set based on the enriched methane and electricity requirements, as well as the intermittency of solar radiation as measured by the availability of molten salt at the required temperature. Pressure was found to adversely effect the production of enriched methane while slightly increasing the electrical output from the steam turbine. While the reformers themselves don't consume large amounts of heat, vaporizing their feedstock does, which puts constraints on the number of reformers that can be used on the same salt circuit. Examining the space requirements for the number solar collectors, the study found that the proposed plant would work for small municipalities but the space requirement could be a drawback for towns larger than 20,000 inhabitants.

Conclusions

Integrating solar thermal decomposition technology into society on a large scale offers both short- and long-term benefits. In the short term, the technology can help reduce CO_2 emissions by creating clean burning hydrogen from carbon-based fuels while prolonging the lifespan of the world's fossil fuel reserves. The extensive long-term use of solar decomposition technology with cellulosic biomass feedstocks has the potential to act as a carbon sink, reducing the amount of CO_2 present in the atmosphere. Solar decomposition technology is unique in that it use carbon-based feedstocks to produce usable energy with little to no CO_2 emissions.

References Cited

Cherubini, Francesco, and Gerfried, Jungmeier., 2010 LCA of a Biorefinery Concept Producing Bioethanol, Bioenergy, and Chemicals from Switchgrass. International Journal of Life Cycle Assessment 15.1, 53–66.

Gokon,, Nobuyuki, Shin-ichi Inuta, Shingo Yamashita, Tsuyoshi Hatamachi, and Tatsuya Kodama., 2009. Double-walled Reformer Tubes Using High-temperature Thermal Storage of Molten-salt/MgO Composite for Solar Cavity-type Reformer. International Journal of Hydrogen Energy 34.17 7143–154.

Kodama, T., Gokon, N., Inuta, S., Yamashita, S., 2009 Molten-Salt Tubular Absorber/Reformer (MoSTAR) Project: The Thermal Storage Media of Na_2CO_3–MgO Composite Materials. Journal of Solar Energy Engineering 131.4 041013.

De Falco, D., Giaconia, A., Marrelli, L., Tarquini, P., Grena, R., Caputo, G., 2009 Enriched methane production using solar energy: an assessment of plant performance. International Journal of Hydrogen Energy 34, 98–109.

Hong, H., Liu, Q., Jin, H., 2009. Solar Hydrogen Production Integrating Low-Grade Solar Thermal Energy and Methanol Steam Reforming. Journal of Energy Resources Technology 131, 012601–012611.

Ozalp, N., Kogan A., Epstein M., 2009. Solar decomposition of fossil fuels as an option for sustainability. International Journal of Hydrogen Energy 34.2, 710–720.

Rodat, S., Abanades, S., Sans, J., Flamant, G., 2009. Hydrogen production from solar thermal dissociation of natural gas: development of a 10 kW solar chemical reactor prototype. Solar Energy 83, 1599–1610.

Maag, G., Zanaganeh, G., Steinfeld, A., 2009 Solar thermal cracking of methane in a particle-flow reactor for the co-production of hydrogen and carbon. International Journal of Hydrogen Energy 34, 7676 –7685.

Liu, Q., Hong, H., Yuan, J., Jin, H., Cai, R., 2009. Experimental investigation of hydrogen production integrated methanol steam reforming with middle-temperature solar thermal energy. Applied Energy 86.2, 155–162.

Shin'ya, O., 2009 Hydrogen production characteristics of a bioethanol solar reforming system with solar isolation fluctuations. International Journal of Hydrogen Energy 34, 5347–5356.

16. Solar Power

Teija Mortvedt

Sunlight is a constant presence in the lives of every creature on earth. There is never a point where our planet is not touched by the sun's golden rays at any given time. Sunlight has the power to warm our earth and enable plant photosynthesis; it is a valuable energy source. It is for precisely this reason that sunlight is an incredibly promising source of clean alternative energy, an energy which is arguably the most abundant natural resource on earth.

Great amounts of energy delivered by sunlight can be harnessed in several different ways, all useful in their own right. Photovoltaic (PV) solar power harnesses sunlight by directly converting it to electricity through a complex process occurring on individual solar panels. Concentrating Solar Power (CSP) uses lenses or mirrors to direct large areas of sunlight onto much smaller surfaces. Sunlight can be used for heating by directly warming water and using that for domestic hot water needs, or for thermal heating in homes. Compressed Air Energy Storages (CAES) and Thermal Energy Storage (TES) are valuable forms of solar energy storage for later use.

Solar power can be generated in any area of the globe and is unique in that respect. Certain areas such as the American Southwest are ideal for solar energy generation because they receive full solar irradiation throughout much of the year. Solar power plants could easily be built in these areas where solar irradiation is high, and with effective transmission lines, be distributed throughout the country. Similar options have been examined in Europe using power generated in Northern Africa or the Middle East. Solar power plants in these areas could take up relatively little space and it is possible for panels to be installed on existing roofs or on bare landscape without disturbing the native plant life much. Concerns have been raised regarding the visual appearance of solar panels, and work is being done to minimize aesthetic impact if that proves to be an important issue.

Solar energy has enormous potential. Save for carbon emission during the manufacturing process, once solar plants are up and running they are entirely clean with zero carbon emissions. Solar power could replace fossil fuels entirely. Even under the worst weather conditions it is shown that solar energy has the capacity to supply 69% of the total electricity needs of the US by 2050 and over 90% by 2100 (Fthenakis *et al.* 2009). A mere 2.5 % of yearly solar irradiation in the Southwest is comparable to total annual US energy consumption; solar energy plants are capable of producing much more energy than daily demand requires.

In addition, there never will be a shortage of solar power, and we currently have methods of energy storage and production to meet any and all energy needs. So why is solar energy not sweeping the nation, or globe for that matter? The answer lies in cost—the situation for almost all new energy technologies—the attempt to be competitive with fossil fuels, particularly the cheap but hugely polluting coal which is now the source of most world energy. Photovoltaic solar panels are made from quartz and metal ores which are expensive to mine and refine, as well as limited in supply. The manufacturing costs and installation processes of solar plants are a weighty obstacle to overcome. The systems are complex and must be well-maintained to remain efficient. Unfortunately solar power has a long way to go to be completely cost competitive with fossil fuels, and, for the most part, is not currently economic without the aid of subsides.

Leaders in the field are researching many creative options to alleviate road-block of high prices; solar panels are being made thinner so they require less raw material in the manufacturing process, we are able to determine optimal ratios of solar field size to powerblock ratios in order to maximize efficiency where the most energy is produced at the lowest cost, and energy storage options are being examined which offer the ability to store energy to be sold at a later time of day when energy prices are higher. We rely on technological advancement in the future to make solar energy a truly competitive option, but the only way it can begin to become a large scale alternative is if we support solar power in the early stages while costs remain high and technology still in development. Carbon finance, tax credits, and subsides implemented by governments are helpful ways to support the development of solar energy in the near term. As technology advances these subsides will become less important, however they are necessary at present.

In this chapter I examine studies involving general solar energy and the various options and scenarios which exist for an energy market increasingly saturated by solar.

Carbon Mitigation is Possible with Growth of the Solar Photovoltaic Power Industry

Drury *et al.* (2009) partitioned carbon mitigation and emissions stabilization over the next 50 years into seven 1.0 Gton C/year carbon reduction wedges. With significant industrial and expected technological growth, solar photovoltaics (PV) could provide at least one of these carbon reduction wedges. This level of reduction can be met by increasing PV installations and manufacturing capacities by less than 1 GW/year annually for the next 50 years. In the short term, PV manufacturing will lead to an increase in carbon emissions, however this increase is small, 0.3% of electric sector emissions, and will be negated in the long run due to PV efficiency and storage capacity.

Easan Drury and colleagues at the National Renewable Energy Laboratory evaluated a series of PV growth scenarios and extrapolated the data onward until 2050, determining that at industry expansion levels, which are well within our capacity, PV has the potential to mitigate a wedge of carbon emissions. In calculation of the PV wedge contribution, 'upstream' components of fuel production are considered, including factors such as the large amount of energy used to transport natural gas, methane leaks and coal transportation. The wedge contribution is primarily from avoided fuel combustion in the electric sector and therefore a reduction of greenhouse gas emissions.

The US share of one carbon wedge can be supplied with 756–774 GW of PV capacity installed by 2050 assuming constant annual growth in the industry. In context, 500–700 GW could be installed on commercial and residential rooftops, the remaining PV capacity located on 1% of current US cropland.

To manufacture various types of PV modules, materials such as quartz and metal ores must be mined and purified then manufactured into the components of each module. This intensive process results in significant carbon emissions, which is why initially PV might have a positive contribution to carbon emissions. However the carbon intensity of manufacturing PV decreases over time as PV displaces other carbon emitting electrical energy sources and as manufacturing technology progresses. The degree to which PV could displace carbon emitting energy sources is dependent on the mix of coal, natural gas, and petroleum used in the market.

Solar Energy as an Overall Economic Option for US Energy Needs

Solar energy is currently only a minor contributor to US renewable energy options due to cost and intermittency issues. But advances in technology have led to drastic cost reductions in the production of photovoltaics (PV). Such advancements open the door for solar energy to become cost competitive with fossil fuels by 2020 (Fthenakis et al. 2009). The issue of intermittency can be solved by integrating PV with compressed air energy storage (CAES) and enhancing thermal storage capabilities. Even under the worst weather conditions it is shown that solar energy has the capacity to supply 69% of the total electricity needs of the US by 2050 and over

90% by 2100. Advances in technology make solar energy a promising renewable energy source. The challenge will be securing enough political foresight to realize this potential.

Vasilis Fthenakis and colleagues have used current data and figures to forecast future energy demand levels in the US and then extrapolated the deployment level of existing solar technologies in order to prove the feasibility of solar energy as a dependable cost effective resource.

With technology comes efficiency in PV production, leading to cost reduction. Module layers can be made thinner to require less material in their production and horizontally merging input production at onsite PV power plants will also decrease cost. Compressed air energy storage will ensure that even on a cloudy day, base level energy needs will still be met because energy is over-produced during sunny periods and stored with CAES. Concentrating solar power (CSP) systems offer a viable option for thermal energy storage if consistent annual deployment takes place resulting lowered costs.

The southwest (SW) United States is ideal for solar energy production. At least 640,000 km^2 (250,000 square miles) of land is suitable for solar power plant construction in this area. The SW receives over 6.4 kWh/m^2 day and 4,500 Q-Btu per year, and a mere 2.5% of this yearly solar radiation equates to the current annual US energy consumption. But production in the SW would require a national transmission network using high capacity lines.

Solar plants must be oversized in order to meet both peak energy needs and base-load solar levels. However this will result in excess energy output, enough to easily allow hydrogen production during the spring, summer, and fall months. This would allow the hydrogen transportation market to open up as a supplement to biofuels.

Technology is growing and will likely continue to do so at a steady to increasing pace. So advancements are of little worry compared to the political factors involved in the implementation of these alternative energy sources. Political planning and foresight will be invaluable to the advancement of solar energy utilization.

What a Looker: Solar Power Plants

Solar energy is a good option for areas of high solar irradiation because it can produce large amounts of electricity at low levels of pollution. One of the only direct pollutants is visual alteration of the landscape where panels are placed. Following EU regulations, Environmental Impact Assessment (EIA) requires a visual impact analysis for large solar power plant constructions. Torres–Sibille et al. (2009) devised a system to judge the aesthetic impact of a given solar power plant. When compared with real subjective human evaluation indicator used in this study generally explains user preferences well and will be useful in determining where to build solar plants and how best to do so to minimize visual impacts.

Torres–Sibille and colleagues at Valencia University of Technology devised their method of aesthetic impact analysis based on expert methodology used to analyze wind power. Solar power is similar to wind in that it dramatically transforms the appearance of a landscape with out dramatically altering the land itself. The effect of solar panels is at a much lower altitude than wind power but still obvious.

The researchers focused on aesthetic impact based on visibility, color, fractality and concurrence between fixed and mobile panels. Relative importance was assigned to each variable and data were combined in mathematical models used to determine how a user might perceive a given power plant landscape. Factors such as color of panels, surrounding flora and layout were important to the public. It was shown that the model was able to match preferences well by giving positive or negative values to several criteria.

Models of this sort and further study will be helpful in determining the visual impacts solar power plants have on people. Perception is very important when matters involve public approval and that may be the case for solar plants. Knowing what appeals to the eye will help developers build the most pleasant systems possible and fewer citizens might complain that a solar power plant has ruined the view.

Prospective Combined Solar-Wind Energy

Wind and solar energy are two of the main renewable energy options. Wind energy is currently much less expensive at 7.5681 c€/kWh than photovoltaics at 43.1486 c€/kWh. Dufo-Lopez *et al.* (2009) examine the feasibility of a combined solar-wind energy production system in Spain in three different forms; Type A in which all energy is sold to the grid, Type B in which some energy is sold to the grid and some is used to produce hydrogen which is also sold, and Type C in which some energy is sold to the grid, some used to produce hydrogen later used in a fuel cell and the electrical energy thus generated is sold. It was found that the intermittent production of hydrogen was only economical in areas with a high wind speed and if the selling price was at least 10 c€/kWh, much higher than currently allowed under Spanish law.

Wind energy would be much less expensive to produce in Spain because of equipment costs, but wind speeds can vary greatly within much of the land that has been determined to have a high enough wind speed is already occupied by wind installations.

Conversely photovoltaics can be installed almost anywhere because solar irradiation does not vary much within a geographical area considered. Economically it makes sense to combine the two technologies because wind power will help bring down costs and solar energy will make for a larger area of production.

The three types of hybrid PV-wind systems considered vary the degree to which hydrogen is used. In type B and C systems hydrogen will be generated when the excess energy generated from the electrical systems exceeds the evacuation capacity of the electrical grid, but are viable options only if wind speed is high enough, and can only be implemented in limited areas of Spain. PV-only systems are the best option for places with sub par wind levels.

Solar Homes Systems in India

Tens of millions of rural households throughout India lack access to grid electricity and of these, about 67 million use kerosene, a hydrocarbon based fuel, for lighting (Chaurey and Kandpal. 2009). Solar home systems (SHS) offer people in rural areas access to energy to run general appliances and provide lighting without the expense, time, and effort of connecting them to the grid as well as eliminating much CO_2 production. SHS would eliminate the need to burn kerosene for lighting as well as prevent much CO_2 that would have been emitted during the process of connecting many of these rural areas to the grid. Carbon finance could also reduce the cost of SHS to the user by an estimated level of 19%. This technology is a low cost carbon mitigation option that brings electricity to areas that may not have the ability to obtain otherwise. However it is arguable that SHS may not me quite economically feasible in these areas even with cost reduction and considering the benefits.

Chaurey and Kandpal of the Centre for Energy Studies at Indian Institute of Technology gather together a compilation of data on SHS systems in order to determine the pros and cons of their integration into areas of India without an electrical grid connection. SHS are sometimes a lower cost option than grid connection for many areas that are very isolated and have low population densities. It would also displace much carbon produced from the burning of kerosene and the use of diesel generators. Despite this carbon mitigation potential, there are few SHS projects that are benefiting from carbon finance.

Due to the high costs of photovoltaics it is unlikely that they will play a large role in world energy contributions until 2020. PV has a high startup cost and poor cost efficiency at low load levels as would be the case in the rural areas in which SHS would be implemented. There for implementing this technology will not be possible unless it is heavily subsidized and technological advancements continue to be made.

SHS diffusion in India has been fairly limited. Policy changes and high upfront costs provide a barrier to integration of this technology. As well as the general lack of financing and a needs to system design incompatibility. These factors have presumably limited diffusion of this technology in the Indian market.

Implementation of SHS technology would have many benefits to the communities in which it is placed, as well as overall carbon mitigation benefits. However in order for this to take place action must be taken to facilitate funding, marketing, technology, manufacturing and delivery of these systems before they are a more practical option.

Implementation of Solar Home Systems in Bangladesh: Feasibility

In Bangladesh the climate, despite the monsoons, seems well suited for solar energy. The form of photovoltaics most attractive to the people of Bangladesh is the solar home system (SHS) which would provide electricity for lighting and other uses to households across the country. Currently the people of Bangladesh burn kerosene for lighting and use dry cell batteries mostly for radio. SHS would eliminate the burning of kerosene and the waste of batteries. It was determined that it would be financially smart for small business and household lighting and entertainment (but not lighting only).

Alam Hossian Mondal of the Center for Development Research the University of Bonn studied three villages, Niz Mawna, Barabo and Dhonua to determine whether it was economically beneficial to use SHS's to provide electricity in order to prevent the use of other non-renewable energy sources.

SHS eliminates the need for kerosene burning lamps, which in turn eliminates large quantities of CO_2 emissions. After considering per ton CO_2 reduction costs it was determined SHS would yield an annual saving of 70 Taka (60 Taka = 1 USD) per household.

A typical SHS includes a photovoltaic (PV) array, and a rechargeable battery for energy storage. This system could be implemented via standard solar application on rooftops. These roofs belong to rural customers who are not in the habit of buying large systems, and usually do not buy everything unless they see the perceived benefits of the purchase. Therefore if SHS is to be implemented it must be seen as a worthy investment by the rural home and business-owners.

It was shown that due to the high initial capital and installation costs, SHS would not be affordable unless subsidized to at least some degree. Once subsidized properly, people would be inclined to purchase the system, resulting in a chain reaction and increased SHS popularity. However the SHS is only economical for households if they are using the electricity for some uses other than lighting. It would almost always be good for small businesses to utilize, decreasing costs in the long run and decreasing CO_2 emissions from halted use of kerosene.

Teija Mortvedt

Concentrating Solar Power and Thermal Energy Storage: Possibilities

As the solar energy movement progresses, the efficiency and cost-benefit ratios can be examined to determine which technologies will serve us best. Unlike photovoltaic generation, which converts light energy directly to electricity, concentrating solar power (CSP) uses thermal energy to produce electricity through steam turbines. Shioshanasi and Denholm (2009) analyzed the potential for CSP at various sites in the American Southwest and showed that CSP is more valuable when implemented in conjunction with thermal energy storage (TES) which allows for increased capacity of plants as well as greater profit by shifting production to hours of higher energy prices. Despite these advantages, it was determined that CSP with TES cannot be justified at current capital costs, but CSP alone will become more economic with further cost reductions.

Shioshansi and Denholm worked to model the capabilities and costs of CSP using data from four sites in the southwest: Gila Bend (Arizona), Daggett (California), Southern New Mexico, and Western Texas. They evaluated plants both with and without TES. With TES a larger solar field could be built and plant layout and size would be dramatically affected. Field size determines plant capacity so this is an important consideration. If the solar field is too small, the power block will be underused and inefficient and capacity will be lower. If the solar field is too large thermal energy will be wasted because the plant will not be able to utilize all the energy collected.

The study analyzed operating profits of CSP plants with different sized solar fields and three different levels of TES. TES always increased operating cost and it was seen that cost varied significantly with location and plant size. Location differences can be attributed mainly to energy price differences by location.

TES makes it possible to hold solar energy overnight for generating electricity the next day. They model used in this paper assumes that prices are known only one day in advance, though predictions of multiple days may be available in the future. This feature allows given amount of energy generation to be sold at the highest price but the analysis was based on the assumption of perfect foresight into the future, which in practice is not true. Regardless, it was determined that this model was profitable without 100% foresight.

CSP with TES is currently not an economic option anywhere but in Texas where energy prices, and therefore profits, are higher. It is assumed that CSP is eligible for investment tax credit (ITC) of 30% currently or a possible reduced 10% in the future due to CSP cost reductions. The 30% ITC makes CSP without TES an economic option only at the Texas site, and with TES economic in Texas and

Daggett. CSP will become a more economic with technological increases and cost reductions in the future.

Could Concentrating Solar Power be Competitive with Coal?

The European Union has challenging targets for reducing its greenhouse gas emissions. A potential solution is concentrating solar power (CSP) in North Africa with electricity transmission to Europe. The feasibility of this option has been examined and it is known that it is possible to generate enough power for transmission, but there has been little work to evaluate the cost of such a project. CSP is much more expensive than its competitor, coal burning power plants. Williges *et al.* (2010) examine the efforts that could be made to make CSP cost competitive with coal and the value of subsides until technology increases. It was found that subsides estimates are feasible for the EU and its energy targets. The cost of subsides and the time for CSP to be competitive with coal were determined positively effected by the inherent sensitivity of CSP to perceived risk and learning rates.

Because Northern Africa has the more solar radiation than Europe and is relatively close, it is a good option for CSP plants. Williges *et al.* examine developed the Mediterranean area renewable generation estimator (MARGE) to estimate costs of implementing CSP plants and bringing the energy to Europe. They examine specific investment costs and interest rates demanded by investors.

The results of this study confirmed previous analyses which suggest a total subsidy of 20 billion dollars and cost parity with coal by 2025 to 2030. The study showed that CSP is sensitive to a range of external drivers which policy makers can influence. CSP was found to be least sensitive to geographic diversification and most sensitive to learning rate. Differences in learning rate could push the time-cost parity with coal back by 20 years.

There is a wide range of numbers for reaching cost parity with coal over the years. A favorable combination of the examined variables could make minimize subsides and time for cost equilibrium to be reached. This study found that CSP could be an effective and affordable way to mitigate climate change and it is for this reason that more research and examination on the topic should be done if we are to reach our current goals for the future.

Conclusions

Human energy demand seems boundless and sunlight is infinite, but is this a match? Solar power can be located on relatively little land and produce a large amount of energy. It is intermittent but there are areas where this factor is negligible, places where we might produce power to be transmitted elsewhere. Once running, solar plants are clean and carbon free. Solar power has many pros, but currently even greater cons due to high cost. We have seen however in the previous discussions that these cons have the potential to fade with time and be contained in the near future until we have time to adjust. Technology will continue to increase and if solar power is implemented and humans will find ways to minimize costs and maximize efficiency as industry grows. In the meantime solar energy can most likely only get the kick-start it needs to become successful if governments provide subsidies or tax credits to allow cost competitiveness with fossil fuels. This is of course entirely dependent on the value society decides to place on this particular technology and its future benefits.

References Cited

Chaurey, A., Kandpal, T.C., 2009. Carbon Abatement Potential of Solar Home Systems in India and their Cost Reduction Due to Carbon Finance. Energy Policy 37, 115–125.

Dufo–Lopez , R., Bernal-Agustin, J.L., Mendoza, F., 2009, Design and Economical Analysis of Hybrid PV-wind Systems Connected to the Grid for the Intermittent Production of Hydrogen, Energy Policy 37, 3082–2095.

Drury, E., Denholm, P., Margolis, R. M., 2009. The Solar Photovoltaics Wedge: Pathways for Growth and Potential Carbon Mitigation in the US. Environmental Research Letters 4, 034010, 1–11.

Fthenakis, V., Mason, J. E., Zweibel, K., 2009. The technical, geographical, and economic feasibility for solar energy to supply the energy needs of the U.S., Energy Policy 37, 387–399.

Mondal, A. H., 2009. Economic Viability of Solar Systems: Case Study of Bangladesh. Renewable Energy 35, 1125–1129.

Sioshansi, R., Denholm, P., 2010. The Value of Concentrating Solar Power and Thermal Energy Storage. iwse.osu.edu.

Torres–Sibille, A. C., Cloquell–Ballester, Viceente–A., Cloquell–Ballester, Victor-A., Ramirez, M. A. A., 2009. Aesthetic Impact Assessment of Solar Power Plants: An Objective and a Subjective Approach. Renewable and Sustainable Energy Reviews 13, 986–999.

Williges, K., Lilliestam, J., Patt, A., 2010. Making Concentrated Solar Power Competitive with Coal : The Costs of a European Feed-in Tariff. Energy Policy 38, 3089–3097.

17. The Promising Future of Vehicle Technology

Blake Kos

With the inception of the personal vehicle in the early 20th century, modern society has relied on these machines for their continued economic growth and advances in technology by allowing people and goods to travel further and faster at relatively low costs. Today, vehicles powered by the internal combustion engine (ICE) dominate the transportation system and are supported by an extensive and well-functioning global infrastructure. However, ICE vehicles still produce environmentally harmful byproducts that have contributed to changes in the global climate. Some fear that if nothing is done to mitigate these negative effects, dramatic and rapid changes in the climate are inevitable, resulting in disastrous consequences to established industries and economies. Thus, scientists and professionals around the world are investigating certain measures that modern society can adopt to address these alarming issues. These potential measures should be adopted in an effective manner insofar as, they do not thwart economic growth or future technological advancement.

Quick, reliable personal mobility has become an integral part of daily life in modern society. Increased personal mobility has enabled the economy of the US to grow and it will be fundamental in its future growth and success. Currently, the US transportation system is the world's largest transportation system with roughly 251 million registered vehicles. However, almost all the vehicles in the US fleet are powered by an internal combustion engine, which operates chiefly on petroleum-based fuels. The domination of the internal combustion engine in American society requires an enormous amount of energy, which has forced the US to be dependent on imported oil from politically unstable regions of the world. Imported oil supplies more than half of US oil needs resulting in billion of dollars leaving the country. Also, the operation of vehicles powered by ICE produces harmful Greenhouse Gas (GHG) emissions. The most important GHG produced by the transportation sector is CO_2, which has been proven to enhance the effects of climate change. Consequently, transportation activities are the second largest portion of US GHG emissions therefore making the US a major source of global CO_2 emissions. Data from the 2010 US Inventory Report show that in 2008, approximately 27% of total US GHG emissions were solely produced by the transportation sector and the largest source of GHG emissions for the transportation sector was passenger vehicles (33%), followed by light-duty trucks, SUVs and minivans (29%). As of now, the US transportation sector consumes 7 out of 10 imported barrels of oil. Without the adoption of countermeasures, transportation energy use and GHG emissions will continue to grow.

Currently, the US transportation sector relies heavily on high-carbon fossil fuels as its principle transportation energy source. In order to decrease the high US transportation energy use and GHG emissions, measures and policies should be adopted to transition the US transportation sector to other energy sources such as renewable and low-carbon energy sources. Unfortunately, such energy sources require more effort and significant advances in technology before they can be commercial available. For example, Canadian tar sands could be utilized without negative externalities if they were used to produce hydrogen and carbon sequestration was incorporated to make it a carbon neutral technology. Although hydrogen is the optimal long-term option to addressing the issues with the current transportation sector, hydrogen-related technology will not transpire for at least a couple of decades due to the necessary technological breakthroughs in hydrogen transportation and the required infrastructure. A near-term alternative proposed by Stone et al. (2009) to reducing transportation energy use and GHG emissions would be developing greater efficiency of the existing transportation energy sources through the use of hybrid technology until the technological and economical challenges of low-carbon energy sources are overcome. Another feasible option offered by several studies would be replacing the current high-carbon intensity energy sources with low-carbon sources such as natural gas, bio-fuel, or electricity. One can already observe increased implementation of natural gas as a transportation energy source for a majority of public transportation vehicles especially in California. In the bio-fuel case, biomass grown on a hectare of land when it is converted to electricity achieves more transportation kilometers and GHG offsets than when it is converted into ethanol (Campbell et al. 2009). When produced by carbon neutral sources like wind, water, solar, and nuclear, electricity generation for electric vehicles can result in nearly zero carbon emissions and can greatly aid in the pursuit of emission reduction targets and independence to the oil addiction. Coupled with US fleet electrification, Guille *et al.* (2009) introduces the concept of an integrated electric vehicle to grid concept in addressing the problems associated with intermittent renewable energy. In addition to hybridization and electrification of the US vehicle fleet, improvements in the logistics, handling of goods, and the optimization of trucks loads and capacity of the commercial trucking industry has the potential to increase transportation system energy efficiency. Necessary technologies should be developed and effective policies need to be adopted for a cleaner, more economically efficient US energy system to transpire without the dependence of oil.

The Future of Automobiles, using Electric, Hybrid and Fuel Cell Technology to meet New Global Demands

The majority of the vehicles currently being operated on the road, whether for personal or commercial use, are equipped with internal combustion engines (ICEs). The ICE is principally powered by gasoline which when burned produces greenhouse gases (GHG). These GHGs, some of which are harmful to human health and all of which induce global warming, have come under tougher emissions regulations by government agencies around the world. In order to resolve the energy crisis and global warming, some believe that battery-powered technology is the solution. Chan (2007) proposes a battery-powered technology that incorporates all electric, hybrid (mix of ICE and electric) and fuel cell powertrain systems.

C.C. Chan at the University of Hong Kong explains why battery-powered technology will be more widely accepted in the automotive industry and by the consumer in order to meet new global pressures about global warming and the potential energy crisis. Currently, the market share of such technologies is insignificant, nevertheless, Chan predicts that these technologies will gain more attractiveness due to superior fuel economy and performance, especially hybrids.

Electric powered vehicles have been around for as long as a century and because pressures about health concerns, global warming, and a future energy crisis persist, automakers are being forced to provide the consumer electrically powered vehicles once again. As of now there exist three types of electrically powered vehicles. Hybrid vehicles (e.g. Toyota Prius), use both an electric motor and an engine. There are four common architectures of a hybrid vehicle: series, parallel, series-parallel, and complex hybrid. The major difference between these systems is whether the electric motor is used to achieve better fuel economy or better performance. A series hybrid uses the ICE output and converts it into electricity using a generator. The electricity produced is then stored in a battery—or if necessary, can bypass the battery storage. Generally, efficiency is lower in a series system hybrid. A parallel hybrid allows both the ICE and electric motor to deliver power in parallel with the vehicle's onboard computer deciding on the mix. The other two systems,

213

series-parallel and complex, are mixtures of the series and parallel systems. Also, there are micro, mild, and full hybrids, depending on the power output of the electric motor (i.e. full hybrids can save about 30%–50% energy and put out about 50 kW of power). The micro and mild classifications are used to achieve a moderate increase in efficiency. All-electric vehicles use only an electric motor and a battery, require time to recharge, and have a limited range. Fuel cell vehicles use hydrogen as the source of power for the vehicle, emitting only heat and water.

At a glance these technologies seem very promising, however, there are some key advances that need to be made before they can become more commonplace. Some issues that automakers are experiencing with the all-electric vehicles are current battery technology, management, and size. The major issues are time required for charging and miles per charge. As of now, our current electric infrastructure cannot sustain charging millions of electric vehicles. Fuel cell vehicles, which do not require charging, address the latter problem. However, concerns regarding fuel cell costs and the hydrogen infrastructure are preventing fuel cell vehicles from widespread consumer use. The most promising technology out of the three is hybrid, but consumers still have issues with the control, optimization, and management from multiple sources of power and battery size. Fortunately, researchers have been able to find solutions to these concerns through the development of better hybrid control technology, power converters, and the mixture of battery and ultra capacitors that once developed will allow these types of vehicles to eventually dominate the market.

Potential Importance of Hydrogen as a Future Solution to Environmental and Transportation Problems

With declining global crude oil supplies, increasing political instability in the regions with large oil reserves, more stringent emission regulations and the threat of global warming, hydrogen has been proclaimed as the future transportation fuel (Balat 2008). The strategic development of hydrogen technology is extremely important in the pursuit of a low-emission, environmental friendly, cleaner, and sustainable energy system which most governments are pursuing. Hydrogen as a future alternative transportation fuel has many advantages. One is that hydrogen can be produced from a wide variety of sources such as biomass-based production, electrolysis of water, and coal gasification. Another key advantage is the special properties of hydrogen. Hydrogen has a rapid burning speed, a high effective octane number, and no toxicity or ozone-forming potential. Also, the only combustion byproduct of hydrogen is water and a minor amount of nitrogen oxide. Unfortunately, its major downfall is the cumbersome and heavy on-board storage tanks required for gasoline-comparable driving range. Given the advantages associated with hydrogen technology, many believe a hydrogen economy will eventually rise, replacing the vast majority of petroleum fuels currently in use.

Mustafa Balat at the University of Mahallasi in Turkey has analyzed the potential importance of hydrogen as a future solution to replacing petroleum-based fuels and he indicates that hydrogen will be viable solution in the long term as the costs related to hydrogen technology diminish.

Hydrogen, a colorless, odorless, tasteless and non-toxic gas, is the most abundant element in the universe. The production of hydrogen can be accomplished from numerous sources through a range of processes. It is believed that eventually, hydrogen will replace most petroleum-based products and give rise to the "hydrogen economy". In order for that to occur, many obstacles will need to be addressed. These obstacles include a cost efficient delivery system, a universal and ubiquitous hydrogen distribution infrastructure, more cost effective hydrogen production, and better on-board storage capabilities. Once these challenges are met, hydrogen will be the answer to combating socially and politically unstable issues like global warming, diminishing oil supplies, stricter emission standards, and increases in health problems associated with air pollution in industrialized and developing nations around the world.

Design, Demonstrations and Sustainability Impact Assessments for Plug-in Hybrid Electric Vehicles

A near-term solution that addresses many of challenges consumers, researchers, automakers, utilities, and government agencies have had historically with conventional and electric vehicles, is the plug-in hybrid vehicle (PHEV)(Bradley *et al.* 2009). The PHEV is a type of hybrid vehicle that uses a portion of its propulsive energy from electricity generated from the power grid. The current PHEV prototypes have successfully demonstrated increased transportation energy efficiency, reduced carbon emissions, reduced criteria emissions, reduced fueling cost, and improved transportation energy sector sustainability. With these beneficial impacts of the PHEV, the transportation sector will be able to displace petroleum as a transportation fuel and access the lower-cost and cleaner energy available via the power grid.

Bradley and Frank analyze the potential of plug-in hybrids to replace petroleum-based transportation fuels for the transportation sector. They claim that PHEVs confront the issues associated with both the internal combustion and electric vehicles and believe that PHEVs are the near-term solution to displacing petroleum as transportation fuel.

PHEVs are similar to conventional hybrid electric vehicles in that they both incorporate an electric and internal combustion drivetrain, however, the main difference is that a PHEV has an additional component called the charger. The charger permits the PHEV to draw and store energy via the electrical grid onto its onboard batteries. Because the PHEV utilizes both an electric and internal combustion drivetrain, it must be controlled by the vehicle's architecture and energy management system. The energy management system regulates the electric and combustion drivetrain systems to provide the most desirable mixture of power and efficiency thus allowing the vehicle to be driven with better performance, higher energy efficiency, lower environmental impact and lower cost than conventional HEVs (hybrid electric vehicle).

Based on data gathered from PHEV prototypes, PHEVs offer dramatic reductions in petroleum consumption, criteria emissions (vehicle evaporation emissions, refueling emissions, electricity generation emissions, and the emissions associated with fuel extraction, processing, production, transportation, and distribution) and carbon emissions. For example, PHEV with a 100 km driving range in electric vehicle mode driven and charged nightly, will result in an 84% decrease in gasoline consumption, compared to a conventional gasoline-powered vehicle. Since PHEVs have less frequent refueling events, the criteria emissions associated with PHEVs are reduced. However, this can be offset depending on means of electricity generation i.e. wind, hydroelectric and solar. If PHEVs are plugged in during off peak hours, grid efficiency will be improved and electricity costs to consumer will be lowered. As of now, the numbers of PHEVs in the market is insignificant; as consumer interest rises and better technology is incorporated into PHEVs, petroleum-based transportation fuels will be displaced.

The Most Efficient use of Biomass: Bioelectricity or Ethanol

Concerns about the stability of crude oil prices and the climate change effects of greenhouse gases (GHG) are influencing investments to develop a viable and more cost-effective alternative energy source within the US transportation sector. Campbell *et al.* claim that bioenergy is a near-term renewable solution to powering the vehicles of the future without affecting food prices or GHG emissions. Currently, the two leading alternative transportation technologies are cellulosic ethanol and electric vehicles, either pure electric or hybrid. Industrial biomass, which is derived from trees and plants including switchgrass and corn, either can be converted into ethanol to power an internal combustion engine or converted into electricity through composition or gasification via turbines and generators for battery-powered electric vehicles. Although there is uncertainty about which option will be technologically and economically possible first, the authors show that biomass converted directly into electricity is more land-efficient than biomass converted into ethanol.

Campbell, Lobell, and Field assess the performance of bioelectricity and ethanol with respect to transportation kilometers and GHG offsets achieved per unit area of cropland. They suggest biomass converted into electricity to power battery-powered vehicles offers much higher efficiency with respect to transportation kilometers and GHG offsets than does biomass converted into ethanol.

Around the world and the US, there is a surging interest in developing alternative renewable energy sources for the transportation sector. In order to meet the many transportation and climate change goals, bioenergy has been regarded as a potential and feasible near-term solution. Given the limited area of land dedicated to growing biofuel crops, bioenergy efficiency should be maximized. Campbell *et al.* show that one can travel farther on biomass grown on a hectare of land when it is converted to electricity than when it is converted into ethanol. Also, the net transportation output, which subtracts the fuel-cycle costs (energy needed to grow the biomass and convert into electricity or ethanol) and the vehicle-cycle costs (energy needed to manufacture, maintain, and dispose of vehicle) per hectare is 56% greater for the bioelectricity option than for the ethanol option. (The vehicle-cycle costs are larger for the battery-powered vehicles than the internal combustion vehicles because of the cost of the batteries.) In addition, several ethanol cases indicate negative net transportation distances because the distance that could be traveled with the net fuel-cycle is greater than the distance that could be traveled with ethanol usage. Coupling carbon capture and sequestration technologies with bioelectricity production could result in carbon negative values that remove CO_2 from the atmosphere.

A Conceptual Framework for Vehicle-to-Grid Implementation

All-electric vehicles (EVs) and plug-in hybrids (PHEVs), which both use batteries for propulsive purposes, are seen as key players to the US energy independence and the pursuit of reducing the effects of global warming. A massive deployment of battery-powered vehicles (BVs) into the US transportation sector, is expected in the coming years, but some questions and doubts have been raised about the effects of full integration of BVs into the national grid. Guille *et al.* (2009) evaluate the concept of a network of aggregated BVs in providing and storing energy for a more efficient and reliable grid. The concept of using BVs as load and generation/storage devices on the national grid is known as vehicle-to-grid (V2G). Under this proposed concept, BVs play an important role in improving the reliability, economics, and environmental benefits of daily grid operations. Unfortunately, the V2G concept is still in the developmental stages and requires a solid framework to overcome some issues before a nation-wide implementation is carried out.

Guille and Gross at the University of Illinois at Urbana-Champaign assess a proposed framework for the implementation of the vehicle-to-grid concept. This concept, which incorporates battery-powered vehicles, is viewed as a direct approach to addressing the issues of US energy independence and the effects of global warming.

A US solution to the concerns of energy independence and the reduction in the effects of global warming is the near-term deployment of BVs. Battery-powered vehicles are able to take advantage of clean, alternative sources of energy and reduce regional emissions by using electricity instead of fossil fuels. Because the average US driver commutes about 32 miles a day, not all the energy stored in the battery is exhausted. Therefore, each BV is considered a potential source of both energy and available storage which can be controlled by the current national grid without new power plant installations (i.e. coal-fired power plants). Once the BV is plugged into the grid, the batteries may be used as an energy resource. In order for the BVs to have an impact on the grid, a large number (thousands to hundreds of thousands) would be needed. The key enabler to realizing the V2G concept is the Aggregator that controls and retains BVs connected to the grid. The aggregation of BVs controlled by the Aggregator allows for the exploitation of possible economic benefits such as purchasing and selling electricity to and from the grid. Also, the Aggregators can work in conjunction with grid operators to use BVs as a useful sink for load levelization during off-peak hours thus reducing energy and reserve requirements. However, the implementation of this proposed concept has one critical prerequisite; the establishment of an infrastructural computer/communication/control network for the integration of the aggregation of BVs into the grid. Regulators must understand the potential impacts of BV integration on the national grid and formulate effective policies (i.e. package deals) to pass this costly but critical requirement.

Recent Challenges of Hydrogen Storage Technologies for Fuel Cell Vehicles

Quick and reliable personal mobility is one of modern society's most increasing desires, especially with the progress of a world economy. However, current personal mobility (i.e. automobiles and airplanes) is powered by "dirty" and environmentally harmful sources derived from fossil fuels. Mori et al. (2009) believe that fuel cell technology will address the issues of unhealthy urban air quality and the threat of global warming associated with the current inefficient and environmentally damaging technology. Fuel cell technology is powered by hydrogen, which can be produced from a wide variety of non-fossil sources such as biomass-based production, electrolysis of water, as well as natural gas and coal gasification. Unfortunately, fuel cell technology faces an enormous barrier of on-board hydrogen storage before it can be commercially viable and cost-effective for the average consumer. Current state-of-the-art hydrogen storage technology can only store 1/10 of energy of gasoline in the same volume due to hydrogen's low-density. In order for a "hydrogen" society to transpire, increased hydrogen storage density will need to be achieved.

Mori and Hirose from the Fuel Cell Development Division of the Toyota Motor Corporation investigate the latest material and system developments to solve some of the difficulties of the on-board hydrogen storage. If the on-board hydrogen storage issue can be successfully addressed, they believe a hydrogen economy will be a near future possibility and the goal of a cleaner, sustainable, and inexpensive energy system will be met.

Hydrogen is expected to be the clean and renewable energy carrier to replace the current dirty and damaging energy source, fossil fuel. Unfortunately, the enormous challenge of on-board hydrogen storage without compromising standard vehicle requirements (i.e. safety, performance, cost, technical adaptation for the infrastructure and scalability) needs to be resolved. To solve this challenge, increases in both storage of hydrogen and efficiency will need to be achieved for a comparable gasoline-powered vehicle range. Researchers have developed a possible solution for extending fuel cell vehicle range. This solution uses a composite high-pressure tank, which is characterized by charge-discharge easiness and a simplified structure. This proposed high-pressured (70 MPa) 180L tank results in 40–50% increases in storage and if coupled with the optimal materials and winding strategies, the tank can result in a 65% increase of storable hydrogen. Hydrogen-absorbing tanks have been examined as another possible solution. These tanks have the advantage of storing about 2.5 times more hydrogen with a higher ratio of hydrogen weight to tank weight, which makes the vehicle much lighter, thus more efficient. With these proposed, more efficient storage tanks, researchers are on the right track to achieving an on-board storage system that incorporates a lighter tank with increases of storable hydrogen.

Mobile Source CO_2 Mitigation through Smart Growth Development and Vehicle Fleet Hybridization

Current population migration models predict that most US cities will experience the most rapid population growth rates since before the Second World War within the coming decades. Therefore, resources such as clean air, water, and constant reliable energy will be significantly strained in these metropolitan areas. The use of "smart growth" strategies within these cities has been determined to measurably reduce per capita demands for these resources through more compact, mixed-use, and transit-supportive patterns of growth. Also, the improvement of vehicle fuel economy through the use of advanced vehicle technologies such as hydrogen vehicles, hybrid vehicles, and plug-in hybrid vehicles is widely accepted as the best approach to reducing urban GHG emissions. However, the universal diffusion of advanced technological vehicles into the US transportation sector will take decades due to their high costs and slow vehicle turnover rate. To accommodate such rapid growth, air quality management programs will need to be adopted today to ensure that clean air is provided to the residents of these metropolitan areas of tomorrow.

Stone *et al.* analyze the results of a study on the effectiveness of reducing emissions of carbon dioxide in various metropolitan areas within the US. They have found that significant emission reductions can be met through the incorporation of smart growth development patterns and vehicle hybridization within the whole US transportation sector.

By 2050, it is expected that populations in large metropolitan areas around the U.S. will drastically increase. The projected rapid population increase will be corresponded with an increase in CO_2 emissions from urbanization as well as tail-pipe emissions. Many believe that management programs should be adopted to maintain healthy air quality and to control for future climate change effects. This study suggests the potential for both smart growth strategies and technological change within the transportation sector to mitigate GHG emissions growth projected to occur in large cities by 2050. The results indicate that the most aggressive smart growth strategy will reduce current GHG emission trends by 8% while full light duty fleet hybridization will reduce it by 18%. In addition, it has been found that a doubling of population density in these metropolitan areas would be more beneficial than full integration of hybrid technology within the US vehicle fleet. In conclusion, to effectively reduce future urban GHG emissions, air quality management strategies should be designed to promote the continued integration of advanced vehicle technologies and to initiate concentrating the new population growth into denser urban centers. In addition to air quality management, cities should develop strategies to address the problems associated with urban growth for example increased traffic congestion and decrease physical activity.

Trends in Truck Freight Energy Use and Carbon Emissions in Selected OECD Countries from 1973 to 2005

In the first decade of the 21st century, the global economy has grown significantly. To sustain the current global trade trends, fast and efficient goods movement typically performed by commercial trucking has been seen as imperative for economic growth. As a result, changes within the trucking sector have been observed. The types of goods being moved and how far or frequently they are transported are examples of the changes that have occurred and will occur in the future.

These changes have an important impact on the energy demanded and the carbon footprint of the trucking sector. As the global goods movement expands around the world, many countries including the US will experience added pressure to control emissions and reduce fuel use of the trucking sector. Historically, reductions in fuel costs have been driven by the adoption of best available technologies and fuel reduction practices. However to address the pressing concerns of declining global oil supplies, Kamakate *et al.* (2009) have concluded that more stringent emission regulations and the threat of global warming, freight transportation will be forced to reduce its energy use and emissions even more. The use of bio-diesel fuel, better logistics and driving, higher load factors, and better matching of truck capacity to load coupled with best available technology will have the largest impacts in reducing truck energy use and emissions around the world.

Kamakate and his colleagues have identified numerous factors and business practices to successfully address global concerns of oil supplies and more strict emissions regulations. Overall freight energy use has increased, driven by both the growth of international trade and the shift towards trucking as the mode of freight transportation, which is more energy intensive than other modes. This increase in higher energy use has put added pressure on the trucking sector to address the global concerns of increased fuel costs and more stringent emission regulations. Unfortunately, there is little opportunity for gains in decreased energy use by shifting from trucking to rail. Instead, the largest gains have been from improvements in logistics, handling of goods, and the optimization of truck loads and capacity. Improved logistics means optimizing the location where goods are produced, loaded, and unloaded. Producers and handling facilities located closer to main roads and rail terminals reduce the use of trucks, and complete loading of trucks to full capacity, better traffic conditions, and other logistical factors could save truckers time and fuel costs over time. Policymakers should include these improved business practices in future policies to achieve greater reductions in energy use and emissions within the freight transportation sector.

Conclusions

To successfully curb the growth of US transportation emissions, and address the threat of global climate change, it will require a thoughtful combination of policies and measures that do not drastically affect US economic growth and technological processes. A successful policy will include specific vehicle efficiency improvements, timelines for transitions to low-carbon energy sources, and the termination of inefficient technologies. Until such policies are adopted, the US transportation sector will continue to be powered by petroleum-based fuels. For now, increases in energy efficiency will allow for more time for technological development in technologies like hydrogen. Over the next 30 years, more fuel-efficient technologies will emerge and the US government will be required to increase its role to facilitate the transition away from petroleum-based fuels. By taking action now, effective strategies can be formulated to reduce the fastest growing source of CO_2 emissions in the US economy and relieve the US of its oil addiction.

Reference Cited

Balat, M., 2008. Potential importance of hydrogen as a future solution to environmental and transportation problems. International Journal of Hydrogen Energy 33, 4013– 4029.

Bradley, T., Frank, A., 2009. Design, demonstrations and sustainability impact assessments for plug-in hybrid electric vehicles. Renewable and Sustainable Energy Reviews 13, 115–128.

Campbell, J., Lobell, D., Field, C., 2009. Greater transportation energy and GHG offsets from bioelectricity than ethanol. Science 324, 1055–1057.

Chan, C., 2007. The State of the Art of Electric, Hybrid, and Fuel Cell Vehicles. Proc. IEEE, 704–718.

Guille, C., Gross, G., 2009. A conceptual framework for the vehicle-to-grid (V2G) implementation. Energy Policy 37, 4379–4390.

Kamakate, F., Schipper, L., 2009. Trends in truck freight energy use and carbon emissions in selected OECD countries from 1973 to 2005. Energy Policy 37, 3743–3751.

Mori, D., Hirose, K., 2009. Recent challenges of hydrogen storage technologies for fuel cell vehicles. International Journal of Hydrogen Energy 34, 4569–4574.

Stone, B., Mednick, A., Holloway, T., Spak, S., 2009. Mobile Source CO_2 Mitigation through Smart Growth Development and Vehicle Fleet Hybridization. Environmental Science & Technology 43, 1704–1710.

Section V—Water and Climate Change

18. The Water Crisis: Wastewater Treatment and Reclamation

Acadia Tucker

Every terrestrial organism depends on fresh water, and although the Earth's surface is nearly two-thirds water, only 0.01% of it is fresh (Goldfarb 2000). Natural waterways have an intrinsic capacity to recover from limited amounts of pollutants but this capacity is often exceeded by wastewater releases from industrial agriculture, manufacturing, and domestic treatment plants. Even though wastewater treatment facilities are designed to reduce the contaminants in wastewater to tolerable levels before release into natural water bodies, many lakes, rivers, and ocean regions are nevertheless polluted by excess macronutrients which can trigger algal blooms and lead to eutrophication. The demand for fresh water resources is beginning to exceed the supply as the human population continues to grow and as the world continues to industrialize.

Before centralized wastewater treatment facilities, hunters and gatherers scattered their waste over large areas of land to prevent pollution from concentrated waste. This land-based waste cycle kept macronutrients tied to the Earth. Nutrients were directly recycled from human waste to the soil, bacteria, plants, and animals instead of washed out to sea. As people began to settle into permanent communities they had to develop new habits to conquer waste. Asian cultures fertilized their fields with human waste while western cultures built communal cesspools and outhouses. In the early 1800s, the invention of water pipes revolutionized the way 19th century households transported water. The convenience of a constant supply of water supported increased exploitation as the average amount of water used for domestic purposes jumped from 3–5 gallons a day to 30–100 gallons a day per person. Waste was also "flushed" into backyard cesspools connected to public sewage trenches. In 1832, as direct result of contaminated sewage systems, nearly 20,000 people died in Paris due to cholera (Rockefeller 1998).

This sparked a serious debate among engineers. They wondered how they could develop a sewage system that would improve public health. Instead of recycling human waste, engineers decided, "the solution to pollution is dilution" (Rockefeller 1998). By 1909 over 25 miles of new sewage pipes were installed and waste was deposited directly into local waterways. Unfortunately, cities downstream from the sewage pipes experienced typhoid outbreaks and, as a direct response, began to filter their drinking water. The sewage systems in America and Europe grew rapidly during the middle of the 20th century as more cities became industrialized. Now community waste was a combination of domestic and toxic industrial waste that was carried straight to local rivers. Natural waterways became heavily polluted in the most industrialized areas and created enough pressure to mandate treating wastewater before it entered the natural environment and gave rise to modern wastewater treatment plants.

Wastewater treatment facilities range from simple treatment techniques to more complicated methods of nutrient removal but they all share the same goal; to remove suspended solids and pollutants for both organic and industrial waste, and they are important for monitoring water quality in densely populated and industrialized areas. All treatment plants have the same basic decontamination processes but the type of treatment depends on the type of waste (Shahabadi et al. 2009). Wastewater enters a primary sedimentation tank where suspended solids precipitate out of the water and settle to the bottom creating a byproduct called sludge. The main purpose of primary treatment is to separate the sludge so that it can be treated separately from the rest of the wastewater. During the secondary stage of treatment the remaining wastewater is aerated and treated biologically. Flocculation is filtered and the final product is effluent wastewater with reduced levels of organic waste and suspended solids. Many wastewater treatment plants offer a tertiary treatment to further improve the quality of effluent wastewater.

Recent studies suggest that wastewater treatment facilities are necessary for public health and ecological preservation but need certain modifications to remain effective. Current wastewater techniques are good at removing organic solids but are less efficient at removing inorganic waste. There are no specific technologies available to remove heavy metals, pharmaceutical drugs, and unattractive odors from treatment plants. In addition, the plants are reservoirs for antibiotic-resistant bacteria (Zhang et al. 2009). Treatment facilities are also so expensive that certain communities can't even afford them. In undeveloped nations, wastewater treatment is virtually nonexistent and millions of people die every year from water-borne diseases (Ojunkule 2009). In developing countries intensified industrial practices place a higher emphasis on industrialization instead of pollution control. In these areas contaminated water resources prove to be the biggest and most dangerous problem.

Today's engineers and scientists are faced with some difficult challenges in wastewater treatment. They are trying to create wastewater treatment facilities that are more environmentally beneficial but certain questions remain unanswered.

What happens to the toxic sludge? What ecosystems can tolerate wastewater discharge? How can wastewater treatment plants become more sustainable? New technology and research strives to reduce the ecological impact of wastewater treatment plants and improve nutrient removal while making treatment available for communities across the globe.

Economic Valuation of Wastewater Treatment is Important for Determining Ecological and Social Costs that are Beneficial for Policy Making

Wastewater treatment plants have many environmental benefits that are often overlooked because water, like other public resources, does not have a large direct market value. The economic valuation of the cost and benefits of wastewater treatment is necessary for the instigation of polices to fight against the degradation and depletion of water resources (Hernández-Sancho et al. 2009). The removal of phosphorus is the most beneficial action to employ in wastewater treatment plants and the removal of suspended solids is the least beneficial action in any type of environment.

F. Hernández-Sancho and colleagues at the University of Valencia, Spain estimated the ecological cost created by wastewater discharge in an unregulated environment. They analyzed the difference between the outputs produced by a wastewater treatment plant and the potential outputs produced by a more efficient process under four different situations that involved rivers, seas, wetlands, and wastewater reuse. The outputs taken into consideration included: treated water, nitrogen, phosphorous, suspended solids, organic matter, and chemical oxygen demand. The inputs considered included: energy, labor power, reagents needed to create chemical reactions, and maintenance of the plant.

Through mathematical manipulation they were able to determine a value for ecological costs created by wastewater treatment plants so successful environmental policies can be made. They discovered that wetland areas are the most susceptible to damage caused by wastewater discharge because they are the most sensitive to pollutants and therefore the most valuable environment to reduce wastewater outputs from entering. Meanwhile, the ocean's large volume has more potential to dilute harmful substances because of the large water volume, and offers the lowest ecological benefit for wastewater discharge reduction. In addition, the removal of phosphorous and nitrogen produces the most environmental benefits for any system and the removal of suspended solids has the least dramatic environmental benefit. Water resources can also be protected by reducing the anthropogenic stresses on surface and ground water by reusing treated water. Not only does this reduce the amount of water pumped out of aquifers, it also reduces the amount of wastewater discharge that enters rivers, steams, and oceans.

The Benefits of Municipal Wastewater Reclamation and Reuse

The amount of municipal wastewater is increasing, as new places across the globe are becoming progressively more populated, industrialized, and urbanized. In order to reduce the amount of stress on water, wastewater reclamation and reuse is necessary. Wastewater is an untapped resource that needs to be exploited because as the demand for water increases, so does the generation of wastewater (Kumar 2009). Wastewater treatment plants can provide water for such tasks as cleaning, toilet bowl flushing, and recreational use without putting pressure on raw water resources. The future of urban water supplies will depend on how effectively people use wastewater discharge for domestic and industrial purposes.

Kumar, of the Technology Information, Forecasting and Assessment Council in India, assessed the efficiency and productivity of wastewater treatment plants in Delhi. He observed the gap between domestic wastewater generation and effective treatment in order to articulate the importance of wastewater reclamation.

Kumar discovered that 20% of wastewater reuse could support 10% of the population of Dehli. The advantages of wastewater reuse include: reduced stress on raw water sources, decreasing the gap between city water supply and demand, and the decrease in pollution due to untreated municipal discharge. Potable water is usually not the ultimate goal of wastewater reuse because of the cost of such a high level of treatment, and general public skepticism about drinking treated sewage. The most resourceful way to reuse wastewater is for daily household and industrial purposes that are water-intensive but don't require potable water.

Kumar suggests that the most economical way to treat wastewater influent is by the up flow anaerobic sludge blanket (UASB) process. This system requires less energy, chemicals, and labor to operate than the conventional methods of treatment. It utilizes a series of biofilters and membranes (instead of microbes) to cleanse the water. However, this system does have limitations associated with poor removal of macronutrients, pathogens and organic materials, which can be improved by post treatment facilities in the form of aerated lagoons or stabilization ponds. The UASB coupled with post treatments can effectively and economically treat wastewater so it can be exploited by any city with any budget.

Sustainable Wastewater Reuse in Northern China

China's effort to increase its standard of living and economic development puts a tremendous stress on water resources. Industrialization and urbanization associated with such development creates large quantities of unregulated water pollution that threatens the health of China's citizens and ecosystems. However, many developing countries lack the funding to support treatment facilities. Wastewater treatment programs need to be affordable enough for local communities to support (Ojekunle *et al.* 2009). Wastewater treatment plants provide not only water suitable for reuse but also other economic benefits that help offset the high cost of operation. Wastewater treatment plants can recycle lower quality water for tasks that don't require "pure" water resources to decrease the stress on the water supply and protect the surrounding ecosystems from pollution.

Ojekunle *et al.* of the Department of Environmental Science at Tianjin University developed an inexpensive treatment plant for the Toacheng district in Northern China to help improve the current water crisis. This system includes: a collection system, primary treatment plant, discharge into natural waterways, constructed wetland area for further purification, effluent reservoir for temporary storage and transportation to a power plant for cooling purposes.

Wastewater treatment plants may seem like a big investment for a community to make, but the cost of treatment operations can be subsidized by the economic benefits produced by the treatment plant. Wastewater facilities can profit from selling reclaimed water to companies for cooling and other services, harvesting and selling reeds from the constructed wetland area that improve the utility of septic tanks, and promoting ecotourism by preserving important landscapes. These three things alone could generate an estimated 200 million RMB a year (approximately 29.4 million USD). Furthermore, treatment plants protect the surrounding ecosystems from polluted discharge and constructed wetlands can create more species diversity.

Constructed wetlands also remove up to 97% of fecal coliform bacteria, 60 to 80% of suspended solids, 25 to 55% of nitrogen and 16 to 42% of phosphorus from treatment plant discharge. This cleans natural waterways and increases the value of the land, providing more areas suitable for living and commercial use. Yet, two risks remain: public health and flood control. Public health can be bettered by the improved water quality if the wetland area is constructed properly with adequate filtration and UV disinfection. Controllable floodgates in the temporary reservoir and buffer zones in the constructed wetland can help maintain reasonable water levels within this system. Although cost is an important factor in the construction and operation of wastewater treatment plants there are other factors that limit the number of treatment plants that are present in urban areas.

Determining Odor Emission Factors for Each Phase of Wastewater Treatment

The odor produced by wastewater treatment plants is a limiting factor in urban areas, but the use of treatment facilities in populated areas is important for the health of the surrounding ecosystems. Odors are released during the biodegradation of sewage and can be quantified by odor emission factors (OEF's) linked to particular treatment processes (Capelli *et al.* 2009). The major source of odors emitted from wastewater treatment plants occurs during the primary sedimentation phase of the treatment process.

Carpelli and colleagues estimated the OEF's produced during each phase of wastewater treatment from the time of water delivery to sludge storage. They used a wind tunnel to generate airflow over each holding tank, measured the resulting odor concentrations, and, using OEF calculations, determined the odor impact on the surrounding areas. The overall odor emission rate (OER) was determined by the sum of OEF's produced by the individual processes of wastewater treatment.

So which phase is the smelliest? Primary sedimentation is the strongest smelling OEF and emits the highest concentration of odor into surrounding areas. Odor concentration decreases as the depuration cycle continues with the exception of sludge thickening, which generates the second highest odor emission. The nitrification process generates the least amount of odor. This suggests that the concentration of odor is the highest before biological treatment. In order to incorporate more treatment facilities in urban areas changes in wastewater transport can be made to reduce odor irritants. Sewage systems determine the quality and odor potential of water entering a treatment plant; correct management of wastewater before it enters a plant can reduce the amount of odors generated. This also suggests that the operation of treatment facilities does not create the majority of odor emissions and therefore more facilities can be placed in urban areas, decreasing the human impact on the surrounding environment.

Life Cycle Assessment for Alternative Technology in Wastewater Treatment Plants

Urban wastewater treatment plants have primarily focused on human health by removing harmful pollutants to levels tolerable by individuals. However, the goals of urban wastewater treatment facilities need to focus not only on human health but also on ecological health and sustainability (Lundin *et al.* 2009). A typical urban treatment plant mixes household waste with industrial waste and urban run off. The availability of new technology allows us to assess our current wastewater treatment systems in an effort to improve the water quality of effluent wastewater entering the environment. Now, separation systems that divide black water from grey water are being explored as an efficient alternative to conventional wastewater treatment. Separation systems decrease the amount of pollution that enters a stream as discharge and recycle macronutrients for agricultural purposes.

Lundin et al. at Chalmers University of Technology in Sweden preformed a life cycle analysis to compare separation treatment methods to conventional treatment methods, and large treatment plants to small treatment plants. Two alternative separation techniques were theoretically applied to each treatment site. The alternative to the large-scale treatment used urine separation through specialized toilets, and the small-scale alternative treatment used liquid composting with the aid of vacuum pumps. A specific set of base parameters and boundaries was established for the LCA, which included resource and energy use in construction and operation, emissions to water and air, and waste generation.

The LCA analyses discovered that in terms of nutrient removal, the liquid composting method preformed the best but required the most resources and energy during construction compared to conventional wastewater treatment facilities. Liquid composting technology requires energy-intensive waste-generating materials such as steel. During operation, the small-scale plant used up to four times as much energy as the large-scale plant due to the energy required to run the vacuum pumps for the liquid composting system. The fossil fuel energy consumed by the machinery used to spread and transport recycled sludge in the alternative treatment methods was greater than the fossil fuel requirements for conventional treatments. However, the use and transportation of recycled sludge for fertilizer in agricultural areas is less than the amount of energy it takes to produce synthetic fertilizer. Results show that there is a clear advantage to alternative wastewater treatment technologies but the practical use of sludge is not feasible at the current time. Most wastewater sludge includes heavy metals and other contaminates that can't be applied to agricultural areas. Measures need to be taken to clean up sewage sludge to make it economically realistic to run more efficient alternative technologies to treat and manage wastewater.

In general, the optimal treatment method is urine separation with conventional treatment for grey water and human feces. The urine is stored and transported directly to agricultural fields as liquid compost. This dramatically reduces the amount of fossil fuels used to produce synthetic fertilizers because urine separation conserves the nitrogen in urine so it is not lost to the air or water. Therefore, emissions to the air and water are dramatically reduced which protects the human population as well as the ecosystems we depend on.

Acadia Tucker

The Impact of Greenhouse Gas Emissions Generated By Industrial Wastewater Treatment Plants

Wastewater treatment plants produce greenhouse gasses (GHG's) including CO_2, CH_4, and NO_x during the wastewater treatment process. Industrial wastewater reclamation plants produce more GHG's than municipal wastewater treatment plants because they contain more suspended solids and have a higher demand for biochemical oxygen (Shahabadi *et al.* 2009). Wastewater treatment plants improve wastewater quality by three main methods: aerobic reactors, anaerobic solid digestion, and hybrid treatments that combine both aerobic and anaerobic methods. The most efficient industrial wastewater treatment process is a hybrid system that harnesses and reuses the biogas expelled by bacteria to supply the energy needs required to operate a treatment facility.

Bani Shahabadi and colleagues at Concordia University measured the GHG emissions created from the three different treatment methods listed above. The GHG calculation was based on both on- and off-site factors which include emissions released during the nitrification and denitrification process, the impact and cost of external materials needed to operate the treatment plant, the amount of electricity consumed during the treatment process, the emissions from the decomposition of wastewater sludge, and the amount of biogas produced to offset the amount of electricity consumed.

The authors discovered that aerobic treatment methods produce the least amount of greenhouse gases (GHGs). Anaerobic and hybrid treatment methods produce the largest amounts of GHGs because they require more off-site materials and power to run the plant effectively. However, GHG emissions alone do not indicate the most productive treatment method. The most productive treatment method for industrial wastewater reclamation is a hybrid system because it offers the highest rate of nutrient and contaminant removal. Hybrid systems can reduce the amount of GHG emissions by recycling the biogas produced from solid waste decomposition to operate the plant and minimize the demand for external electricity. In addition, lowering the temperature of the anaerobic solid digestion process and producing all the materials needed for treatment on-site instead of transporting them can further reduce emissions. Hybrid treatment methods can be both efficient and environmentally conscious, and therefore the best option for industrial wastewater facilities. However, not even the best-designed hybrid treatment plant can remove every contaminant.

Increase of Antibiotic-Resistant Bacteria in Wastewater Treatment Plant Discharge

Wastewater treatment plants are the perfect breeding ground for antibiotic-resistant bacteria because they create an environment in which bacteria and antibiotics interact regularly (Zhang *et al.* 2009). There is a growing concern about the prevalence of antibiotic-resistant bacteria released from wastewater discharge into surrounding environments because they dramatically reduce the numbers of effective antibiotic treatments available for humans and create a problem for pharmaceutical companies and public health. The impact of antibiotic resistant bacteria in influent and effluent wastewater was investigated for two different scenarios: high temperature high flow water, and low temperature low flow water. The concentration of resistant bacteria released from wastewater discharge consistently increased the longer the wastewater was retained within the treatment plant reactors.

Zhang *et al.* at the Department of Environmental Health Sciences, University of Michigan, investigated the probability of antibiotic resistance in *Acinetobacter spp.* and the spread of resistant bacteria into natural environments through wastewater discharge. They looked at 366 strains of *Acinetobacter spp* in adjunction with 8 different commonly used antibiotics at 5 different wastewater treatment facility sites, comparing the concentration of resistant bacteria from both upstream and downstream locations for each treatment plant.

They discovered that although wastewater treatment plants effectively reduce the concentration of bacteria that enter an ecosystem, the remaining bacteria released in discharge have a higher potential to be resistant to antibiotics. Commonly, bacteria present in wastewater discharge are resistant to at least one or two antibiotics, while some are resistant to up to five or six different ones. Zhang and colleagues discovered that the concentration of resistant bacteria increased downstream from wastewater treatment plants, which suggests that the wastewater discharge is directly responsible for higher concentrations of resistant bacteria. Furthermore, the concentration of antibiotic resistant bacteria increased in effluent wastewater treated by low temperatures and low flow compared to treatments of high temperature and high flows. This implies that the best way to reduce the concentration of resistant bacteria in discharge is to treat wastewater at high temperatures and to limit the amount of time the wastewater is retained in the plant. Unfortunately, wastewater treatment plants are more efficient at removing other contaminants the longer the water and sludge remain in the treatment facility.

Acadia Tucker

The Efficiency of Pharmaceutical Removal of Wastewater Treatment Plants and Environmental Risk Assessment

The presence of Pharmaceutical drugs in aquatic environments is a hazard to the integrity and health of ecosystems, and the main source of pharmaceuticals in river and ocean water comes from the discharge of wastewater treatment plants. Modern treatment facilities are highly effective in the removal of nitrogen and carbon, but there is no specific technology designed for the removal of micro-pollutants like pharmaceuticals (Gros *et al.* 2009). Pharmaceuticals appear in effluent wastewater because they generally have a low tendency to absorb onto the sludge produced during the treatment process, and the rate of biodegradation is not fast enough to be completed in current treatment water retention times. The removal rates of pharmaceutical compounds depend on the temperature of operation, the degradation rates of compounds, the hydraulic retention time, and the sludge retention time. The pharmaceuticals detected the most in wastewater discharge are antibiotics, serotonin reuptake inhibitors, and antiepileptics.

Gros *et al.* at the Department of Environmental Chemistry in Barcelona, Spain monitored seven wastewater treatment plants that operated under primary and secondary treatment processes. They tracked 73 predetermined pharmaceutical compounds by attaching signal isotopes that could be easily tracked downstream from the treatment plants. They also calculated a hazard index to predict the harmful effects of pharmaceuticals on organisms, specifically algae, daphnids, and fish.

The most abundant pharmaceutical drugs that appeared in influent wastewater prior to treatment were non-steroidal anti-inflammatories and analgesics. However, these drugs had the highest removal rates (81–98%) in wastewater discharge. Drugs like lipid regulators, cholesterol-lowering statin drugs and anti-diabetics showed either no removal rate in some instances or a medium rate (40–60%). Antibiotics, serotonin reuptake inhibitors, and antiepileptic drugs actually increased in wastewater discharge although the reason for this is unclear. Gros determined that compounds with a high biodegradability and a low tendency to absorb onto sludge are influenced the most by hydraulic retention time; the longer the wastewater remains in the treatment plant, the less pharmaceuticals that will appear in effluent wastewater. Compounds that are less biodegradable but have a high tendency to absorb onto sludge are influenced more by the sludge retention time; the longer the sludge sits in the wastewater treatment plant, the more time the pharmaceuticals have to decompose. The risk/hazard quotient showed that algae were harmed the most by pharmaceutical-rich discharge, followed by daphnids and fish. Results suggest that diluting wastewater discharge is a viable mitigation technique to decrease the amount of harm done to an aquatic ecosystem from contaminated discharge.

Conclusions

Wastewater management has improved dramatically from the time of medieval civilizations to the present day. We depend of wastewater treatment facilities to protect the health of the general public and the natural waterways people depend on. They are becoming increasingly important as the Earth's fresh water becomes scarcer. Wastewater management emphasizes the efficiency of water use instead of increasing water supply. New advances in wastewater technology allow communities to recycle nutrients back into the soil and reduce their dependence on fossil fuels by harvesting biogas. Although no society today has a perfect method for waste disposal, there is a future for sustainable wastewater treatment.

References Cited

Capelli L., Sironi S., Del Rosso R., Ce´ntola P,. 2009. Predicting odour emissions from wastewater treatment plants by means of odour emission factors. Water Research 43, 1977–1985

Gros, M., Petrović, M., Ginebreda, A., Barceló, D., 2009. Removal of pharmaceuticals during wastewater treatment and environmental risk assessment using hazard indexes. Environment International 36, 15–26

Goldfarb T. 2000. Notable Selections in Environmental Studies. Second edition, 181–190

Hernández-Sancho F., Molinos-Senante M., Sala-Garrido R,. 2009. Economic valuation of environmental benefits from wastewater treatment processes: an empirical approach for Spain. Science of the Total Environment 408, 953–957

Kumar M, 2009. Reclamation and Reuse of Treated Municipal Wastewater: an Option to Mitigate Water Stress. Current Science 96, 886–889.

Lundin M., Bengtsson M., Molander S., 2009. Life Cycle Assessment of Wastewater Systems: Influence of System Boundaries and Scale on Calculated Environmental Loads. Environmental Science and Technology 34, 180–186

Ojekunle O., Zhao L., Li R., Tan X. 2009. Ameliorating water crises through sustainable wastewater reuse in Hengshui, China. American Water Works Association. Journal10. 71–79

Rockefeller A. 1998. Civilization and sludge: Notes on the history of the management of human excreta. Capitalism Nature Socialism 9, 3–18

Shahabadi B., Yerushalmi L., Haghighat F., 2009. Impact of process design on greenhouse gas (GHG) generation by wastewater treatment plants. Water Research 43, 2679–2687.

Acadia Tucker

Zhang Y., Marrs C., Simon C., Xi C., 2009. Wastewater treatment contributes to selective increase of antibiotic resistance among *Acinetobacter* spp.. Science of the Total Environment 407, 3702–3706.

19. Managing Water Resources in the Face of Climate Change

Shae Blood

Water is one of the earth's most precious natural resources, given that it is essential for socio-economic development and the maintenance of healthy ecosystems. As populations grow and ever rising demands for groundwater and surface water in agriculture, industry, and households continue, the pressure on water resources is aggravated. Stress on freshwater resources is also intensified by other factors, such as anthropogenic climate change, the degradation of water quality, intersectoral competition, and interregional and international conflicts. In recent decades, water use has been growing at more than twice the rate of population increase, leading to an increasing number of regions that are subject to chronic water shortages. In 2007 the Food and Agriculture Organization (FAO) estimated that 1.2 billion people live in countries and regions that are classified as water-scarce. Projections for the future of water resources appear to be even more dismal: by 2025, the number of people affected by water scarcity is expected to reach 1.8 billion. The problem of water scarcity, therefore, is of serious concern and needs to be addressed at both a local and global scale.

Evidence of water scarcity is abundant and can be classified into two types: physical and economic. The former occurs when available water resources are meager, while the latter refers to the inability of water resource managers to make the investments needed to keep up with increasing demand. Although fresh water resources are influenced by a wide array of factors, this chapter primarily focuses on the implications of climate change on water resources. Scientists observe that climate change coupled with rapid development has been affecting hydrologic patterns in many regions of the world, particularly in semi-arid and arid regions. This, in turn, has increased concern among the water resource community. Increasing average temperatures, fluctuating patterns of precipitation, and changes in the fre-

Shae Blood

quency and magnitude of weather anomalies have the potential to impact water resources, and thus the maintenance of several important sectors, in unpredictable ways. Policy makers must therefore be well-informed about the potential impacts of changes in climate. Though climate change is apparently inevitable, global models tend to disagree on how much temperatures will rise and at what rate. Climate change due to global atmospheric concentrations of greenhouse gasses such as CO_2 and methane has been at the forefront of current research in recent years; yet such efforts provide varying results as they each utilize different emissions scenarios in their climatic models. As a consequence, the degree to which climate change will impact water resources remains uncertain. This uncertainty may have dire consequences for management decisions, potentially hindering the incorporation of the implications of climate change in water resources planning initiatives. An experiment conducted by Buytaert *et al.* (2009) explores the uncertainties associated with global climate models (GCMs), which typically combine climatic and hydrological models. This particular study highlights the importance of prediction ranges in future precipitation, emphasizing the need to develop and implement better downscaling techniques when creating these models. De Fraiture *et al.* (2009) elaborate on a similar topic, but delve deeper into the agricultural sector. This study further explains the differing views of how to address future challenges involving livelihoods and natural ecosystems.

Finally, Langsdale *et al.* (2009) note the potential of a new initiative to affect future policies in water management—participatory modeling. Participatory modeling emphasizes the importance of stakeholder participation throughout the model building process, as it creates a shared learning experience and increases participants' trust in the system. While the problems of water scarcity are great, the potential solutions, participatory modeling included, provide hope for the future of water resources.

Explaining the Link between Climate Change, Water Scarcity, and Local Livelihoods in the Greater Himalayan Region

Current projections of the effects of climate change in the Greater Himalayan region of Asia remain ambiguous (Xu *et al.* 2009). Although it is certain that there will be significant changes in temperature, shifts in ecosystems, and increased frequency and duration of extreme events such as landslides and flash floods, a framework to guide further quantitative assessments and appropriate policy responses needs to be established. Hence Xu *et al.* examine the cascading effects of climate change on water resources, biodiversity, and local livelihoods across alpine, montane, and lowland zones in the Greater Himalayas.

The authors studied the Greater Himalayas due to the area's great climatic variability, rich diversity of species and ecosystems, and the 1.3 billion people that the river basins provide water for. Given that glaciers, snow, and ice cover close to 20% of the region and are receding more quickly than the global average, the supply of future downstream water is at risk. Current warming patterns demonstrate that temperatures at high elevations are already occurring at approximately three times the world average, and thus could be potentially catastrophic for Greater Himalayan peoples and ecosystems. If such trends continue, glaciers in the region may shrink by 400,000 km^2 by 2035, limiting the freshwater supplies for downstream communities in the long-run. These fluctuations in glacial retreat will also likely result in a decline of endemic species that have a limited geographic range and alter the composition and distribution of other vegetation types, such as forests. Himalayan forests serve a number of functions; they foster biodiversity, anchor soil and water, and act as an important carbon sink. While forest areas are expected to increase in some regions of the Greater Himalayas, they are projected to decrease elsewhere. Therefore, the impact of these shifts is still unknown.

The authors focused on four categories of cascading effects: ecological, local livelihoods, downstream watersheds, and global feedbacks. Xu *et al.* note that while research on ecological responses is scarce, predator-prey relationships are likely to be disrupted, and thus result in secondary extinctions in the alpine ecosystems. Though the effect of glacial ice and snow melting cannot be completely predicted, both local and global communities will be affected, given that downstream water supplies and agricultural land will eventually decrease due to rising global sea levels and coastal salinity levels. In order for humans to adapt to such changes, the authors highlight the need for adaptive capacity—the ability to recover from change through learning and flexibility so as to maintain a desirable state. Thus, increased regional collaboration in scientific research and policymaking is needed if the local communities are to address the effects that climate change will have on the Greater Himalayas in the upcoming decades.

The Feasibility of Sustainable Water Deliveries from the Colorado River

The persistence of the Colorado River is essential, given that it irrigates over three million acres of farmland and provides water to some 27 million users in the southwest United States and Mexico (Barnett and Pierce 2009). According to a number of global climate models, however, anthropogenic climate change is expected to reduce runoff in this region by 10 to 30% in the near future, thus putting the Colorado River at a substantial risk. In order to determine whether or not currently scheduled water deliveries from the Colorado River system can be sustained under such changes, Barnett and Pierce develop a model that provides quantitative information on the size and timing of future delivery shortfalls. Although the results indicate that currently scheduled future water deliveries are not likely to be sustainable, the situation may be mitigated through a program of water reuse, conservation, transfers between users, and other measures.

The hydrological cycle of the Colorado River has been under the pressure of climate change for several decades, and has experienced further stress due to rapid population growth. As a result of these changes, the flow of the Colorado River is expected to decrease between 10 and 30 percent. Two of the region's reservoirs, Lake Powell and Lake Mead, are man-made and operated by the United States Bureau of Reclamation (USBR), indicating that future deliveries will be reduced to protect their elevation following such reductions. Nonetheless, the numbers on expected river flow and sustainable water deliveries have not yet been explored. The authors, therefore, study the effects of climate change on Colorado River water deliveries while maintaining a 305-m (1,000-ft) elevation of Lake Mead. An updated version of the Colorado River Budget Model (CRBM)—a model that calculates the net effects of in- and out-flows on a monthly basis—is used to compare the total amount of water available each year to the number of scheduled deliveries in that same year. This model, therefore, allows for a projection of when the shortfalls might occur and ignores the complicated legal rights to the water. As climate change and economic development evolve, full deliveries will become rare. This is due to the temporal autocorrelation of the Colorado River flow and the El Niño Southern Oscillation (ENSO) cycle, in which reservoirs can be up to 80 percent full for a period of time and then become unable to replenish during subsequent dry years.

The authors find that if the climate changes as predicted, the currently scheduled future water deliveries will not be met. While the model with a 10% reduction in runoff projects that requested deliveries will exceed sustainable deliveries by 2040, the same scenario occurs by 2025 in the 20% reduction model. Thus, the only solution at this time is to aim to reduce future deliveries up to 20%. Barnett and Pierce note that an operational model to predict river flow at 10 to 20 year time-scales should be implemented in order to facilitate the decision-making process of the severity and timing of future deliveries to avoid substantial droughts.

Water Scarcity in the West Bank: Evidence for the Need of Regional Cooperation in Coping with Climate Change

Global climate change is expected to increase temperatures by 2–6°C in future years and may lead to a reduction of precipitation of up to 16% in the Mediterranean basin. As a result of a reduction in rainfall or an increase in evapotranspiration, water resource availability and agricultural water demands will experience severe effects (Mizyed 2009). The West Bank, which heavily relies on agriculture to stimulate its economy, will be subject to such effects and is thus used as a case study from the Mediterranean basin to explore the effects of several climate change scenarios on future water scarcity. The results reveal that a reduction in precipitation will have dire socioeconomic and possibly health impacts on the inhabitants of the West Bank, and an even more serious outcome when combined with an increase in temperature.

The West Bank was chosen by the author not only because groundwater is the main source of water in the region, but because water availability is naturally low due to a number of political constraints. Agriculture also plays a major role in the area, given that it employs 18% of the Palestinian labor force, accounts for 13% of GDP, and uses over half of the West Bank's water resources. The limited availability of water resources coupled with increasing domestic water demands have the potential to not only damage water quality, but to intensify water use conflicts. Therefore, Mizyed evaluates the impacts of climate change on water scarcity and agricultural water demands in the West Bank using three different temperature scenarios (an increase of 2, 4, and 6°C) and two separate precipitation scenarios (no change and a 16% reduction). The climate model was created by collecting data for temperature and precipitation, two variables that have a direct effect on evapotranspiration and precipitation. Based on the data from the seven different weather stations, monthly values of evapotranspiration were estimated using the FAO Penman-Monteith method and then compared with monthly precipitation depths to determine the changes in the natural recharge depths for groundwater aquifers—an indicator of the availability of water resources.

The results demonstrated that reduced precipitation due to climate change has a greater impact on groundwater recharge than increased temperatures. While an increase in temperature of 6°C has the potential to increase evapotranspiration and agricultural water demands by up to 17% and reduce water availability by 21%, a 16% reduction of precipitation alone led to a 30% reduction in groundwater recharge. Moreover, if both temperatures increase and precipitation decreases, water availability in the future will only be half of its quantity today. Hence Mizyed highlights the need for national action plans and cooperation among neighboring states to utilize all current knowledge and experience to ameliorate the effects of climate change on water scarcity.

Investments in Agricultural Water Management: Optimality Varies Across Basins and Regions

The combination of increasing food prices, rapid population growth, and excessive water use in agricultural production in recent decades has the potential to lead to water shortages in many parts of the world (De Fraiture *et al.* 2010). Although agricultural water management faced similar issues in the past, the current situation is threatened by a number of new challenges, such as differences in diets, urbanization, agricultural transformation, climate change, energy policy, and environmental restoration. In order to fill knowledge gaps in the relationship between food production, ecosystems, and livelihoods, the authors focus on the analysis behind a number of policy options for agricultural water management, and conclude that the tradeoffs for optimal implementation plans will vary both across water basins and regions.

Agricultural productivity has experienced a dramatic increase in past years due to the expansion of investments water usage. As a result, food security and poverty have been impacted in a positive way—employment opportunities flourished, food prices fell during certain periods, and rural output was maintained. Despite the effects that investments in agricultural water management have had on ameliorating poverty, the allocation of benefits has not necessarily been even. In particular, natural resources and environmental amenities have been adversely affected because of poorly planned management, land appropriation, and the diversion of water from aquatic ecosystems. As a way to meet this challenge, the authors analyze all of the components of the Comprehensive Assessment of Water Management in Agriculture (CA), an extensive research program comprised of 700 professionals.

Although the authors discuss an array of findings from the CA, they specifically highlight the recommendations for future water management that achieve the three-part objective of alleviating poverty, maintaining ecosystems, and ensuring food security. While the authors stress that decision makers be better informed about the impacts of water use and allocation, several tradeoffs between investment options exist and vary by region. Therefore, public perspectives and decisions will heavily depend on geography, water resource allocation, and incomes. Such issues include the increase in water storage due to volatile rainfall patterns resulting from climate change and the decreased instream flows; water use rights; and the tradeoff between using water resources today versus the future.

Water Footprint Calculation Methods Revisited

Pressure on freshwater resources has increased in recent years as a result of climate change, population growth, economic development, and demands made by industry, specifically in the agricultural sector (Ridoutt and Pfister 2010). In order to make the use of global freshwater resources more sustainable, indicators that involve the impacts of production systems and consumption patterns need to be developed. In the current water footprint calculation method, results are often misleading and footprints of different products and services cannot be meaningfully compared. Therefore, Ridoutt and Pfister attempt to provide a solution by incorporating water stress characterization factors into the existing water footprint calculation methods.

Ridoutt and Pfister calculated the stress-weighted water footprints of two specific products consumed exclusively in Australia: Dolmio's pasta sauce and Peanut M&M's. In order to obtain characterization factors about the level of water stress relevant to each location of water consumption, a water stress index (WSI) was used with a range from 0.01 to 1. Given that specific coordinates could only be identified in some circumstances, such as for individual factories, the WSI values were averaged to produce a relevant characterization factor. The authors then calculated the stress-weighted water footprints by multiplying water consumption at each point in the product life cycle by the representative characterization factors.

Although the volumetric water footprint of Dolmio's pasta sauce was substantially lower than that of Peanut M&M's, its stress-weighted water footprint was over 10 times greater, suggesting the differences in current calculation methods and thus corporate action. Significant differences in volumetric and stress-weighted water footprints were also found when considering product ingredients: while tomatoes were of the greatest concern in the stress-weighted water footprint, the simple volumetric method primarily focused on the amount of water used by the agricultural stage of production of cocoa derivatives. Tomato production, however, has a greater potential to contribute significantly to local water scarcity, as they are typically are grown under irrigation systems in areas with hot and dry climates. Furthermore, a majority of the stress-weighted water footprint occurred outside of Australia, emphasizing that the actual potential for harm can exist in locations far from the product's local environment. Thus, the new approach encourages product manufacturers and retailers to reduce the negative effects their products have on the global water cycle. Despite the many advantages the revised water footprint calculation method provides, the authors highlight the need for alternative approaches to environmental management since the method described does not necessarily account for all types of water consumption.

The Effects of Global Circulation Models (GCMs) on Management Decisions

A strong relationship exists between policy makers and scientists, as the former continue to demand accurate projections of future climate change in order to design adaptation strategies. A popular approach utilized by scientists in forecasting such changes often involves integrating environmental models. Climatic and hydrologic models, therefore, are commonly combined for the purpose of predicting the impacts of climate change on water resources, yet this approach is prone to large uncertainties (Buytaert *et al.* 2009). The authors attempt to assess the uncertainties associated with these global circulation models (GCMs) that are downscaled to smaller scale hydrological models by focusing on four catchments in the Andes. Prediction ranges are shown to be very wide, highlighting the need for the development of better hydrological models for the use of planning adaptation mechanisms.

The uncertainties related to GCM projections on future changes are due to a number of factors—oversimplification of climate representation, inaccurate assumptions about climate processes, limited spatial and temporal resolution, and errors in the forcing data. However, GCM results continue to be used for hydrological and ecological models, potentially having an adverse effect on management decisions. Though a large number of studies addressing the impacts of climate change on water resources have incorporated data from GCMs, such studies typically only use data from one GCM, and thus mask potential uncertainties of the projections. As a solution, the authors focus on four mesoscale hydrological catchments in the Paute River basin in south Ecuador using the entire GCM set of the IPCC's Fourth Assessment Report. Given that the Paute River is the main source of water for the city of Cuenca and hosts the largest hydro-power plant in Ecuador, there is a need to explore the effects that climate change will have upon this resource.

Buytaert *et al.* gathered data from the four separate catchments for precipitation, discharge, and potential evapotranspiration, while GCM projections for the A1B scenario for the period 2011 to 2030 were used. Despite the consistent average projections in temperature ranging from an increase in 0.72 to 1.12°C, average projections of precipitation anomalies diverged widely and predictions in the direction of change were contradictory. The results further demonstrated that an increase in temperature will lead to a change in potential evapotranspiration in the future, though this change may be negative or positive. The authors explain that this discrepancy is due to the ambiguous predictions for future precipitation, which has an effect on the soil moisture deficit and actual evapotranspiration. Therefore, future hydrological models should incorporate such factors in order to avoid jeopardizing management decisions for the sustainability of water resources.

Uncertainty of Climate Change Impacts on Groundwater Resources

Climate change is expected to have detrimental effects on water resources, and groundwater resources in particular. Although the majority of global communities depend heavily on groundwater as a source of drinking water and an agricultural input, the percentage of groundwater that accounts for global freshwater use is still not well known (Doll 2009). Given its many advantages over surface water, however—better protection from pollution, greater accessibility, and increased availability—the impacts of climate change on groundwater resources are a great concern to policy makers. The author, therefore, addresses such impacts by quantifying renewable groundwater resources and computing the number of people affected for four climate scenarios in the 2050s. Global maps of vulnerability to the impact of decreased groundwater recharge during this time period were also generated. The maps showed discrepancies in spatial distributions due to climate model uncertainty rather than different emissions scenarios, suggesting that climate change scenarios should not be used to quantitatively predict the future of groundwater resources.

Groundwater is characterized by both water volume (groundwater storage) and water flow (groundwater recharge). Water flow recharges groundwater storage, and can therefore be used as a measure of renewable groundwater resources. Doll first determined the impacts of climate change on groundwater recharge and quantified the number of affected people with the global water resources and use model, WaterGAP, and four climate change scenarios resulting from the A2/B2 emissions scenarios and two global climate models. However, since vulnerability of populations to decreased groundwater resources relies on the degree of the decrease and the sensitivity of the population to such a decrease, the author also created and combined a sensitivity index with the model of changes in groundwater resources due to climate change. The sensitivity index comprised three indicators: water scarcity, dependence of water supply on groundwater, and generic sensitivity or adaptation capacity of the human system. These three indicators ranged from 1 to 5, with 1 indicating maximum adaptive capacity and 5 indicating maximum sensitivity. Sensitivity of the human system and adaptive capacity were not evaluated for future conditions because of increased complexity in modeling.

Despite the fact that all scenarios determined that future groundwater resources will decrease anywhere between 30–70% in currently semi-arid regions, such as northeastern Brazil, the A2 emissions scenario projected that a decrease of groundwater resources by more than 10% will not only span a larger area of the globe (18.4–19.3%), but affect a greater proportion of the global population (10.7 billion) in comparison with the B2 emissions scenario. The highest sensitivities were found in countries such as India, Pakistan, and Iran, yet the highest vulnerabilities were found in other regions, including southwest Africa and the central Andes. This discrepancy highlights the uncertainty that results from utilizing different climate models. As a concluding remark, Doll further emphasizes that although local vulnerability assessments allow for more tailored results, multi-scale vulnerability assessments should be pursued in the future to ensure consistency across the globe.

Participatory Modeling: An Effective Strategy for Adapting to Climate Change

Despite the impacts that climate change may have upon water resources in the future, most North American municipalities have failed to incorporate such information into their water management practices. This may be due to the fact that the data gathered by global climate models is not readily accessible or applicable to current watershed-scale hydrologic assessments (Langsdale *et al.* 2009). As a way to encourage incorporation of climate change within water planning and policy developments, the authors used the Okanagan Basin in British Columbia, Canada as a case study for engaging various stakeholders in a participatory group modeling exercise. Though the authors found the overall process to be beneficial in terms of exploring plausible water management plans for the basin, they emphasize the impossibility of measuring its long-term significance over such a short time period.

Given that climate change will have varying impacts depending on geographic region, new methods for assessing water resources are necessary in order to encourage adaptation to reduce future vulnerabilities. Although there is an urgent need to incorporate aspects of climate change into water planning initiatives, decision makers must overcome a number of obstacles in order to successfully maintain the future of water resources. Such challenges include awareness of and concern for the adverse effects of climate change on water resources in the community, availability of information in relevant terms, and evaluation of water resources in an integrated system context. Therefore, the study focused on the Okanagan Basin, an arid region prone to natural hydrologic variability, to meet each of these challenges by increasing stakeholder participation in the development of models for decision making in the water resource community. In general, participatory modeling promotes team learning, allows for the exchange of information between stakeholders, and supports consensus. However, the authors set more specific goals in this project. First, the authors assembled a diverse group of stakeholders not only to provide a networking system within the basin, but to ensure that all opinions were accounted for. Second, the system dynamics modeling tool was used in order to guarantee effective communication within the group of basin stewards. Lastly, the authors emphasized the importance of stakeholder participation throughout the entire process in order to establish a sense of ownership in the model.

The process was conducted by a team of representatives from all major interests and agencies, including academic and federal government researches, and consisted of five full day voluntary workshops held within the basin between February 2005 and January 2006. Participants went through six phases of model development—brain storming, system mapping, qualitative modeling, quantitative modeling, calibrating, and future options—and then evaluated the overall exercise during the final session. The survey results reveal that while the process improved participants' understanding of water resource management, fostering a sense of ownership over the model proved difficult because of inconsistent participation and limited participation in the actual building of the model. Therefore, the communication and evaluation aspects of the process should be re-examined if the long-term impact of such an exercise is to be determined.

Conclusions

Although a myriad of uncertainties in global climate modeling exist, current research demonstrates that the availability of water resources will be adversely affected by climate change, among other contributors. Addressing water scarcity, therefore, will require an unprecedented level of action at the local, national, and river basin levels. International cooperation will also be essential, which will ultimately translate into integration across all sectors. Such a multidisciplinary approach to managing water resources is twofold: maximization of the economic and social welfare of the community, and resilience of the ecosystems that sustain the world population.

References Cited

Barnett, T., Pierce, D., 2009. Sustainable water deliveries from the Colorado River in a changing climate. Proceedings of the National Academy of Sciences of the United States of America 106, 7334–7338.

Buytaert, W., Célleri, R., Timbe, L., 2009. Predicting climate change impacts on water resources in the tropical Andes: the effects of GCM uncertainty. Geophysical Research Letters 36, 1–11.

De Fraiture, C., Molden, D., Wichelns, D., 2010. Investing in water for food, ecosystems, and livelihoods: an overview of the comprehensive assessment of water management in agriculture. Agricultural Water Management 97, 495–501.

Doll, P., 2009. Vulnerability to the impact of climate change on renewable groundwater resources: a global-scale assessment. Environmental Research Letters 4, 1–12.

Langsdale, S., Beall, A., Carmichael, J., Cohen, S., Forster, C., Neale, T., 2009. Exploring the implications of climate change on water resources through participatory modeling: case study of the Okanagan Basin, British Columbia. Journal of Water Resources Planning and Management 135, 373–381.

Mizyed, N., 2009. Impacts of climate change on water resources availability and agricultural water demand in the West Bank. Water Resources Management 23, 2015–2029.

Ridoutt, B.G., Pfister, S., 2010. A revised approach to water footprinting to make transparent the impacts of consumption and production on global freshwater scarcity. Global Environmental Change 20, 113–120.

Xu, J., Grumbine, R., Shrestha, A., Eriksson, M., Yang, X., Wang, Y., Wilkes, A., 2009. The melting Himalayas: cascading effects of climate change on water, biodiversity, and livelihoods. Conservation Biology 3, 520–530.

20. Water Supplies: How Climate is affecting the Availability of Fresh Water

Eric Van Oss

Water resources are a pivotal resource that cannot be substituted. Dependency on water encompasses all aspects of life and shapes human development. Food production, economic activity and quality of life are essentially dictated by water quantity and availability. Water management is becoming an increasingly important field as challenging global water issues arise.

Globally, water resources are being placed under increased stress, largely because of human development and global climate change. Increased population growth and higher living standards require more water and place existing reserves under stress. Additionally, high growth and development rates are taking place in arid regions with existing water challenges. The major problem with current patterns is that growth rates are not sustainable. Many major watersheds are under stress, and trends indicate that future demand will exceed current levels. In arid Northwest China, Fang and Xie (2009) found that rapid urbanization and inadequate infrastructure significantly impact the region's water security. In many cases, inadequate storage facilities and infrastructure exacerbate existing water scarcity.

In addition to human activity, climate change significantly alters the availability of water by influencing the frequency and amount rainfall. In the Caribbean, Cashman *et al.* (2010) found that climate change reduces rainfall throughout the entire region and is especially pronounced in already arid areas. Rajagopalan *et al.* (2009) found that in the American Southwest, drought-like conditions have caused water reserves to fall to historic lows. Climate change increases the likelihood of large-scale drought by decreasing rainfall as human activity depletes existing reserves. Prolonged drought, in Jordan for example, forces governments to import water to ensure that minimum demand is met (Abdulla *et al.* 2009). Climate trends indicate that potential droughts and decreased rainfall are likely in these arfid areas in the future, signaling increased threats to once-stable water supplies.

Many governments face significant challenges combating and changing the effects of water scarcity and transitioning to sustainable practices. One of the major challenges is balancing local water needs with economic growth. Cashman *et al.* found that although the Caribbean is badly water-stressed, the governments that rely heavily on tourism and are unwilling to impose water restrictions on resorts. In many cases, local government and policymakers are unwilling to address water sustainability at the expense of economic growth; Phillips *et al.* commented on the difficulty of balancing residential growth—Phoenix's main economic engine—with the reality of water scarcity. This trend is especially pronounced in economically emerging counties that are experiencing new found wealth and have not felt the full effects of water insecurity.

The second major factor, found in developing regions, is the lack of sufficient water infrastructure. Many areas cannot properly store or transport water, which contributes greatly to water scarcity. In some cases, like the Caribbean, governments simply lack the cohesion and funding to implement the necessary changes (Cashman *et al.* 2010). In other areas infrastructure has simply not kept pace with regional development. This is demonstrated in Northwest China, where development has strained infrastructure in a previously sparsely populated and rural area (Fang and Xie, 2010).

The path towards water sustainability can be made in several steps. One is ensuring that regional water systems can efficiently coordinate water storage and transportation. This would include providing adequate aquifers and streamlining how water is transported. Additionally, Cashman *et al.* suggest that governments should encourage individual infrastructure improvements, such as installing household rain collection bins. Secondly, significant water reductions can be made in the agricultural sector. Agricultural systems use large amounts of water and increasing their efficiency would relieve pressure on water reserves. Many of these changes could be made by enhancing irrigation systems and implementing new watering techniques. Lastly, Larson *et al.* found that governments can impose water restrictions upon residents with relatively little public resentment.

Water Scarcity in the Caribbean

In the Caribbean, access to adequate stores of fresh water is a major concern. The region's two major economic sectors, tourism and agriculture, use large amounts of water, and increases are expected in the future. Population growth and continued urbanization have also increased regional water usage and will continue to do so. Climate modeling for the region has shown that climate change will produce dry conditions, more frequent droughts, salt-water intrusion, and water scarcity (Cashman *et al.* 2009). Particular events that especially pertain to the region, such as rising sea level and tropical storms, will significantly increase due to climate change. Already, several counties lack year-round water reserves and many do not have adequate storage techniques, causing seasonal demand to exceed supply. This coupled with the affects of climate change will continue to threaten the already vulnerable Caribbean fresh water supplies. Decreased access to fresh water can have severe adverse health-related and economic impacts across the region.

Adrian Cashman uses the assessment reports from the Intergovernmental Panel on Climate Change (IPCC) to show the effects of climate change in the Caribbean region. The report projects significant increases in sea level. Additionally, the IPCC projects regional warming of up to 5°C, and the IPCC SRES scenarios indicate increased water stress due regional drying caused by climate change. Annual precipitation is expected to decrease across the region as a whole, but will be especially pronounced in the more arid regions.

These projections show significantly reduced accessibility to fresh water on a number of islands. Rising sea levels disproportionately affect low-lying coastal areas and will threaten already land-constrained aquifers. Water storage by aquifers is limited by an island's size and rising sea levels would put many aquifers as risk for salt-water intrusion, significantly affecting year-round water access, especially for islands that rely heavily on rain collection. Most Caribbean nations rely on stored rainwater during the dry seasons, however, with projected lengthened dry seasons and decreased rainfall these reserves are increasingly put under stress. There is less rain for immediate consumption and even less for future use. Furthermore, IPCC studies found that climate change increases the likelihood and severity of hurricanes and flooding, the secondary effects of which include aquifer contamination and disrupted water distribution. Both natural disasters and rising sea levels have the potential to contaminate water supplies creating health concerns.

Climate change will also prompt significant economic concerns. Agriculture will be adversely affected by decreased water supplies. Land and crop productivity will drop, and harvest yields will decrease throughout the region. Tourism uses large amounts of water, notably at resorts, and water scarcity will put this mega-industry in competition with local water needs. Serious water management policy changes are needed to ensure that the region is water-secure, however, the region currently lacks the basic data and human resources needed to effectively implement the necessary changes. Solutions must include increasing and maintaining water storage, enhancing water harvesting, and increased water efficiency with the ultimate goal being water sustainability.

Eric Van Oss

Water Supplies in Arid Northwest China

Fang and Xie, (2009) looked at urbanization trends and their effect on fresh water availability in He-Xi province in Northwest China, which is arid and increasingly vulnerable to the effects of climate change. He-Xi has experienced rapid urban growth rates, but access to urban water supplies has not kept pace with population growth. Climate change will further reduce water supplies in the region and further population growth, and increased economic activity will place more stress on water resources. Furthermore, this will prompt an increase in water contamination, soil salinity, and desertification. The paper emphasizes the need for a sustainable water supply to counter the adverse affects of human activity and climate change.

C-L. Fang and Y. Xie conducted a field survey to find the current water use by economic sector as well as the region's current water resources. They calculated the water change rates based on regional development goals and future water usage trends. These calculations were integrated with demographic and economic predictions to determine the region's water sustainability.

The study focuses on increased water consumption in urban areas and economic sectors. He-Xi province will experience high urbanization growth rates and development within the next 20 years. The region has an arid climate that already suffers from strained water reserves. The calculations show that based on future trends, urban water supplies will increase and rural water reserves will decrease. Every sector, except for agriculture, will increase water usage. Better irrigation and water management will reduce the percentage of water used by the agricultural sector, but for economic growth to continue the study found that use of irrigation water, forestry water, industry water, and urban domestic water all must be reduced. This can be achieved through less consumption and better technologies in industry and agriculture. Additionally, larger cities with diversified economies also have the highest water usage efficiency. The study concludes that as the region's economy develops further, the new technologies and better infrastructure will increase overall regional water efficiency. In addition to increased efficiency the paper also concludes that policy changes are necessary to ensure the region maintains a sustainable water supply.

Water Stress on the Colorado River

The Colorado River is a major water source for the Southwest US and is being placed under increasing stress by rapid population growth and climate change. Rajagopalan et al. (2009) determined the risk of the Colorado River drying up under several different water management scenarios, attempting to analyze the reliability of water resources until 2057. Development and population growth are expected to continue, and climate change will have adverse drying effects in the already arid region. The threat of water scarcity after 2026 increases significantly and highlights the necessity to change current water management policies.

The authors modeled the annual risk to the Colorado River between 2008 and 2057. Projected growth is superimposed upon projected climate variability to determine the annual depletion. The study also takes into account several different management practices that significantly change the annual depletion predictions.

The Colorado River is the major water source for the American Southwest. The reservoir storage capacity is four times the average flow of the river, which historically has provided a stable water supply even in times of excessive drought. Currently the water reserves are under increasing stress due to rapid regional growth and climate change, and the major water reserves of Lake Mead and Lake Powell have hit historic lows. The study found that the risk of the Colorado drying up is unlikely before 2026. After 2026 the effects of climate change significantly increase the risk. After 2026, population increases coupled with increased drought likelihood and decreased water flow will place existing water reserves under significant stress, and annual flow in the Colorado River could be reduced by 20%. The authors found that several water management practices would decrease the annual depletion and significantly increase reserves to more sustainable levels. While no serious shortages are likely to occur before 2026, the authors make it clear that immediate changes in management are necessary to minimize future risks. If policies are not amended in the near future, the entire Colorado basin will potentially face severe water shortages.

Water Scarcity in Northern Jordan

Jordan is one of most water-insecure countries in the world and increased demand, population growth, and climate change threaten already insufficient water reserves. The Zarqa River is the major water reserve for the populous northern region and its arid Mediterranean climate significantly increases the threats posed by climate change. Abdulla *et al.* (2009) modeled several scenarios using different temperature increases and rainfall projections to determine future amounts of runoff and water reserves. Reduced rainfall and increased temperature do not greatly alter runoff scenarios; however they significantly reduce ground water reserves that provide the majority of stream flow for the Zarqa River. Jordan already cannot meet water demand and further reduction in reserves will threaten economic growth, food production, and human health.

Fayez Abdulla and colleagues modeled climate change scenarios using the EPA's BASINS-HSPF. They used two sources of water records spanning 1980–

1994 and 1995–2002, to determine long-term water and temperature trends. Using several temperature and rainfall projections they were able to determine potential reductions in Jordan's water reserves.

Jordan already faces a significant water shortage. About 1000 m³ of water is needed per person per year, and Jordan's water reserves can only supply 870 m³ of renewable water. Furthermore, most of the population resides in the northern region, but most water must be imported from the south at high costs. Assuming that rainfall remains stable and temperature increases by 3.5°C, water runoff and underground reserves will decrease by 1.2% and 3.6% respectively. If temperature changes occur with a 10% decrease in rain fall, runoff will decrease by 15.5%, but underground reserves will drop by more than 30%. The study clearly shows that Jordan's water security is linked more to rainfall than temperature increases. For example, when rainfall drops by 20%, a 52.4% reserve reduction occurs; when temperature increase is included reserve depletion only increases by 5%. Furthermore, increased industrial and population growth in the northern region will contribute to the depletion of Zarqa River reserves. These climate effects will severely reduce the Zarqa River's reserves and recovery, given that most of the flow comes from underground reserves and not run-off. The study shows that Jordan must implement significant policy and water management changes to ensure the future sustainability of its water reserves.

Water Resources in the Nile River Basin

Hamouda *et al.* (2009) discuss water resources and potential scarcity for the three countries in the Nile River watershed. Water scarcity in Egypt is more threatening than potential scarcity in the Sudan and Ethiopia where water resources are more stable. The entire basin, however, faces several problems that could exacerbate the threat of water scarcity. This is mostly caused by environmental degradation, lack of infrastructure, and (in the case of Egypt) lack of water resources. In general the entire Nile region is characterized by weak water management practices that can have severe future implications.

The authors compiled existing literature and studies to analyze the region's water resources using the Water Availability Index, Water Poverty Index, Water Stress Indicator, and the Dry Season Flow Index to determine overall water stability.

Water scarcity in the Nile Basin is a serious concern. All of Egypt is essentially water- stressed and its current ground water extraction is unsustainable in the long term. Water scarcity in Sudan and Ethiopia is not as serious an issue, but there are concerns over water supply and stress in addition to availability. In all of Egypt and parts of Ethiopia and Sudan, the climate is arid and rainfall is infrequent. Furthermore, the area suffers from high rates of deforestation, which can decrease precipitation, increase droughts, and contribute to erosion, which decreases reservoir life and increases downstream sedimentation. Lack of infrastructure and funding contribute to poor regional access to water, and Sudan and Ethiopia have more serious problems than actual water scarcity. The authors suggest that in order to combat these issues, NGO's must help governments install water harvesting mechanisms in order to prevent scarcity during droughts and dry seasons. Additionally there is a need for better management practices to ensure increased water quality and future sustainability.

Water Management Concerns in the American Southwest

The Salt River Project (SRP) was formed in the early 1900's to ensure a sustainable water supply for Arizona's Salt River Valley (roughly metropolitan Phoenix). Population increases and urbanization placed increased pressure on water sources and forced the SRP to find additional water resources. The general water management practices, however, have remained unchanged, raising concerns about the management and sustainability of water supplies. Phillips *et al.* (2009) suggests that the current climate change-induced drought has rendered the current management policies ineffective and in need of serious change. The uncertainty of climate change and its effect on water resources emphasizes the need to implement a new SRP management object in the near future.

The authors observed the historical water management practices of the SRP starting in the 1970s. They compared the current polices with the expected environmental conditions (namely drought and declining surface water) to calculate the sustainability of current management practices.

The SRP has historically ensured water sustainability by treating each filling of a reservoir as the beginning of a historic drought. The SRP gets most water from dams along the Salt and Verde Rivers and groundwater wells. The amount of water is highly dependent of snowmelt and runoff. Additionally, SRP can draw upon surface water from the Colorado River. Water allocation is determined by using the Storage Planning Diagram, which takes into account water storage, inflow, and groundwater pumping as a percentage of demand and allocation. This model, however, has been unchanged for the last 30 years. Climate change, severe drought, and population constraints have significantly increased the demand upon strained reserves. Less water is being taken from the principle river and SRP is increasingly reliant on buying or exchanging water from the Colorado River. Groundwater pumping is at the maximum level and reservoir storage continues to decrease. Without the Colorado River and increased pumping, the area's reservoirs would have been nearly empty in the early 2000s. Furthermore, reliance on the Colorado

River has allowed SRP to maintain current water allocation amounts. Trends are that further severe drought will persist in the region and water reserves will be placed under further stress. SRP must reduce reliance buying water, but reducing the amounts of allocated water. Part of the problem is that SRP did make policy changes when the area developed from an agricultural site to a major urban center. The current allocations allowed per acre do not reflect the needs of an urban metropolitan area. To ensure water stability, especially during uncertain environmental conditions, SRP must reduce water allocations in the Phoenix area, while replenishing its own reserves and decreasing dependence on outside water sources.

Water Footprints in Food Production

Ridoutt and Pfister (2009) studied water footprints of two products, Dolmio Pasta Sauce and Peanut M&M's. Their methods took into account location, existing water reserves, and ingredient water consumption to show both high-use and high-risk food production activities. The results clearly showed differences between total volumetric and water stress calculations, and the water stress footprints were especially helpful at identifying regions with a high risk of water scarcity This was dramatically apparent when comparing particular ingredients'water footprints— particularly that of tomatoes—which accounted for the majority of the pasta sauce's water footprint. The results provide a good indication to sustainable use practices and how to achieve more efficient ones.

Bradley G. Ridoutt and Stephan Pfister from CSIRO Sustainable Ecosystems and the Institute of Environmental Engineering calculated the water footprint of Dolmio Pasta Sauce and Peanut M&M's. They compared the Green (land use related), Blue (irrigation and process water) and Grey (high contaminant concentration) water percentages needed to produce the pasta sauce and M&M's respectively. Using the water consumption amounts at each location the revised Water Stress Index to evaluated the stress and harm on regional water sources as well as individual product water usage.

The stress water footprints of the pasta sauce and M&M's were 141 and 131 respectively, with a large percentage of each product's total consumption coming from grey water. Agricultural production was shown to be the dominant factor for both products' water footprint, while food processing and other activities contained a negligible water footprint. The total volumetric water footprint for the pasta sauce was significantly less than the M&M's, however the pasta sauce's water stress foot print was over ten times greater than the M&M's. These calculation differences highlight the substantial differences between volumetric and stress related water footprints. It also addresses the issue of how water reporting can be misleading due to the differences between total water consumption and actual water scarcity risk.

Of the ingredients used, tomatoes contributed 95% of the total water stress footprint of the pasta sauce; there were no ingredients of the same water footprint magnitude in peanut M&M's production. This highlights the difference in agricultural production. Tomatoes are usually grown in arid climates relying heavily on irrigation and chemical fertilizers, contributing more to regional water scarcity than peanuts, furthermore the pasta sauce has a larger grey water percentage due to high chemical fertilizer usage. Peanuts are grown in tropical locations and use relatively little irrigation methods or chemicals.

Using the revised calculations to account for water stress footprints better identifies what processes most adversely affect water supplies. Additionally it provides more accuracy for sustainability reporting as well as allowing consumers to make informed purchases by highlighting activities causing water stress. The study also underlines the growing conflicts between food production and water usage and touches upon sustainable processing alternatives.

Public Perception of Water Management in Greater Phoenix

Larson *et al.* (2009) examine the water use perceptions between residents, policymakers, and scientists in the Greater Phoenix region. Phoenix is a semi-arid rapidly growing Southwestern US city that is facing increasingly stressed water resources. The authors examine the three groups' opinions to determine support for water use reduction policies. They analyzed responses to ecological and water scarcity concerns in addition to water policy alternatives and implementation. Overall, there was wide concern for water management issues, especially water scarcity and drought. There was, however, no consensus between groups regarding the reasons for water stress, or policy alternatives.

The authors collected data from a series of surveys conducted throughout the Phoenix metropolitan area. The responses were categorized into three distinct groups; residents, policymakers, and scientists. The groups represented a wide range of income level and ethnicities. The questionnaire measured the concern for water related issues and the response to water management policies.

The Phoenix region has been growing rapidly for the last several decades. Population growth has greatly increased regional water demand. Residential uses such as landscaping, pools, and recreation are expected to surpass agriculture as the single largest water consumption activity. All three groups expressed concern about wide-scale scarcity and drought. Additionally, all groups acknowledged that climate change and further development would increase stress on water resources. Residents tended not to view their own water usage as a significant threat to water security, but instead pointed to large-scale projects, such as man-made lakes. Policymakers were least likely to want to impose stricter water restrictions or increase water prices due to their perceived belief that residents were staunchly opposed to such measures. Residents, however, were not nearly as opposed to water restrictions as policymakers initially believed, showing the feasibility of implementing such options. This study highlights the differences between the different groups' differing notions regarding water management. Scientist were most likely so support drastic restrictions, and policymakers overwhelming supported the status quo, with the residents falling somewhere in between. The findings could be useful for restructuring water management polices by allowing all groups to understand each other's concerns

Conclusions

Water scarcity is a problem that can potentially affect all regions across the globe. Studies show that climate change trends will continue, placing further stress on water resources. This, coupled with human activity will surely continue to place more water resources under increased stress. Many governments and communities, for a variety of reasons, have failed to take the necessary steps to ensure water security. Studies emphasize the need for local water restrictions, increased infrastructure, and increased efficiency as the best way to achieve water sustainability. The effects of water management are not immediately felt in the short term, but the practices have serious long term repercussions.

References Cited

Abdulla, Fayez, Tamer Eshtawi and Hamed Assaf (2009). Assessment of the impact of potential climate change on the water balance of a semi-arid watershed. Water Resource Management 23, 2051–2068.

Cashman, Adrian, Leonard Nurse and Charley John, 2010. Climate change in the Caribbean: the water management implications. The Journal of Environment & Development XX(X), 1–26.

Fang, C.-L. and Xie, Y., 2009. Sustainable urban development in water-constrained Northwest China: A case study along the mid-section of the Silk-Road – He-Xi corridor. Journal of Arid Environments 74, 1–9.

Hamouda, M. A., Mohamed M. Nour El-Din and Fawzia I Moursy, 2009. Vulnerability Assessment of Water Resources Systems in the Eastern Nile Basin. Water Resources Management 23, 1–29.

Larson, K. L., D. D. White, P. Gober, S. Harlan and a. Wutich (2009). Divergent perspectives on water resource sustainability in a public-policy-science context. Environmental Science and Policy 12, 1012–1023.

Phillips, Daniel H., Reinink, Yvonne, Skarupa, Timothy E., Ester, Charles E. and Skindlov, Jon (2009). Water resources planning and management at the Salt River Project, Arizona, USA. Springer Science 23,109–124.

Rajagopalan, B., K. Nowak, J. Prairie, M. Hoerling, B. Harding, J. Barsugli, A. Ray, and B. Udall, 2009. Water supply risk on the Colorado River: Can management mitigate? Water Recourses 45, 1–7.

Ridoutt, Bradley G. and Stephan Pfister, 2010. A revised approach to water footprinting to make apparent the impacts of consumption and production on global freshwater scarcity. Global Environmental Change 20, 113–120.

21. Climate Change Considerations for Water Management

Winnie Wong

Water is a natural resource essential for the survival of all living organisms and water ecosystems provide food, shelter, breeding areas and nursery areas for a wide variety of organisms. The importance of protecting water resources is directly linked to our survival, and the range of stakeholders in the quantity and quality of freshwater resources is far-reaching. The development of water resources can enhance the provisioning, regulatory, and cultural services of aquatic ecosystems that are important to society and biodiversity alike. In order to optimally manage water resource services, it is necessary to understand the current and possible future condition of our water resources in the face of changes in freshwater availability due to climate change.

Water exists as either surface water or underground water, both of which are utilized as sources for human consumption. Surface water is naturally replenished by rainfall and lost due to evaporation and percolation into the soil. Groundwater is water located beneath the surface in soil pore spaces. Groundwater is naturally recharged when rain, snow melt, or surface water in lakes and rivers moves downward from the surface. Despite the categorization, water can freely flow from one regime to the other since the two are part of an interrelated system.

Lakes, rivers, and underground sources of freshwater are already under intense pressure from multiple competing uses, pollution, and habitat degradation. Many vulnerable aquatic ecosystems are put under additional stress due to the effects of climate change which directly impact freshwater supplies. The issue is no longer whether or not climate change exists, but how to deal with the inevitable effects of climate change. Society's extensive exploitation of natural resources and widespread environmental degradation has committed us to a future of rapid changes in climate and resource availability.

Some of the effects being studied include reduced groundwater inflow, changes in water temperature, and greater seasonal fluctuations in precipitation which will drive changes in nutrient cycles, food chains, water level, and water quality. According to global model runs, some places will experience a 10% decrease in groundwater recharge, but a fifth to one third of the global population will experience a groundwater recharge increase of more than 10% by the 2050s. (Petra Döll 2009). It is difficult to generalize the exact changes to water supplies caused by climate change because there is a great degree of variation depending on the location. A study on Finland groundwater predicted that the changes in the timing and height of surface and groundwater levels due increased seasonal fluctuations in precipitations, evapotranspiration, and recharge may impact water quality (Okkonen *et al.* 2009). A study on the Colorado River looked at the effects of decreased recharge on risk of reservoir depletion (Rajagpalan *et al.* 2009). The authors modeled how a 20% reduction of inflow by 2057 can significantly raise the risk of annual reservoir depletion by 2057 by 51% compared to no climate-induced reductions in inflow. Effects of changed nutrient cycles on water quality will impact water availability, and freshwater systems will be subject to more pressure due to elevated levels of nitrogen and phosphorus, degrading soil and freshwater resources (Heathwaite 2010). Furthermore, the significance of local management shouldn't be underestimated as land management decisions can drastically impact water supplies The type of vegetation on overlying land above groundwater aquifers can alter groundwater recharge (Været *et al.* 2009). Lake Biviere di Gela experienced a complete rearrangement of its phytoplankton community due to significant increases in temperature and nutrient availability driven by climate change and land management decisions (Barone *et al.* 2010). Therefore, it is imperative more research is done to untangle effects of climate change on water resources and to understand how to develop sustainable water management systems.

Successfully navigating through the possible changes in water supply and quality requires accurate monitoring and models to predict future conditions. There has been extensive research into the future of water supplies through the use of climatic and hydrological models to better understand the complexities of water systems. Despite the widespread use of these models to simulate future conditions, there is a high degree of uncertainty in model predictions of future water supplies. Global models do not correlate strongly with localized models due to the interconnectedness of hydrological, biological, and physio-chemical processes that make water supply predictions much more difficult than carbon emissions predictions. Furthermore, the most commonly relied on proxies to infer water availability fail to take into account a wide range of biological factors. The water availability predictions based on precipitation, annual water deficit, and evapotranspiration significantly differed from results obtained from ecosystem models LPJ-GUESS and LPF-

DGVM in 32% of one study area (Hickler 2009). Parallel to carbon footprinting, the concept of water footprinting has been emerging to encourage responsible water consumption, but even the measurement of current water consumption impact is imprecise due to the various types of water sources and different purposes to which water is employed (Ridoutt and Pfister 2009). This becomes problematic when inaccurate predictions and measurements are used to guide policies and management strategies.

Global Vulnerability to Change in Groundwater Recharge

Petra Döll (2009) of Goethe University Frankfurt studied the vulnerability of different regions to the impact of climate change on renewable groundwater resources. Four different climate change scenarios projected for the 2050s were considered using IPCC SRES scenarios A2 and B2 using two global climate change models ECHAM4/OPYC3 and HadCM3. According to these model runs, most places with high population density and high sensitivity will likely experience less than 10% decrease in groundwater recharge, but a fifth to one third of the global population will experience a groundwater recharge increase of more than 10%. The paper found that the regions most vulnerable to decreased groundwater flow are at the North Africa rim, southwestern Africa, northeastern Brazil, and in the central Andes.

Döll used the amount of decrease in groundwater recharge and the sensitivity of human system to that decrease to derive the degree of vulnerability. The impact of climate change on groundwater resources was quantified using the WaterGAP Global Hydrological Model WGHM (Döll and Florke 2005). A sensitivity index of each region was determined using levels of water scarcity, dependence on water supply on ground water and adaptive capacity of the human system. All the scenarios agree that groundwater recharge will increase in the northern latitudes while semi-arid zones will see strong decreases, anywhere from 30% to 70%. Scenario A2 predicts that in the 2050s, groundwater recharge will have decreased more than 10% on 20.4–21.5% of the global land mass, affecting 18.4–19.3% of the 10.7 billion global population. Scenario B2 predicts that groundwater recharge will decrease more than 10% on 18.3–20.4% of the global land mass, affecting 16.1–18.1% of the 9.1 billion global population.

The scenarios suggested by the two climate models for the 2050s indicate that anthropogenic change may have already caused a decrease in renewable groundwater resources of more than 10% on more than one fifth of the global land mass. The sensitivity of the human system to decreases in groundwater recharge show strong spatial variability because many highly populated areas such as India, Pakistan, Iran, Saudi Arabia, Jordan, Morocco, and eastern China are not expected to have significant decreases in groundwater recharge by the 2050s. Because of such variability, vulnerability should be considered a local phenomenon that can be responsive to specific societal and physical variables and actions to solve water resource management problems.

Impact of Climate Change on Finland Groundwater

Jarkko Okkonen and Bjorn Klove of the University of Oulu, Finland and Mikki Jyrkama of the University of Waterloo, Canada developed a conceptual framework to understand the impact of climate change on groundwater, and they applied it to the case study of eskers in northern Finland (Okkonen *et al.* 2009). Impacts of predicted climate change on groundwater were not based on numerical modeling, but from information accumulated from previous studies in similar environments to evaluate the impacts of climate change in cold regions on near-surface hydrological regime, surface-water bodies, and groundwater. The advantages of Okkonen's conceptual framework is that it is easy to use and helps to identify linkages between different parameters impacting groundwater systems. Their results from northern Finland show that increased winter precipitation and decreased soil frost are expected to enhance groundwater recharge leading to a rise in water levels. Warmer summer temperatures will increase evapotranspiration, decrease recharge, and lower water levels. The heightening of seasonal fluctuations will impact water quality more in cultivated land than in land with no human use.

The paper looks at the responses of surface and subsurface hydrology to climate change by looking at how groundwater is affected by changes in precipitation and temperature. Climate change affects hydrological processes such as evapotranspiration and recharge change during the summer and winter, which ultimately influence groundwater quality and water levels. In the case study of northern Finland, the A2 emission scenario by 2050 was used to predict a winter temperature increase by 4.6°C and summer temperature by 2.1°C. Climate change is expected to increase groundwater recharge and water levels during the winter and decrease both during the summer. Higher temperatures in the summer will potentially increase direct evaporation from surface water bodies and the ground surface, enhance transpiration through vegetation, and result in decreased groundwater recharge and water levels. In the winter, rainfall would increase and snow accumulation would decrease. Increased winter precipitation will initially increase snow depth but as the amount of rainfall increases, snow depth will begin decreasing. Decreased snow depths will lead to a decrease in protective snow and enhance groundwater recharge and water levels. The quality of water is expected to increase due to increased oxygen-rich water from snowmelt during the winter, while groundwater quality is expected to worsen during the summer. The increase in winter recharge and higher groundwater levels may increase solute leaching and capture pesticides and other pollutants that will decrease groundwater quality. Agricultural areas are especially influential as the seasonal changes in recharge might accentuate pesticide concentrations in groundwater.

Depletion of Colorado River Reservoir by Climate Change

Climate change and growth in demand will greatly impact the water supply of the Colorado River. Rajagpalan and his colleagues at the University of Colorado found that the risk of depleting reservoir storage increases significantly over time while alternative management policies can help reduce the risk (Rajagpalan *et al.* 2009). The paper sought to evaluate the risk of future water storage failure under existing management policies by taking into account demand growth, known historical climate variability, and projected reductions in Colorado River flow due to climate change. Taking into consideration annual inflows and outflows of the Colorado River and historical and paleoreconstructed flow variations, two scenarios of climate change were considered: a linear reduction in annual average flow of 10% and 20% over the 50 year period from 2008–2057. Under each scenario, various alternative management policies were simulated and the probabilities of depleting active system reservoir storage were calculated. The study found that the effects of climate change-induced flow reductions increases the risk of reservoir depletion significantly over time although alternative management policies can help mitigate the risk.

In the scenario that there is no climate change-induced average annual flow reduction with existing practices, shortage risk increases to 7.5% by the 50 year mark due to increase in demand. In the scenario that there is a 10% average annual flow reduction due to climate change, the risk significantly increases over the 50 year period to about 26%. In the scenario that there is a 20% average annual flow reduction, the risk is significantly higher at about 51%. Although shortage strategy and demand growth management can reduce the risk in all scenarios, the risk remains very high in the cases when there are climate change-induced average flow reduction of 10% and 20%. Even under more aggressive strategies, the risks stand at 11% and 33%, respectively. Most notably, the risk per year does not increase linearly. After around the 20 year mark, the rate of increased risk rises significantly faster than prior years, demonstrating the importance of preemptive management strategies. The study shows that management alternatives can greatly mitigate increased risks and should be implemented well before significant detection of local climate change. The paper warns policy makers to not be lulled by the relatively small risk of depletion in the first 20 years. If people wait until 2027 to confirm detection of climate change, the availability to options may be limited.

Winnie Wong

Multiple Stressors on Water Quality and Availability

Ann Louise Heathwaite (Heathwaite 2010) of Lancaster University looked at multiple stressors that impact fresh water availability—changing climate, land use, demands on water resources and nutrient cycles because it is important to sustain the long-term quality, not just quantity, of water from rivers and groundwater. The paper focuses on diffuse pollutants which are characterized by sources that are generally widespread, hard to detect, and by highly variable fluxes. Elevated levels of nitrogen and phosphorous compromise the ecosystem services that we depend on, degrading soil and freshwater resources. Heathwaite also points out the need to better understand in-stream transitional processes that impact diffuse pollutants.

Environmental systems are undergoing a period of unprecedented change due to climate change and associated human-induced changes. Human activities have increased nitrogen and phosphorus cycles by an average of 100 and 400%, respectively. The importation of nitrogen and phosphorous from land to water has been of considerable concern because the human-induced changes in nutrient cycles are becoming evident at the ecosystem level. Elevated levels of nitrogen and phosphorous promote algal growth at the expense of higher plants. Prior research confirms that we can no longer assume a hydroclimatic stationarity basis for models of water resource availability and management. For freshwater ecosystems, hydrological connectivity and diffuse pollution risk may change under a changing climate. Predicting ecosystem response to diffuse pollutants is challenging due to the multiple factors that regulate biogeochemical transformations in freshwater systems. There is a lack of understanding of internal in-stream processes that may transform, immobilize, or eliminate diffuse pollutants. These relationships deserve further research because riverbeds are transitional environments between groundwater and surface water that serve as a sink for sediment and pollutants. The focus of restoration measures on the riparian zones may not deliver sustainable solutions for freshwater ecology. There needs to be better understanding of the spatial controls on the delivery of diffuse pollutants to better understand how restoration measures would give the best return. This requires advances in sensor technologies and the development of cyber infrastructure to make simultaneous observations at appropriate ranges of time and space scales. Unforeseen consequences for land and freshwater systems could result in assumptions being built into predictions of climate change impacts that are misleading.

Land Use Management Effects on Groundwater in Lake St. Lucia

Lars Været (Været et al. 2009) looked at the effects of land management and climate variations on groundwater resources in Lake St. Lucia, South Africa. The study area had been cleared of its pines and the forest replaced by grassland over the past decade. The change in land use led to a general rise of the water table. The study found that because deep-rooted plants such as pines lower groundwater levels through evapotranspiration, the reduction of deep-rooted plants can mitigate potential effects of reduced water resources. The modeling simulations suggest that positive local land management impacts outweighed the negative effects of sea-level and precipitation changes predicted for the area.

Modeling information was simulated through the MODFLOW groundwater model developed by the US Geological Survey. Climate change-induced sea level change of +0.4 m, and precipitation change of ±10% were simulated together with different land uses (pine plantation versus grasslands). Twelve different combinations of sea level, land use, and rainfall scenarios were simulated. Simulations with grassland resulted in considerable rises of the water table.

Increased rainfall leads to greater levels of evapotranspiration because there is an increase in water level that penetrates further into the rooting zone of the vegetation. Deep-rooted plants such as pines further increase evapotranspiration levels because deeper roots are able to access more water. Grassland has a more shallow rooting depth and results in less evapotranspiration losses, so change from pine plantations to grasslands causes a greater increase in outflow into Lake St. Lucia. A change in land use from pine plantations to grassland will cause a greater increase in total outflow from the aquifer compared to the effect of increased rainfall alone. The expansion of pines will likely reduce groundwater recharge drastically.

Climate Change and Management Impacts on Phytoplankton in Biviere di Gela, Sicily

Rosella Barone (Barone *et al.* 2010) and her associates at the University of Palermo looked at the effects of climate change and management procedures on the phytoplankton community on the Mediterranean lake Biviere di Gela in Sicily. The increased need for water coupled with climate change will interfere with the hydrological cycle and pose a threat to Mediterranean aquatic ecosystems. In Bieire di Gela, the phytoplankton community underwent a complete rearrangement from the period between 1987 and 2007. The study found the lake experienced the appearance and dominance of new phytoplankton species due to climate change-induced effects over the last 20 years. The lake has also been subject to further modification because freshwater from a nearby dam supplied a source of artificial inflow to maintain the lake's water level. Shallow aquatic ecosystems such as Lake Biviere di Gela, are more prone to dramatic changes in biota as a result of a modification in their water supply.

Data came from monthly collections of phytoplankton samples between 1987–1988 and 2005–2007. Weight biomass of different species of phytoplankton and different water properties were recorded for the two time periods. The study found that there was a time-shift in the occurrence of rain, significant increases in average air temperature, and proportional increases in evapotranspiration and eva-poration levels. Temperature and precipitation data recorded for over 40 years were used to evaluate climate variability. The data showed that the total amount of water flowing into the lake from the catchment has significantly decreased despite precipi-tation levels being relatively steady. The lowered water level disrupted the littoral zone, but the lake's water level was maintained by adding freshwater from a nearby dam which increased nutrient availability. The increase in water temperature, tur-bidity and nutrient availability, and reduced salinity level is believed to have helped cyanobacteria to outcompete previously dominant macrophyte species.

The current phytoplankton community in the coastal lake Biviere di Gela is the result of inadequate management and climate changes interfering with hydro-logical processes. Biviere di Gela was transformed from a clear, macrophyte-dominated lake to a turbid one, dominated by cyanobacteria in the summer. Fur-thermore, the effects of climate change encourage blooms of cyanobacteria in the shallow lake. Cyanobacteria pose a multitude of water quality concerns because of the toxins they produce that can poison humans and animals. Biviere di Gela does not serve as a freshwater reservoir of drinking water, but the case illustrates the po-tential danger climate change poses in exacerbating toxic contamination of bodies of freshwater.

Ecosystem Model Predicts Water Availability

Species distribution models typically use four common proxies for water in order to predict how water availability will impact future species distribution. However, the affects of changes in vegetation structure and function on the water balance of terrestrial ecosystems are not accounted for. Hickler (2009) sought to assess whether the water availability measure commonly used in species distribution models properly account for hydrological effects of changes in vegetation structure and functioning. His study used the ecosystem models LPJ- GUESS and LPF-DGVM which took into account soil water content along with variables based on climate. The projections for future water availability from four common proxies for water and the soil water content predicted by ecosystem models differ substantially.

The paper focused on water availability in Europe. The LPJ-GUESS model includes a number of factors that influence water availability not accounted for in common proxies for water. LPJ- DGVM is a simplified ecosystem model that was also assessed. The four commonly used proxies for water availability used were total annual precipitation, total precipitation during water scarce periods (June, July and August), annual water deficit, and sum of actual evapotranspiration divided by equilibrium evapotranspiration. Water stress experienced by plants is a function of water availability and both soil after and atmospheric variables are biologically meaningful. For tree species, the water content of soil is a more direct measure of water availability than variables purely based on climate.

The changes projected by the four proxies correlated with each other while these variable showed no or very weak correlations with the two ecosystem models. Projected changes in the four proxies for water availability indicate a net effect of increasing temperate and annual rainfall in many areas with drying over most of Europe. In contrast, in the ecosystem models, the sign of change (positive or negative) differs in 32% of the total study area. These significant differences in results are important because results from species distribution models have been used as guiding policies for adaptation to climate change.

Revised Approach to Water Footprinting

A revised water footprint method devised by Ridoutt and Pfister takes into consideration the type of water source and different usages during stages of production to determine how much Dolmio® pasta sauce and Peanut M&M's® contribute to water scarcity (2009). Existing water footprint calculations use the volumetric summation of all water content in the product at all stages of production and consumption. Under the existing method, the products Dolmio® pasta sauce and Peanut M&M's® have water footprints of 202 and 1153, but the revised water footprints offer a drastically different relationship. The stress-weighted water footprints of Dolmio® pasta sauce and Peanut M&M's® are 141 and 131.

Bradley G. Ridoutt of the Australian Commonwealth Scientific and Research Organization and Stephan Pfister of the Swiss Federal Institute of Technology Zurich demonstrated a revised water footprint calculation method using brand products, Dolmio® pasta sauce and Peanut M&M's®. Ridoutt disaggregates water according to the different sources: blue water which is surface and groundwater sources, and green water which is rainwater that is consumed through crop evapotranspiration. Because some places have a higher degree of water scarcity than others, location and level of stress imposed by different activities are considered in calculating a product's water footprint. Therefore, the water consumption at specific locations at each point in the product life cycle and the water stress index (WSI) by Pfister (2009) were used to determine the level of contribution to water scarcity of both products.

In both cases of Dolmio® pasta sauce and Peanut M&M's®, the agricultural stage of production contributed the greatest, followed by operations, ingredients processing, and packaging. The study found that blue water sources are typically directly consumed at rates exceeding short-term replacement; therefore processes heavily using blue water sources contribute significantly to stress-weighted water footprints. A main ingredient of Dolmio® pasta sauce is tomato. Due to the stress-heavy consumption of blue water in agriculture, tomatoes contributed more than 95% of stress-weighted water footprint. Therefore, efforts to reduce water footprint should focus on stress-heavy processes and not necessarily processes that use more water.

The study argues that the simplistic existing volumetric method is une-quipped to accurately depict how production impacts water scarcity. This method is misleading and confusing as these water footprints do not accurately reflect a product's impact on the water supply. A revised water footprint method would allow quantitative comparisons between products in terms of potential to contri-bute to water scarcity. Water footprint assessment methods need to accurately re-flect the impact of consumption and this requires a revised approach that considers the incorporation of water stress characterization factors. The revised method will help corporations direct optimal actions to reduce negative impact of water supply and help consumers to make more informed purchases.

Conclusions

The world community has looked to global leaders to take charge of the cli-mate change situation to initiate corrective policies; it has been largely let down by the lack of concrete action thus far. Effective action will be facilitated when better data is available, though, and the papers summarized in this chapter are examples of current attempts to get those data. The research features a wide range of different analytical frameworks and terminology. The science and analysis is still young and no standardized method has been developed yet, and there is still a deep lack of understanding between the hydrological, biological, and economic relationships of our water systems. Improving water management requires accurate measurement of water use, better and more consistent monitoring of critical variables, and better understanding of the mechanisms underlying atmospheric and hydrological processes in order to mitigate the uncertainty of the impacts of climate change. We must be ready to deal with the consequences of our decisions because, undoubtedly, there will be significant changes due to climate change on freshwater supplies.

References Cited

Barone, R., Castelli, G., Naselli-Flores, L., 2010. Red sky at night cyanobacteria delight: the role of climate in structuring phytoplankton assemblage in a shallow, Mediterranean lake (Biviere di Gela, southeastern Sicily).Hydrobiologia 639, 43–53.

Döll, P., 2009. Vulnerability to the impact of climate change on renewable groundwater resources: a global-scale assessment. Environmental Research Letters 4, 1–12.

Döll, P., Florke, M., 2005. Global-scale estimation of diffuse groundwater recharge. Frankfurt

Hydrology Paper 03, Institute of Physical Geography, Frankfurt University, Germany.

<http://www.geo.uni-frankfurtde/ipg/ag/dl/f publikationen/2005/FHP 03 Doell Floerke 2005.pdf>

Heathwaite, A. L., 2010. Multiple stressors on water availability at global to catchment scales: human impact on nutrient cycles to protect water quality and water availability in the long term. Freshwater Biology 55, 241–257.

Hickler, T., Stepan F., Miguel B. A., Oliver S., Wilfried T., and Martin T. S., 2009. An ecosystem model-based estimate of changes in water availability differs from water proxies that are commonly used in species distribution models. Global Ecology and Biogeography 18, 304–313.

Okkonen, J., Jyrkama, M., Klove, B., 2009. A conceptual approach for assessing the impact of climate change on groundwater and related surface waters in cold regions. Hydrogeology Journal. DOI: 10.1007/s10040-009-0529-9.

Rajagopalan, B., K. Nowak, J. Prairie, M. Hoerling, B. Harding, J. Barsugli, A. Ray, and B. Udall, 2009. Water supply risk on the Colorado River: Can management mitigate? Water Resources Research. DOI: 10.1029/2008WR007652.

Ridoutt, B., Pfister, S., 2010. A revised approach to water footprinting to make transparent the impacts of consumption and production on global freshwater scarcity. Global Environmental Change 20, 113–120.

Været, L., Kelbe, B., Haldorsen, S., Taylow, R. H., 2009. A modeling study of the effects of land management and climatic variations on groundwater inflow to Lake St Lucia, South Africa. Hydrogeology Journal 17, 1949–1967.

Section VI—Biological Effects of Climate Change

22. Overfertilization of Crops: Consequences and Solutions

Maria Harwood

The overfertilization of crops by farmers has been a historic problem since the creation and widespread distribution of inexpensive nitrogen, phosphorus, and potassium fertilizers. Overfertilization of agricultural commodities continues, despite the abundance of research that demonstrates the harmful effects of this practice on the crops, the environment, and humans. The wide reaching effects of overfertilization has prompted some government intervention to regulate the application levels to crops, but long-standing government subsidies towards agriculture and the provision of fertilizer at almost no cost to farmers has undermined regulation efforts (Ju *et al.* 2009). Solutions to the problem are almost as numerous as the effects on the environment, ranging from low cost soil tests for farmers, to highly expensive measures like the development of fertilizer application maps for every agricultural field in production.

Overfertilization with N, P, and K fertilizers has negative effects on human health, nature, and the farmers' crop yield. The loss pathways of nutrients to the environment are the root causes of the negative effects industrial agriculture has on nature (Oenema *et al.* 2009). The loss of nutrients can occur through volatilization, surface runoff, and leaching into the groundwater (Ju *et al.* 2009). In nature, overfertilization causes the disruption of nutrient cycles, eutrophication of surface water bodies, accumulation of nutrients in the soil, acid rain, and soil acidification. Added negative effects of eutrophication include the resulting algal blooms from high nutrient content in water. When algae dies, it sinks to the bottom of the water body and begins to decompose, a process which can use up most of the oxygen content in the water, resulting in anoxic conditions which cause massive fish die-offs. Overfertilization of crops can also result in human health issues when the leaching of nutrients into the groundwater pollutes the water table, or runoff pollutes surface potable water supplies. Human health effects from excessive nitrate content in water include blue baby syndrome and gastrointestinal cancer in adults (Kundu and Mandal 2009). Overfertilization also has a marked effect on the crops themselves, as the presence of too much fertilizer can stunt growth and result in lower yields (Ju et al. 2009). For some reason, even knowledge of all these negative effects from overfertilization has not resulted in a decrease in farmer's usage of fertilizer.

The causes of overfertilization vary depending upon the geographical region. In China, where the government provides chemical fertilizers at a very low cost, the farmers have no cost incentive to limit their use, and often don't know that excessively high rates of fertilizer can reduce yield (Ju et al. 2009). Since the farmers experienced remarkable growth in yields with increased use of fertilizer, they fail to see the harm from applying more. Farmers may also purposefully fertilizer their crops beyond the crop requirements, because of the loss pathways for nutrients. If farmers do not take measures to accurately apply fertilizers, much of what they apply ends up washed away or volatilizing to the atmosphere, so to overcompensate for this problem fertilizer is over-applied (Oenema et al. 2009). By identifying the causes of overfertilization, solutions may be developed.

Solutions to overfertilization vary greatly in cost. Low cost solutions revolve around education of farmers about the harmful effects of overfertilization and soil tests that can be distributed to farmers so that they can be knowledgeable about the nutrient requirements of their own fields. Policy directives have been implemented in some nations, but simple enactment of the laws does not mean that they will be effective at combating overfertilization (Oenema et al. 2009). Best practices need to be identified and distributed to the farmers in a practical manner, one that is low cost or supported by government subsidies to offset the high upfront costs of combating the loss pathways of nutrients to the environment.

Overuse of N Fertilizers Leads to Nutrient Imbalance and Acidification of Soil in Zhangjiagang County, China

Darilek et al. (2009) conducted a study of the soil fertility parameters in conjunction with information from the county of Zhangjiagang, China, on the amounts of nitrogen, phosphorus, and potassium fertilizers used from 1980 to 2004. Within this county, which is part of the Yangtze River Delta area, there are two dominant types of soil, Cambisols and Anthrosols. Cambisols are found in the northern region near the river, while Anthrosols are prevalent in the southern plains region. Anthrosols experienced such a large acidification of the soil (a decrease in pH), due to over-application of N fertilizers and an increase in industrial effluents that the area will be rendered useless for crop production in 25 to 30 years.

Jeremy Darilek and his colleagues collected soil samples of both Cambisols and Anthrosols from around the county in 1980, then again in 2004. These samples were analyzed for pH, organic matter, cation exchange capacity, total nitrogen, total phosphorus, available phosphorus, and available potassium. These data combined with information supplied by the county on the rates of N, P, and K fertilizer applied annually were used to determine the effects of the different fertilizers on the soil fertility parameters. The effects of the fertilizers on the environment were not evaluated directly, but were inferred from present knowledge on overuse of fertilizers and how this can lead to N leaching and eutrophication of surrounding water bodies.

The ratio of N:P:K fertilizer applied to the rice and wheat crops grown in this region has increasingly contained excessive amounts of N, above the needed requirements for the crops since 1990. P fertilizer rates have increased, but remain at levels beneficial to the growth of the crops due to a lack of P accumulation in the soil. Also over the years there has been a phasing out of the use of organic fertilizers, and an increased reliance on inorganic fertilizers. Among the two soil types, Anthrosols were found to have a greater decrease in pH—an acidification of the soil—which if left unchecked will deplete the metal bioavailability, fertility, and microbiology of the soil to such an extent it will be inhospitable to crops in 25 to 30 years. The cause of this acidification is largely an increase in the application of N fertilizer, but also a result of the rapid industrialization of the county, which has led to greater numbers of factories, which spew industrial effluents that contribute to the rise of acidification. These nutrient imbalances in the soil resulting from incorrect application of fertilizer cause non-point pollution of N into the surrounding water bodies, endangering both human and ecosystem health.

Despite Heavy Agricultural Cultivation, the Groundwater of Nadia District of West Bengal, India, Remains Safe for Human Consumption

Kundu and Mandal (2009) conducted a study of the nitrate and fluoride concentrations found in the drinking groundwater in an area of heavy agriculture within the Nadia district of West Bengal, India during November 2007. They looked for differences in concentrations from spatial variations among aquifers, type of crops planted, and rate of fertilizer application. All of the samples analyzed for N and F content were below the maximum limit determined safe for drinking water according to WHO guidelines, indicating no groundwater contamination of the drinking water sources for the sample area. The amount of N varied significantly based on the depth of sampling aquifers (wells), type of crops in cultivation (shallow versus deep rooted), and the rate of N fertilizer application. In contrast, F concentrations varied only slightly due to the uniform geological composition of the area, which is the main contributing factor to F content.

Kundu and Mandal collected 342 samples during the month of November only, avoiding the monsoon season in India, which brings intense rainfall. They chose the Nadia district of West Bengal because it is one of the areas in India with the highest usage of pesticides and fertilizers, with an average fertilizer application rate of 177.4 kg/ha. The samples were taken from different types of wells that had varying depths.

It was found that in areas where people lived there were higher levels of N in the water than in the agricultural areas—a result of N contamination from sewage systems. The N content in the water varied greatly based on region within the study area, but was higher where use of N fertilizer was also high and where crops were grown that had shallow root systems, like potatoes. The N content was also dependent on the depth of the well tested; deeper wells had lower amounts of N due to the greater restriction on the movement of N in water within the soil profile. Fluorine did not demonstrate the same variations as N because the main source of F comes from the geological composition of the area, not the use of fertilizers. The geology of the area was found to be homogenous, explaining the relative uniformity of the concentrations of F, but there was an increase in F with the use of phosphatic fertilizers. Despite the fact that the levels of N and F found in the drinking water were too low to cause human harm, the N levels were building up in areas with cultivation of shallow rooted plants, which do not absorb the N fertilizer as well once the N mixes with water and begins to percolate through the soil, below the reach of their roots.

Reductions of 30–60% of Applied Synthetic N Fertilizer Possible in Intensive Chinese Agriculture Systems

The increased availability and overuse of synthetic N fertilizers worldwide over the past 40 years has led to demonstrated negative environmental consequences in the form of disrupted N cycles, eutrophication of surface water, nitrate pollution in the groundwater, acid rain, and soil acidification (Ju et al. 2009). This study closely monitored double crop rotations in different locations within China to determine the extent of N fertilizer overuse and how much synthetic fertilizer was actually needed for growing either the wheat and maize or wheat and rice combinations. It was found on the whole that Chinese farmers apply N fertilizer in excess of 30 to 60%.

Xiao-Tang Ju and his colleagues studied double crop rotations of maize and wheat, as well as wheat and rice. The later combination is farmed using an alternating flood and drain system of the fields. Their experiment determined that with increased N inputs, there was an increase in N losses due to leaching from the top 1 meter of soil, ammonia volatilization, and denitrification. The wheat/maize rotation of crops had higher N recovery rates and N retention rates, as well as lower N loss rates than the wheat/rice rotations. One implication of this finding for Chinese farmers is that growing wheat/maize is more effective at preventing leakage of N than growing rice/wheat; providing the benefit that more N is left in the soil for later crops,. The Chinese soil was also found to have a high natural N content, so large applications of N fertilizer are not needed. Such a reduction would lead to a decrease in the amount of ammonia volatilization in the soil, preventing the deleterious effects on the surrounding ecosystems. An overall reduction of 30–60% of synthetic N fertilizer could be applied to the fields with no loss in crop yield and with beneficial effects to the natural ecosystems.

^{15}N Content in Plants Can Be Used as an Indicator of Excess Compost Application

Yun and Ro (2009) conducted an experiment using Chinese cabbage plants to determine whether the amount of ^{15}N within the plant tissues can be used to indicate the overuse of compost in soil. Compost is an important inexpensive alternative to chemical fertilizers, although the overuse of compost can lead to the same environmental impacts that overuse of N fertilizers have. The amount of nutrients in compost varies depending upon the source, therefore the concentrations of N and P need to be determined before application to soils in order to avoid overuse. Four different amounts of compost were used in the experiment and three areas of plant tissue and the soil were analyzed for ^{15}N content. The study determined that the amount of ^{15}N found in the plants along with the soil nitrate content can be used to tell if the level of compost application was too high.

Yun and Ro used potted Chinese cabbage plants grown for 42 days in soil amended with a compost made of pig manure mixed with sawdust. Four different rates of compost were applied to the soil; 0, 500, 1000, 1500 mg N/kg. The outer, middle, and inner leaves of the Chinese cabbage plants were analyzed for N content to determine whether the source of N found in the plants was from the compost or the indigenous N soil content. This distinction is key to figuring out if ^{15}N can be used as an indicator of the amount of compost used or if it is only showing the N usage from the soil.

Compost application increased the amount of dry mass accumulation of the cabbage with the lowest application rate, but successive increasing amounts of compost produced no increase in dry mass. Although the amount of dry mass did not increase with added compost, the uptake of N by the cabbage plants did increase in proportion to the amount of compost. The increasing compost amounts also produced greater amounts of ^{15}N found in the cabbage for all applications except the lowest. The inner, younger leaves of the cabbage showed a strong correlation of the ^{15}N levels being derived from the compost, therefore the authors determined the ^{15}N levels found in plants can be used as an indicator of the amount of compost being applied to the soil.

Use of Modeling to Predict P Accumulation in Winter Wheat and Maize Crop Rotations

Ma et al. (2009) conducted an experiment which involved creating a model to predict the Olson-P levels in soils under cultivation for winter wheat and maize crops in China. The model used over 15 years worth of data from crop rotations among five provinces of China with varying soil composition and climate. Both crops that were fertilized with P and those that were not were included in the study to examine the level of extraction of Olson-P by the crops in the form of grain yield. The unfertilized crops quickly exhausted the soils' Olson-P content until a level of approximately 3 mg/kg was reached at which removal plateaued. When P fertilizer was applied to the crops, the amount of Olson-P rose and accumulated within the soil at an average rate of 1.21 mg/kg/yr. The model created was determined to be accurate in predicting rates of Olson-P in the soils.

Ma et al. used measurements of Olson-P levels and P fertilizer application rates from five experiment sites around China spanning over 15 years. Three treatments used no fertilizer, N and P fertilizer, or N, P, and K fertilizer. The initial value of Olson-P in the soils is important to know so that further calculations can be performed to predict the future levels after crop removal and added P fertilizer so the authors modeled levels of Olson-P in the soils based on P application rate, crop grain yield or removal, and soil pH and validated the model by comparing its results to another series of long-term studies of crop rotations from around China and India. The model accurately predicted the amount of Olson-P found in the soils for the unfertilized crops, but not for crops fertilized with a combination of N and P, or N, P, and K.

Savings of 19% Net GHG Flux to Atmosphere Possible with Fertilization of Crops in Early Spring

Phillips *et al.* (2009) conducted an experiment to determine whether the timing of fertilizer application to a maize crop in Central North Dakota affects the greenhouse gas (GHG) fluxes during the growing season. Plots were fertilized either in early spring (April 1) or in late spring (May 13). It was hypothesized that the plots fertilized in early spring would produce lower net GHG emissions, due to the lower air and soil temperatures which inhibit the microbial production and consumption of GHG. The three GHGs measured include: methane, carbon dioxide, and nitrous oxide. Fertilization of the plots in early spring had a net GHG flux of 19% less than the plots which were fertilized in late spring. Over 98% of the GHG emissions came from CO_2, as opposed to methane or nitrous oxide.

Phillips *et al.* measured methane, CO_2, and nitrous oxide gases, in conjunction with soil pH, electrical conductivity, texture, bulk density, total C and N, water holding capacity of the soil, air temperature near soil surface, and soil temperature 10 cm below the surface. The plot measurements were taken between 1000 to 1200 hr—the time period that is most representative of the daily fluxes—1 to 4 times per week. These factors were measured to determine what was producing the changes in GHG emissions. The experiment was conducted over five months on the northern Great Plains in five plots, each 0.30 ha, that were fertilized with urea in early spring, and five plots fertilized in late spring.

Both methane and CO_2 emissions showed effects from the early versus the late fertilization of the maize crop. The fluxes were greater within the soil for the plots that were fertilized in late spring. The time-integrated net GHG flux for soils that were fertilized in late spring was greater than the soils fertilized in early spring. Nitrous oxide did not show any difference in flux between the two treatments, and CO_2 was responsible for over 98% of the total GHG flux emissions. A net GHG flux lost to the atmosphere of 19% could be avoided in central North Dakota if fertilizer were applied to fields in early spring, before temperatures rise above 10°C. When the soil and air temperatures rise above 10°C, the microbial activity in the soil gets stimulated with the addition of urea fertilizer, producing greater GHG emissions.

The Three Best Practices to Decrease N Losses in EU-27 Cause High Costs to Farmers, but are Successful

Oenema *et al.* (2009) performed a modeling-based experiment to determine the environmental and economic costs of implementing the three most promising measures to abate N losses in agricultural production within the 27 Member Nations of the European Union (EU-27). The three general categories of measures include balanced fertilization (BF), low-protein animal feeding (LNF), and ammonia emissions abatement (AEA), with preferred order of implementation BF, LNF, and AEA. Both practices of BF and LNF were found to decrease N inputs as they simultaneously increased N output in useful products. AEA caused a decrease in ammonia emissions, but this was coupled with an increase in other types of N emissions, therefore not seen to be effective when used alone without other measures. All three measures were not without additional costs to the farmer in time and lost income, as well as to society in the form of higher priced goods.

To determine the environmental effects of the different measures, the MITERRA-EUROPE model was used, along with the CAPRI model to determine the economic costs (Oenema *et al.* 2009). These three measures were selected based upon their evaluated effectiveness to increase N use efficiency and decrease N losses through ammonia and nitrous oxide emissions to the atmosphere and N leaching into groundwater and surface waters. Nitrogen use efficiency (NUE) is defined as the N output in useful products (harvested crops, milk, meat) as a percentage of the total N inputs (N fertilizer). The three measures were evaluated against the N losses and NUE increases from "business as usual" in 2000 and 2020.

AEA was only considered in conjunction with the other measures because a decrease in ammonia emissions results in "pollution swapping" where N increases in other areas. All three measures were found to have varying degrees of effectiveness across EU-27 given the differences in the type of crop or animal production and soil types, although implementation always resulted in reduction of N losses, but not without costs to farmers and consumers in the form of lost profits and welfare. BF was determined to be the best measure to implement because of its low relative cost and large benefits in the form of decreased N losses, mostly in areas determined as nitrate vulnerable zones (NVZ). LNF had high costs associated with it because in the baseline measures there already was a relatively low amount of N in the animals' excretion, therefore lower protein content feed is not a viable solution because the feed already contains close to the optimum amount. AEA also had high costs associated with implementation, but due to the phenomenon of pollution swapping, this measure could only be implemented when coupled with the other measures, further increasing the overall costs. These measures all have been proven to have demonstrable effects on lowering N losses to the environment, but not without decreases to farmers' income as high as 25% of the total EU spending on agriculture.

Use of Computer Systems to Tailor Slurry Application to Specific Agricultural Fields Proves Effective

Schellberg and Lock (2009) conducted a study that designed software and hardware systems to control the application of cattle slurry to grasslands and agricultural crops. They theorized that if the application process of the slurry, utilized as a crop fertilizer, could be controlled to a high degree of accuracy based on a fertilizer application map specific to the field of cultivation, large N losses to the environment and over-fertilization of the crops would be avoided. This study did not evaluate the effectiveness of their site-specific slurry application techniques in the form of crop yield or spatial distribution of N. Instead, it examined the effectiveness of the software and hardware systems working together to produce accurate application levels as determined in the application map.

Schellberg and Lock used cattle slurry in their two field application experiments on a grassland used for forage and a field of corn. The key issues in applying this technique lay in the ability to determine the local nutrient demand of the plants and the need for an advanced on-field monitoring system tracking the release of the slurry. The authors tackled the latter problem by creating a software and hardware system to actively control the flow rate of the slurry during application. The various parameters that they measured include the dry matter yield, the dry matter content in the harvested material, the plant N content, the estimated N extraction by plants, the mineralized N in the fields, and the calculated N fertilizer. These data were used as input parameters to their software system to ultimately determine the correct amount of N fertilizer, or slurry, to be applied to the varying locations within the field.

This article pointed to the accuracy of the application map as the key to the site-specific application of slurry, although it noted that the size of the grid cells within the field for slurry application must be small to produce accurate results. There also was a time lag noted within the equipment as it attempted to adjust as it entered a geographic region of the field that required a varying amount of slurry.

Conclusions

The current status of research on overfertilization has substantially demonstrated the negative effects on humans, the environment, and crop yield. The loss pathways of nutrients have been identified and best practices to combat those losses have been shown to be effective. Future research on the topic of overfertilization will revolve around the creation of models of nutrient accumulation in soils to replace the high costs of continued soil tests to farmers.

References Cited

Darilek, J., Huang, B., Wang, Z., Qi, Y., Zhao, Y., Sun, W., Gu, Z., Shi, X., 2009. Changes in soil fertility parameters and the environmental effects in a rapidly developing region of China. Agriculture, Ecosystems and Environment 129, 286–292.

Ju, X., Xing, G., Chen, X., Zhang, S., Zhang, L., Lui, X., Cui, Z., Yin, B., Christie, P., Zhu, Z., Zhang, F., 2009. Reducing environmental risk by improving N management in intensive Chinese agricultural systems. Proceedings of the National Academy of Sciences 106, 3041–2046.

Kundu, M. C., Mandal, B., 2009. Agricultural Activities Influence Nitrate and Fluoride Contamination in Drinking Groundwater of an Intensively Cultivated District in India. Water, Air, and Soil Pollution 198, 243–252.

Ma, Y., Li, J., Tang, T., Liang, Y., Huang, S., Wang, B., Liu, H., Yang, X., 2009. Phosporus accumulation and depletion in soils in wheat-maize cropping systems: Modeling and validation. Field Crops Research 110, 207–212.

Oenema, O., Witzke, H.P., Klimont, Z., Lesschen, J.P., Velthof, G.L., 2009. Integrated assessment of promising measures to decrease nitrogen losses from agriculture in EU-27. Agriculture, Ecosystems and Environment 133, 280–288.

Phillips, R., Tanaka, D., Archer, D., Hanson, J., 2009. Fertilizer Application Timing Influences Greenhouse Gas Fluxes Over a Growing Season. Journal of Environmental Quality 38, 1569–1579.

Schellberg, J., Lock, R., 2009. A Site-specific Slurry Application Technique on Grassland and on Arable Crops. Bioresource Technology 100, 280–286.

Yun, S., Ro, H., 2009. Natural ^{15}N abundance of plant and soil inorganic-N as evidence for over-fertilization with compost. Soil Biology and Biochemistry 41, 1541–1547.

23. Agriculture in the Midst of Global Climate Change

Patricio Ku

When discussing the issue of global climate change the conversation is usually centered on fossil fuels, renewable energy, or other "green" technologies. One of the leading industries of the world that nourishes every human is commonly overlooked—the agricultural sector. Without a perennial agricultural base, the human population would collapse. The relationship between agriculture and climate change is interesting because the two influence each other. Agriculture, which accounts for up to 15% of global greenhouse gas (GHG) emissions (World Bank 2007) is one of the leading GHG contributors, but at the same time, crops sequester CO_2 as they grow. Conversely, unpredictable weather and rising temperatures due to the onset of climate change have an impact on agriculture itself. As a result, crop production needs to adapt to warming and to shifting weather patterns.

There is no way to know absolutely the different weather patterns that climate change will bring about, but with today's climate models it is increasingly possible to predict and simulate weather patterns as well as future crop output. Crop output simulations are normally based on a combination of multiple climate and crop models. There is no quick way to test how accurate these models are since they are essentially predicting the future, but they are increasingly validated as time progresses and climate change becomes more evident.

The effects that agriculture has on climate change are much easier to discern than crop adaptation processes. At its core, climate change is affected by agriculture through the emission of GHGs into the atmosphere. Large-scale farms use many chemicals to enhance crop productivity and resilience. Many of these are made from, or use energy from fossil fuels; for example, synthetic fertilizers and pesticides are both GHG contributors. Furthermore, large quantities of fossil fuels are burned to transport grains, fruits, and vegetables from different corners of the world. The majority of the GHGs produced by agriculture are methane and nitrous oxide. Methane release into the atmosphere is mostly attributed to rice paddies, where warm waterlogged soil provides ideal conditions for methanogenesis. The release of nitrous oxide into the atmosphere comes mainly from the over-use of synthetic fertilizers.

Climate change is also affected indirectly through agriculture by a number of secondary processes. The vast fields dedicated to farming have deforested land all over the world and have correspondingly altered the Earth's land cover, causing a rise in global surface temperature (IPCC 2007). Deforested land, whether for agriculture or not, also takes away from carbon sequestration potential.

While these effects that agriculture has on climate change have already begun to be noticed, evidence of effects of climate change on agriculture is still preliminary. Scientists have been able to simulate some of the expected changes and in general, agricultural production will be affected most by changes in temperature, CO_2, glacial run-off, precipitation, and different interactions between these elements (Challinor et al. 2009). Whether the effects of climate change will be positive or negative varies greatly according to region.

Positive effects of climate change will be seen mainly throughout the higher latitudes where a rise in temperature could lead to longer growing seasons. It may also be possible to grow crops in regions that are presently too cold or do not have enough frost free days. Another positive effect that almost all agriculture will benefit from is the increased concentration of CO_2 in the atmosphere. Since plants need CO_2 in order to photosynthesize, an increase in carbon emissions should be beneficial to crops everywhere. If organic agriculture were to increase relative to conventional industrial agriculture, this intake of CO_2 by the agricultural sector could even reduce atmospheric CO_2.

But it is likely that most of the effects of climate change on agriculture will be negative. The majority of countries will experience much drier climates leading to increased soil erosion and lower crop productivity. Areas around the middle-latitudes and tropical and sub-tropical regions will be affected the most. Places like southern Africa could have up to 30% reductions in maize production by 2030 (Lobell et al. 2008).

The effects of climate change on agriculture and *vice versa* are still being analyzed as more data about climate change become available. Increasingly unpredictable weather will force farmers to adapt to climate change in order to maintain current production levels. Selected genetically modified crops are also being selected by farmers because of their tolerance to drought or excess heat, and more such crops are in the research pipeline.

There is no single solution to the problems that climate change will bring to crop production and the agricultural industry. What follows is a series of summaries based upon the most current scientific analyses on agriculture and climate change. First, crop and climate simulations are assessed to gain an understanding of where crop yield may be heading. As the chapter progresses, adaptation scenarios are developed for certain regions of the world, and alternative agriculture techniques are also introduced.

Simulating Effects of Climate Change on Crops

Since crop yield can vary greatly according to changes in weather and climate, it is increasingly important to simulate the effects climate change will have on the world's agriculture (Challinor et al. 2009). In order to simulate and predict the impact of rising atmospheric GHGs on crops, scientists used two basic climate simulation models that systematically represent future climate scenarios and their effects on crops. The first simulation is a climate model where current data about GHGs, climate change, and ecosystems are compiled to come up with a predicted climate scenario. The climate scenario is then used in conjunction with a large-area crop model to forecast the alterations climate change will have on crop yield. Combining multiple models, called ensemble modeling, is a mix of multiple climate scenarios, and seems to be the best way to understand the effect climate change may have on crops. One of the largest problems facing crop simulation is the number of variables that must be accounted for. Mean temperature, the interaction between water stress and CO_2, and the interaction between ozone and a range of environmental variables must all be considered. There are so many variables used when assessing the affects of CO_2 on crops that these variables must be studied further so that they can be applied to each individual scenario. Socio-economic factors were also found to play a huge role in crop yield and productivity. Productivity relies on capital and labor inputs, so the type of adaptive response that is met with shifting weather patterns will have a tremendous influence on a crop's response to climate change.

Andrew Challinor, along with the help of his colleagues, studied how climate change could affect crops. This included the progress made so far as well as challenges that scientist face in attempting to simulate different crop scenarios as well as methods for adapting plants to the steadily increasing carbon emissions. Socio-economic factors around the world were also studied and found to have a significant correlation to climate change and could also play a role in affecting crop yield. Over 140 scientific articles on how different scenarios and variables could affect crop yield were analyzed.

The knowledge of how to simulate plant-climate interactions is steadily increasing. Once estimates of climate change impacts are reliable, the information can be used to create valuable information relevant to plant adaptation. Plant adaptation will be a key role in combating the effects climate change will have on our world's agriculture. But, before action can be taken based on crop simulations, there are a number of factors that must come together in order for simulations to be accurate enough to be used. Reliable quantification, consistent techniques for combining diverse modeling approaches, and appropriate calibration of models must all be fine-tuned so that accurate quantitative data can be derived from these controlled experiments.

Agriculture and Global Warming

Agriculture and climate change have strong influences on each other. Global warming of more than $4°C$ expected in many areas will increase crop vulnerability and surpass the adaptive capacity of many crop systems. Also, agriculture currently accounts for approximately 15% of the world's GHG emissions (Minimakawa et al. 2009). Negative impacts of temperature increase have already been reported all over the world. There is also tremendous potential to help mitigate atmospheric CO_2 by sequestration in agricultural soils

Minimakawa, Yagi, and Nishimura from Tsukuba, Japan, studied the interaction between agriculture and global warming, and how they affect each other. Irreversible impacts on the adaptive capacity of the Earth were evaluated. An understanding of the "big picture" was considered the top priority which would permit quantitative objectives for coping with global warming.

Temperature increases of up to $3°C$ in the mid to high latitudes are projected to slightly increase crop productivity. However, moderate temperature increases ($1–2°C$) in the lower latitudes are very likely to reduce major cereal yields. Rice is one crop that has already seen a negative response to global warming resulting from pollination failure. Rice sterility in Japan increases about 16% with each $1°C$ increase in air temperature above $35°C$ during the growing period. There are many ways agricultural practices can be adapted to global warming, such as by using cultivars with heat tolerance, changing crops, and shifting the cropping period. Several choices can be made by governments regarding agriculture that could help lower anthropogenic climate change impacts.

Organic Agriculture: Reducing GHGs

Changes to modern agriculture are important in fighting global climate change because the agricultural sector is currently responsible for over 20% of the world's anthropogenic GHG emissions (Khanal 2009). Organic agriculture is being contemplated as an appropriate farming system that could serve dual functions for climate change mitigation and adaptation. In comparison with conventional agriculture, organic agriculture is reportedly more efficient and effective in reducing GHGs, mainly attributed to less use of chemical fertilizers and fossil fuels. Specifically, the primary features responsible for lower CO_2 emissions in organic agriculture are maintenance and increase in soil fertility by use of farmyard manure, the omission of synthetic fertilizers and pesticides, and the lower use of energy-intensive animal feeds. Furthermore, this method of farming provides benefits for resilience of soil quality, which is susceptible to climate change, by complementary use of soil nutrients and water, increased total productivity through appropriate polyculture mixtures, pest protection, the creation of microclimates suitable for beneficial insects, and strengthening the genetic traits of local landscapes.

Ram Chandra Khanal explored research findings that focused on the impact of organic and non-organic agriculture on climate change. Organic agriculture will help the environment and climate change in a variety of ways. First, organic agriculture is much more resilient to the effects of climate change. Ecological resilience, improved biodiversity, and healthy management of farms and the surrounding environment are all positive factors that are achieved through organic farming. Second, organic farming will help offset GHG emissions produced by modern commercial farming techniques. Agriculture presently contributes 65–80% of the world's N_2O, mainly from the use of nitrogenous fertilizers on cultivated soils, and from cattle and feedlots. Agriculture is also believed to account for about two-thirds of the total man-made methane emissions. With a switch to organic agriculture, these high rates of GHGs from food production could all be drastically reduced. As an overall healthier alternative to commercial farming, both in terms of nutrition and for the environment, organic agriculture is a very attractive substitute to current farming practices.

Climate Change and its effects on Mediterranean Agriculture

Agriculture in the Monegros region of Spain is marginal and the effects of climate change could be economically and socially very costly (Mestre-Sanchís and Feijóo-Bello 2009). A multicriteria decision making process is used to identify the impacts of climate change. Different climate and irrigation scenarios are evaluated in order to determine the best cultivation plan for the farmer. Compromise programming is later added to the different scenario outcomes, taking into consideration other environmental, social, and cultural aspects which involve different levels of risk aversion. None of the simulated climate change scenarios reach the profit levels of the reference scenario. In an attempt to reach present-day net margin values in the future, farmers will need to increase their risk in order to obtain equivalent economic return. Social impacts that can be foreseen include lack of viability of the farms, which could be threatened by the permanent reforms of the European Union.

Mestre-Sanchís and Fejóo-Bello, Spanish scientists from the University of La Rioja and University of Zaragoza, analyzed marginalizing effect of climate change on agriculture in the Monegros region of Spain. The overall evaluation of the different crop portfolios is carried out using a multi-objective approach which centers around four flow-diagram blocks which show the different models considered. Block I is based on the different scenarios studied which depend on climate- and soil-related factors and specific crop characteristics. Block II shows the net margin of the crop simulation incorporating the key components of the proposed methodology which are grouped into six categories: economic, technical, political, environmental, water, and others. Block III helps to present a better understanding of the behavioral models for farmers in the different climate change scenarios. Finally, block IV exemplifies proposed scenarios based on the adequate inputs for the crop simulation and other multi-criteria decision models. Through the integration of these four blocks, a multi-objective simulation model is created to model farm owners' decisions in different scenarios.

According to results, the effect of climate change in the Monegros area will be greater than in other regions in the European Union. Developments in technology will be able to solve some of the problems facing climate change adaptation, but the costs surrounding technological adaptation would be unaffordable in an open market. The results show that climate change will have an effect on many aspects of the world's societal entities, not just the economy. The highest additional costs will come from the increases of water consumption that must be added to make up for lost net margin. In general, the risk factors associated with running a farm will all increase as farmers try to adapt to climate change. These risks, along with all the other variables that go into farming, will soon enough determine if the Monegros area will continue to be feasible as an agricultural region. Nobody can say for sure what the effects of climate change will be, but it is almost certain, according to the model, that the effects here will be negative.

Adaptations to Maize and Wheat Production in Response to Climate Change

Agricultural systems are susceptible to changes in meteorological variables such as solar radiation, water, and CO_2 levels (Meza and Silva 2009). The effects that climate change will have on crops around the world will be location-specific, but they will also depend on a variety of adaptation strategies used by farmers. To calculate different adaptation strategies that may need to take place, researchers have performed impact assessments and alternatives evaluation based on a wide variety of methodologies. These impact assessments simulate weather conditions as well as crop yields of maize and wheat according to an array of supposed adaptation strategies. If climate change does not produce abrupt and sudden changes in weather patterns, it is probable that agricultural practices can be modified and negative effect can be partially or even completely avoided. Dynamic adaptation is crucial if farmers would like to maximize their gross margin.

Francisco Meza and Daniel Silva calculated whether it would be possible to adapt to the new weather and environment that climate change will bring. In order to predict the weather for the next 70 years, simulations from the HadCM3 global circulation model were used. The crop yield simulations were derived as a function of current as well as future climatologically conditions using DSSAT v 4.0. The two locations used in the experiment were Curicó and Temuco, Chile. After simulations were run, another experiment calculating dynamic adaptation was conducted to analyze the effects of different periods of evaluation on the ability of farmers to introduce adaptation strategies as climate changes progressively.

Many adaptation techniques were seen to be responsive and successful. Although the spring wheat species that was tested did not show any potential for adaptation, the maize and winter wheat species did. Earlier sowing dates were seen to be an extremely effective strategy of adaptation to climate change. The rise in temperature will allow many crop species to have a longer growing season. The maize and winter wheat species also displayed a positive response to the increase of CO_2. The authors concluded that combinations of sowing dates and fertilization rates are two simple and cost-effective way to cope with climate change. As the effects of climate change become more visible and understood, alternative adaptation techniques will become much more prominent. The more flexibility and options a farmer has when dealing with climate change, the more possibilities for adaptation can be evaluated and utilized.

Soil Acidification in China

The biogeochemistry of ecosystems can be altered by acidification and can adversely affect biota (Guo *et al.* 2010). Soils take hundreds of years to acidify under natural conditions because they are strongly buffered by reactions, weathering of soil minerals, and aluminum and iron interactions. Since the 1980s Chinese agriculture has greatly intensified with large inputs of chemical fertilizers and other resources. Whether or not degraded soil and environmental quality in south China also causes significant soil acidification at a national scale is investigated. National soil surveys that measured pH in all topsoils in the early 1980s and from 2000 to 2008 were compared on the basis of six soil groups according to geography and use, with cereal crops and cash crops as two subgroups. All topsoils, except the highest pH soils, were found to have significant acidification, with acidification in cash crop systems always being greater. Information on soil pH for 10 long-term monitoring field (LTMF) sites was also summarized. Data analysis shows that high-N fertilizer inputs and the uptake and removal of base cations by plants are the main reason for soil acidification.

Guo and his colleagues examined whether the increasing acidification of soil in southern China affects the whole nation. Two data sets were compiled that compare the pH of 154 topsoils in the 1980s versus the 2000s. Ten LTMF sites were also analyzed and summarized

Comparisons revealed that acidification in group I soils are approaching pH values such that toxic metals such as aluminum and manganese could be mobilized. Even though soils in group V are considered resistant to acidification, they still acidified significantly with pH decreases averaging 0.27 and 0.58 under cereals and cash crops, respectively. Topsoils were significantly acidified, with an average pH decline of 0.50. The LTMF summaries showed that significant soil acidification occurred only on conventional fertilization plots and not on no-fertilization and fallow plots. This means that decreasing pH levels are exclusively attributed to conventional fertilization. The excess of N fertilizer used contributed substantially to regional soil acidification in China. It is possible, with optimal nutrient-management strategies, to reduce N fertilizer rates without decreasing crop yields. Acidification in soils all over China is increasing at an alarming rate. Knowledge-based N management practices are essential for sustainable agriculture in China and should be implemented immediately.

Rain-fed Agricultural Enterprises and their Resistance to Climate Change

Climate change is expected to increase the frequency of dry conditions around south-eastern Australia. Traditional rain-fed agricultural land management has operated with the intent of maximizing yield in good seasons, but with climate change it may be more feasible to adjust to the increasing amount of dry seasons instead (Reid, 2009). The effect of climate change on resilience thresholds pertaining to dry conditions is not uniform to the landscape. As a result, during dry periods, certain areas will call for different management strategies. A property planning tool was developed to make properties more resilient to climate change by encouraging production in dry seasons by limiting land degradation and financial exposure. The planning tool takes into account the drying order of different segments of property, grading the soil types of each segment, and tailoring a water retention and utilization strategy for each segment. A training program to help ease the farmers into using the adaptation program was also implemented. When used in the property planning extension program the planning tool proved to be highly effective. If farms are to remain productive their focus must shift from maximum yield in good conditions to sustainable yields in drier conditions.

Gregory H. Reid studied the use of target strategies for differing land areas within the same landscape as a way of adapting to drier conditions brought on by climate change. Reid mapped out different soil fertility in conjunction with moisture retention to produce a guide to investment priorities. The resulting map code can then be used as an adjustment guide to seasonal weather conditions based on fertility and moisture limitations in each area. The guide will help avoid land degradation that would limit future production.

The planning method implemented proved to be very successful. Many farmers who participated in the study have already noticed changes in yield and production. After the study, the number of participants willing to adapt to climate change through this planning tool rose from 43% to 84%. Surveys indicated that 91% of the participants felt better equipped to deal with climate change. It is also estimated that the program will encourage the sequestration of more than 100,000 tons of carbon into soils and trees. The likely benefits through using this planning tool are reduced degradation costs, less feed supplementation, delayed destocking beyond market lows, and better long term stocking capacity. With the onset of climate change, rain-fed agriculture will eventually require this method of integrated property planning with an emphasis on soil moisture as a diminishing resource in order to adapt to unpredictable seasons.

Phytoremediation Methods and their Potentials

Two phytoremediation techniques are being developed to harness the ability of plants to absorb or secrete various substances (Gleba *et al.* 1999). The first is called phytoextraction, in which complex underground root systems extract and concentrate essential elements and compounds from soil and water. Plant roots that are hydroponically grown can also directly absorb, precipitate, and concentrate toxic metals from polluted effluents or sewage water. The second type of phytoremediation, rhizosecretion, capitalizes on the opposite effect of phytoextraction; instead of removing unwanted contaminants, rhizosecretion relies on a plants ability to make valuable compounds and deliver them into their environment. This could potentially replace solvents as a means for extracting chemicals from plants.

Doloressa Gleba and Colleagues at Cook College and Rutgers University performed a biochemical analysis of root exudates from 120 plant species. These analyses gave evidence that roots followed an "extroverted" path in their relationship with soil, while the evolution on plant shoots primarily followed "introverted" paths by perfecting physical barriers between themselves and the environment. With this knowledge, phytoremediation techniques can be used in order to perfect and expand technology about soil remediation, drug discovery, and molecular farming.

When analyzing the rood exudates from the 120 plant species, a number of notable observations were made. First, for each plant, a distinct set of compounds was exuded, giving each species a unique biochemical character. The root exudates in themselves were relatively simple mixtures, making the isolation of active molecules relatively easy. These exudates also did not contain any pigments or tannins, known to interfere in activity screens. Lastly, the chemical composition of root exudates is very different from that of conventional methanolic extracts of root tissue.

The future development of phytoremediation techniques lies in the development of effective and safe pharmaceuticals derived from the compilation of biologically active lead molecules secreted by the roots, and in large-scale, cost-effective manufacturing of recombinant proteins. A growing need and demand for pharmaceuticals should foster the development of these techniques. As a result, more effective utilization of biosynthetic capacity of plants based on their cheap and renewable nature will present many opportunities for scientists in the future.

Conclusions

Current scientific literature on climate change and agriculture show that it is only a matter of time before the effects of climate change become more and more noticeable. Although initially there may be some positive effects that vary regionally, the majority of the agricultural sector will most likely face drastic consequences. Nevertheless, there is increasing potential for crop adaptation to changes in the world's climate. New sustainable technologies being developed will hopefully increase the crop productivity that is lost through climate change. In order for these technologies to be effective, shifts in weather patterns must be anticipated and put in place immediately so that plant adaptation may be transitioned from older agricultural practices. It is also important to be mindful of the contributions that commercial agricultural practices are having to climate change. There are many ways to lessen the impact of conventional agriculture, such as switching to organic farming, but they must actually be practiced for there to be a reduction in GHGs. It is clear that global climate change is having a significant effect on the world's agriculture and that the world's agriculture is also contributing to climate change. Adaptive steps must be put into place as soon as possible if consequences are to be offset.

References Cited

Challinor, A., Ewert, F., Arnold, S., Simelton, E., Fraser, E., 2009. Crops and climate: Progress, trends, and challenges in simulating impacts and informing adaptation. Journal of Experimental Botany 60, 2775–2789.

Gleba, D.,Nikolai, B., Ludmyla, B., Ralph, K., Alexander, P., Marina, S., Slavik, D., Sithes, L., Yuri, G., Ilya, R., 1999. Use of Plant Roots for Phytoremediation and Molecular Farming. Proceedings of the National Academy of Sciences of the United States of America 96, 5973–5977

Guo, J., Liu, X., Zhang, Y., Shen, J., Han, W., Zhang, W., Goulding, C., Vitousek, P., 2010. Significant acidification in major Chinese croplands. Science 327, 1008–1010

Khanal, R., 2009. Climate change and organic agriculture. The Journal of Agriculture and Environment 10, 116–127.

Lobell, D., Burke M., Tebaldi, C., Mastrandrea, M., Falcon, W., Naylor, R., 2008. Prioritizing Climate Change Adaptation Needs for Food Security in 2030 Science 319, 607–609

Mestre-Sanchís, F., Feijóo-Bello, M., 2009. Climate change and its marginalizing effect on agriculture. Ecological Economics 68, 896–904.

Meza, F., Silva, D., 2009. Dynamic Adaptation of Maize and Wheat Production to Climate Change. Climactic Change 94, 143–156.

Minimakawa, K., Yagi, K., Nishimura, S., 2009. Agriculture and global Warming: Their Interaction and other problems of sustainability. Journal of Developments in Sustainable Agriculture 4, 79–81.

Parry, M., Canziani, O., Palutikof, P., van der Linden, P., Hanson, C, 2007. Contribution of Working Group II to the Fourth Assessment Report of the Intergovernmental Panel on Climate Change. Cambridge University Press, Cambridge, UK, 976

Reid, G., 2009. Building resilience to climate change in rain-fed agricultural enterprises: An integrated property planning tool. Agric Hum Values 26, 391–397.

World Bank, 2007. Adaptation to and mitigation of climate change in agriculture. World Development Report 2008: Agriculture for Development. World Bank, Washington, 200–201.

24. Deforestation and Climate Change

Martin Selasco

Forest ecosystems play an important role in the global carbon cycle by capturing and storing large quantities of carbon, and they can be very useful tools in reducing anthropogenic climate change. When they are damaged, however, as is the case in deforestation and forest degradation, they can contribute significantly to the global carbon emissions; this is what is happening today. With such an emphasis on carbon emissions from the burning of fossil fuels, it is easy to overlook deforestation and forest degradation as contributors to global warming, but policy makers have been considering ways to reduce forestry-related emissions in developing countries. The Forest Carbon Partnership Facility (FCPF) has been adopted by several countries as a mechanism for reducing carbon emissions from deforestation and forest degradation (REDD). Through this program, developing countries are provided with incentives to cut back forestry-related carbon emissions.

In order for such programs to be effective, accurate measurements of forest biomass and forestry-related carbon emissions are needed. Without accurate measurements, it would be difficult to decide whether or not a country should receive compensation. In addition, it is important to consider how implementing REDD policies will affect the communities and economies of participating countries. Such considerations can help reduce leakage and ensure participation at a local level.

The studies summarized in this chapter look at the effects of forest degradation and deforestation on forest carbon storage and carbon emissions, the effects of forest degradation and deforestation on regional climate change, and the effects of policies aimed at reducing carbon emissions due to forest degradation and deforestation. The studies are not limited to participating REDD countries, nor are they limited to tropical deforestation, but rather they look at how the management of forests worldwide contribute to the global carbon cycle.

Boosted Carbon Emissions from Amazon Deforestation

The continued deforestation of the Brazilian Amazon is likely to result in increasing annual carbon emissions because of higher biomass densities in remaining unprotected forests (Loarie et al. 2009). While the average area deforested annually has not changed significantly since the 1990s, previously cleared forests in the southeastern Amazon had a lower biomass, and the observed patterns of deforestation indicate an encroachment on higher biomass regions found in northwestern areas. Such an encroachment suggests that without a significant reduction in the area deforested annually, annual carbon emissions will continue to increase.

Scott R. Loarie, Gregory P. Asner, and Christopher B. Field used satellite images to determine the different biomass concentrations in the Brazilian Amazon. Then, they looked at deforestation records and logging patterns to calculate carbon loss over time. While the average area of forest cleared annually has not changed much since the 1990s, they found a significant increase in carbon loss in recent years, from an average of 183 million grams per hectare in 2001 to an average of 201 million grams per hectare in 2007, and correlated this increase with the deforestation of higher biomass areas.

A better understanding of the distribution of biomass in forest ecosystems would help reduce the impacts of deforestation. In the Brazilian Amazon, deforestation in high biomass areas will not only significantly increase carbon emissions, but it could also negatively affect biodiversity and water cycles. If Brazil were to significantly slow the rate of deforestation in the coming years, it could dramatically reduce its carbon emissions and help preserve a precious ecosystem.

Carbon Storage in Old-Growth and Second Growth Western Larch Forests of the US Inland Northwest

The deforestation of old-growth western larch forests in Montana has been shown to significantly reduce the total amount of carbon storage in the regional ecosystem (Bisbing et al. 2010). In a study that compared the amount of carbon stored in old-growth and second growth larch forests, old growth forests were found to have about three times more carbon than second growth forests.

S.M. Bisbing, P.B. Alaback, and T.H. DeLuca sampled 15 pairs of adjacent old-growth and second growth larch stands in Flathead National Forest, Montana. The second growth forests had been clear-cut between 1961 and 1979. The authors measured the amount of carbon found in mineral soil, forest floor, coarse woody debris, overstory, understory, and coarse roots, and then used the data to calculate the ecosystem carbon total.

For old growth larch forests, the average total carbon captured was 305 million grams of carbon per hectare, but for second growth forests, this total was only 98 million grams of carbon per hectare. While the average amount of carbon stored in the understory was greater in second growth forests than in old-growth forests, it is less than 0.1% of the total carbon captured by the ecosystem. The differences in the amount of carbon found in mineral soil were statistically insignificant, but the forest floor, the overstory, coarse roots, and coarse woody debris were all found to store significantly more carbon in old growth larch forests. The results also demonstrated the amount of carbon in the different parts of old growth and second growth larch forests. In old growth forests, the majority of the carbon is in the overstory, but in second growth forests the biggest source of carbon is mineral soil. Overall, the significant loss of stored carbon from clear-cut logging suggests a need to preserve the old-growth larch forests, and that there be increased retention of large structural elements to help reduce carbon loss.

Rainforest Biomass Stocks and Carbon Loss from Deforestation and Degradation in Papua New Guinea

Papua New Guinea, a small country located in the South Pacific, contains large areas of tropical forest that play an important role in the global carbon cycle. A recent study estimated that in 2001 deforestation and forest degradation in Papua New Guinea was responsible for somewhere between 2 and 7% of global tropical carbon emissions (Bryan *et al.* 2010). More importantly however, this study suggests that there is a great deal of uncertainty in estimating carbon fluxes due to a lack of field measurements in this area. Furthermore, it suggests that in order to reduce carbon emissions caused by tropical deforestation, accurate and reliable biomass measurements are needed Papua New Guinea's rainforests.

J. Bryan, P. Shearman, J. Ash, and J.B. Kirkpatrick used 22 unlogged biomass measurements to estimate the carbon stock of unlogged forests, and relied on tree censuses set up by the International Tropical Timber Association to calculate the biomass densities of logged forests. They then used high-resolution maps to calculate the amount of deforestation that occurred between 1972 and 2002. Using these data, they estimated that 1178 million tons of carbon were lost due to deforestation and degradation between 1972 and 2002.

While the researchers were able to generate a range of estimates on the carbon flux of Papua New Guinea, they expressed a large degree of uncertainty in these estimates. They attributed much this uncertainty to the measurements of unlogged biomass. Part of the problem was that these unlogged biomass measurements were not collected in range of environments, but rather tended to focus on commercial species because of their harvesting potential. They suggest that stands of *Nothofagus* may be over-represented in their study. Furthermore, they point out a lack of a standard approach for measuring biomass. In response to this, the researchers propose a national field survey that uses a standardized methodology to collect biomass data in unlogged forests. Acquiring such measurements would be extremely helpful in effectively reducing Papua New Guinea's carbon emissions due to tropical deforestation.

Harvest Impacts on Soil Carbon Storage in Temperate Forests

Researchers have looked at data from 75 different studies to analyze the impacts of forest harvest on soil carbon storage, and they found that harvesting caused an 8% average decrease in the overall soil carbon of temperate forests (Nave *et al.* 2010). When they looked at different soil categories they found that forest floors had a 30% decline in carbon storage after harvest, while minerals soils showed no significant overall change. For some soil orders, such as Inceptisols and Ultisols, carbon storage in mineral soil significantly declined after harvest. Furthermore, the researchers suggest that losses in forest floor carbon have a greater effect on Spodosols because this order tends to have larger forest floor carbon pools.

L.E. Nave, E.D. Vance, C.W. Swanston, and P.S. Curtis conducted a meta-analysis of 432 soil carbon response ratios from 75 papers written between 1979 and 2008. They chose studies that reported soil carbon values of both harvested and unharvested temperate forests, defining unharvested forests as those which had not beet harvested for the last 30 years. Various factors such as harvest type, harvest intensity, and soil layer, and soil taxonomic order were taken into account to help explain variation within the data. They found that soil layer and soil taxonomic order, more than any other categories, accounted for a significant amount of variation.

Overall, this study suggests that harvesting has a significant impact on soil carbon storage in temperate forests, and that various factors such as species composition, soil taxonomic order, and time since harvest affect carbon losses. For example, forest floors showed themselves to be more vulnerable to carbon loss than mineral soils. Also, hardwood stands lost more forest floor carbon than coniferous/mixed stands. The researchers suggest that knowing the effects of species composition and soil taxonomic order on harvest-induced carbon losses can be a useful tool in understanding forest management effects on soil carbon storage.

Effects of Deforestation on the Regional Climate of the Maya Lowlands in Guatemala

The Petén basin of northern Guatemala, often referred to as the Maya lowlands, is experiencing massive deforestation. From 2000 to 2008, 2.64% percent of this region has been deforested. Such large-scale deforestation has been shown to affect regional surface temperatures and moisture (Manoharan *et al.* 2009). While forested areas do not differ much from deforested areas in the wet season, in the dry season deforested areas experience much higher surface temperature and lower moisture contents. Such regional climatic changes could make the restoration of deforested areas increasingly difficult.

V. Manoharan, R. Welch, and R. Lawton measured surface temperature, soil moisture, and vegetation in twelve regions of the Petén basin, each with an area of 30 square kilometers. Out of the twelve regions studied, six are considered forested, three are considered partially forested, and three are considered deforested. The measurements were taken from 2000 to 2008 on clear days. The researchers found that the surface temperatures were similar during the wet season regardless of habitat or year, but during the dry season, forested areas were 3–4°C warmer than in the wet season, a measurement that remains relatively constant from 2000 to 2008. However, deforested areas were an average of 8°C warmer than forested regions during the dry season in 2000, and 4°C warmer than forested regions in the dry season in 2008. Soil moisture was found to be high in forested areas in the wet season regardless of year. However, deforested areas and partially deforested areas had noticeably lower soil moisture in the wet season during this period. As would be expected, forested areas were found to have less soil moisture overall during the dry season. Comparatively, deforested and partially deforested areas had much lower soil moisture in the dry season (an average of 36% saturation for deforested and partially deforested areas in 2008 compared to an average of 70% saturation for forested areas in 2008). In addition to these findings, a 9.3% decrease in forest cover was found in partially deforested areas from 2000 to 2008.

Overall, the findings suggests that forested regions have a relatively stable environment, but that deforestation leads to increased seasonal variations in soil moisture and surface temperature, with particularly noticeable effects during the dry season. Such climatic changes could negatively affect forest regeneration in affected areas.

Deforestation in Panamanian Protected Areas: Protection Effectiveness and Implications of Reducing Emissions

Implementing policies that favor reduced greenhouse gas emissions from deforestation and forest degradation (REDD) in countries with tropical forests can be useful in limiting anthropogenic climate change. Such policy strategies could include the implementation of sustainable forest management and forestry certification, payment for ecosystem services, fiscal and trade policies, and protected areas (PAs). Panama was used as a case study to investigate the effectiveness of PAs at conserving forest integrity and curbing deforestation (Oestreicher *et al.* 2009). Researchers found that some PAs were effective at controlling deforestation while others were not. While some PAs were well staffed, especially ones near the Panama Canal Watershed, other PAs, such as La Amistad, and Palo Seco, lacked a sufficient number of guards. Limited availability of transportation and inadequate numbers of bases were also noted as factors limiting the effectiveness of PAs.

Jordan S. Oestreicher and his colleagues conducted 28 interviews in 9 PAs, representing 43% of the PAs in Panama. They conducted semi-structured interviews with PA stakeholders in San Lorenzo, Soberanía, Charges, and Altos de Campana. They also conducted structured interviews with ANAM representatives from Volcán Barú, La Amistad, Darién, Cerro Hoya, and Palo Seco, supplementing their data with PA management plans and physical maps. They analyzed PA effectiveness through five research categories, which include personnel, transportation, infrastructure, NGOs, and funding.

In this study, the researchers suggest increasing personnel, transportation, funding and infrastructure as ways of increasing the effectiveness of PAs. However, they also suggest that NGOs play an important role in developing community-based forest management that help prevent leakage while encouraging sustainable resource use.

Simulating the Impacts of Reconstructing the BR-319 Highway in the Brazilian Amazon

Brazilian researchers have suggested that the reconstruction of the BR-319 highway, which was once the principal route to the State of Roraima, would cause a large migratory influx to the area that could increase both deforestation rates and carbon emissions (Barni *et al.* 2009). This study estimated the total deforestation and carbon emissions from 2007 and 2030 for three different scenarios. The baseline scenario, which assumes no highway reconstruction, results in 3478 square kilometers of deforestation and 59.1 million tons of lost carbon. In the Business As

Usual (BAU) scenario, which assumes highway construction with no conservation strategy, 5100 square kilometers of forest are lost, along with 86.5 million tons of carbon. In the conservation scenario, which assumes highway reconstruction but includes the implementation of preservation policies, only 2134 square kilometers of forest are lost, and carbon emissions amount to 35.3 million tons of carbon.

P. Barni, P. Fearnside, and P. Lima de Alencastro Graça from the National Institute for Research in the Amazon (INPA) used INAMICA-EGO land-use and land-cover change simulation and modeling software to simulate deforestation and carbon emissions under three different scenarios. They based their baseline simulation on historical rates of deforestation from 2004 and 2007. For the BAU simulation they took into account incentive policies that would attract migration, such as the creation of new settlement projects and land donations, by looking at deforestation rates that followed the implementation of similar projects in the past. In the conservation scenario, they proposed the implementation of conservation units, which totaled to about 695 thousand hectares. In this scenario, they also assumed no creation of new settlement projects, no expansion of current settlement projects, high control and inspection of logging, and the enforcement of ecological economic zoning.

The results of this study show that reconstructing the BR-319 highway without the implementation of a conservation strategy could lead to much higher rates of deforestation and increased carbon emissions. Furthermore, they suggest that if the proposed conservation strategies were implemented, deforestation rates and carbon emissions would decrease. Regardless of whether or not the highway is reconstructed, the State of Roraima could decrease deforestation and carbon emissions by implementing these strategies.

REDD and Decentralized Forest Management

At the 2009 climate change conference in Copenhagen, a mechanism for reducing climate emissions from deforestation and forest degradation (REDD) was adopted to provide incentives for developing countries to reduce forestry-related carbon emissions. Irawan and Tacconi (2009) have expressed concerns about the implications of decentralized forest management for the implementation of REDD within participating countries. On the one hand, decentralization helps meet local needs and encourages increased participation. However, a decentralized implementation model is difficult to monitor and there is a greater risk of leakage. In a top-down model of REDD implementation, the central government has the ability set reference levels and monitor emissions more easily. However, in such a case, local needs are more likely to be ignored and there may be decreased local participation.

Researchers at the Australian National University, S. Irawan and L. Tacconi, analyzed the possible modes for the involvement of local governments in implementation of REDD. They classified the possible modes as Option 1, Option 2 and Option 3. Option 1 describes a top-down approach, in which the central government sets national reference levels and prescribes targets and activities. Option 2 entails a 'bidding mechanism' in which the central government sets reference levels, and local governments submit expressions of interest along with project proposals. Option 3 embodies a more decentralized approach in which central and local governments work together to set a national reference level, and local governments are allowed develop their own implementation programs. All three of these options would require financial incentives at the local level to encourage participation. While there is no single correct way to implement REDD, the researchers suggest that each country assess these options according to its own needs and political structures.

Conclusions

These studies demonstrate how deforestation and forest degradation negatively affect carbon capture and storage in forest ecosystems, and they express the need for more studies quantifying the effects of deforestation and forest degradation. While the need to preserve forest ecosystems seems to be clear, the effective implementation of REDD policies could be a challenge. Financial incentives may encourage some forest preservation, but land development and commercial harvesting of forests continue to be profitable. In addition to this, there are significant costs to effectively preserving protected areas, such as providing adequate guards, staff, and transportation. However, allowing local communities to manage forest resources could help reduce some of these costs and help increase participation in deforestation reduction programs by providing direct benefits to the participants.

References Cited

Barni, P., Fearnside, P., Lima de Alencastro Graça, P., 2009. Deforestation and Carbon Emissions in Amazonia: Simulating the Impact of Connecting Brazil's State of Roraima to the "Arc of Deforestation" by Reconstructing the BR-319 (Manaus-Porto Vulho) Highway. XIII World Forestry Congress, Buenos Aires, Argentina.

Bisbing, S., Alaback, P., and DeLuca, T., 2010. Carbon storage in old-growth and second growth fire-dependent western larch (*larix occidentalis* Nutt.) forests of the Inland Northwest, USA. Forest Ecology and Management 259, 1041–1049

Bryan, J., Shearman, P., Ash, J., Kirkpatrick, J., 2010. Estimating rainforest biomass stocks and carbon loss from deforestation and degradation in Papua New Guinea 1972–2002: Best estimates, uncertainties, and research needs. Journal of Environmental Management 91, 995–1001

Irawan, S., Tacconi, L., 2009. Reducing Emissions from Deforestation and Forest Degradation and decentralized forest management. International Forestry Review 11, 427–438

Loarie, S., Asner, G., and Field, C., 2009. Boosted carbon emissions from Amazon deforestation. Geophysical Research Letters 36, L14810

Manoharan, V., Welch, R., Lawton, R., 2009. Impact of deforestation on regional surface temperatures and moisture in the Maya lowlands of Guatemala. Geophysical Research Letters 36, L21701

Nave, L., Vance, E., Swanston, C., Curtis, P., 2010. Harvest impacts on soil carbon storage in temperate forests. Forest Ecology and Management 259, 857–866

Oestreicher, J., Benessaiah, K. Ruiz-Jaen, M., Sloan, S., Turner, K., Pelletier, J., Guay, B., Clark, K., Roche, D., Meiners, M., Potvin, C., 2009. Avoiding deforestation in Panamanian protected areas: An analysis of protection effectiveness and implications for reducing emissions from deforestation and forest degradation. Global Environmental Change 19, 279–291

25. Effects of Climate Change on Native Species

Ashley Scott

Warmer temperatures, modified precipitation patterns, and increasing CO_2 concentrations may have large implications for species dynamics. Understanding the effects of climate change on other organisms, particularly in their natural environments, is crucial. In addition to the direct climatic variations that result from global climate change (i.e. precipitation, temperature, and timing of snow melts), range limitations that inhibit migration to cooler areas (including land slope and inherent nutrients), effects of climate change on invasive species populations, emergence period durations, adaptability, and ambient CO_2 concentrations largely impact the viability of a native species.

The two genera studied by Miller-Rushing and Inouye (2009) were affected differently by the various climatic variables studied. One genus exhibited decreasing flower abundance over time, the other did not. However, the genera shared certain similarities, such as a relationship between snowmelt and flowering timing.

Likewise, uncertainty prevented conclusive predictions for the population dynamics certain invasive species in North American forests (Dukes *et al.* 2009), but the study concluded that most species are shifting northwards and increasing in prevalence throughout their ranges. In general, invasive species migrate and evolve more quickly than native plants; this is the reason they thrive in the foreign environment. Pathogens and insects also evolve and proliferate much more quickly than plant species, due to faster life cycles and metabolic rates that increase with temperature, respectively.

Plant species in Italy's Trento Province exhibited similar trends (Marini *et al.* 2009) with the growth of each species positively correlated with temperature. Native species richness, however, decreased with increases in temperature, whereas alien species richness increased. In addition, native and alien species were

Ashley Scott

affected by different variables. Though alien plant species richness in the region mostly depended upon temperature and human population density, native species abundance was most related to availability of calcareous bedrock.

A study of the volcano rabbit and European mountain hare in Britain yielded glum findings. Models based on field results predicted their near eradication by the year 2100 (Anderson *et al.* 2009). Because minimal adaptation was observed by organisms located at the range fringes, the populations' outer margins are expected to reduce the most quickly. Randin *et al.* (2009) found similar results in a study of Swiss Alpine vegetation. Upward shifts in elevation, accompanied by range reductions, are expected to decrease species diversity in their Diablerets and Zermatt study plots between 12.3% (based on the B2 IPCC scenario) and 51.8% (A1 scenario).

Likewise, European caddisfly taxa located in springs, constrained niches, high altitudes, and the south were deemed most susceptible to global climate change (Hering *et al.* 2009). In those areas, the ranges are restricted. Though many species require cold temperatures, nearly half have limited distribution capabilities: this will likely diminish caddisfly diversity.

Because temperature sensitivity is a crucial determinant of ecological prosperity, the most temperature-adaptive species have a comparative advantage. An amino acid substitution, which altered the enzyme cMDH's structure and function, was found to impact limpet species' abilities to withstand increasing temperatures (Dong and Somero 2009). It is seemingly counterintuitive that species located at high latitudes and vertically high intertidal zones were deemed the most adaptive. However, the cooler environments in which these species live prevent them from being subjected to temperatures at their upper thermal limits, which can permanently diminish cMDH function.

Lastly, increasing atmospheric CO_2 concentrations may enhance biomass accumulation (Souza *et al.* 2010) with woody species becoming more prevalent than herbaceous species.

Hence, changes in native and invasive species dynamics can be anticipated to accompany climatic variation. Many populations are enhanced by warmer temperatures and increased CO_2 concentrations, which may advance certain plant and insect populations. However, species incapable of adaptation to variables related to global climate change, such as heat and altered precipitation patterns, could be driven into extinction.

The *Mertensia* and *Delphinium* Genera Show No Significant Differences between Early- and Late-Flowering Plants

Climate change could compromise the livelihood of many plant species. Miller-Rushing and Inouye (2009) looked at two species each of the *Mertensia* and *Delphinium* genera, and found a statistically significant relationship between time of flowering and of snowmelt for all four species. However, the *Delphinium* species' peak flowering occurrences appeared to have been best explained by mean temperatures. In addition, both *Mertensia* species showed declining peak flower abundance over time. The study's main conclusion was that specific case studies are necessary to know the impacts of climate change on each species.

Early- and late-flowering plant species of the *Mertensia* and *Delphinium* genera were observed in 8 rocky meadow plots and 12 wet meadow plots at the Rocky Mountain Biological Laboratory. The observations were collected from 1973 to 2006 and include frost, snow pack, and temperature data, in addition to plant numbers and times of occurrence. The *Mertensia* species were most affected by the time at which the snow melted, whereas the *Delphinium* species were most affected by mean temperatures.

Three of the four species studied (both an early- and a late-flowering species each for the *Mertensia* and *Delphinium* genera) flowered significantly earlier over time (Miller-Rushing and Inouye, 2009), with the early-flowering species impacted most. This could be a result of a statistically significant increase in mean spring temperatures of 2.0°C between 1973 and 2006. However, each of the four species flowered earlier in springs with early snowmelt. The two *Delphinium* species' peak flowering occurrences were best explained by mean temperatures, whereas those of the *Mertensia* species were best explained by the snowmelt timing, though the impacts of mean temperature change or snowmelt occurrence on peak flowering were not constant among species. Both of the *Mertensia* species exhibited declining peak flower abundance over time, though this was not seen in the *Delphinium* species. There did not appear to be differences in flower abundance patterns between the early- and late-flowering species of each genus. However, *M. ciliata* and both *Delphinium* species had lower flower abundance during years of early snowmelt (which is expected to progressively advance during the next century). Hence, this study showed that two species within the same genus can have traits linked to different climate variables, concluding that specific case studies are needed to determine how each species is impacted by climate change.

This study considered only the effects of spring weather upon the flowers, and precipitation data were not included. The fact that three of the four species are flowering earlier even though the number of frost days has not changed significantly, leads to more freeze damage.

Global Climate Change may Increase the Prevalence and Range of Invasive Plants, Pests, and Pathogens in North American Forests

Since invasive plants, pests, and pathogens are the main biotic disturbers of North American forests, those populations' responses to anticipated climate change will have large implications (Dukes *et al.* 2009). In this study, the general effects of anticipated climate change are modeled for six species that typically disturb North American forests. Though uncertainty prevented conclusive predictions from being drawn for some of the species, many showed northward range shifts and increased prevalence, mostly due to increased temperatures throughout their ranges. This study also emphasized the need for models of whole systems instead of specific species (due to the complex interactions among species), but this would be extremely difficult to accomplish.

The six nuisance species studied (two each of insect pests, plant pathogens, and invasive vegetation) were chosen based on how representative they are of important nuisance species and to spread light on species that had not been studied extensively (therefore, they are "not necessarily the most damaging species"). The population growth rate of the hemlock wooly adelgid (an insect pest) appears to only be affected by temperature, so warmer winters would cause the population size to increase dramatically. The growth rate of the other pest species studied, the forest tent caterpillar, is governed by more complex variables; it increases with temperature as well, but not as quickly as the adelgid.

Armillaria root rot, a secondary pathogen (meaning it only kills weakened hosts), will kill more trees in climate change conditions, as the weather conditions will stress more trees (due to higher temperatures, worse droughts, and increased pest prevalence) and enable the root rot to function for a greater portion of the year (since it is dormant during the winter). Beach bark disease, which is due to interactions between an introduced scale insect (*Cryptococcus fagisuga*) and a fungus, can only thrive when winter minimum temperatures consistently exceed $-34°C$. Hence, global warming has been expanding the range northward in which this disease is apparent. In addition, increased tree growth rates (which occur at higher temperatures and CO_2 concentrations) increase susceptibility to the disease, due to the subsequent effects on phenol and nitrogen concentrations in the bark and leaves.

Glossy buckthorn, an invasive plant species from Eurasia covering a very wide range in North America, "exclude(s) native understory species" and "change(s) ecosystem… dynamics". Though the species is relatively cold-tolerant, warming would likely expand the species' range further north. Historical European pollen data suggest that the species has spread north more quickly relative to other species after the warming at the beginning of the Holocene, but there is limited and inconclusive data, so there is no consensus regarding the expected effects of climate change on the glossy buckthorn in North America. Oriental bittersweet, an invasive vine originating from southeastern Asia, severely damages adult trees and inhibits growth of new trees. This species prefers warmer temperatures and higher average precipitation, and its high photosynthetic rate and versatility is expected to make it more successful in climatic change conditions. Because all models that predict future behavior are necessarily extrapolations, there is much uncertainty, due to limited abilities to predict future human behavior (i.e. land-use patterns) and biological changes (i.e. the relationships between species, feedback, etc).

Insect metabolic rates increase drastically as temperature rises, increasing consumption, rate of reproduction, and dispersal. Hence, insects tend to thrive in warmer climates. Because the coldest world regions are expected to be warmed the most with climate change, this could greatly increase pest populations of North American forests. However, pathogen population dynamics are more complicated; many factors impact their population sizes directly and indirectly. Pathogens can adapt more easily than host plants to climate change. Though climate change drives evolutionary change in both pathogens and plants, the faster life cycles of pathogens give them the upper-hand. Invasive plant species adapt better to climate change than native plant species, since they are by nature more resilient to changes in climate and can evolve much more rapidly. However, it is hard to tell what role migration will play; invasive species tend to migrate more quickly than native plants. However, it is unclear how climate change will affect the roles of dispersers and pollinators to both native and invasive species.

Invasive Plant Species in the Italian Alps may Benefit Disproportionately more from Global Climate Change than Native Species

The effects of climate change on alien and native species could have large implications; alien plant species can disrupt native species' community dynamics, since they can drive native species into extinction and promote biological homogenization. Marini *et al.* (2009) found that the density of all types of plants (as well as that of the the local human population) exhibited a positive relationship with temperature, but native species richness declined as temperatures increased, whereas the species richness of naturalized and casual aliens increased. Variation in richness of alien plant species in Italy's Trento Province is "almost entirely explained by temperature and human population density", whereas native species abundance is most related to the abundance of calcareous bedrock. The conclusion is that a stronger response to predicted global climate change is expected from alien species than native species, but colder and population-sparse areas of higher altitudes are less prone to invasion from alien species.

Cells of 3' x 5' in the Province of Trento were studied. Since this is at the southern border of the Alps, elevation ranged between 66 and 3769 m. Several variables, categorized as environmental energy (which is determined by annual average temperatures and cumulative radiation), propagule pressure and disturbance, and other environmental factors (including precipitation, slope, and coverage by calcareous bedrock and grasslands) were measured. Regression analyses were performed for the measured variables to determine autocorrelation, colinearity, and correlation. In addition to ordinary least squares regression and simultaneous autoregressive models, hierarchical partitioning was used to determine the variables most likely to affect variation in species richness and their relative importance, thus considering all possible multiple regression models.

Human population density in itself affects the distribution and niche health of plants, but it is also very strongly related to energy availability: this is why humans tend to live at lower elevations. Therefore, high colinearity was found between temperature and human population density. High positive correlation was observed between temperature and human population density, proportion of urban elements, road density, and agricultural land. Temperate mountains were studied to differentiate between the effects of energy availability changes due to elevation and human population density. The relationship between human population density and species diversity may be attributed to initial settlements in areas of high biodiversity or species introductions. However, once population density exceeds a certain level, plant species richness declines. Mountains are expected to become warmer and more populated due to climate change, which may enhance alien species invasion. The mean level of invasion was 4% overall, though it varied between 0 and 14%.

In Response to Global Climate Change, Species are Expected to Ascend in Altitude and Latitude and Decrease in Number

The migrations to higher altitudes and elevations of the volcano rabbit and European mountain hare in Britain, as a result of vegetation responses to climate change, are expected to decrease both species' range sizes; soil conditions and other factors often limit range shifts (Anderson *et al.* 2009). The organisms at both the trailing and leading edges of the range appear to respond more slowly to climate change than the overall population. While the probability of population decline, abundance, and average position is not expected to change drastically in the near future, the two populations studied are predicted to shift and decline drastically (due to shrinking ranges) by 2060.

B. J. Anderson and colleagues studied two lagomorph species, *Lepus timidus* and *Romerolagus diazi*. Environmental suitability maps were created with GIS mapping, based on the conduciveness of climate and habitat to survival. Simulations were used to predict future environmental suitability maps through the year 2100. From the environmental suitability maps, the "distribution of suitable patches" was modeled (a patch is not deemed "suitable" if it cannot support at least 50 females). The simulations were run under two conditions: a stable climate baseline and predicted climate change. These data were then used to determine the populations' range limits.

Based on the models, both populations are expected to be adversely affected by climate change. Female abundance (the prevailing metapopulation metric used in this study) is expected to decline into near eradication at the end of the prediction period (near year 2100) so the entire population will collapse shortly thereafter. Additionally, range limits are expected to be greatly impacted. Though the outer margins of the population are predicted to change most drastically, the metapopulation's range is expected to change and shrink, though somewhat sporadically.

High Plant Species Diversity Losses in the Swiss Alps are Expected, regardless of Modeling Discrepancies

Upward elevation shifts and range reductions observed in Swiss Alpine trees and other plant species (due to global climate change) are problematic. Previous studies predicted high plant diversity loss in western European mountain ranges—up to 60%. Randin *et al.* (2009) which created species distribution models (SDM), found similar results, with mean diversity losses estimated to be between 12.3% (B2 IPCC scenario) and 51.8% (A1). However, models created at the European and local scales had different limitations and subsequently yielded different habitat persistence results, with higher persistence predicted for the locally scaled models. The study concludes that species distribution models must consider both local and macro scales to be accurate.

Two regions in the Swiss Alps were studied: Diablerets (Canton de Vaud) and Zermatt (Canton de Valais). The elevation ranges from 375m to 3210m at

Diablerets and from 1480m to 4634m at Zermatt (43% of the Zermatt study area holds glaciers). Some species distribution data were collected from the AFE, since 2089 AFE plots (sized 50km x 50km each) are in the Diablerets and Zermatt sampling areas. Models were developed based on those data for 78 species (appearing in one or both studied regions), 42 species appearing in the Diablerets region and 51 appearing in Zermatt. The plots in this study were much smaller (ranging between 10m^2 and 64m^2). Seven "climatically derived variables" were used (from Climatic Research Unit and MeteoSwiss data): growing degree days; mean annual temperature; minimum temperature of the coldest month; mean annual, winter, and summer precipitation; and potential evapotranspiration. These climate predictors were fitted to the large AFE plots then projected and fit to the small study plots. SDM were generated, using the latest version of the BIOMOD program. GLM, GAM, and GBM were calibrated with 70% of the data (which were chosen randomly), and the remaining 30% of the data evaluated these models. The best model for each species and scale was then selected. Although this study downscaled, which "can generate additional uncertainty", this was necessary to compare this study to others. This is because habitat and subsequent biodiversity loss rates vary greatly among studies (due to differences in location, resolution, and species composition), and results of studies from different resolutions (local scales and macro scales) in the same regions are rarely compared.

The frequencies with which species are expected to appear in a given area due to habitat suitability were calculated. These local habitat persistence coefficients are based on the number of suitable and unsuitable plots within the larger cells (a maximum value of 100 would be obtained if all species were predicted to have sufficient habitat persistence). Because species higher in elevation are expected to be most vulnerable to climate change, species were categorized as montane, subalpine, or alpine/nival and the frequencies with which the species' habitats persisted within these categories were modeled. Finally, predictions of the percentage of species expected to become extinct in each plot for each of the four IPCC scenarios were also generated.

The mean predicted species losses, aggregated from all of the plots studied, were 51.8%, standard deviation of 14.5% (based on the A1 IPCC scenario); 17.3%, SD 12.8% (A2); 14.4%, SD 5.6% (B1); and 12.3%, SD 8.3% (B2). These findings are compatible with those of other studies. However, local habitat persistence coefficients were high, ranging between 69% (A1) and 74% (B2) for the Diablerets region and at 100% for Zermatt. Because of this, elevation range was found to be the main (local) habitat persistence determinant. In addition, at smaller (local) scales, some habitats were expected to persist that the larger (European) scales predicted would disappear. Since small and large scales capture different variables, this study concludes that both should be considered in models. It is also worth noting that the local model predictions were based on the unrealistic assumption that species would exhibit unlimited dispersion.

The Least Mobile European Tricoptera taxa may be Hard Hit by Global Climate Change

The caddisfly family, which is vital to aquatic ecosystems, is expected to be adversely effected by global climate change (Hering *et al.* 2009). The sensitivities of 1134 European caddisfly (Tricoptera) taxa to climate change were studied, based on five criteria: presence in ecoregions, stream zonation preference, temperature range preference, emergence period duration, and feeding specificity. Between 21.9 and 47.9% of the European caddisfly taxa were found to be very susceptible to climate change.

Only the five categories were used because other climatically impacted variables were not present in significant proportions of the population. Species found in only one of the 23 European ecoregions studied were deemed "endemic". If at least 50% of a species was "eucrenal" and "hypocrenal" (of the 10 categories describing stream zone preference), the species was classified as preferring springs. Species sensitive to temperature increases were categorized as stenotherms. Emergence periods were deemed short if they were less than 50 days long. Feeding type specifies how the animal eats—some examples are as a parasite, predator, grazer, and miner.

The number of taxa per ecoregion varied between 12 and 373, but most ecoregions contained between 200 and 300 taxa. The criteria measures found 47.9% of species to have limited abilities to distribute, 23.1% strongly prefer springs (and therefore cannot move upstream as in large rivers), 21.9% dwell in cold water ("stenotherms"), 35.5% have short emergence periods, and 43.7% have restricted ecological niches due to feeding types. In addition, 84.1% of taxa met at least one sensitivity criterion. This is disconcerting, since the study finds climate change to place the majority of taxa at risk.

Species richness has a south-north gradient, since species only inhabited southern Europe when glaciers covered the continent during the Pleistocene. However, most of the sensitive taxa are also located in southern Europe and at high altitudes, for all sensitivity parameters. Though there are knowledge gaps regarding the species' distribution, a study with finer resolution would be nearly infeasible, due to the size of the study area and number of species. Limited taxonomic knowledge also hindered the study. Lastly, this study's definition of "endemic" was quite arbitrary.

Ashley Scott

Cold-Adapted Limpet Species are Best-Suited for Temperature Increases

Species that adapt best to higher temperatures will thrive, whereas non-adaptive species will likely be driven into extinction due to global warming. Since limpets are ecologically important and widespread marine animals, thermal sensitivities of six species of limpets from the *Lottia* genus having different vertical and latitudinal distributions were studied (Dong and Somero 2009). The ability to survive and adapt to high temperatures, as indicated by the structure and function of the enzyme cMDH, was found to be impacted by a substitution of one amino acid. Because low-latitude warm-adapted species live close to their upper thermal limits, they are most vulnerable to further temperature increases. It follows that vertically high-intertidal species were found to be more heat tolerant than low- and mid-intertidal species—high-intertidal species are the most submerged, so they typically experience cooler temperatures.

All of the limpets were collected from sites off the central Californian coast. They were then acclimated to 14°C seawater for two weeks. During this process, they were immersed in 14°C seawater twice a day for 6 hour intervals to simulate high tide. Then, cMDH was purified from a tissue sample extract. Michaelis-Menton constants were determined and activity was found with a spectrophotometer. RNA was also purified from the muscle tissue. Reverse transcriptase reactions and PCR were performed, and RACE was then used to create full-length cDNA. The cMDH coding regions were then amplified, and the sequences were assembled to create three-dimensional models of the protein structures. From that, the amino acid sequences were deduced.

Amino acid substitutions were studied, along with the effects on the enzyme's structure and function. The Michaelis-Menton constant is an index of function, and resistance to denaturation is indicative of structure. The enzyme cMDH was studied because it is widely distributed among organisms and is crucial for many metabolic pathways. All Michaelis-Menton constants—and therefore cMDH function—increased with increasing temperatures. However, at higher temperatures, warm-adapted species' Michaelis-Menton constants increased much less than those of cold-adapted species. Low-intertidal species were found to be less thermally stable than high-intertidal species. The three-dimensional models showed that amino acid substitutions can also affect hydrogen bonding among nucleotides, impacting protein folding. Conformational mobility can be induced by one amino acid substitution at many sites, which results from changes to adapt to temperature.

Changes in CO_2 Concentration may Affect Plant Biomass and Species Dynamics

Changes in CO_2 concentration may affect biomass accumulation and plant species composition (Souza *et al.* 2010). Both understory and overstory plant species dynamics—namely the relative amounts of herbaceous and woody species—are affected by an increasing ambient CO_2 concentration, which increases the prevalence and composition of woody species in forest understories.

The study compared plants grown with supplemental CO_2 (eCO_2) to those grown in ambient CO_2 conditions (aCO_2) in a "free-air" CO_2 enrichment facility of a monoculture of sweetgum. In providing CO_2 to the eCO_2 plots, all other factors (such as pH, light, temperature, and moisture) were kept equal. The plots, which were established in 1998, were studied for ten years.

Total aboveground understory biomass was found to be 25% greater in eCO_2 plots than aCO_2 plots. Woody biomass drastically increases with CO_2 concentration; though woody biomass was initially unchanged for the first two study years, it drastically increased as the study continued. Woody plants may fare comparatively better than herbaceous species because they are perennial. Though woody species comprised only 7% of total understory biomass in 2001–2003, woody species comprised 50% of total understory biomass in 2008, and woody biomass was 60% greater in eCO_2 plots than aCO_2 plots. Herbaceous biomass was found to be 30% greater in eCO_2 plots than aCO_2 plots except for one year. However, only 6 to 14% of the total variation in understory community composition could be explained by eCO_2, though more significant effects were noticed in species-specific studies. Net primary productivity was 23% greater in eCO_2 than aCO_2 rings in the overstory during the first six years of the experiment, but after that, the difference between the two types diminished.

Conclusions

A common theme in these studies is need for further research. Randin *et al.* found discrepancies in habitat persistence results between models scaled at European and local levels. A holistic system model is also recommended by Dukes *et al.* to capture the complexities of inter-species relationships. Similarly, the study by Miller-Rushing and Inouye determined that predicting anticipated effects on a particular species requires case-specific studies. Hence, current knowledge of particular species and ecological systems is severely lacking. Not only does proper understanding require thorough study of specific organisms, but larger models need to capture interactions within ecosystems. Climate models at the macro and micro levels are also necessary to capture overarching trends without ignoring important geographical intricacies, like varying gradients in mountainous and hilly areas (which affects exposure to light and wind).

References Cited

Anderson, B. J., Akcakaya, H.R., Araujo, M.B., Fordham, D.A., Martinez-Meyer, E., Thuiller, W., and Brook, B.W., 2009. Dynamics of range margins for metapopulations under climate change. The Royal Society 276, 1415–20.

Dong, Y. and Somero, G.N., 2009. Temperature adaptation of cytosolic malate dehydrogenases of limpets (genus *Lottia*): differences in stability and function due to minor changes in sequence correlate with biogeographic and vertical distributions. The Journal of Experimental Biology 212, 169–177.

Dukes, J.S., Pontius, J., Orwig, D., Garnas, J.R., Rodgers, V.L., Brazee, N., Cooke, B., Theoharides, K.A., Stange, E.E., Harrington, R., Ehrenfeld, J., Gurevitch, J., Lerdau, M., Stinson, K., Wick, R., and Ayres, M., 2009. Responses of insect pests, pathogens, and invasive plant species to climate change in the forests of northeastern North America: What can we predict? NRC Research Press 39, 231– 248.

Hering, D., Schmidt-Kloiber, A., Murphy, J., Lucke, S., Zamora-Munoz, C., Lopez-Rodriguez, M.J., Huber, T., and Graf, W., 2009. Potential impact of climate change on aquatic insects: A sensitivity analysis for European caddisflies (Tricoptera) based on distribution patterns and ecological preferences. Aquatic Science 71, 3–14.

Marini, L., Gaston, K., Prosser, F., and Hulme, P., 2009. Contrasting response of native and alien plant species richness to environmental energy and human impact along alpine elevation gradients. Global Geology and Biogeography 18, 652–661.

Miller-Rushing, A.J. and Inouye, D.W., 2009. Variation in the impact of climate change on flowering phenology and abundance: An examination of two pairs of closely related wildflower species. American Journal of Botany 96, 1821-1829.

Randin, C.R., Engler, R., Normand, S., Zappa, M., Zimmermann, N.E., Pearman, P.B., Vittoz, P., Thuiller, W., and Guisan, A., 2009. Climate change and plant distribution: local models predict high-elevation persistence. Global Change Biology 15, 1557–1569.

Souza, L., Belote, R.T., Kardol, P., Weltzin, J.F., and Norby, R.J., 2010. CO_2 enrichment accelerates successional development of an understory plant community. Journal of Plant Ecology 3, 33–39.

26. Changes in Distributions of Invasive Species with the Changing Climate

Sanami Nakayama

Climate change has a profound effect on species and ecosystems around the world. It can have drastic effects on the phenology and physiology of organisms, composition of and interactions within communities, structure and dynamics of ecosystems, and ranges and distributions of species (Walther *et al.* 2002). The range and distribution of a species is influenced by climatic factors, such as temperature and precipitation, through physiological thresholds of temperature and precipitation tolerances of organisms. It is generally expected that with warming, ranges of species will shift poleward or to higher altitudes because organisms will be forced to move to areas that are within their temperature tolerances (Root *et al.* 2003). With shifts in ranges of species around the world, biological invasions are becoming a growing concern.

Biological invasions occur when a species is introduced to areas that it is not native to, usually through unintentional or intentional introduction by human activities. A common vector of species introduction that is examined in this chapter is the aquarium trade (Chang *et al.* 2009). With climate change, however, non-native species can also naturally expand into adjacent areas (Walther *et al.* 2002). Once introduced, if the new habitat is environmentally suitable, invasive species may rapidly increase in number and become widespread, causing the composition and functioning of the ecosystem to change. Invasive species are also of concern because they are the cause of major economic losses in agriculture, forestry, and other segments of the economy. For instance, the tomato red spider mite *Tetranychus evansi* is a widespread pest that has caused crop losses up to 90% in the last decade in South-East Africa and West Africa (Migeon *et al.* 2009). In the US alone, invasive species have caused major environmental damage and losses adding up to $120 billion per year (Pimentel *et al.* 2005).

According to Bethany A. Bradley and her colleagues (2009), one of the fundamental reasons why we expect invasion risk to increase with climate change is because invasive species are well suited to succeed in novel environments, and novel environments are created by climate change. Changes in environmental conditions due to climate change can cause an area to become suitable for a species that did not previously occupy the area. For species native to the area, however, changes in environmental conditions may make the habitat less suitable. Invasive species are typically characterized by high adaptability and tolerance of wide ranges of environmental conditions compared to native species. Invasive species can thus pose major threats to native biodiversity by being competitively dominant and by altering fundamental properties of ecosystems (Dukes and Mooney 1999). Generally, it is expected that with warming, overall ranges of invasive species will expand. Recent studies of several invasive species, such as the flatworm *Platydemus manokwari* in Japan (Sugiura 2009), species of hawkweeds in Australia (Beaumont *et al.* 2009), and the pacific oyster *Crassostrea gigas* along the European Atlantic coast (Dutertre 2010), have found this expectation to be true.

Most elements of global change have been found to favor invasive species over natives, further exacerbating the impacts of invasion on ecosystems (Dukes and Mooney 1999). For example, in the Andes of central Chile, as temperature increases, the invasive beetle species *H. Variegata* is likely to increase in abundance and drive the native species *H. variegata* to extinction because the invasive beetles are successful in a wider range of temperatures and can adjust more quickly to environmental changes compared to the natives. It has also been found that rising CO_2 levels are more advantageous for invasive plants compared to native plants (Bradley *et al.* 2009, Raizada *et al.* 2009).

As the climate continues to change rapidly, the monitoring and management of invasive species is becoming more crucial, especially of those that can cause major harm to native biodiversity and to our economy. Current research focuses on the use of models to predict the distributions of invasive species under future climate conditions. Experimental and observational studies have also been conducted to look at the effects of climate change on the abundances and distributions of invasive species over the past few decades. An understanding of how climate change affects invasive species and the use of models to predict distributions of harmful species will greatly aid in effective management of these species. Models can also be used for the restoration of native species. Though it is generally thought the ranges of invasive species will expand with climate change, some studies have found the ranges of some to contract, creating restoration opportunities for native species (Beaumont *et al.* 2009, Bradley *et al.* 2009). Models can be used to predict the areas from which invasive species contract, and native species can be re-introduced into these areas before undesirable species take advantage of these opportunities.

Introduction of Non-Native Species through Aquarium Trade

A growing vector for the introduction of non-native aquatic species to new environments in the US is the aquarium trade. Andrew L. Chang and his colleagues (2009) studied this vector by surveying pet stores in the San Francisco Bay-Delta region to determine which fish species being sold have the potential to become invasive if introduced to the Bay-Delta. Using a conservative model, the researchers found that 5 species sold throughout the region could survive in the Bay-Delta if introduced. Using a less conservative model, they found that up to 27 species could survive in the Bay-Delta.

The researchers first identified 168 stores in the San Francisco Bay-Delta area that sold aquarium fish. They then separated these stores into three regions based on the store's proximity to freshwater or saltwater regions of the Bay-Delta and they classified each store as either independent (individually owned and operated) or a chain store (stores that are part of a chain with multiple retail stores and centralized management). They then randomly selected nine independent and nine chain stores in each region to survey. At each store, they conducted an inventory of all of the fish being sold and for each tank, they recorded the species listed on the tank, the species actually present in the tank, and any additional labeling information that was available. In addition, they conducted telephone surveys to ask store representatives about their knowledge of invasive species and their willingness to address threats posed by these species.

To determine whether a species has the potential to survive in, and invade, the Bay-Delta region, the researchers separated the region into marine and freshwater subregions and developed a model to compare temperature and salinity tolerances of each species to environmental data for each salinity region. Because minimum temperature tolerance is a major limiting factor in fish survival, they chose to use the warmest minimum temperature in each salinity region as the criterion for determining survival potential. Because preliminary models gave results that underestimated invasion potential of aquarium fish, the researchers came up with two models: a more conservative, colder, scenario, and a less conservative, warmer, scenario. Under the colder scenario, they compared lowest recorded temperature tolerances of each species to the warmest minimum temperature of the Bay-Delta in each salinity region. Under the warmer scenario, warmest minimum temperatures of the regions were increased by 3°C and fish temperature tolerances were reduced by 3°C.

Of the 867 fish species that the researchers identified, under the colder scenario, three freshwater and two saltwater species had the potential to become invasive if introduced to the Bay Delta. Under the warmer scenario, nine freshwater and eighteen saltwater species had the potential to become invasive. Nearly all independent and chain stores sold at least one of these species. Under the colder scenario, chain stores sold a significantly greater number of potentially invasive species compared to independent stores. Under the warmer scenario, there was no difference. It was also found that a greater percentage of fish species were labeled correctly in chain stores compared to independent stores. A majority of the respondents of the telephone surveys had some knowledge of invasive species and most were willing to sell different species in place of those that are potentially invasive.

The results of this study suggest that as global temperatures continue to increase, an increasing number of fish species in the aquarium trade are likely to have the potential to survive and become invasive if introduced to the San Francisco Bay-Delta Region. It is thus becoming more imperative for management of potentially invasive species in the trade to reduce the risk of introducing these species to the Bay-Delta. The researchers suggest that two management actions should be taken to reduce the risk of invasion: the implementation of programs to enhance invasive species awareness and education among store representatives, and improvement in fish labeling practices. If store representatives are knowledgeable about invasive species, they can relay important information to their customers and advise them of the risks of their purchases. Improving labels by including information such as life history traits and warnings about the potential hazards of releasing pets can help customers avoid buying fish that they will be unhappy with and reduce inappropriate disposal of unwanted fish into local waterways.

Potential Distribution of the Invasive Pest *Tetranychus evansi*

Tomato red spider mite (*Tetranychus evansi*) is an invasive pest of solanaceous plants that has caused major crop losses throughout the world. The change in distribution of this species with climate change is becoming a growing concern. Alain Migeon and his colleagues (2009) developed a model to predict the potential distribution of the species under current climate conditions and to determine the climate factors that limit its distribution. They found that *T. evansi* has the potential to survive in areas that it does not currently occupy; various climate factors such as dryness, excess moisture, and cold stress limit their distribution.

The main hosts of *T. evansi* are solanaceous plants, including tobacco, tomato, and eggplant. The mites cause serious damage to these crops throughout the world, including North America, Indian Ocean Islands, countries in sub-Sarahan Africa, the Mediterranean, Hawaii, and Taiwan. Because *T. evansi* is a cause of major economic loss, it is crucial to prevent its expansion. Migeon and his colleagues used a CLIMEX model to predict the potential distribution of *T. evansi*. This model uses four stress indices (cold, heat, dry and wet) and their interactions (cold-wet, cold-dry, heat-wet, heat-dry) to determine a species' ability to persist in a certain location, based on environments that the species occupies. Minimum and maximum temperature thresholds of 10°C and 38°C and dry stress and wet stress thresholds, based on soil moisture holding capacity, were used in the model. A cold-wet stress temperature threshold of 12°C and a hot-wet stress temperature threshold of 32°C were also used.

The model shows that areas that are not currently occupied by the mites but are climatically suitable include parts of Asia, all of the Australian coasts, and many parts of Central America and the Caribbean. Cold stress, dry stress, wet stress and hot-wet stress are the limiting factors of the distribution of *T. evansi* in South America. In temperate zones, dry stress, wet stress, and cold-stress limit its distribution. In the Mediterranean Basin and Japan, the distribution of *T. evansi* is limited by cold climatic conditions and cold stress. In the Mediterranean Basin, the mites are restricted to coastal areas where minimum temperature is relatively high. In Japan, the mites are restricted to climatically mild areas. These areas represent their northern-most limit because north of this limit, temperatures become too low for successful development.

In most areas, temperature stress plays an important role in determining the distribution of *T. evansi*. As the climate continues to warm, it is likely that more areas will become climatically suitable for the mites. The researchers suggest that we should determine the pathways by which *T. evansi* disperse as a first step in the management of the species.

Projected Ranges of Invasive Hawkweeds in Australia with Climate Change

Management of invasive species is crucial within conservation reserves in Australia because many species listed under the Threatened Species Conservation Act of 1995 are threatened by them. Beaumont and his colleagues investigated the projected distributions of three invasive hawkweeds (*Hieracium* spp.) under current and future climate conditions using ecological niche models (Beaumont *et al.* 2009). They found that the hawkweeds still have the potential to increase their ranges under current climate condition but as the climate warms, their ranges are likely to contract overall. Though the hawkweeds have not established in the Australian Alps, much of the conservation reserves in the Alps are currently climatically suitable for the weeds and they will remain suitable until at least 2070.

The two main goals of this study were to 1) assess the potential distributions of three hawkweed species *Hieracium pilosella*, *H. aurantiacum*, and *H. murorum* under current and future climate conditions and 2) determine whether the potential ranges of these invasive species coincide with conservation reserves. The researchers used eight ecological niche models to assess the potential distributions of the hawkweeds under current and future climate conditions in 2030 and 2070. Ecological niche models are commonly used to generate projections of ranges of exotic species by determining the areas that are likely to remain climatically suitable for a species. The researchers obtained information about areas that are set aside for conservation in every Australian state and territory, and they used ArcGIS to determine the extent to which the projected distributions of hawkweeds coincide with these reserves.

Results show that the three hawkweed species have the potential to increase in range and occupy larger areas than those they currently occupy. The researchers suggest that the weeds have not expanded into areas that are currently climatically suitable for them because they have not had enough time since they were introduced to Australia. All three species were introduced to Australia less than 20 years ago, and within the next few years, the weeds may realize their invasive potential and expand into larger areas. The researchers also suggest that the ability of the weeds to expand into suitable areas may be limited by their poor dispersal.

As the climate warms, it is projected that the ranges of the hawkweeds will contract overall. However, about a fifth of the areas that are projected to be currently suitable for the weeds are contained within conservation reserves in the Australian Alps, which are home to many endemic species. As temperature increases, a larger fraction of suitable areas are projected to be contained within reserves. The results of this study emphasize the need for control and management of the hawkweeds to minimize the possibility of these species moving into conservation reserves.

Alien Beetle Species Takes Over Native Beetle Species in a Mountain-Top Environment

High-elevation mountain environments are some of the most sensitive ecosystems to the warming climate because they are characterized by low temperatures. Because plants and animals that live in these environments must be able to tolerate harsh conditions created by low temperatures, it was believed that these environments are not likely to experience biological invasions. However, with the modern world's increasing temperatures, researchers have become concerned that high-elevation mountain environments are becoming more prone to invasions. Marco A. Molina-Montenegro and his colleagues investigated the effects of global warming on two ladybird species, *Eriopis connexa* and *Hippodamia variegata*, in the Andes of central Chile (Montenegro *et al.* 2009). *E. connexa* is native to Chile, while *H. variegata* is an alien species. The results of this study show that as the climate warms, the alien species will increase in abundance and drive the native species out of their mountain-top habitats.

The researchers looked specifically at the differences in abundances of the two ladybird species in two different habitats- one at exposed sites on the mountain-top and one in open-top chambers (OTCs). OTCs are chambers that prevent heat loss, and the temperature inside a chamber is 4–5°C higher than the surrounding environment. Twelve cushions plants, plants on which the ladybirds live, were randomly chosen. OTCs were placed around six of them; the other six were left exposed to the mountain-top environment. The abundance of the two ladybird species were estimated once a month, from November to March. The soil moisture and abundance of other arthropods at each site were also estimated.

The researchers found that the abundance of ladybirds were higher at sites with OTCs compared to sites without, for both species. At sites without OTCs, the abundance of *H. variegata* and *E. connexa* did not differ. However, at sites with OTCs, the abundance of the alien species was 13 times greater than that of the native species. Soil moisture at sites with and without OTCs did not differ, suggesting that the difference in abundance of the two species at sites with OTCs is due to the temperature inside the chambers. The researchers also found a total of eight arthropod species at sites with OTCs, most of which are alien species. They found that the abundances of all of these species were higher at sites with OTCs compared to those without. Only five of these species were found at sites without OTCs.

The results of this study suggest that global warming will have an effect on the abundance of both *H. variegata* and *E. connexa*. With increasing temperature, the alien species will increase in abundance, while the native species are driven to possible extinction. The researchers believe that the alien species are benefiting from the warmer temperature because they can be successful in a range of temperatures. These beetles have been found to be more adaptive in behavior and metabolism compared to the native species, allowing them to adjust quickly to changing temperatures. Thus while the native species struggles to adapt to the change in their environment, the alien species may out compete the native species and drive them out of their habitats. The results of this study also suggest that we should be cautious about possible invasion by other alien, arthropod species in high-elevation mountain environments with the warming climate.

Possible Invasion of Temperate Areas by *Platydemus manokwari* with the Warming Climate

The warming climate of our modern world has been advantageous for many invasive species, including the snail-eating flatworm *Platydemus manokwari* (Sugiura 2009). This flatworm species was first discovered in New Guinea and is typically a tropical species, but it has recently been introduced by humans both intentionally and accidentally to subtropical regions and is quickly spreading throughout, posing serious threats to endemic gastropod species; the worms feed on any living gastropods. Though low winter temperatures have so far restricted invasion by *P. manokwari* in temperate areas, there is growing concern that warmer winters may prevent this restriction.

Shinji Sugiura looked closely at the effects of seasonal variations in predation rates of *P. manokwari* on the land snails *A. despecta* in the field, and the effects of temperature on feeding activities of the flatworms in the laboratory. All experiments were conducted in Chichijima Island, located 1000 km south of the Japanese mainland. To investigate the effects of seasonal variations in predation rates of *P. manokwari*, Sugiura experimentally placed nylon bags containing *A. despecta* on the forest floor during 7-day time periods in February, April, May, June, July, September, and December. He checked to see how many snails were still alive after various lengths of time in the forest, and this varied by month.

In the laboratory, Sugiura investigated the effects of temperature on *P. manokwari* survival and predation rate, and the effects of *P. manokwari* density on *A. despecta* survival. To study the effects of temperature on feeding activities of the flatworms, he placed individual flatworms in containers at each of 5 different temperatures (10, 14, 18, 22, and 26°C). If they survived for a week, Sugiura placed a snail in the flatworm's container and checked whether or not any of the snails had been eaten after 7 days.

Sugiura found that there is a difference in predation rates of *P. manokwari* among seasons. Predation rates of the flatworms were highest in July, September, and November. No snails were preyed on in February. Sugiura also found that snail survival is positively correlated with mean daily temperature in the field. He suggests that at higher temperatures, a rapid population growth of *P. manokwari* can occur. This may explain why predation rates were highest after the summer. Sugiura also mentions that though he could not test for the effects of moisture on *P. manokwari*, high humidity and precipitation are required for these flatworms to survive.

In the laboratory, Sugiura found that temperature influences the survival and feeding activities of *P. manokwari*. Only about a quarter of them kept at 10°C were able to survive after 14 days and no snails placed in the containers with these flatworms were eaten. At the other four temperatures, almost all individuals were still alive after 14 days. About half of the *P. manokwari* kept at 14°C attacked snails and almost all *P. manokwari* kept at 18, 22 and 26°C attacked snails. In sum, higher temperatures are favorable for *P. manokwari* because their survival and predation rates increase with temperature. Sugiura also found that the higher the density of *P. manokwari*, the lower the survival of *A. despecta*.

The results of this study suggest that with the rapidly changing climate, temperate regions should be cautious of possible invasion and establishment by *P. ma-*

nokwari. Low temperatures of winters in temperate zones have kept *P. manokwari* from being able to survive but with globally increasing temperatures, it is becoming more likely that the flatworms will be able to disperse out of the tropical and subtropical regions that they have been limited to and successfully invade and establish populations in temperate regions. Sugiura thus suggests that these regions should take necessary precautions, such as quarantine procedures of soil containing materials that could carry *P. manokwari*, in order to avoid invasions by these invasive flatworms.

Northward Expansion of *Crassostrea gigas* with Climate Change

The invasive pacific oyster, *Crassostrea gigas*, was once limited to the southern Atlantic regions of Europe, and southern Bourgneuf Bay in France marked its northern-most limit. However, over the past 10 years, the oysters have spread north and have established populations throughout northern European Atlantic regions. They have been causing declines in performances of farmed oysters in these regions. Michaël Dutertre and his colleagues (2010) of the University of Nantes studied the environmental variables, reproductive physiology, larval development, and post-larval recruitment of *C. gigas* to investigate the causes of its recent spread into northern temperature environments. They found that there has been a trend of warming in the northern Atlantic and increased temperatures have allowed successful reproduction, larval development, and recruitment of the oysters into these regions.

The researchers surveyed *C. gigas* from a northern, high-turbidity mudflat site, and a southern, sandy-muddy bottom site, in Bourgneuf Bay from 2005–2006. To analyze reproductive physiology of the oysters, slices of visceral tissue were examined and oocyte diameters measured to determine the gonadal developmental stage. Water quality probes were installed at each site to record temperature, salinity, suspended particular matter concentration (SPM, the total amount of particles), particulate organic matter concentration (POM, potentially digestible particles) and chlorophyll-a concentration (amount of available phytoplankton) of the water. Ratios of POM:SPM, which gives an indication of food availability, and of Chl-a:POM, which gives an indication of the quality of food, were calculated. D-larva and post-larval densities at each site were determined from water samples. Daily water and atmospheric temperatures from 1970 to 2006 were also calculated.

The results of this study show that the expansion of *C. gigas* northward coincided with a marked increase in water temperature. Optimal larval development requires a period of at least two weeks during which water temperature is higher than 22°C. Massive recruitment of *C. gigas* in the northern site occurred when summer temperatures started reaching over 20°C. Oocyte diameters of oysters at both sites showed that reproductive cycles are timed by water temperature thresholds. The oocyte growing stage begins when spring water temperature reaches 8–10°C. The mature stage was reached more quickly in 2006 than in 2005 because 2006 was marked by reduced daily amplitude of water temperatures and greater spring food quality (i.e. higher Chl-a:POM). Maximum d-larva density was observed during the summer periods in which water temperature was higher than 20–22°C, and the northern site showed greater numbers of larvae and post-larvae than the southern site. Post-larval recruitment was much higher in 2006 than in 2005 at both sites. At the northern site, chlorophyll-a levels were found to control post-larval recruitment.

Reproductive and developmental processes are thus very sensitive to temperature and an increase in water temperature has allowed for successful oocyte growth, larval development, and greater post-larval recruitment in the northern Atlantic regions of Europe. As temperature continues to increase, it is expected that *C. gigas* will expand further north, into coastal areas that are used for oyster farming. Active management of this species should be considered to prevent the invasive oysters from causing further damage to oyster farms.

Effects of Decadal Climate Oscillations on the Distribution of an Invasive Mussel Species

There have been shifts in biogeographic ranges of many plant and animal species due to global warming. For some of these species, scientists have been able to predict the direction in which they will shift with increasing temperature. Thomas J. Hilbish and his colleagues at the University of South Carolina investigated whether changes in distribution of two mussel species, *Mytilus galloprovincialis* and *Mytilus trossulus*, and their hybrids along the coast of California follow the predictions made by the global warming hypothesis (Hilbish *et al.* 2010). *M. trossulus* is native to the coast of California while *M. galloprovincialis* is a warm-water species that was introduced to this region via ballast water. The two species have hybridized and formed a hybrid zone throughout the coast of California. The global warming hypothesis predicts that *M. galloprovincialis* are moving poleward while *M. trossulus* are moving towards the equator with the warming climate. The researchers found that shifts in ranges of these species are in directions opposite of those predicted by the global warming hypothesis, but these shifts can be explained by the effects of decadal climate oscillations.

To determine whether there have been changes in the biogeographic ranges of the two mussel species, the researchers sampled mussels from various open-coast locations in California, running from south of Monterey Bay to North of Humboldt Bay. They compared their findings to those of an earlier study, conducted 10 years earlier by Paul D. Rawson and his colleagues. All mussels collected were genetically analyzed at three nuclear gene loci and were classified as either *M. galloprovincialis* or *M. trossulus*, depending on which species-specific allele they were homozygous for. All other mussels were classified as hybrids. The researchers also looked at changes in upwellings and sea surface temperatures (SST) at the study sites within the last 10 years, using upwelling indices and data from the National Data Buoy Center from the National Oceanic and Atmospheric Administration (NOAA).

Contrary to predictions made by the global warming hypothesis, *M. galloprovincialis* and the hybrid zone have shifted their geographic ranges south, towards the equator. They are almost completely absent from the northern-most sites, where they were abundantly present 10 years ago. At every site north of Monterey Bay, *M. galloprovincialis* are less abundant than *M. trossulus*. South of Monterey Bay, the sites are still dominated by the invasive species. The geographic range of *M. trossulus*, however, has remained unchanged over the past 10 years.

The researchers believe that the shift in the range of *M. galloprovincialis* and the hybrid zone to the south is due to decadal climate oscillations. In the 1990s, the western coast of the US was experiencing a warm phase of the Pacific Decadal Oscillation (PDO) and strong El Niño activity. Recently, this region is experiencing a cool phase of the PDO and mild El Niño activity. At most of the buoy sites, SST were lower by about 1°C from 1999–2005 compared to SST from 1982–1987. Upwellings, which get stronger during cold phases of a PDO, have also been greater in central and northern California from 1999–2005 compared with 1982–1987. Upwellings are events that cause loss of warmer surface waters from on-shore regions, which are then replaced by colder, deeper waters from offshore. Consequently, SST of near-shore regions decrease during times of great upwellings.

The researchers believe that the most probable explanation for the shift in the ranges of *M. galloprovincialis* and the hybrid zone is due to the declining SST of the northern and central coast due to the current phase of the PDO. SST of the study sites south of Monterey Bay have not significantly changed over the past 10 years, thus the abundance of *M. galloprovincialis* at these sites has remained relatively unchanged. A decrease in SST by 1°C was not significant enough to have an effect on *M. trossulus*. The researchers also suggest that other explanations may explain the shift in range of *M. galloprovincialis*, such as increased larval mortality at lower temperatures, low larval recruitment due to stronger upwellings, and northwards dispersal of larvae during a strong El Niño event that occurred 10 years ago. None the less, this study shows that it is important to take into account decadal climate oscillations when trying to understand the long-term effects of global warming on ecological communities.

Sanami Nakayama

Changes in Growth Rates of Invasive and Native Plant Species in Response to Elevated CO_2 Levels

Rapidly increasing global CO_2 levels will have profound effects on the growth of many plant species by directly impacting photosynthetic processes. Purnima Raizada and her colleagues (2009) investigated whether invasive and native dry deciduous species of India respond differently to elevated CO_2 levels. They grew seedlings of two invasive and four native plant species under ambient and elevated CO_2 levels and compared the growths of each species. They found that growth response to elevated CO_2 levels varied among species but biomass, relative growth rate, and net assimilation rate of invasive species were higher than those of native species.

The researchers used the invasive species *Lantana camara* and *Hyptis suaveolens,* the two most important invaders in dry deciduous forests of India. They used the four native species *Acacia catechu, Bauhinia variegate, Dalbergia latifolia,* and *Tectona grandis.* They planted seedlings of each species under ambient (375–395 μmol/mol) or elevated CO_2 levels (700–750 μmol/mol). To expose plants to elevated $CO_2,$ the researchers used decomposed manure as a source of CO_2 and grew the seedling in trenches that were covered with polythene frames. Seedlings grown under ambient conditions were planted in trenches that were left uncovered, without organic matter. The researchers used three plants of each species under each treatment.

Initially, before being grown under a treatment, randomly chosen plants of each species were harvested to measure initial growth data. After 60 days of exposure to ambient or elevated $CO_2,$ the researchers measured biomass partition parameters (root shoot ratio, root mass fraction, stem mass fraction, leaf mass fraction, and leaf area ratio) and growth parameters (specific leaf area, relative growth rate, and net assimilation rate) of each plant. These parameters were then used to compare biomass accumulation and growth of each species.

Growth performance of seedlings in response to elevated CO_2 levels differed across species. Elevated CO_2 significantly promoted growth of seedlings of all six species, but increase in height was greater for the invasive species than the natives. The invasives also accumulated more biomass under elevated CO_2 compared to the natives. Net assimilation rates and relative growth rates were also higher in the invasives. The researchers suggest that higher relative growth rates in the invasive species will give them relative advantage over the natives and may help them become competitively dominant under different environmental stresses.

The results of this study show that as global CO_2 levels increase, we can expect the invasive species *L. camara* and *H. suaveolens* to perform better than many native species in dry deciduous forests of India. The invasive plants may become competitively dominant, changing competitive hierarchies and the structures and functions of these forests. Management of the invasives may become more difficult as CO_2 levels increase because of their rapid growth and adaptability under these conditions.

Possible Restoration of Native Plant Species with Climate Change

It is widely expected that with global warming, invasive plant species will expand in range and pose further threats to native species. Bethany Bradley and her colleagues at Princeton University, however, examined possible reductions in invasive plant competitiveness with climate change because conditions may become climatically unsuitable for some invasive species (Bradley *et al.* 2009). The researchers used bioclimatic envelope modeling to predict the range shifts of five invasive plant species in the western US by 2100. From these models, they found that two of the species will expand in range, two will shift in range, and one will contract. Shifts and contraction in ranges of invasives may create opportunities for restoration of native species.

The researchers used bioclimatic envelope modeling, an approach used to predict species distributions based on geographical relationships between current distributions of the species and future climate conditions, to predict the ranges of five invasive plant species: *Bromus tectorum*, *Centaurea biebersteinii*, *Centaurea solstitialis*, *Tamarix* spp., and *Euphorbia esula*. They used these five species because they are some of the most problematic invasive species in the western US. They are currently widespread, they outcompete native species, and they have been able to dominate and alter ecosystems. In their models, the researchers used climate conditions that best predict the presence of a species, and these climate variables were determined by identifying climate conditions that most constrained a species distribution. Future climate conditions were derived from a compilation of 10 atmosphere-ocean general circulation models (AOGCMs) of precipitation, minimum temperature, and maximum temperature change by 2100. Using four climatic variables, bioclimatic envelopes were created to predict the distributions of the five invasive plant species by 2100.

Based on predictions made by these models, by 2100 only two of the species will expand in range. One will contract, and two will expand in some places and contract in others. The two likely to expand, *C. solstitialis* and *Tamarix* spp., also are likely to prevent restoration in areas they currently occupy. *B. tectorum* and *C. biebersteinii* are likely to shift in range because climatically suitable areas for these species are likely to move northwards, thus they will expand into some regions while they contract from others. *E. esula* are likely decrease in range and contract from the regions it currently occupies.

There are restoration opportunities for native plant species in regions from which invasive species contract. The researchers suggest that modeling and experimental work should be done to determine whether it is possible for native species to occupy these areas. They may not be able to re-establish because of climate change but if restoration of native species is possible, we should attempt to re-introduce the species soon after the invasive species have retreated, to prevent new invasive species from establishing in these areas.

Conclusions

Climate change is breaking down barriers created by temperature and precipitation tolerances that have confined invasive species within certain areas. Over the past few decades, many invasive species around the world have begun to expand in range and pose serious threats to biodiversity of native species and to our economy. Under future climate conditions, most invasive species are expected to expand in range. Some species, however, are predicted to contract in range. It easy to predict the potential distributions of species with respect to change in one climatic factor, such as temperature. However, many factors that affect species distribution can interact in complex ways and simple correlations with one climatic factor are not always observed. Other factors unrelated to global climate change can also affect species distribution. Thus, it is important to note that generalizations about how climate change affects invasive species do not always apply. One thing is certain: the management of invasive species is crucial to prevent further loss of biodiversity and further economic losses.

References Cited

Beaumont, L., Gallagher, R., Downey, P., Thuiller, W., Leishman, M., Hughes, L., 2009. Modelling the impact of *Hieracium* spp. on protected areas in Australia under future climates. Ecography 32, 757–764.

Bradley, B., Blumenthal, D., Wilcove, D., Ziska, L., 2009. Predicting plant invasions in an era of global change. Trends in Ecology and Evolution, DOI 10:1016.

Bradley, B., Oppenheimer, M., Wilcove, D., 2009. Climate change and plant invasions: restoration opportunities ahead? Global Change Biology 15, 1511–1521.

Chang, A., Grossman, J., Spezio, T., Weiskel, H., Blum, J., Bury, J., Muir, A., Piovia-Scott, J., Veblen, K., Grosholz, E., 2009. Tackling aquatic invasions: risks and opportunities for the aquarium fish industry. Biological Invasions 11, 773–785.

Dukes, J., Mooney, H., 1999. Does global change increase the success of biological invaders? Tree 14, 135–139.

Dutertre, M., Beninger, P., Barillé, L., Papin, M., Haure, J., 2010. Rising water temperatures, reproduction, and recruitment of an invasive oyster, *Crassostrea gigas*, on the French Atlantic coast. Marine Environmental Research 69, 1–9.

Hilbish, T., Brannock, P., Jones, K., Smith, A., Bullock, B., Wethey, D., 2010. Historical changes in the distributions of invasive and endemic marine invertebrates are contrary to global warming predictions: the effects of decadal climate oscillations. Journal of Biogeography 37, 423–431.

Migeon, A., Ferragut, F., Escudero-Colomar, L., Fiaboe, K., Knapp, M., de Moraes G., Ueckermann, E., Navajas, M., 2009. Modelling the potential distribution of the invasive tomato red spider mite, *Tetranychus evansi* (Acari: Tetranychidae). Experimental and Applied Acarology 48, 199–212.

Molina-Montenegro, M., Briones, R., Cavieres, L., 2009. Does global warming induce segregation among alien and native beetle species in a mountain-top? Ecol Res 24, 31–26.

Pimentel, D., Zuniga, R., Morrison, D., 2005. Update on the environmental and economic costs associated with alien-invasive species in the United States. Ecological Economics 52, 273–288

Raizada, P., Singh, A., Raghubanshi, A., 2009. Comparative responses of seedlings of selected native dry tropical and alien invasive species to CO_2 enrichment. Journal of Plant Ecology 2, 69–75.

Root, T., Price, J., Hall, K., Shneider, S., Rosenzweigk, C., Pounds, A., 2003. Fingerprints of global warming on wild animals and plants. Nature 421, 57–60.

Sugiura, S., 2009. Seasonal fluctuation of invasive flatworm predation pressure on land snails; implications for the range expansion and impacts of invasive species. Biological Conservation 142, 3013–3019.

Walther G., Post, E., Convey, P., Menzel, A., Parmesan, C., Beebee, T., Fromentin, J., Hoegh-Guldberg, O., Bairlein, F., 2002. Ecological responses to recent climate change. Nature 416, 389–395.

Section VII—Health Effects of Climate Change

27. Biofuels, Fossil Fuels, and Human Health

Christina Mainero

Biofuels have come into vogue fairly recently, offering what many self-proclaimed environmentalists and environmental scientists deem to be a plausible alternative to traditional petroleum-based fuels. The idea that we potentially can power our cars, trains, planes, and the like with the unused remnants of biological materials that we are producing as food already, appears to be the perfect solution to several environmental concerns. Some of the materials that otherwise would be left behind (for example, corn husks and corn stover) may be promising sources of fuel, allowing what would otherwise be agricultural waste to be used productively by society.

However, there are some concerns about the use of biofuels, including their economic feasibility and their ability to be equally effective and efficient energetically as petroleum-based fuels. One of the primary concerns also associated with traditional fuels is their effects on human health. In order to truly assess whether biofuels are good alternatives to traditional petroleum-based fuels, all their potential environmental impacts will have to be considered, along with economic and energetic considerations.

Researchers are studying the ways in which these fuels impact air quality, and, thus, human health. Hill *et al.* (2009) examined the environmental impacts of different types of biofuels compared with gasoline. Specifically, they looked at the climate change and health costs of greenhouse gas (GHG) and fine particulate matter ($PM_{2.5}$) emissions and determined that cellulosic ethanol is less costly than corn-based ethanol and gasoline, though there are regional differences in these shifts due to divergent production systems.

Pearce *et al.* (2009) also examined the potential danger to human health associated with biomass combustion in Cusco, Peru. They compared the CO and $PM_{2.5}$ emissions associated with food preparation in the morning, afternoon, and evening produced by several types of fuels. They determined that dung emits the greatest amount of pollutants, followed by wood, kerosene and gas.

Similarly, Orru *et al.* (2009) did a case study examining the threat of particulate matter to human health in Tartu, Estonia. Their research specifically investigated the dispersion and deposition of emissions from the combustion of peat biofuel and determined an estimate for the years of life lost (YLL) due to such emissions. They concluded that the threat to air quality by particulate matter emissions from peat biofuel combustion was marginal in comparison to the overall emissions induced by all pollutant sources in the city.

Some researchers have examined the hazards associated with the production of sugarcane as a biofuel, determining that fires associated with the cultivation and harvest of sugarcane are detrimental to human health. For example, Uriarte *et al.* (2009) considered the relationship among sugarcane production, fire occurrence, and the respiratory health of the children and the elderly in São Paolo, Brazil. Moreover, they predicted how the expansion of sugarcane cultivation would affect the number of fires and, thus, the respiratory health of the children and the elderly in the region.

Along the same lines, Kyu *et al.* (2009) analyzed the effects of exposure to maternal smoking, non-maternal smoking, and biofuels on the height of children under the age of five across seven developing countries. Although there were mixed results regarding the effects of maternal smoking on the height of the children, height was negatively correlated with both non-maternal smoking and biofuel exposure. Furthermore, biofuel exposure specifically was strongly connected with stunted or severely stunted growth among these children.

Hewitt *et al.* (2009) examined the effects of converting rainforests to oil palm plantations in Malaysia, discovering that oil palm plantations actually emit a far greater amount of volatile organic compounds and nitrous oxides than rainforests. These nitrous oxides and volatile organic compounds often react to form ozone in the presence of sunlight, which negatively impacts human health. In order to mitigate this potential threat, the researchers proposed the creation of nitrogen management schemes, controlling and managing nitrogen levels, in order to protect air quality.

Other researchers have studied the concentration of mutagenic and carcinogenic polycyclic aromatic hydrocarbons (PAH) emitted by various types of fuels combusted in diesel engines. Krahl *et al.* (2009) inspected the mutagenic effects caused by such diesel engine emissions, comparing rapeseed oil, rapeseed methyl ester, gas-to-liquid, and petrodiesel fuels. Their study concluded that rapeseed oil, which has increasingly been used as a traditional fuel alternative in Germany, had much more strongly mutagenic extracts and condensates than all of the other fuels. Furthermore, the researchers speculated that such mutagenic effects would also be present when using other types of vegetable oils bearing similar fatty acid components.

Similarly, Ballesteros *et al.* (2009) investigated the carcinogenic effects of PAHs emitted by three biofuels compared with a conventional fuel. The researchers used a fairly new method for conducting a chemical speciation of the sixteen PAHs considered to be the most threatening to human health. In examining the relationship between the type, the amount, and the carcinogenic potential of these PAHs in fuels and biofuels, the researchers concluded that biofuels emit far less total PAHs and are less hazardous to human health than traditional fuel emissions.

With increased investigation of the potential consequences of the production and utilization of biofuels, our society will be better informed when comparing and contrasting the advantages and disadvantages of biofuels and traditional fuels. Such research will allow us to determine the hidden health hazards of various biofuels and fuels. With this knowledge, we can determine whether or not certain biofuels are as effective as traditional fuels in light of environmental, economic, and health considerations.

Cellulosic Ethanol Has Lower Climate Change and Health Costs than Corn Ethanol and Gasoline

Hill *et al.* (2009) analyzed the environmental impacts of several different types of biofuels and petroleum-based fuels. Their study concluded that the climate change and health costs of greenhouse gases (GHG) and fine particulate matter ($PM_{2.5}$) emissions of cellulosic ethanol were significantly lower than those of corn ethanol and gasoline. They also determined that the health impacts due to $PM_{2.5}$ emissions vary by region according to the magnitude of fuel production. This study calculated these costs by looking at the three methods for producing corn ethanol in biorefineries (through natural gas, coal, or corn stover heating) and comparing them with the costs of the four methods of producing cellulosic ethanol (corn stover, switchgrass, diverse prairie biomass, or *Miscanthus*). The cost of producing these biofuels was then compared with the cost of producing gasoline.

Hill *et al.* determined the cost of emissions incurred from these different types of fuels and demonstrated the existence of regional disparities in these costs caused by production system differences. They made a number of assumptions in order to compare the seven methods for producing these different types of fuel, including that all of the fuel production occurred in the United States, that there were no significant land-use changes in order to produce the biofuels, and that no crops were displaced due to biofuel production. Furthermore, they used the Greenhouse Gases, Regulated Emissions, and Energy Use in Transportation (GREET) model to analyze the bulk of the GHG and $PM_{2.5}$ emissions, conducting separate analyses to track both emissions caused by $PM_{2.5}$ formation and GHG emissions caused by land-use changes.

To estimate the costs of the GHG emissions created by production of corn ethanol, cellulosic ethanol, and gasoline, Hill *et al.* used estimates of carbon mitigation costs, carbon market prices, and the "social cost of carbon," a term which they defined as the estimated cost to society of potential carbon-related damage in the future. The "social cost of carbon" was the most variable of these three terms since there is much dispute over the way to analyze the cost-benefit ratio of future costs of carbon damage.

Unlike GHG emissions, $PM_{2.5}$ emissions cannot be considered on a global scale. Instead, they must be considered on a much more regional scale that accounts for factors such as population density as well as the density of fuel and biofuel production sites. To estimate the $PM_{2.5}$ emissions for each county in the United States, the researchers used a model called the Response Surface Model (RSM), which uses equally-sized cells to quantify changes in the emissions levels throughout the country while demonstrating the community health impacts of such emissions in a particular area.

Hill *et al.* concluded that all of the methods for producing cellulosic ethanol have lower GHG emissions than the methods of producing corn-based ethanol and gasoline. Additionally, they found that corn ethanol does not always emit fewer GHGs than gasoline. Instead, the amount of greenhouse gases produced depends on several factors, including technological assumptions, significant changes in land use, and the type of heat source used in the biorefineries.

Similarly, the RSM spatial data indicated that cellulosic ethanol also has the lowest $PM_{2.5}$ emissions of the fuels examined. Additionally, the research indicated that all of the methods used to produce corn ethanol have higher health costs than gasoline due to $PM_{2.5}$ emissions.

Overall, the data suggested that the relative climate change and health costs of a billion ethanol-equivalent gallons of fuel were $123–208 million for cellulosic ethanol, $469 million for gasoline, and $472–952 million for corn ethanol. Although methods of producing cellulosic ethanol must become more economically feasible in order to be a practical alternative to traditional petroleum-based fuels, this research is important because it suggests a strong link between biofuels, fuels, and health, while enumerating some of the economic consequences of their interactions with one another.

Biomass Fuel Combustion is a Potential Danger to Human Health in Cusco, Peru

Pearce *et al.* (2009) studied the use of biofuels for household energy in Cusco, determining that the combustion of these fuels resulted in potentially dangerous levels of $PM_{2.5}$ and CO emissions. Combined with the hypoxic stress of high-altitude living, this is a very real threat to human health. The study concluded that the levels of $PM_{2.5}$ emissions present in kitchens were 4.4 times higher than those in secondary rooms and 9.4 times higher than those in outside entryways. Similarly, the CO concentrations were highest in kitchens, with concentrations averaging 4.8 times more than secondary rooms and 3.3 times more than outdoor entryways. They found that the highest levels of CO and $PM_{2.5}$ emissions occurred with the combustion of dung, followed by wood, kerosene, and gas, respectively.

The goal of this study by Pearce *et al.* was to measure the average indoor and outdoor CO and $PM_{2.5}$ emissions at 41 residences in Cusco during the preparation of meals in the morning, afternoon, and evening. Measurements of CO and $PM_{2.5}$ emissions were taken at breathing level to mimic human exposure to these pollutants. The measurements were taken in three different locations in each residence—the kitchen, the room designated as the second most used room, and the front entryway outside each home. To minimize any discrepancies, the concentration levels of both CO and $PM_{2.5}$ were collected simultaneously.

Statistical analyses of the data on $PM_{2.5}$ emissions demonstrated that emissions caused by the combustion of wood are significantly higher than those caused by kerosene, while those from dung are significantly higher than those caused by gas. Furthermore, in secondary rooms, $PM_{2.5}$ emissions from wood combustion were significantly higher than those from gas. Similarly, wood emissions of CO in kitchens were significantly higher than gas emissions. Overall, the median CO and $PM_{2.5}$ emissions were highest for the combustion of dung, followed by wood, kerosene, and gas, respectively. Kitchens, where the food preparation occurred, tended to have the highest concentrations of CO and $PM_{2.5}$, followed by the secondary rooms and then the outdoor entryways. Furthermore, the general trend seemed to show that the greatest concentration of pollutant emissions occurred in the morning, which the authors suggested was due to the fact that large meals tend to be prepared in the morning and simply reheated throughout the rest of the day in Cusco.

However, Pearce *et al.* noted that there were several limitations in their study, including the small sample size, the shortness of the data collection period, the lack of an even distribution of measurements across the different fuel types, and the fact that the measurements of pollutant concentrations did not actually measure the number of human exposures to CO and $PM_{2.5}$ emissions. Despite these limitations, this study is interesting in that it notes the potential dangers of the combustion of biofuels and fuels in the preparation of food, particularly in developing countries, such as Peru.

Health Hazards Caused by Peat Biofuel Combustion are Minimal in Tartu

Orru *et al.* (2009) investigated the potential health impacts of the increased combustion of peat biofuel in Tartu, Estonia, by calculating the dispersion and deposition of particulate matter emissions and estimating the number of years of life lost (YLL) caused by such emissions. Using the AEROPOL model and AirQ software to illustrate and identify the effects on health, the researchers concluded that peat biofuel combustion caused an average of 55.5 YLL each year per 100,000 individuals. However, this value was marginal in comparison to their estimated value of 1539 years of life lost from all environmental sources of pollution in Tartu each year. Thus, they concluded that the hazards to human health caused by increased emissions from peat biofuel production were insignificant when compared with overall particulate matter emissions from traffic pollution and local heating.

Orru *et al.* sought to assess whether or not the transition from gas to peat biofuel combustion would seriously impact the health of individuals due to potential changes in air quality. To calculate and estimate these effects, their model included the following measurements: a calculation of emissions, an assessment of the ambient air quality, the identification of at-risk individuals, and a quantification of the health effects. Because peat content varies widely in composition, which can affect its health implications, they determined the percentages of ash, sulfur, trace elements, and heavy metals prior to conducting the study. The AEROPOL model was used to calculate the average emission of pollutants from boiler houses. The researchers created dispersion maps and compared them with population density information to determine the boundaries of the exposure area near the boiler houses. The AirQ software then calculated the average YLL in the area. To assess base-line air quality, Orru *et al.* conducted official air pollution monitoring of PM, SO_2, NO_2, and CO emissions in five different areas throughout the city.

The results of this study demonstrated that the most health hazardous emissions from the boiler houses, the $PM_{2.5}$ emissions, dispersed in a fairly small area and persisted for only a short period of time. According to the researchers, the mean annual pollutant concentrations from other sources were well over 20 times higher than those from boiler houses. For those individuals in the more highly exposed areas, the calculated YLL per year was 36, while it was 19.5 for those outside the exposed area. However, these values seem almost negligible when considering the fact that the total YLL induced by all pollution sources each year has an estimated value of 1539. The concentrations of SO_2, CO, and O_3 from the boiler houses were low.

However, the researchers noted that there were some shortcomings in their analysis. For example, the air quality in Tartu was measured only once each year over a two-week period, which may not have allowed the most accurate characterization of air quality. Additionally, the 95% confidence interval on the YLL was large, which was partially due to the fact that YLL was determined by a number of different factors. Although there were some uncertainties associated with this study, the researchers concluded that the YLL caused by peat burning was not a significant threat to air quality or human health.

Sugarcane-Associated Fires Are Detrimental to Respiratory Health: A Case Study in São Paolo

Researchers in São Paolo, Brazil investigated the current effects of sugarcane-associated fires on the respiratory health of the children and the elderly in the region. Additionally, Uriarte et al. (2009) predicted how the recent expansion of sugarcane land might impact the number of fires in the region, and, thus, the respiratory health of the populace. They used data from a variety of sources in addition to the data that they collected themselves to show that seasonal variations in respiratory morbidity could be attributed to sugarcane-associated fire occurrences. Thus, they determined that burning sugarcane fields is a significant health hazard for the children and the elderly in the region and suggested that the recent expansion of sugarcane-dedicated land would lead to an increase in respiratory hospital admissions related to sugarcane fires.

Uriarte et al. (2009) explored the relationship among sugarcane production and cultivation for biofuel, fires associated with harvesting this sugarcane, and the respiratory health of the children and the elderly in São Paolo. Additionally, they predicted how increases in sugarcane-dedicated land would affect the prevalence of fires and the respiratory health of the population in the region. The researchers gathered data regarding the cultivation and production of the major crops in each municipality; statistics on the occurrence of fires standardized by municipality; monthly air quality data on the concentrations of smoke, particulate matter ($PM_{2.5}$), and total suspended particles in a subset of municipalities; hospital admissions for respiratory diseases of children and the elderly, and meteorological data on the total monthly precipitation and average monthly maximum temperature.

Although a greater number of children than elderly were admitted to hospitals for respiratory illnesses during the course of the year, fire-associated respiratory morbidity was roughly 1.8% for both populations. In municipalities where over 50% of the land was dedicated to sugarcane production, this morbidity percentage rose to 15% of cases among the elderly and 12% of cases among children. Furthermore, the authors suggested that 38% of respiratory cases among children were likely caused by current or chronic fire exposures caused by previous fires in the area.

The researchers looked at the data regarding the expansion of sugarcane-dedicated land and anticipated that such an expansion would lead to an additional 672 fires in the region. Their model predicted that these additional fires would cause an increase in the overall number of cases of respiratory illness of 4.8% among the elderly and 3.0% among children. However, this model also suggested that between 2003 and 2006 the number of cases of fire-associated respiratory illnesses would increase by 224% among the elderly and 177% among children.

The authors noted, though, that there were some limitations to their study, specifically that the fire occurrence data collected over the years was captured by two different satellites and that they could not access complete data for respiratory illnesses during some of the years. To account for and mitigate these issues, they used statistical modeling tools.

This research is important because it suggested that a vast array of different social, economic, health, and labor factors must be considered in assessing the viability of biofuel production in particular regions. Considering the societal and environmental costs of various biofuels is important given the interest in such fuels as a potential short-term solution to our world's energy needs.

Exposure to Cigarette and Biofuel Smoke May Negatively Affect the Height of Young Children

Various studies have proposed that exposure to carcinogenic fumes, traditional fuels, and biofuels may negatively affect the growth and development of children. Especially within developing countries, childhood exposure to cigarettes, tobacco, fuels, and biofuels is widespread. Kyu et al. (2009) specifically investigated whether or not the exposure of children under five years old to cigarette smoke and biofuels is correlated with their height relative to their age. Using multilevel regression analyses, the researchers determined that exposure to maternal smoking negatively affected the height of the children in only three of the developing countries studied while biofuel exposure negatively affected height across all seven countries. Moreover, for children under five years old, biofuel exposure is connected with stunting and severe stunting in height. Thus, this study demonstrated that such exposures to cigarettes and biofuels might hinder childhood growth for young children in developing countries.

In this study, Kyu et al. sought to examine the effects of maternal smoking and biofuel exposure on young children due to the rise of smoking and biofuel use in developing countries, the fact that maternal smoking may increase a child's likelihood of exposure, the paucity of information regarding the effects of maternal smoking on children under five years old, and the increased use of biofuels in developing countries. For the seven developing countries studied, data were collected between 2005 and 2007. In setting up their sampling scheme, the researchers divided each country into clusters of roughly fifteen to twenty women. Within each cluster, they measured the heights of the children and also conducted interviews with their mothers. In some clusters, they questioned a subset of men regarding their daily activities and habits. In doing this, the researchers were able to assess the effects of maternal smoking, exposure to smoking by other members of the house, and biofuel exposure on the height of the children. Factors such as child age, child gender, breastfeeding initiation, mother's age, mother's educational history, estimated birth size of the child, household wealth and country acted as covariates.

Based on the data collected, Kyu *et al.* concluded that the children of women with fewer financial resources, less education, and more children tend to have increased smoking and biofuel exposure. Additionally, their regression models indicated that maternal smoking correlated negatively with height in Cambodia, Namibia, and Nepal; correlated positively with child height in Moldova; and showed no significant correlation either way in the remaining countries. Exposure to non-maternal smoking and biofuels, however, demonstrated a significant negative correlation with the height of young children. Moreover, biofuel exposure appears to be connected with stunting and severe stunting within all of the countries studied.

However, the researchers also noted several limitations of this study. Specifically, they mentioned the fact that there were no data regarding maternal smoking and biofuel exposure during pregnancy, which may be an important factor influencing the height of the children. Furthermore, actual biofuel exposures were measured indirectly rather than directly based on the type of biofuel used for cooking and daily activities. Additionally, the study lacked information regarding the duration of exposure. Studies such as these, though important for looking into potential correlations, do not conclusively establish causation. Yet, this study is significant because its conclusions suggested that there might be notable detrimental health effects associated with biofuel use as well as maternal smoking. Such heath effects must be considered in evaluating whether or not biofuels are plausible alternatives to traditional, petroleum-based fuels.

Christina Mainero

NO$_X$ Emissions from Malaysian Oil Palm Plantations May Lead to Unhealthy Levels of O$_3$

Hewitt *et al.* (2009) examined the effect of converting rainforests to oil palm plantations in Malaysia. The production of palm oil has increased, partially due to the fact that the biofuel has been touted as "environmentally-friendly." However, using various measurements and models, the researchers discovered that oil palm plantations actually emit a far greater amount of nitrous oxides and volatile organic compounds (VOCs) than rainforests. This is especially problematic as nitrous oxides and VOCs can react in the presence of sunlight to create O$_3$, which is classified as an air pollutant with the potential to seriously damage human health, among other things. Should nitrous oxides in Malaysia reach levels comparable to those over rural North America and Europe, it is likely that O$_3$ levels could reach over 100 ppbv, well above the level known to be dangerous to human health. Thus, the authors concluded that nitrogen emission management schemes must be developed.

In their investigation, Hewitt *et al.* took fully integrated and comprehensive biosphere-to-atmosphere flux measurements and modeled the atmospheric chemistry of rainforests and oil palm plantations in the tropics. They determined that VOC emissions from both types of land tend to be dominated by isoprene, though the plantations emit five times as much of it as the rainforests, evidently because of biogenic emissions from oil palm trees. The researchers suggested that the emissions of VOC compounds from the oil palm plantations were greater than those of European cities, such as London. Moreover, their measurements suggested that oil palm plantations emit roughly 2.5 times as much nitrous oxide as rainforest land, a result of vehicle exhaust, combustion, and soil nitrogen fertilization.

Thus, the researchers demonstrated that land use change for the purpose of producing more "environmentally-friendly" biofuels can be problematic. Their results supported the notion that converting rainforest land to oil palm plantations for biofuel production purposes leads to increased emissions of nitrous oxides and volatile organic compounds (VOCs). Although levels of O$_3$ have not yet increased substantially, Hewitt *et al.* believed that ozone emissions will rise with the increased industrialization and production of nitrous oxides in the area. Such an increase in emissions will negatively impact human health. Moreover, the researchers noted the importance of controlling and managing nitrogen levels at local and regional scales in order to prevent significant changes in the air quality. Because of its potential cost to human health and crop productivity, the researchers argued that oil palm biofuel production might be fairly short-lived.

Rapeseed Oil Emits Significantly More Mutagenic and Carcinogenic PAH than Petrodiesel Fuel

With the increasing economic viability of a diverse array of biofuels, researchers in Germany measured the concentrations of polycyclic aromatic hydrocarbons
(PAH) in a variety of fuel and biofuel emissions since PAH are hazardous to human
health. Krahl *et al.* (2009) investigated the diesel engine emissions of rapeseed oil,
rapeseed methyl ester, gas-to-liquid fuel, and traditional petrodiesel fuel, noting the
mutagenic and carcinogenic content of these emissions for each fuel. To test the
mutagenicity of condensates and extracts from these fuels, the researchers used two
strains of the *Salmonella typhimurium* mammalian assay. The study determined that
rapeseed oil extracts and condensates were significantly more mutagenic than traditional petrodiesel. Furthermore, rapeseed methyl ester also exhibited significantly
higher mutagenic effects than the petrodiesel, whereas the gas-to-liquid fuel did
not.

Krahl *et al.* (2009) examined how the combustion of various fuels impacts the
overall mutagenicity of diesel engine emissions. To conduct their investigation, the
researchers used a Mercedes-Benz OM 906 LA engine and collected, gravimetrically
massed, and analyzed emissions of hydrocarbons, carbon monoxide, nitrogen
oxides, and particulate matter. In order to determine the mutagenic effects of these
different emissions, they collected three sets of condensates and particulate matter
extracts for each of the fuels. The researchers tested each of the extracts and condensates from the various fuels for mutagenic properties using the mammalian mi-
crosome assay, *Salmonella typhimurium,* which detects mutagens through reverse
mutation strains. They used those strains of *S. typhimurium,* which had previously
shown the greatest sensitivity in detecting frameshift mutations and base-pair substitutions in diesel fuels, where an increased number of revertant colonies indicated a
mutagenic response.

The study by Krahl *et al.* (2009) indicated that emissions of hydrocarbons and
carbon monoxide were well below limits set by Euro 3 for all of the tested fuels and
biofuels. Rapeseed methyl ester had the lowest carbon monoxide emissions, followed by the rapeseed oil, petrodiesel, and gas-to-liquid fuels, respectively. Although the emissions levels of nitrogen oxides from petrodiesel and gas-to-liquid
fuels remained just below those allowed by Euro 3, the emissions from rapeseed oil
and rapeseed methyl ester exceeded this limit. Particulate matter emissions were
below the outlined limits for all of the fuels, with gas-to-liquid and rapeseed methyl
ester demonstrating significant reductions in these emissions. Rapeseed oil emitted
a far greater amount of nitrogen oxides and particulate matter than the traditional
petrodiesel fuel, indicating that rapeseed oil, while economically viable, may not be
the best alternative to petrodiesel when considering its impacts on human health.

Unlike the other fuels, the condensates and extracts of the rapeseed oil emissions led to a significant increase in mutagenic effects when tested with the *S. typhimurium* strains.

Although rapeseed oil exhibited a much higher mutagenicity of its diesel engine emissions than the other fuels, the researchers noted that rapeseed oil is not particularly disadvantageous when examining regulated exhaust emissions, such as carbon monoxide, nitrogen oxides, particulate matter, and total hydrocarbons. However, its emissions do have relatively strong mutagenic effects in comparison to the other fuels, which is likely due to the fact that it is a triacylglycerol, meaning that it decomposes at high temperatures such as those experienced during combustion. Products formed by this decomposition pose particularly dangerous hazards to human health. This study clearly indicated that other considerations beyond economic viability, such as health impacts, must be considered in order to ascertain which biofuels are the best substitutes for traditional fuels.

Biofuels Significantly Reduce the Health Hazards Caused by Polycyclic Aromatic Hydrocarbons

Several previous studies have suggested that various fuels emit carcinogenic polycyclic aromatic hydrocarbons (PAHs). Ballesteros *et al.* (2009) examined the relationship between the amount of oil, the type of oil, and the carcinogenic potential of three biofuels and a conventional fuel. The researchers conducted a chemical speciation of the sixteen most hazardous PAHs associated with fuel combustion using a newly developed method combining processes of thermal extraction, solid-phase micro-extraction (SPME), and GC/MS analysis. The researchers found that using biofuels rather than conventional fuels reduced total PAH emissions as well as the risks to human health from these emissions. Furthermore, they determined that PAH emissions depend on the oil used for the transesterfication process.

Ballesteros *et al.* inspected the mutagenicity of the sixteen PAHs considered to be hazardous to human health. To determine the impact on human health of the type and origin of vegetable oil used for transesterfication compared with a reference fuel, the researchers conducted a chemical speciation on these compounds. Additionally, they collected data on the gaseous non-methane hydrocarbons emissions, the diesel particulate matter emissions, volatile organic matter emissions, mean particle diameter, and particle opacity for the biofuels and the reference fuel. In order to properly compare the emissions for these different fuels, the researchers made sure that the exhaust gas recirculation ratio remained constant. Moreover, they examined all of the fuels in two different operating modes: extraurban and urban. The three biofuels used in this study were rapeseed methyl ester (RSM), waste cooking oil methyl ester (WCOM), and waste cooking oil ethyl ester (WCOE), which were then compared to the conventional reference fuel.

To accurately gauge the health risks associated with the different fuels, Balles-teros *et al.* used a conversion factor, called the toxicity equivalent factor (TEF). This conversion factor provided them with a carcinogenic equivalence sum (KE) that represented the inherent carcinogenicity of each of these PAHs. All three biofuels showed a reduction in KE, indicating that biofuel emissions are less hazardous to human health than conventional fuels. For the RSM WCOM, and WCOE, there was a notable reduction in the emissions of the PAHs with higher molecular weights, which tend to have more carcinogenic potential. Unlike the RSM, the biofuels originating from cooking waste oils emitted significantly higher levels of lighter PAHs than the conventional fuels. However, the health risk to humans was still lower than that associated with the use of conventional fuels because PAHs with lower molecular weights tend to be far less carcinogenic than those with high molecular weights. The researchers concluded that using biofuels not only reduces the overall amount of PAH emissions, but also diminishes negative health impacts when compared with conventional fuels. Moreover, they determined that the type of oil used for the process of transesterfication significantly influences the emission of heavy or light PAHs, which, in turn, dictates their effects on human health. Thus, this study suggested that certain biofuels may be less toxic to human health than conventional biofuels, advancing the case for biofuels as plausible alternatives to conventional fuel sources.

Conclusions

In recent years, our society has seen the advent of first and second-generation biofuels as possible alternatives to traditional petroleum-based fuels. Because of the scarcity of traditional fuels and the deleterious effects that they can have on the health of the environment and of the population, there has been a considerable amount of interest in the use of biofuels as viable fuel alternatives. However, before our society jumps headlong into the production of various types of biofuels, it is necessary that we research their effects and consequences on the environment and the health of the population. Such consequences are essential in weighing the ad-vantages and disadvantages of using these different types of fuels to power our so-ciety.

Various studies have demonstrated that biofuels can, in fact, pose serious health hazards. More research must be done to investigate and understand the po-tential health hazards of creating and using biofuels, so that these hazards can be taken into consideration alongside their environmental and economic impacts. For example, various types of biofuels and mechanisms of biofuel production have different consequences for the environment and health. Many studies have compared the emissions of CO_2, fine particulate matter, ozone, other greenhouse gases, and polycyclic aromatic hydrocarbons among various types of fuels and biofuels. Some studies have looked at these emissions in the context of combusting fuels in car engines while others have looked at the effects of emissions produced from fuel use in food preparation and agriculture. In conducting further research, we will be able to garner a much better and more complete understanding of the positive and negative consequences of switching from traditional fuel to biofuel production for energy. Such information will vitally influence the direction of biofuel research, development, and utilization in the years to come.

References Cited

Ballesteros, R., Hernandez, J.J., Lyons, L.L., 2009. An experimental study of the influence of biofuel origin on particle-associated PAH emissions. Atmospheric Environment 44, 930–938.

Hewitt, C., MacKenzie, A., DiCarlo, P., Di Marco, C., Dorsey, J., Evans, M., Fowler, D., Gallagher, M., Hopkins. J., Jones, C., Langford, B., Lee, J., Lewis, A., Lim, S. McQuaid, J.. Misztal, P., Moller, S., Monks, P., Nemitz, E., Oram, D., Owen, S., Phillips, G., Pugh, T., Pyle, J., Reeves, C., Ryder, J., Slong, J., Skiba, U., and Stewart, D., 2009. Nitrogen management is essential to prevent tropical oil palm plantations from causing ground-level ozone pollution. PNAS 106, 18447–18451.

Hill, J., Polasky, S., Nelson, E., Tilman, D., Huo, H., Ludwig, L., Neumann, J., Zheng, H., Bonta, D., 2009. Climate change and health costs of air emissions from biofuels and gasoline. PNAS 106, 2077–2082.

Krahl, J., Knothe, G., Munack, A., Ruschel, Y., Schröder, O., Hallier, E., Westphal, G., Bünger, J., 2009. Comparison of exhaust emissions and their mutagenicity from the combustion of biodiesel, vegetable oil, gas-to-liquid and petrodiesel fuels. Fuel 88, 1064–1069.

Kyu, H.H., Georgiades, K., and Boyle, M.H., 2009. Maternal smoking, biofuel smoke exposure and child height-for-age in seven developing countries. International Journal of Epidemiology 38, 1342–1350.

Orru, H., Kaasik, M., Merisalu, E., Forsberg, B., 2009. Health impact assessment in case of biofuel peat—Co-use of environmental scenarios and exposure-response functions. Biomass and Bioenergy 33, 1080–1086.

Pearce, J., Aguilar-Villalobos, M., Rathbun, S., Naeher, L., 2009. Residential exposures to $PM_{2.5}$ and CO in Cusco, a high altitude city in the Peruvian Andes: A Pilot Survey. Archives of Environmental and Occupational Health 64, 278–282.

Uriarte, M., Yackulic, C., Cooper, T., Flynn, D., Cortes, M., Crk, T., Cullman, G., McGinty, M., Sircely, J., 2009. Expansion of sugarcane production in São Paulo, Brazil: Implications for fire occurrence and respiratory health. Agriculture, Ecosystems and Environment 132, 48–56.

28. Natural Sources of Medicine and Possible Effects of Climate Change

Kevon White

Medicines have always been an important tool for human civilizations, especially in current times when more diseases are emerging and there are less effective ways of combating them. Though synthetic medicines are commonly used for medical treatments, the potential of natural medicine resources have led scientists to discover new ways of treating and curing diseases. Different forms of natural medicines have been applied to a variety of health-related issues; food items can be used to prevent "flesh-eating" bacteria, antioxidants can be extracted from biofuels, and bacteria can used to eliminate dangerous pollutants. Natural medicines include any medicine source that is derived from compounds produced by animals, plants, bacteria, or any other living organism. The effects of global warming and climate change can therefore limit the availability of these medicines and even increase the rates of human disease. Owing to environmental destruction, fewer natural medicines will be become available for human use, severely limiting the potential for finding new cures and treatments. The studies in this chapter focus on how natural medicines are used by local populations, what type of natural resources are currently available, the impacts of natural medicine on the environment and human health, and the impacts of climate change on human health.

Humans have used natural medicines for thousands of years, incorporating a myriad of plants and animals to treat health problems, but the use of locally grown or harvested natural medicines has been restricted primarily to rural populations in modern times. Even so, a number of the species used in making natural medicines have been listed as either endangered or vulnerable, limiting their availability. R. Alves and colleagues studied the effects of locally obtained natural medicines on rural cultures in Brazil and and M. Panghal and colleagues studied them in India. A survey and several interviews were conducted in both studies to determine how the local populations used a particular plant or animal species to treat certain illnesses.

Alves and colleagues found that 36 local animal species were favored for medical use in the regions of northeastern Brazil, and 22 of these were listed by different organizations as endangered. M. Panghal and colleagues found that out of the 57 plant species used to treat illnesses—including poisonings from snake bites—29 were listed as vulnerable or data deficient. Both studies reported that more information would be needed about cultural perceptions and medical knowledge in order to protect the local species or determine if they have any use in western medicine.

New sources of natural medicine have been identified with promising results; in particular those that come from already known resources have shown new medical potential. Two examples of renewable natural medicine resources include switchgrass and *Leptospermum* honey. N. Uppugundla and colleagues found that the antioxidants rutin and quercitrin could be extracted from switchgrass (*Panicum virgatum*)—a perennial grass native to North America—before the plant was turned into biofuel. E. Blair and colleagues showed that *Leptospermum* honey has profound implications in modernized medicine. This honey, derived from the *Leptospermum* species of "tea" tree, has been used in Australia and the United Kingdom as a medicine called Medihoney® that prevents and treats MRSA and other antibiotic-resistant bacteria from infecting open wounds (Blair *et al.* 2009). It is especially useful in hospital environments where open surgical wounds can likely be infected by antibiotic-resistant bacteria leading to more complications in a patient. The findings may lead to new potential pharmaceutical uses of natural medicines in both food and drug industries.

Recently, human health has been threatened by toxins from environmental pollution. Of the different forms of pollution, water pollution is one of the most difficult to eliminate from the environment. In particular, freshwater sources provide drinking and tap water which are recycled in sewage treatment facilities. However, not everything is filtered out in these facilities; among other things, pharmaceuticals may remain intact in treated wastewater, and heavy metals may not be removed either (Elkarmi *et al.* 2009). Toxins produced by marine algal blooms can enter commercial fisheries through bio-accumulation from fish and shellfish that have previously consumed the algae (Donovan *et al.* 2009). Environmental pollutants entering human food markets and water systems can cause devastating health effects which range from birth defects to instant paralysis (Donovan *et al.* 2009 and Elkami *et al.* 2009). However several remedies, in particular bacteria, have been discovered that can eliminate environmental toxins by completely degrading them into an innocuous form. Elkarmi and colleagues found that the bacterium *Pseudomonas alcaligenes* was able to completely biodegrade the waste compound 2,4-dichlorophenol (DCP), a waste product of pharmaceutical industries. In another study, Donovan and colleagues found that the bacteria genus *Pseudoalteromonas* were effective at biodegrading toxins from the toxic algae *Alexandrium tamarense*.

The bacteria, which can found in blue mussels, exhibited the ability to completely break down paralytic shellfish toxins (PST).

Climate change from global warming has been an increasing concern of environmental agencies because of the potential devastation it can cause to the world's ecosystems. In the case of medicine, increasing global temperatures could mean an increase in the number of human disease cases. Two studies included in this chapter looked into the potential damaging effects of climate change as it involved disease incidence rates. One, by Patrick Rydén and colleagues, modeled the incidences of tularemia disease in Sweden from 2010–2100. The model they used was based on preliminary data obtained from the incidences of tularemia disease in the years 1997–2008. Their study found that the duration of tularemia disease outbreaks increased due to a 2°C increase. The other study by Lampouguin Bayentin and colleagues determined if there was a relationship between temperature extremes and the rates if ischemic heart disease (IHD). For their study they analyzed all of the reported hospital cases of IHD in Quebec, Canada between the years 1989–2006 for people between the ages of 45–64 and those 65 years and older. The data showed that the rates of IHD were exacerbated by the prevalence of smoking, and longer periods of temperature extremes increased the number of IHD hospitalizations than short periods of dramatic temperature change. Based on these studies an increase in temperature could mean an increase in the duration of disease onset, thus diseases with naturally reoccurring periods such as influenza may have those periods prolonged. A prolonged period of disease onset means more incidences of disease, which would eventually affect health care and medicine.

Utilizing Animals as Materials for Indigenous Medicines in Brazil

The local human populations in northeastern Brazil use the nearby wild and domesticated fauna to create animal-based remedies that have had little known clinical analysis in western medicine. However, these medicines involve many different endangered species. Therefore, the use of these medicines can have severe environmental and ecological impacts, not only on the ecosystem but also on the native culture of Brazil. Brazil possesses 70% of the world's cataloged animal and plant species and contains between 15% and 20% of the world's biodiversity (Alves et al. 2009). Thus it is important to find the proper economic and ecological solution in which the species can be maintained without major damage to the ecosystem and in which the animal resources are economically sustainable for the local population.

Rômulo R.N. Alves and his colleagues from various biology departments held interviews with eleven merchants of different medicinal shops in the municipality of Caruaru. They conducted interviews in which the owner stated the type of animal that was used in the medicine, the parts of the animal used, its vernacular name, the mode of preparation, administration of the medicine, and the intended use of the product. The colloquial names were then verified with the scientific name to determine the actual species used in the product. The reported therapeutic effects were categorized into ten separate classifications based on known diseases. Then the informant consensus factor (ICF) was calculated to determine which taxa were consistently needed for any particular ailment. The relative importance (RI) of the species was lastly calculated to determine how useful a particular species was in creating a variety of medicines.

Thirty-six species were found to be used in the production of local medicines including 26 vertebrates and ten invertebrates. Of the 36 species, 28 were obtained from the wild and 22 are listed as endangered under various organizations. The rest include domesticated species such as fowl, cows, and donkeys. The trade for medicinal fauna in Brazil is widespread, allowing for many remedies to spread across the country. The body parts of the fauna are used by locals to clinically treat multiple diseases, even though there are insufficient studies to support claims of efficacy. Of the body parts used most often, fat was found to be used for multiple purposes; gastrointestinal and respiratory issues were the most quoted illnesses that required animal medicines; and skin disease was found to have the highest informant consensus factor. The placebo effects of the medicines are generally agreed upon by the Brazilian merchants, however, and this agreement implies that folk remedies are entwined with Brazilian culture. The use of animal remedies in Brazilian culture suggests that more research be placed in understanding the actual effects of folk remedies. In addition, more efforts are needed in creating a balance between the preservation of the ecosystem and the continuation of Brazilian culture. The relationship between the two concepts may lead to future improvements in modern medicine and may provide significant insight on the importance of preserving wildlife.

Threatened Plant Species in Northern India Provide Medical Treatments for Snake-Bites

Snake-charmers in the Jhajjar District, Haryana, India used over 57 medicinal plant species from 35 families and 51 genera for treating various diseases. Nineteen of the 57 medical plants were used to treat snake bites, which were found to be more prevalent during rainy seasons (Manju Panghal *et al.* 2010). Thirty-eight of the plant medicines were used to treat 18 different types of ailments ranging from mouth ulcers to sexual impotence. The potential of these folk medicines as antivenoms or treatments for various diseases is important for several economic and medical reasons. However, 29 species were stated to be vulnerable, sporadic in distribution, or data deficient, thus the effects of habitat destruction could potentially and inevitably affect this community due to a loss of resources.

Manju Panghal and colleagues from University Rohtak conducted interviews with 42 "Nath" community medical practitioners consisting of 41 males and one female. A survey was issued requesting information about the sources of plant materials, descriptions of the plant species including common names, the parts of the plants used for curing ailments, medical recipes obtained from plant material, and administration of the plant derived drugs. Several plants were collected from the Jhaj-jar District then analyzed and identified by the Forest Research Institute in Dehradun, India. Plant samples were compared with known plant populations found around Haryana, India, then classified according to growth type, spatial distribution patterns, and relative abundance.

Fifty-seven native plant species comprising of 35 families and 51 genera were used by local medicine practitioners with 27 of those species found to be safe, while 29 were found to either be vulnerable or data deficient. Of the 35 plant families, 13 families consisting of 19 species were used to treat snakebites, while 34 families consisting of 48 species were used in the treatment of 18 other diseases and ailments. The most common families used by practitioners included *Fabaceae* with eight species, *Liliaceae* with five species, followed by *Laminaceae* and *Asteraceae* with three species each. The different plant species included 20 herbs (36%), 16 trees (28%), 10 climbers (18%), 9 shrubs (16%) and one creeper (2%). The most common parts of the plants used were the leaves (27%), roots (23%), fruits (10%), seeds (10%), stem barks (9%), whole plant (7%), latex (6%), root bark (4%), flower (3%), and gum (1%). Drugs were applied in the forms of infusion at 23%, powder at 16%, decoction at 10%, and paste at 10% of the total drug application varieties. The different plant-derived drugs were administered through oral tract (63%), on the skin (23%), through the eyes (6%), topically in the mouth (5%), and nasal tract (3%). Of the plant medicines used to treat snake bites, 80% were applied orally from infusion or decoction and 20% were applied topically on the snake bite area. The use of traditional medicine is threatened by a further westernizing society due to wildlife concerns, thus increased efforts in recognizing the potential economic use of traditional medicinal plant species are needed for improving modern medicine.

Is Honey an Effective Medicine for Antibiotic Resistant Diseases?

Leptospermum honey is effective against various types of antibiotic resistant bacteria including *Staphylococcus aureus,* (MRSA), *Acinetobacter calcoaceticus,* and *Escherichia coli.* Additionally the bacteria show no resistance to *Leptospermum* honey even after repeated exposure (Blair *et al.* 2009). *Leptospermum* honey was found to be effective at low concentrations from 4% to 14.8%. It acts differently from other antimicrobial agents by providing moisture, sugars, and hydrogen peroxide as well as an unprecedented number of compounds that have yet to be fully researched. As there are few scientific studies that support the use of honey in wound treatment, more will be needed to understand all of the effects of using honey to treat or prevent infections caused by antibiotic resistant diseases.

S.E. Blair and Colleagues from the University of Sydney and the University of Technology in Sydney conducted several tests using four different types of honey: Medihoney®, *Leptospermum* honey, Lucerne Blueweed honey, and a controlled artificial honey made from several sugars. The Medihoney® was added slowly to various agar plates containing 13 different types of infectious bacteria. The MIC was then recorded from the results. A marcodilution method test was done later in which all four honeys were diluted with water and was slowly added to the bacteria to determine the MBC of the bacterium. The results of the different honeys were compared with those of Oxcallin, Tetracycline, and Ciprofloxacin. The different honeys along with the three antibiotic medicines were tested repeatedly over the bacterial strains to determine resistance capabilities. Lastly, a macroarray analysis was performed on 6% honey solutions of Medihoney® and the inactive *Leptospermum* honey. A culture of E. coli was then combined with the honeys to determine the gene expression of the two samples.

The Medihoney® inhibited the growth of bacteria significantly compared to the artificial control honey. The MIC for the Medihoney® ranged from 4%–16% while the artificial honey's MIC ranged from 20% to beyond 25%. Of the bacteria in the first experiment, MRSA had the least resistance to honey, but it resisted the artificial honey by nearly five times that value. Though the honey is less effective at first, the bacteria do not seem to develop any resistance to it, even after being subjected to repeated trials of honey. When compared to Oxacillin, Tetracyclinen and Ciprofloxacin the percentage of honey needed to inhibit bacterial growth initially was much higher; however, unlike the previous three medicines, the honey does not allow the bacteria to develop a resistance to it. The expression of several E. coli genes when mixed with honey indicates that it may cause a significant change in the protein and binding structures of the bacteria. One-hundred-twenty-four genes were found to be upregulated or downregulated by the presence of honey. Of these genes, most were associated with stress responses in the bacteria. This indicates that honey may have an effect on the bacterial gene sequence and may interfere with protein synthesis. Another suggestion by Blair *et al.* is that the complex nature of the honey and a yet discovered compound could account for its effectiveness in eliminating antibiotic resistant bacteria. *Leptospermum* honey has demonstrated the ability to treat an unusually broad number of antibiotic resistant bacteria, and most importantly it is resilient against these strains. Thus its use in western medicine will be important in combating increasingly deadly strains of evolving bacteria.

Switchgrass: A New Source of Antioxidants

Switchgrass was found to contain the flavonoids rutin and quercitrin, providing antioxidant properties that inhibit human low-density lipoprotein (LDL) oxidation. Antioxidants from switchgrass (*Panicum virgatum*) were extracted using water and methanol, revealing several potential antioxidants that were identified through high-performance liquid chromatography (HPLC). The inhibition of oxidized LDL was found to be significant in both flavonoids in concentrations greater than 9 μM after 24 h (Uppugundla *et al.* 2009). Extraction of flavonoids using hot water in switchgrass could have potential industrial and economic uses, such as providing antioxidants for human consumption. It was also reported from Uppugundla *et al.* that switchgrass can be used as a biofuel; in which case the antioxidants from switchgrass would be extracted before the switchgrass is processed into fuel.

Nirmal Uppungundla and colleagues at the University of Arkansas lyophilized and pulverized *Panicum virgatum* and *Albizia julibrissin* plant material into 4 mm particles. Two types of switchgrass samples were prepared, one with water and another with a 60% methanol solution. Two grams of particulate switchgrass were blended with 30 mL of the respective extraction medium at 1000 rpm for 5 min in a blender; the blended mixtures were then filled with additional 30 mL extraction solution and heated in a water bath at 50, 70, 80, or 90°C for 20 min. The extracts were filtered, frozen at –20°C for 24 hours, immersed in liquid nitrogen and eventually lyophilized. The extracts from both procedures were analyzed by liquid chromatography and mass spectrometry. The *Panicum virgatum* extractions were performed in parallel with the *Albizia julibrissin* extractions to compare antioxidant compound identities. Both sets of extracts were then prepared and placed in a high-performance liquid chromatograph (HPLC) along with a photodiode array (PDA) for identifying the unknown antioxidant compounds. The solutions were then quantitatively analyzed by dissolving two milligrams of each extract in methanol to determine the highest yields of rutin and quercitrin. Centrifugal partition chromatography was used to purify and concentrate the rutin and quercitrin extracts, which were eventually analyzed for purity. The extracts were tested with copper mediated thiobarbituric acid reactive substances (TBARS) assay to determine inhibition of oxidized LDL. Purified switchgrass samples were prepared in dimethylsulfoxide (DMSO) with concentrations varying from 9, 19, 38, to 150 μM. The samples were separated further into 0 h wells and 25 h wells. The amount of TBARS formed was determined from the difference between the 0 h and the 24 h well samples. An ANOVA, student t-test, and a least squared fit were used to determine significance.

The LC-MS analysis of the switchgrass showed peaks at m/z 303, 465, and 611 for the rutin and m/z 303 and 449 for the Quercitrin, confirming their identities when compared to literature values and reference compounds. The 60% methanol extraction had a greater yield than the water extraction ranging from 502–620 mg/kg for rutin and 554–732 mg/kg for quercitrin at 50–90°C respectively. However, based on the student t-test and least-squares fit analyses the 60% methanol does not show a significant relationship between yield and temperature. The water extraction had a far lower yield ranging from 82–186 mg/kg for rutin and 37–193 mg/kg for quercitrin from 50–90°C respectively. However, the t-tests and least-squares fit analyses did indicate a significant relationship between yield and temperature. The purity of the isolated rutin and quercitrin was 61.4% and 76.7% respectively. Both the rutin and quercitrin showed a significant reduction of LDL oxidation by 70% in concentrations as low as 9 μM (with one exception from rutin at 9 μM). The feasibility of using water extraction over methanol extraction for flavonoids from switchgrass could have profound economic implications in food industry and its consumption as well as bio-fuel energy resources.

Paralytic Shellfish Toxins can be degraded by Bacteria found in Blue Mussels

Pseudoalteromonas, a genus of bacteria found in the toxic blue mussel, has the ability to almost completely degrade (≥90%) Paralytic Shellfish Toxins (PST). PST is a condition that arises from consuming shellfish that have been rendered poisonous due to toxins produced by marine algae, plankton and other forms of marine life. There were 7 species of bacteria in the genus *Pseudoalteromonas* isolated from toxic blue mussels which could degrade and detoxify PST efficiently. Though the exact mechanism of degradation is not fully understood, several tests indicated that the PST completely degraded instead of just transforming into an innocuous form (Donovan, *et al*). The 7 bacteria involved for the test showed over a 90% elimination of the PST in only 5 days. The efficiency of the bacteria could have implications in medicine, such as in providing a new medicine against PST or eliminating PST from the shellfish in the environment. However, more research will need to be conducted in order to understand the exact mechanism of degrading PST by *Pseudoalteromonas.*

Carrie J. Donovan and colleagues from Dalhousie University first collected toxic blue mussels from the Canadian Food Inspection Agency off the Atlantic Coast of Canada near Nova Scotia. Sixty-nine distinct bacteria were isolated from the digestive glands of the toxic blue mussels and separated into two types, clear and opaque, of nutritional marine 2216 agar plates. The 69 bacterial isolates were then tested with 600 μl of marine broth 2216, 100 μl of toxic algae *Alexandrium tamarense* extract, and 300 μl of toxic blue mussel extract. A control was made with 100 μl sterile water instead of algae extract. The bacteria were inoculated by centrifuge, and then allowed to incubate at 25°C in a shaking incubator. Samples from the starting day to the fifth day were analyzed using high-performance liquid chromatography (HPLC). The samples were then injected in live mice to determine the effectiveness of the detoxification. Gene sequencing, RNA tests, electron microscopy, biochemical tests, and physiological tests were all employed to determine the morphological characteristics of the bacteria.

Of the 69 isolated bacteria found in the digestive systems of the blue mussel, only one-third of them were found to have a detoxifying effect on PST. Out of that third, only seven—all in the genus *Pseudoalteromonas*—were found to quickly and effectively remove PST and they eliminated over 90% of it, ranging from 92.28–98.51%. The bacteria did not grow on pure agar plates, possibly indicating that the PST is cometabolized by the bacteria and completely degraded. The exact method of PST's elimination is not well known but it occurred in both oxygen rich and aerobic environments. Rats injected with a lethal dose of toxin died in just seven minutes whereas rats that were given any of the seven bacteria lived for at least an hour. One useful possibility might be to use the bacteria to eliminate biotoxins in shellfish before they are consumed.

Pharmaceutical Waste 2, 4-dichlorophenol is Biodegradable by *Pseudomonas* Bacteria.

Pseudomonas alcaligenes was found to be an effective biodegrader of 2,4-dichlorophenol(DCP), a waste product of pharmaceutical industries, at pH 7 and 35°C after ultraviolet light exposure . The chlorinated aromatic compound 2,4-dichlorophenol is an environmental pollutant that can be synthesized into larger phenols, pesticides, and herbicides. *Pseudomonas alcaligenes* extracted from sewage sludge were tested for growth and biodegradation based on various 2,4-DCP concentrations, UV radiation exposure, temperature at pH 7, and pH in 25°C. The amount of 2,4 DCP that degraded from *Pseudomonas alcaligenes* correlated significantly with increasing values of these four factors, in particular the amount of 2,4-DCP that degraded increased significantly after 144 hours of UV radiation exposure (Elkarmi *et al. 2009*). The degradation of 2,4 DCP by *Pseudomonas alcaligenes* would be highly effective in bioremediation programs for reducing the amount of pharmaceuticals in the environment, especially in sewage treatment plants where most pharmaceuticals are not eliminated during the cleaning process.

Ali Z. Elkarmi and colleagues from Hashemite University extracted and identified *Pseudomonas alcaligenes* from the wastewater of two pharmaceutical and healthcare industries. The sewage was centrifuged for 30 minutes to obtain 200 mg of sludge, which was then added to sterilized flasks containing 20 ml of chlorophenol enrichment media and 100 mg/l 2,4-dichlorophenol. The mixture along with a second mixture from 50 ml of nutrient broth and 0.5 ml of the first suspension incubated were incubated 30°C for four days. Nutrient agar plates containing 100 ml/I 2,4-DCP were inoculated with 0.3 ml of the second mixture and both were incubated at 37°C for four days. The results were sent to the Jordan University hospital, which confirmed the identity of the bacterial species *Pseudomonas alcaligenes*. The colonies of *Pseudomonas alcaligenes* were placed in nutrient agar plates of 1 g/l cetrimide where they were tested for 2,4-DCP concentrations in increments of 20 mg/l starting from 120 mg/l to 300 mg/l. Isolated colonies of *Pseudomonas alcaligenes* were then subjected to UV radiation for 24, 48, 72, and 96 hours in 2,4-DCP concentrations at increments of 20 mg/l starting from 240 mg/l to 400 mg/l. The UV irradiated samples were then cultivated in a bioreactor were biodegradability of 340 mg/l 2,4-DCP was tested from temperatures of 25, 30, 35, and 40°C and pH values ranging of 6.5, 7.0 and 8.0. The final results were compared for statistical significance using one-way ANOVA test.

Without UV radiation the amount of bacteria that grew in the 2,4-DCP culture decreased with increasing concentration. From 180 mg/l to 220 mg/l 2,4-DCP, the bacteria exhibited weak growth decreasing from 9.60 to 6.07 $\log_{10}$ of CFU/ml respectively. The amount of 2.4-DCP after UV radiation was added, however, increased the limit for tolerance and biodegradation of 2,4-DCP significantly; at a concentration of 200 mg/l of 2,4-DCP, the growth of bacteria increased from 8.40 mg/l to 9.08 mg/l $\log_{10}$ of CFU/ml. After UV radiation exposure the limit for the concentration of 2,4-DCP to decrease growth was raised to 380 mg/l at 6.80 $\log_{10}$ of CFU/ml. At a pH of 7.0, growths were best at a temperature of 35°C after 168 hours. At a temperature of 25°C, growths were best at a pH of 7.0 after 168. The ANOVA test indicated that there were significant correlations between pH, UV radiation, concentration of 2,4-DCP and temperature. A possible use for the *Pseudomonas alcaligenes* would be in bioremediation and sewage treatment where pharmaceuticals are often not eliminated from the wastewater treatment process.

Are Rising Temperatures Responsible for the Rates of Tularemia in Sweden?

The number of reported human tularemia cases will steadily increase from 2010 to 2100 in the five high-endemic counties of Dalarna, Gävleborg, Norrbotten, Värmland, and Örebro. The predicted increase in the incidences of human tularemia has been linked to the steadily warmer climate of Sweden enabling certain parasites to proliferate. The parasites that spread the bacterium *Francisella tularensis* include ticks, mosquitoes, fleas, horse flies, and deerflies. Though the level of precipitation was predicted to remain stable and constant throughout the 2010–2100 periods, indicating that the increase in parasites is not due to increased rainfall, the rate of tularemia still increased as the climate became warmer (Rydén *et al.* 2009). The high localization of tularemia, the population patterns of its vectors and its incidences on the local population will need to be further researched in order to understand the reasons why increased tularemia epidemics correlate with increased temperature.

Patrick Rydén and colleagues from Umeå University analyzed data about human tularemia outbreaks in Sweden from 1997–2008. A 140-year model for simulation data was constructed and performed. Scenario data was taken using a climate model RCA3 and the IPCC Special Report on Emissions Data. The data were arranged into 50 x 50 km square regions. Empirical data of disease onset from 379 individuals during 1981–2007 were collected from Dalarna County and used to determine the temperature and time parameters of human tularemia epidemics. The monthly average values were calculated for temperature and precipitation using the 50 x 50 km square regions. The duration of a tularemia epidemic was determined using the mean temperatures from May to October and time plots from the first and last human tularemia case for each year, region, and local outbreak area.

Investigations on the five high tularemia-endemic areas showed that the incidences of human tularemia from 1997–2008 ranged from 40.1 to 81.1% of the total tularemia incidences in Sweden. All five counties contain 14.61% of the Swedish population at 1,352,558 human inhabitants. The number of incidences during the 1997–2008 range from 0 in the Värmland and Örebro counties in 1997 to 216 in Dalarna County in 2003. However, the distribution in the five counties was uneven, mainly due to the high localization of the disease. The tularemia prediction model indicated that the summer conditions will last longer due to an increase in temperatures by 2° C during 2010–2100. The precipitation was stable throughout the period and did not increase significantly. The duration of the temperate sensitive outbreaks will vary from 3.5 weeks in Norrbotten to 6.6 weeks in Värmland during 2010–2100. An exact relationship between the temperature and the rate of transmission has not been clearly documented; however, because precipitation is stable throughout the 2010–2100 periods then the amount of rainfall is insignificant to the rate of transmission. More analyses will have to be taken in order to determine the exact causes of the disease's restrictive locality, the vector populations that house the bacterium *Francisella tularensis*, and the responses of the flora, fauna, and transmission rates to increased temperature.

Kevon White

Duration of Extreme Climate Periods from 1989-2006 affects Ischemic Heart Disease Hospitalization Rates in Quebec, Canada

Incidences of ischemic heart disease (IHD) increased with the duration of hot or cold temperature periods from 1989–2006 in Quebec, Canada. Longer periods of higher or lower temperatures were more effective, raising the cases of IHD by up to 12%, than sudden dramatic temperature changes (Bayentin *et al.* 2010). The rates of hospitalization for IHD were most prominent in men ages 45–65 and women ages 65 and over. Differences in latitude gradient also affected the rates of IHD, specifically less incidences occurred moving from northeast to southwest of Quebec. Other factors including smoking preferences, behaviors, and deprivation levels exacerbated the effects of climate change on IHD admissions (Bayentin *et al.* 2010). This preliminary study concluded that climate change, in addition to a myriad of other behavioral factors, can significantly affect the incidences of heart disease.

Lampouguin Bayentin and colleagues from various institutions collected data on reported cases of IHD hospitalizations of all ages from April 1st, 1989 to March 31st, 2006. The data were then plotted linearly by age and gender with respect to time. Smoking prevalence data by age and gender were also plotted for the periods 1998, 2000-2001 and 2003. Meteorological data was collected from the years 1989–2006. A generalized additive model (GAM) was then used to compare the two sets of data. Variable selection was conducted using an F-test and a forward stepwise selection technique. A lag search was conducted using a generalized cross-validation (GCV) criterion. A parameter lambda (λ) was estimated by comparing the Akaïke information criterion (AIC) with several λ values. The excess risk, the rate of which IHD increased with respect to a change in $\pm1°C$, was then calculated.

The greatest incidences of IHD were found in men ages 45-64 and women ages 65 and over. The rate of IHD showed an increasing trend from 1989–1999 and a decreasing trend from 2000–2006. The incidences of IHD decreased from the northeastern regions of Quebec to the southwestern regions. A lag was present in the models used to determine meteorological variables; which implied that the previous climates have more impact on IHD than climates on the day of admission. The increases in averaged daily mean temperature for a given lag and same day admission resulted in more averaged daily IHD admissions for both genders; however, there was a more pronounced effect for men's IHD admission rates than women's IHD admission rates. The risks of IHD in men ages 45–64 ranged from 1.03% to 12.32% compared to men ages 65 and older with IHD risks from 0.53% to 2.98%. Women had higher IHD incidences in hot temperatures but had lower IHD incidences in cold temperatures. For both genders the 65 and older age group had an earlier onset of IHD compared to any other age group. Incidences of IHD also increased with precipitation, humidity, dew point, and ground snow for both genders. The effects of meteorological variables alone decreased over time. Smoking prevalence in both genders was twice the amount the in groups aged 45–64 compared to the 65 and older range. Regions with significant smoking prevalence and high levels of deprivation had significant excess risks; however some regions of low smoking prevalence also showed high excess risk. The combined effects of climate change, behavioral factors, age, and gender have the greatest impact on the incidences of ischemic heart disease. Applying this study to other forms of medicine may help predict certain patterns that increase the risks of cardiovascular diseases.

Conclusions

Natural medicines are important resources needing further research as they have the potential to become novel medicines with use in western medicine. New conservation efforts for endangered species can be implemented by monitoring natural medicines in areas where the native flora and fauna are harvested by local cultures. In addition, the human health effects from using naturally occurring organisms have great implications in modern society. Many of these organisms, including bacteria and fast-growing plants, are cheap to produce as they proliferate on their own, and are easy to maintain due to a lack of specialized care. However, the availability of natural medicines is in jeopardy thanks to habitat destruction; in conjunction with global warming, the changing environment will likely affect human health due to prolonged periods of disease outbreak exacerbating the rates of disease .With the problem of rising global temperatures, more disease outbreaks will mean more financial costs in health-care, and less accessible medicines will mean that cures or treatments will become scarce. Natural medicines are therefore an important resource to research because new potential resources can be found while current resources are optimized for new uses.

Resources Cited

Alves, R., Leo Neto, N., Brooks, S., Albuquerque, U., 2009. Commercialization of animal-derived remedies as complimentary medicine in the semi-arid region of Northeastern Brazil. Journal of Ethnopharmacology 124, 600-608

Bayentin, L., Adlouni, S., Ouarda, T., Gosselin, P., Doyon, B., Chebana, F., 2010. Spatial variability of climate effects on ischemic heart disease hospitalization rates for the period 1989-2006 in Quebec, Canada. International Journal of Health Geographics. doi:10.1186/1476-072X-9-5.

Blair, E., Cokcetin, N., Harry E., Carter D., 2009. The unusual antibacterial activity of medical-grade *Leptospermum* honey: antibacterial spectrum, resistance and transcriptome analysis. Eur J Clin Microbiol Infect Dis 28, 1199–1208

Donovan, C., Garduño, R.., Kalmokoff, M., Ku, J., Quilliam, M., Gill, A., 2009. *Pseudoalteromonas* Bacteria Are Capable of Degrading Paralytic Shellfish Toxins. Applied and Environmental Microbiology 75, 6919–6923.

Elkarmi, A., Abu-Elteen, K., Atta, A., Abu-Sbitan, N., 2009. Biodegradation of 2,4-dichlorophenol originating from pharmaceutical industries. African Journal of Biotechnology 8, 2558–2564.

Panghal, M., Arya, V., Yadav, S., Kumar,S., Yadav, J., 2010. Indigenous knowledge of medicinal plants used by Saperas community of Khetawas, Jhajjar District, Haryana, India. Journal of Ethnobiology and Ethnomedicine, doi:10.1186/1746-4269-6-4.

Rydén, P., Sjöstedt, A., Johansson, A., 2009. Effects of climate change on tularaemia disease activity in Sweden. Citation: Global Health Action. DOI: 10.3402/gha.v2i0.2063.

Uppugundla, N., Engelberth, A., Ravindranath, S., Clausen, E., Lay, J., Gidden, J., Carrier, D., 2009. Switchgrass Water Extracts: Extraction, Separation and Biological Activity of Rutin and Quercitrin. Journal of Agricultural and Food Chemistry 57, 7763–7770.

About the Authors

The authors of this book are students at the Claremont Colleges. The book is a work product of Biology 159: Natural Resources Management taught by Emil Morhardt in the Joint Science Department of Claremont McKenna, Pitzer, and Scripps Colleges. Each student picked a topic, did a full literature search, and selected ten papers written within the past year that exemplified the state of the science.

Their task was to write journalistic summaries capturing the essence of the papers but eschewing technical terms to the extent possible—to become, in effect, science writers. The summaries were due weekly and were returned with editorial comments shortly thereafter. The chapters are compilations of the individual summaries with additional introductory and conclusionary material.

The editor is Roberts Professor of Environmental Biology at Claremont McKenna, Pitzer, and Scripps colleges, and Director of The Roberts Environmental Center at Claremont McKenna College. He remembers how difficult it is to learn to write and appreciates the professionalism shown by these students.

Index

global circulation model (GCM), 186, 244, 247
global warming potential (GWP), 48, 145
glycerin, 142
grassland, 162, 167, 171, 174, 267, 283
grazing, 161, 162, 168
Great Barrier Reef, GBR, 34
Greenland Ice Sheet (GIS), 28, 29, 122, 133
Guatemala, 303, 307
Gulf of Mexico, 82, 84
HadCM3, 186, 263, 293
helium, 30
Hiernacium aurantiacum, 325
Hiernacium murorum, 325
Hiernacium pilosella, 325
Himalayas, 13, 20, 238, 239, 248
Hippodamia variegata, 326
Hirundo rustica (barn swallow), 40, 42
Holocene, 28, 29, 32, 36, 313
hurricane, 189, 251
hybrid, 159, 206, 212, 213, 214, 215, 216, 220, 222, 232, 330, 331
hybrid vehicle, 213, 215, 220
hydraulic fracturing, 60, 67, 68, 69, 70, 72, 102
hydropower, 23
ice core, 18, 28, 29, 32, 36
ice sheet, 27, 28, 30, 31, 33, 35, 37, 76, 122, 123, 189
India, 26, 40, 41, 46, 114, 206, 210, 228, 246, 263, 277, 278, 281, 284, 332, 355, 358, 359, 368
insolation, 29, 30
Intergovernmental Panel on Climate Change (IPCC), 12, 13, 54, 80, 81, 106, 186, 244, 251, 263, 288, 297, 310, 315, 316, 365
intertropical convergence zone, ITCZ, 41, 46
invasive species, 309, 310, 313, 321, 322, 323, 324, 325, 327, 331, 332, 333, 334, 335
IPCC A1F1 scenario, 106
IPCC A2 scenario, 81, 124, 125, 128, 186, 245, 263, 264, 316
IPCC B1 scenario, 81, 106, 316
IPCC B2 scenario, 186, 245, 246, 263, 310, 315, 316
iron, 70, 71, 78, 79, 80, 293
isobutanol, 173

isotope, 11, 27, 30, 32, 33, 34, 35, 36, 44, 234
ITCZ, 41, 46
Jatrohpa curcas L. (jatropha), 154, 155, 160
Kyoto Protocol, 111, 114
landfills, 170
Last Glacial Maximum (LGM), 30, 36
Lead-210 (^{210}Pb), 83
leaf area index (LAI), 146
lichen, 21
life cycle assessment (LCA), 145, 149, 151, 152, 154, 162, 165, 166, 183, 199, 231
lignin, 147
lignocellulose, 139, 140, 144, 147, 168
Little Ice Age, 17, 19, 20, 21, 26, 31, 32, 36, 48, 51, 52, 56
Little Ice Age (LIA),, 17, 19, 20, 21, 26, 31, 32, 36, 48, 51, 52, 56
Lupinus perennis, 171
macrophytes, 268
maize, 165, 279, 280, 281, 284, 288, 292, 293
manure, 280, 291, 332
Marcellus Formation, 70
Medieval Warm Period (MWP), 31, 52
Mertensia, 311
methane (CH_4), 47, 48, 60, 67, 68, 112, 113, 117, 118, 141, 145, 148, 170, 189, 191, 192, 193, 194, 195, 196, 197, 198, 199, 200, 203, 232, 238, 281, 287, 291, 350
methyl halide transferase (MHT), 144
Michigan, 233
Miscanthus x giganteus, 146
monsoon, 40, 46, 207, 278
Mount Hood, 24
mussel, 330, 362, 363
Mytilus galloprovincialis, 330
Mytilus trossulus, 330
Nannochloropsis sp, 143
NAO, 43, 52
Neochloris oleabundans, 143
Net Ecosystem Exchange, NEE, 49
net energy value (NEV), 166
Net Erosion Model (NER), 53
New York, 14, 183
New Zealand, 19, 183, 184, 187
Nile, 254, 258
nitrogen, 6, 36, 43, 52, 55, 56, 72, 82, 95, 116, 119, 129, 139, 142, 143, 145, 146, 149, 155, 156, 171, 187, 200, 214, 227,

www.ingramcontent.com/pod-product-compliance
Lightning Source LLC
Chambersburg PA
CBHW031458270326
41930CB00006B/141